CHRISTIAN MY

This book introduces students to Christian mysticism and modern critical responses to it. Christianity has a rich tradition of mystical theology that first emerged in the writings of the early church fathers, and flourished during the Middle Ages. Today Christian mysticism is increasingly recognised as an important Christian heritage relevant to today's spiritual seekers.

The book sets out to provide students and other interested readers with access to the main theoretical approaches to Christian mysticism – including those propounded by William James, Steven Katz, Bernard McGinn, Michael Sells, Denys Turner and Caroline Walker-Bynum. It also explores postmodern re-readings of Christian mysticism by authors such as Jacques Derrida, Jean-Luc Marion and Jean-François Lyotard. The book first introduces students to the main themes that underpin Christian mysticism. It then reflects on how modern critics have understood each of them, demonstrating that stark delineation between the different theoretical approaches eventually collapses under the weight of the complex interaction between experience and knowledge that lies at the heart of Christian mysticism. In doing so, the book presents a deliberate challenge to a strictly perennialist reading of Christian mysticism.

Anyone even remotely familiar with Christian mysticism will know that renewed interest in Christian mystical writers has created a huge array of scholarship with which students of mysticism need to familiarise themselves. This book outlines the various modern theoretical approaches in a manner easily accessible to a reader with little or no previous knowledge of this area, and offers a philosophical/theological introduction to Christian mystical writers beyond the patristic period important for the Latin Western Tradition.

For Ann

Christian Mysticism
An Introduction to
Contemporary Theoretical Approaches

LOUISE NELSTROP
Oxford University, UK

With

KEVIN MAGILL
Bristol University, UK

BRADLEY B. ONISHI
University of California, Santa Barbara

ASHGATE

Published by
Ashgate Publishing Limited
Wey Court East
Union Road
Farnham
Surrey, GU9 7PT
England

Ashgate Publishing Company
Suite 420
101 Cherry Street
Burlington
VT 05401-4405
USA

www.ashgate.com

British Library Cataloguing in Publication Data
Nelstrop, Louise.
  Christian mysticism : an introduction to contemporary theoretical approaches.
  1. Mysticism – History – Middle Ages, 600–1500. 2. Mysticism – History – Middle Ages, 600–1500 – Study and teaching.
  I. Title II. Magill, Kevin J., 1972– III. Onishi, Bradley B.
  248.2'2'0902-dc22

Library of Congress Cataloging-in-Publication Data
Nelstrop, Louise.
  Christian mysticism : an introduction to contemporary theoretical approaches / Louise Nelstrop, Kevin Magill, and Bradley B. Onishi.
      p. cm.
  Includes bibliographical references and index.
  ISBN 978-0-7546-5732-3 (hardcover : alk. paper)—ISBN 978-0-7546-6990-6 (pbk. : alk. paper)
  1. Mysticism. I. Magill, Kevin J., 1972– II. Onishi, Bradley B. III. Title.

  BV5082.3.N45 2009
  248.2'2—dc22

                                                                          2009019657

ISBN 9780754657323 (hbk)
ISBN 9780754669906 (pbk)
ISBN 9780754686958 (ebk)

Mixed Sources
Product group from well-managed forests and other controlled sources
www.fsc.org Cert no. SA-COC-1565
© 1996 Forest Stewardship Council

Printed and bound in Great Britain by
MPG Books Group, UK

Contents

Preface and Acknowledgements

This book was inspired by a series of undergraduate classes on Christian mysticism. The first question students almost invariably ask is: 'So what is mysticism?' When the only answer they receive is 'Wait and see. You need to make up your own mind!' they think we are being deliberately obtuse. The point of writing this book is to ease some of this frustration but also make it clear why you really do have to 'wait and see'. The student who asks this question wants a one-line answer; a lens through which to view the material. They do not realise that they probably already have such a one-line answer in mind – and *that* is the problem. Popular thinking about Christian mysticism is influenced by theories of mysticism that were developed at the beginning of the twentieth century. Even though students are not normally aware of these theories, more often than not, they subconsciously bring them to the texts. The challenge of teaching Christian mysticism is to help students become aware of their own assumptions (and those of other scholars). It is also about being able to hold the question in suspense, while still diving into the mystery of mystical texts. Only by doing this can they become equipped to reflect on the right way to understand Christian mysticism. The aim of this book is to help readers to do the same.

One of the difficulties with trying to work out our own assumptions is that the theories from which they originate are complex and the theories which challenge them are often even more so. It is off-putting for students to feel that they have to wade through pages of philosophy before they can begin to do this. It is easier to stick with their assumptions. We hope that this book makes this a less daunting task. By rendering contemporary theories of mysticism accessible, this book aims to make it much easier to reflect on our presumptions about Christian mysticism. We have also tried to link the theories to key themes and motifs within Christian mysticism to show how they relate to and affect our thinking about mystical texts on numerous levels.

We begin the book with a brief outline of four theoretical approaches that have developed over the last hundred years. These are perennialist accounts, sometimes referred to as experientialist accounts, (which hold mystical writing to be concerned with ineffable experiences); contextualist positions (which still hold mystical writing to be concerned with experiences, just not ineffable ones); performative language readings (which focus on the language of these texts and wonder whether mysticism is primarily about experiences at all); and, finally, feminist readings (which challenge the way that perennialist accounts privilege human intellect over human embodiment). Having introduced these theories briefly, and some of the key scholars who discuss them, we then turn to look at each of these approaches in more detail by reflecting on how each understands the themes that dominate Christian mystical texts within the tradition of Christian mysticism that developed in the Latin West. In doing so, we will highlight both the benefits and disadvantages of viewing Christian mysticism through these different lenses.

Part I contains six chapters that focus on themes and motifs that are often taken as definitive of Christian mystical writing. Both Augustine and Pseudo-Denys figure highly since they were central to the development of the Christian mystical tradition in the Latin West. Chapter 1 looks at the relationship between Christian mysticism and various forms of Platonism. It explores different theoretical responses to the fact that a relationship really does exist between the Founding Fathers of Christian mysticism and Platonism. For some theorists this is a problem. Take, on the one hand, feminist hostility to the negative portrayal of women that enters into Christian spiritual practice as a result. On the other hand, those who favour a performative language approach delight in the way that this leads negative language to become part of Christian expression of the divine. Chapter 2 further explores this idea of negative or 'apophatic' language, as it is often called. It considers why it is that mystical texts can talk of God in terms of negatives, such as 'God is not good'. Is this language related to certain experiences or is it a language game? The chapter concentrates on the writings of Pseudo-Denys, an author who is important for shaping subsequent use of negative language. Chapter 3 then looks at the idea of interiority and selfhood. It focuses particularly on Augustine and his idea of the prayerful journey as a movement within the self. Perennialist readings find it difficult to account for the mystical encounter that Augustine shared with his mother Monica. The chapter considers whether other theoretical approaches do any better.

Chapter 4 turns to another important element of Christian mystical texts – erotic language. Mystical texts are often filled with erotic discussions of God. This strange phenomenon is considered from different theoretical perspectives. Contextualists are unsurprised by the use of this language, since it is prevalent in the Bible. Performative language readings however consider its use to be a purposeful strategy to reveal the otherness of God to the reader. Chapter 5 considers another central idea within Christian mysticism, the notion of hierarchy. The chapter focuses on Pseudo-Denys's development of this idea and how different contemporary theorists have explained its centrality in mystical texts. The final chapter in Part I, Chapter 6, looks at why mystics talk about a 'mystical' sense of scripture. It outlines the complicated notions of exegesis that leads Christian mystics to believe that Scripture should be understood on a variety of levels. The chapter reflects on how scholars have incorporated allegorical exegesis and the sacramental understanding of the physical world into their theories of mysticism.

Following this exploration of some of the key themes and motifs that we find within Christian mystical writing, Part II sets out to consider slightly later developments. Chapter 7 looks at the idea that mystical writing is gendered. Caroline Walker Bynum has presented the most famous challenge to perennialist ideas about mysticism by suggesting that women approach mysticism differently. Rather than using their minds, she argues, they use their bodies. This chapter considers whether the mystical writing produced by women is distinctively feminine and really a different order of mystical writing to that produced by men. Chapter 8 follows this up by focusing on the role that visions play within mysticism. Visionary mysticism is most often associated with female writers and the chapter explores how theorists have dealt with the idea that a vision can be mystical. Chapter 9 then turns to look at the role performed by images in later mysticism, focusing on three English Mystics: Richard Rolle, Walter Hilton and *The Cloud*-Author. The final chapter in Part II considers the idea that mysticism is sometimes heretical: Chapter 10 investigates the accounts of two writers, Meister Eckhart and Marguerite Porete, and various responses to them found in contemporary thought.

No book on Christian mysticism would be complete without some reflection on postmodern considerations of Augustine and Pseudo-Denys, since these are becoming increasingly dominant in the contemporary Christian landscape.[1] These readings differ to the four approaches that we concentrate on in the rest of book. To give some understanding of the similarities and differences, Part III explores postmodern re-readings of Pseudo-Denys and Augustine. Chapter 11 looks at how Jean-Luc Marion and Jacques Derrida have understood the negative language employed by Pseudo-Denys. In Chapter 12 we consider Augustine's interior quest from the perspectives of Marion, Derrida and Jean-François Lyotard. We hope to show that, while different, there is also overlap between postmodern approaches and the four contemporary theoretical perspectives we focus on, especially as some scholars draw on both. The book finally concludes by reflecting on the question with which we began: 'what is Christian mysticism?' It encourages us not to forget that in the midst of all these theoretical discussions Christian mysticism is first and foremost a form of Christian prayer, a devotional activity that tries to reach out to the divine and help others do likewise. We hope that by approaching these devotional texts in this way we will provide a picture of some of the complexities that surround modern discussions of Christian mystical texts and why it is that modern commentators sometimes disagree about who is and who is not a mystic.

The current climate seems like a good one in which to write a book on Christian mysticism and contemporary assumptions about it. The Western world is finally reawakening to the idea that Christianity really does have a mystical tradition of its own. Christian practitioners in the Emerging Church are turning to it with enthusiasm, asking how a spirituality like this can simply have been forgotten. Continental philosophers are drawing on it for inspiration. Writers like Hildegard have developed huge followings amongst the general public. Her musical compositions have even become best-sellers. Therefore, although this book is meant for beginners rather than experts, we hope it will prove a useful reference book for readers with a more advanced knowledge of mysticism or theology. We

---

[1]   See, for example, P. Rollins, *How (Not) to Speak about God* (Brewster, MA: Paraclete Press, 2006).

also hope it will be valuable to devotional readers who want to gain greater insight into the way in which the vast tradition of Christian mystical writing has been understood by scholars, at least over the last hundred years.

This book would never have been written without the support and encouragements of the staff and students of Regent's Park College Oxford. A few people deserve particular mention: Mark Atherton, Read Marlatte, Timothy Lightfoot and Chris Victor-Jones. Special thanks must, however, go to Eddie Howells, whose comments on an earlier draft vastly improved the development of the argument surrounding the various theoretical approaches to mysticism, as well as to Ted Phillips for his tireless help with proofreading. We would also like to extend our thanks to Sarah Lloyd at Ashgate Publishing for all her patient help in its production, and to Mary Murphy whose eye for detail has made this a much more readable text.

L. N.

Introduction
Contemporary Theoretical Approaches

It is a surprising but significant fact that, while medieval Christian mystics talk about both 'mystical' theology and a 'mystical' sense of scripture, they never talk about 'mysticism' or refer to each other as 'mystics'. The term 'mysticism' is a modern coinage, first used in English, according to the *Oxford English Dictionary*, in 1736. As Mark McIntosh comments:

> Today we often use the term 'mysticism' though this is really something of an academic invention; earlier eras referred to the most intimate and transforming encounter with God as 'contemplation'.[1]

The primary concern of this book is something that the writers themselves referred to as 'contemplation' or 'mystical' theology. These terms appear to cover a very diverse set of devotional activities. Take, for example, the following passages from Margery Kempe and Pseudo-Denys, which describe intimate encounters with God. In the first passage Margery fondles Christ's feet in her mind's eye in a rather erotic manner as he addresses her as his lover.

> Therefore must I needs be homely with you and lie in your bed with you. Daughter, you desire greatly to see me, and you may boldly, when you are in your bed, take me to you as your wedded husband, as your most worthy darling, and as your sweet son, for I will be loved as a son should be loved by the mother and will that you love me, daughter, as a good wife ought to love her husband. And therefore you may boldly take me in the arms of your soul and kiss my mouth, my head, and my feet as sweetly as you will.[2]

Pseudo-Denys, on the other hand, provides a kind of exegesis of Exodus 19:18–19. He tells of how Moses encountered God on Mount Sinai in a dark cloud. Pseudo-Denys states that Moses experiences more than a simple sight of heaven. At a certain point, he envisages Moses breaking free and plunging into the darkness of unknowing:

---

[1]   M.A. McIntosh, *Mystical Theology: The Integrity of Spirituality and Theology* (Cambridge: Blackwell, 1998), p. 11.

[2]   *The Book of Margery Kempe: New Translation, Contexts, Criticism*, trans. and ed. L. Staley (New York: W.W. Norton and Co., 2001), p. 66.

When every purification is complete, he [Moses] hears the many-voiced trumpets. He sees the many lights, pure and with rays streaming abundantly. Then, standing apart from the crowds and accompanied by chosen priests, he pushes ahead to the summit of the divine ascents. And yet he does not meet God himself, but contemplates, not him who is invisible, but rather where he dwells. … But then he breaks free of them, away from what sees and is seen, and he plunges into the truly mysterious darkness of unknowing.[3]

Why do both these authors refer to their writing as 'contemplation'[4] and is this really the same thing as 'mysticism'? This complicated question is the one that our book seeks to unpack.

While some scholars believe that the notion of 'contemplation' and the idea of 'mysticism' are interchangeable, others, like McIntosh above, are far less convinced. This book sets out to raise questions about the assumed relationship between contemplation and mysticism that we find in much modern scholarly writing. First, there is the difference between accounts of contemplation to consider. Is contemplation one, easily defined, activity? Then there is the question of whether, even if some accounts of contemplation are mysticism, are all of them? The answers to these questions hinge on different ideas about the nature of mysticism. To really understand the problems posed by such questions we need to consider what scholars have meant by this idea of 'mysticism'. We also need to be aware that this term is modern and subject to modern theoretical debate. So long as we do this there is no reason why we cannot legitimately describe either or both writers above as 'mystics' or refer to what they are doing as 'mysticism'. If we are going to call both Margery and Pseudo-Denys mystics, however, we *must* be aware of our reasons for doing so.

Each chapter in this book aims to build a clearer picture of the issues at stake in modern interpretations of 'mysticism'. This introduction sets up the framework for the chapters that follow by outlining the main theoretical approaches to Christian mysticism that we believe are found in contemporary scholarship. We argue that four broad theoretical approaches to Christian mysticism have largely come to dominate the modern interpretation of Christian mysticism in the Latin West.[5] These are **perennialist**[6], **contextualist**, **feminist** and what we will call

---

[3]   Pseudo-Denys, 'The Mystical Theology', in *Pseudo-Dionysius: The Complete Works*, trans. C. Luibhéid and P. Rorem (London: Paulist Press, 1987), pp. 136–7. (See Chapters 2 and 3 for further discussion of this passage.)

[4]   The Greek word 'theoria' literally meaning 'seeing' gets translated in the Latin as 'contemplatio' which means 'to view' or 'to contemplate'.

[5]   In suggesting this we are aware that a more philosophical reading would break these categories down further. For an introduction to a reading of mysticism from this approach see the *Stanford Encyclopedia of Philosophy* at http://plato.stanford.edu/entries/mysticism/.

[6]   We have chosen this term over the more descriptive 'experientialist' because it is widely recognised in philosophical literature on mysticism. However, the term

'performative language' readings.[7] 'Performative language' is used to try to encapsulate a general approach to Christian mysticism for which no adequate terminology currently exists.[8]

Before we consider these four theoretical approaches, it is important to stress that most of the scholars that we will consider in the course of this book will not fit neatly into just one of these categories. If they did it would be easy to answer the question 'What is Christian mysticism?' We would simple choose one of the four possible answers after a brief consideration of their various merits. Christian mysticism and the scholarship that surrounds it is, however, more nuanced that this. As we move through the book we will see that what is truly interesting in terms of the question 'What is Christian mysticism?' is the movement and dialogue between these four categories, and that even scholars who hold formative positions within the development of these categories at times themselves move outside the strictures of their own taxonomy. What will hopefully become apparent is that there are many overlapping methods of approaching Christian mysticism, all of which are, however, informed by these categories, which act as poles around which arguments revolve and in relation to which interesting and nuanced discussions take place. With this in mind we will now turn to the first of the four categories.

Perennialist Readings

William James

Without doubt, the father of the modern study of mysticism is William James. James is not the originator of the word 'mysticism', which as noted in the *OED* was first used in English in 1736. However, James published a series of lectures in 1902 under the title *The Varieties of Religious Experience: A Study in Human Nature.*

'experientialist' perhaps better encapsulates the scholars who fall within this category and privilege experience of a certain type.

[7]   Postmodern approaches are addressed separately in the final two chapters of the book.

[8]   Bernard McGinn splits the different approaches up into 'theological', 'philosophical' and 'psychological'. B. McGinn, 'Theoretical Foundations: The Modern Study of Mysticism', in *The Foundations of Mysticism: Origins to the Fifth Century*, The Presence of God: A History of Western Christian Mysticism, vol. 1 (SCM Press: London, 1992), Appendix pp. 265–343. His survey of the range of different readings of mysticism is extremely useful. The reason for adopting different categories is to focus particularly on the issue of experience and the place that it has been given within medieval accounts of mysticism. For an interesting consideration of the debate about mysticism, also see E. Howells, 'Mysticism and the Mystical: The Current Debate', in *The Way Supplement*, 102 (2001), 15–27.

In one lecture, James focused on what he termed 'mystical states of consciousness' and it was his discussion of these which first popularised the idea that there were other kinds of consciousness to those experienced during normal waking life, which could be referred to as 'mystical'.[9]

James, whose training was in psychology and philosophy, defined religion in highly individualistic, psychological language. For James, what mattered most was personal religion. He had little time for the authoritarian claims of religious communities:

> Religion, therefore, as I now ask you arbitrarily to take it, shall mean for us the feelings, acts, and experiences of individual men in their solitude, so far as they apprehend themselves to stand in relation to whatever they may consider divine.[10]

Theology (that is, the systematic presentation of an individual's relationship to the divine) and ecclesial organisation (that is, the creation of a Church and clerics) are for James secondary to true religion. Personal experience of the divine is what allows organised religion to exist. In part, James was reacting to rationalist theories of religion; particularly that of Immanuel Kant (1724–1804). According to Kant, only the accuracy of knowledge claims that rely on the evidence of the senses can be analysed properly. Religious beliefs and experiences, by contrast, have no distinct sensory content. They refer only to supernatural objects, and, as such, Kant regarded such beliefs as having practical consequences only. This means, strictly speaking, that we cannot *know* that God exists. This is because claims to know God are not based on sensory experience. However, we can act out morally commendable lives *as if* there were a God.

Against this, James postulates the existence of a faculty in human beings that is deeper than the senses – which allows an intuitive grasp of reality beyond that which the evidence of our senses can provide. The highest expression of personal religious experience, its root and centre, are what James calls 'mystical states of consciousness'.[11] James argues that these special states of consciousness are marked by certain similar characteristics that allow them to be grouped together under the umbrella 'mystical'. Two of these characteristics are particularly pronounced and, if present, indicate that an experience *is* mystical. They are: ineffability and noesis. In addition, two less well pronounced characteristics are also often present as an aspect of a mystical experience: transiency and passivity.

---

[9]   W. James, *The Varieties of Religious Experience: A Study in Human Nature: Being the Gifford Lectures on Natural Religion Delivered at Edinburgh 1901–2* (London: Burns and Oates, 1952), pp. 371–420.

[10]   Ibid., p. 31.

[11]   Ibid., p. 379.

Ineffability James argues that mystical states of consciousness are characterised by their total difference from states of consciousness that occur as part of our ordinary waking lives. He holds that these make them experiences that defy verbal description because they are not like anything that the experiencer has ever encountered before. Both in reports of states of consciousness brought about through experimentation with anesthesia and in accounts found in religious texts, he finds discussions of experiences that cannot be fully recounted or recalled, although they appear to be recognised in the event that they recur. James argues that these states of consciousness tend to be imageless experiences and that, as such, the recipient is unable to convey them to those who have no knowledge of this type of experience.

When discussing the inadequacy of language to express the mystical encounter, James makes particular reference to the writings of a Christian author, Dionysius the Areopagite, or Pseudo-Denys as he is commonly known. He identifies Pseudo-Denys's use of negative and contradictory language as a trait of mystical texts to use language in a way that indicates that the description of the experience exceeds a single frame of reference, which would limit it in some way. For example, he considers paradox to be used as a means of passing beyond the limits of either the positive or the negative description to what he calls 'a higher kind of affirmation'.[12] By this James means that the Absolute that is experienced in mystical consciousness is experienced as neither a 'this' nor a 'that', but as something that transcends such conceptualisation. James's understanding of negative language has been extremely pervasive within modern Christian scholarship.

Noesis James describes noesis as the belief that this totally other form of consciousness actually offers knowledge of a higher truth value than that which can be obtained during normal conscious experience. Noetic experiences can be viewed as a flash of inspiration in which the recipient is left with the impression that they have encountered knowledge of a highly authoritative nature.

Closely related to noesis is a sense of monism. By this James means a belief that there is an ultimate union or oneness within all things. This is often accompanied by fundamental optimism as recipients are overwhelmed by the belief that they are part of a greater whole.

Transiency The quality of transiency categorises the way in which mystical experiences are often said to be fleeting, like flashes of inspiration that suddenly appear and just as suddenly depart.

Passivity Passivity is the feeling of the will being surrendered and overwhelmed by a superior power. This does not mean that James held that mysticial experiences could not be facilitated by purposeful acts. The examples of passivity James cites include those derived from the use of the breathing practices that are connected

---

[12] Ibid., p. 321.

with Yoga, and the Buddhist meditative states of *dhyāna* where the mind is focused on one particular point as a means of invoking a mystical state of consciousness. Likewise he sees anaesthesia as a means of bringing about such experiences. James views mystical religious writings as evidence of religious attempts to cultivate what anaesthesia and sudden moments of awareness bring about in a more haphazard fashion.

Given the emphasis that James places on the experience, James holds that any doctrines reported in relation to a mystical state of consciousness do not so much reflect the experience of the mystic as indicate individual preference and pre-existing belief systems, which they have subsequently applied to the experience, that is *after* the event. He considers them to be part of the interpretation rather than the experience itself and, as such, ultimately disposable because not connected with the broader mystical issues which concern him. J.E. Smith comments that for James these were states that exemplified the essence of religion, over which doctrinal claims had subsequently been built.[13]

James discusses the extent to which these mystical states of consciousness should be seen as authoritative. He concludes that although it is possible for a mystic to be mistaken about a mystical experience, in the same way that is possible for a person to be mistaken about an ordinary conscious experience, this is not a reason for the experiencer to doubt the truth value of their experience. Even though he accepts that those who have not themselves experienced a given mystical encounter do not necessarily need to accept the truth value of its noetic message, it seems clear that James himself bestowed great authority on these experiences, viewing them as the core of religion.

James's ideas have been developed and critiqued by those who also hold perennialist approaches to mysticism, that is, who believe that mystical texts are primarily concerned with accounts of experiences that defy everyday language. One very important development of James's approach to mysticism is found in the writings of Rudolf Otto.

Rudolf Otto

In his book *The Idea of the Holy* (subtitled *An Inquiry into the Non-Rational Factor in the Idea of the Divine and its Relation to the Rational*), Otto, like James, argues that religion cannot be limited to rational understanding in the way that Kant suggests. While Otto accepts the importance of conceptual understandings

---

[13]   J.E. Smith, 'William James's Account of Mysticism; A Critical Appraisal', in S.T. Katz (ed.), *Mysticism and Religious Traditions* (Oxford: Oxford University Press, 1983), pp. 247–79, at p. 247. For further discussion of James's approach, see, G.T. Alexander, 'Psychological Foundations of William James's Theory of Religious Experience', *Journal of Religion*, 56 (1976), 421–34.

of God, he suggests that these become dangerous if valued to such an extent that they are considered to encapsulate the essence of God. A religion that denies the possibility of non-rational, non-conceptual knowledge of God is, in Otto's opinion, a greatly impoverished one.

For Otto, treatments of religion like these forget that the God they conceptualise as a subject is also beyond subjectification and rational comprehension. Deep knowledge of God requires a comprehension of a different sort; conceptionless knowing that Otto refers to as the 'numenous' (from the Latin '*numen*' – to do with a spiritual place, force or influence). He believes that such knowledge is found in mysticism. Yet while in this sense Otto agrees with James, he is generally critical of James's four-fold interpretative schema of ineffability, noesis, transiency and passivity because he believes that James tries to fit what is non-rational into a rationalist framework. For Otto, this is not being true to the nature of the mystical experience, which he considers to be a 'mental state' that is 'irreducible to any other'.[14] At the same time, he agrees with James that mystics assert that mystical knowledge is ineffable. However, Otto does not believe that this means that we cannot talk about them, it is only that we cannot conceptualise them:

> Yet, although it eludes the conceptual way of understanding, it must be in some way or other within our grasp, else absolutely nothing could be asserted of it. And even Mysticism, speaking of it as … the ineffable, does not really mean to imply that absolutely nothing can be asserted of the object of the religious consciousness; otherwise, Mysticism could exist only in unbroken silence, whereas what has generally been a characteristic of the mystics is their copious eloquence.[15]

The Idea of the Holy, sets out to try to solve this conundrum – how we can talk about mystical experiences. Otto's solution is to suggest that feelings and experiences in our everyday lives already hint to us that non-conceptual knowledge is possible. For Otto, these feelings in some way relate to human appreciations of 'holiness' and as such provide us with a means to talk about them. He identifies three main areas of such appreciation which he calls 'mysterium', 'tremendum' and 'fasciens'.

Mysterium This is a sense of mystery. It is the feeling that there is something 'Wholly Other' that exists beyond our ideas of substance and analyses. It brings

---

[14] R. Otto, *The Idea of the Holy: An Inquiry into the Non-Rational Factor in the Idea of the Divine and Its Relation to the Rational*, trans. J.W. Harvey (London: Oxford University Press, 1931), p. 7. Otto says that it is a kind of knowledge that is *sui generis* – that is, of its own type – a phrase which William of St Thierry, the contemporary of Bernard of Clairvaux, also used to describe mystical knowing.

[15] Otto, *The Idea of the Holy*, p. 2. See also, R. Otto, *Mysticism East and West: A Comparative Analysis of the Nature of Mysticism*, trans. B.L. Bracey and R.C. Payne (New York: The Macmillan Co., 1932).

with it a sense of being stupefied and overwhelmed. It is a sense of lack, but at the same time Otto argues that it has a positive aspect as that which almost overflowing itself, that is so great that it cannot be contained within itself. Otto maintains that it is related to and underlies concepts like the 'supernatural' and the 'transcendent' that we find in religion. We come across mysterium then when we come across that which astonishes us within religion.

Tremendum This is a sense of the awfulness of the holy, in that it engenders dread within us. It is that which makes us tremor before it. He relates this to a sense of creatureliness or 'creature-feeling' that mystics sometimes describe. This is not a sense of being created but of being in the presence of that which totally transcends one's self. Otto argues that mystics report this experience when they say that they are brought to an awareness of their own nothingness. They also report it in relation to a sense that their very self becomes unstable, such that they begin to question whether there is such a thing as an independent self at all.

Fasciens This is a sense that there is something fascinating about this kind of knowledge. Even though it engenders a sense of dread and mystery, it is something wonderful, like the feeling of intoxication.

Otto is critical of James for not fully realising these non-rational elements that he feels are apparent in the examples of mystical experience that James provides in *The Varieties of Religious Experience*. Otto suggests that this is because James is still too empiricist to really understand the human capacity to grasp the numenous that lies deep within human beings, waiting to be awakened in relation to notions of the holy. Otto's emphasis on the holy, however, also betrays his deeply Christian commitments, something which James does not share. Unlike James, Otto is a strong defender of doctrine, organised religion and the Christian religion in particular. His aim is to open up doctrinal religion to a greater awareness of its non-rational dimension, which he already sees it containing, but not fully embracing, holding this in tension with, rather than as an alternative to, the more structured rational aspects of religion. Otto tries to draw us into this middle ground – the tension between ineffability and comprehension – that he sees encapsulated in mystical experiences.

Other Perennialist Readings

A number of other writers have also critiqued aspects of James's account of mysticism while still retaining a broadly perennialist approach. F.C. Happold, for example, argues that the sense of union which these states engender is much more of a defining feature than James's four characteristics of ineffability, noesis, transciency and passivity. Happold in fact considered James's four characteristics to be rather difficult to separate from one another.[16] Also focusing more on the idea of union, Evelyn Underhill is critical of James's view that drug-induced states should be viewed as the same thing as religious mystical states. She insists that they are fundamentally different and that drug-induced experiences should be excluded from any definition of 'mysticism'.[17] Scholars such as W.T. Stace and R.C. Zaehner have further critiqued James's account of mysticism by questioning the extent to which a mystical experience can be disassociated from so-called normal conscious states.[18]

It should by now be apparent that there is not *one* set position that can be defined as the perennialist, or as it is sometimes known the experientialist, reading of mysticism (the same is true of the other three approaches discussed in this book). Otto's approach stresses experience over consciousness in a way not found in James's approach. Later writers, such as Stace, Happold and Underhill, stress the importance of a feeling of union in a way that is also not found in James. Yet, despite such arguments, what these writers, and a large number of others, have in common is their shared belief that there are certain types of experience which defy everyday language, which can collectively be referred to as mystical.[19] For them, mystical experiences still represent an 'other' mode of consciousness, and

---

[16]   F.C. Happold, *Mysticism: A Study and An Anthology* (Harmondsworth: Penguin, 1963).

[17]   E. Underhill, Mysticism: A Study in the Nature and Development of Man's Spiritual Consciousness (New York: E.P. Dutton, 1911).

[18]   W.T. Stace, *Mysticism and Philosophy* (Philadelphia: J.B. Lippincott, 1960); W.T. Stace, *The Teachings of the Mystics* (New York: New American Library, 1960); and R.C. Zaehner, *Mysticism: Sacred and Profane: An Inquiry into Some Varieties of Praeternatural Experiences* (Oxford: Oxford University Press, 1957). Zaehner moves closer to a contextualist position. However, contextualists such as Gimello argue that Zaehner does not manage to escape from the perennialist position. See R.M. Gimello, 'Mysticism in Its Contexts', in S.T. Katz, *Mysticism and Religious Traditions* (Oxford: Oxford University Press, 1983), pp. 61–88.

[19]   Scholars who fall into this category include, C. Butler, *Western Mysticism*, 2nd edn (London: Constable, 1927); E. Colledge (ed.), *The Medieval Mystics of England* (London: John Murray, 1962); M. Glasscoe, *English Medieval Mystics: Games of Faith* (London and New York: Longman, 1993); W. Riehle, *The Middle English Mystics*, trans. B. Standring (London: Routledge and Kegan Paul, 1981). Also see P. Dinzelbacher, 'The Beginnings of Mysticism Experienced in Twelfth-Century England', in M. Glasscoe (ed.), *The Medieval Mystical Tradition in England: The Exeter Symposium IV: Papers Read at Dartington Hall, July 1987* (Cambridge: D.S. Brewer, 1987), pp. 111–31; G. Epiney-Burgard and E. Zum Brunn, *Women Mystics in Medieval Europe*, trans. S. Hughes (New York: Paragon, 1989); and arguably N. Pike, *Mystic Union: An Essay in the Phenomenology of Mysticism* (Ithaca, NY: Cornell University Press, 1992), although Pike's argument is more subtle than this, arguing for mystical experiences in terms of analogy from sense perception in relation to which he makes connections between his own approach and that offered by Steven T. Katz.

it is this idea that we mean when we talk about perennialist readings in this book. Robert Forman, whose discussions of mysticism are carefully considered in this volume, can arguably be described as extending a perennialist-type position.

The majority of modern scholarly readings of Christian mystics have tended in large part to read accounts of Christian contemplation as descriptions of ineffable mystical experiences. Most of these readings in fact simplify James's reading, approaching mystical texts from a narrower experiential perspective than James himself seems to have advocated. Some of these scholars do pay attention to the language of the texts and the cultural/historical context in which the authors lived and by doing so challenge the confines of this taxonomy. However, for all the attention given to traditions, texts and contexts, scholars within this tradition do not seriously question the very Jamesian idea that a deep and personal experience underlies the essence of the text. This ultimately undermines the importance of studying the texts and contexts, since the study of them, rather than being an end in itself, is undertaken primarily to move the reader closer to the underlying experience. For these scholars then, mysticism *is* mystical experience and it is those who have *experienced* such deep truth who are 'mystics'. Thus, while there are differences of nuance amongst such scholars, which will hopefully become more apparent as we move through the various chapters of this book, there is also enough commonality for us to classify them as one broad school of interpretation. It seems fair to say that this is still the predominant reading of at least male contemplative literature from the Latin West.

However, over the course of the last fifty years, James's general understanding of mystical consciousness has been subjected to a far more rigorous criticism than that offered by the likes of Otto, Stace and Zaehner. These criticisms have made a number of scholars of Christian mysticism radically reassess their understanding of this literature. Three general approaches have emerged, which we will refer to throughout this book as contextualist, feminist, and performative language readings. They owe a great deal to the work of four scholars: Steven T. Katz, Caroline Walker Bynum, Denys Turner and Michael Sells. We will very briefly consider the views of each of these writers, although for the most part both their thinking and that of other scholars who follow but also challenge these theories of mysticism will be allowed to unfold through the various themes explored in this book.

Before turning to these writers it is worth stressing that there are a number of scholars who differ from the perennialist position outlined above, but do not really fit into the categories outlined below. They accept that a pre-linguistic experience of God or immediate contact with God is possible and believe that this is expressed in mystical texts. They do not, however, disregard context in the same way that James does. Bernard McGinn, an extremely important figure in the modern study of mysticism, falls into this category, even though as noted he is better aligned with a revised contextualist category. Thus, writers like McGinn can be said to straddle the categories discussed in this chapter in a subtle way that highlights the complexity involved in trying to answer the question 'What is Christian mysticism?'[20]

Contextualism

Steven T. Katz

Contextualism largely owes its origins to the thought of Steven T. Katz.[21] Katz has edited four books of articles, in which he and others explore the issue of mystical experience from similar positions.[22] His articles in each of these books are now regarded as seminal within the philosophy of mysticism for the manner in which they challenge James's general understanding of mysticism.

Katz is not satisfied with James's interpretation of mystical texts since he believes that there cannot be experiences that are not mediated through cultural context. This means that not only our interpretation but also the experience itself

---

[20]   These writers hold an understanding of mysticism, which, although valuing the role of experience, involves a much more questioning approach to experience than that arguably offered by James. They consider context but not from the strictly contextualist position posited by Katz, who rejects the idea of pre-linguistic experience. While it can still be argued that this focus on experience mitigates against a serious consideration of the language of these texts such as we find in performative language readings, the nuanced positions held by writers like Bernard McGinn brings such an assumption into question. Scholars who arguably fit in this category include: L.E. Bouyer, '"Mysticism": An Essay on the History of the Word', in A. Plé et al. (eds), *Mystery and Mysticism: A Symposium* (London: Blackfriars, 1956), pp. 119–37; G. M. Jantzen, *Power, Gender and Christian Mysticism* (Cambridge: Cambridge University Press, 1995), pp. 278–321; Baron F. von Hügel, *The Mystical Element of Religion as Studied in Saint Catherine of Genoa and Her Friends*, 2 vols (London: J.M. Dent and Sons, 1908); W.R. Inge, *Mysticism in Religion* (London: Hutchinson University Library, 1947); O. Davies, *Meister Eckhart: Mystical Theologian* (London: SPCK, 1991); E. Howells, *John of the Cross and Teresa of Avila: Mystical Knowledge and Selfhood* (New York: Crossroad, 2002).

[21]   This approach is also sometimes known as 'constructivism'; Robert Forman uses this term when he criticises Katz's position. However, Katz does not feel that those who classify his approach as constructivism offer a fair account of it and prefers the terms 'contextualism' and 'contextualist'. For a discussion of his approach as contextualism, see B. McGinn, *The Foundations of Mysticism: Origins to the Fifth Century*, The Presence of God: A History of Western Christian Mysticism, vol. 1 (New York: Crossroad, 1991), p. 323. Also see J.B. Hollenback, *Mysticism: Experience, Response, and Empowerment* (University Park, PA: Pennsylvania State University Press), pp. 8–12.

[22]   The four volumes edited by Katz are: *Mysticism and Philosophical Analysis* (London: Sheldon Press, 1978); *Mysticism and Religious Traditions* (Oxford: Oxford University Press, 1983); *Mysticism and Language* (Oxford: Oxford University Press, 1992); *Mysticism and Sacred Scripture* (New York: Oxford University Press, 2000).

is shaped by who we are and what we believe. Katz is basically arguing that we cannot escape from ourselves and touch some kind of ineffable or divine Absolute or God.

> There are NO pure (i.e. unmediated) experiences. Neither mystical experience nor more ordinary forms of experience give any indication, or any grounds for believing, that they are unmediated. That is to say, *all* experience is processed through and organised by, and makes itself available to us in extremely complex epistemological ways.[23]

Katz therefore argues that attention must be paid not only to the post-experiential reports of the mystic but also to pre-experiential mediating conditions.

Unlike James, who argues that mystical states of consciousness from any religious tradition can be identified under four characteristics, Katz believes that all human experience, in which he includes so-called 'mystical' experience, is shaped or determined by cultural categories. A Hindu and a Christian do not both have unmediated experiences of *x* which they then describe at a later stage in the familiar language of their respective religious traditions. Rather, the Hindu has a pre-formed, anticipated Hindu experience, and the Christian has a pre-formed, anticipated Christian experience. Furthermore, the conceptual background that the mystic brings to his or her experience excludes in advance what cannot be experienced within that religious tradition. A Hindu, epistemologically speaking, does not have the mediating conditions to report experiences of the Virgin Mary, any more than a Christian can report experiences of Vishnu. Katz notes, however, that a religious tradition's conceptual resources are diverse enough to produce a plurality of experience. In such cases, Katz says, attention must be paid to historical development and shifts in ideology in order to study the effect of such changes on mystical experience. In fact, he argues that there is no such thing as 'perennial philosophy' – by which he means a philosophy that exists across all cultures and contexts.[24] This said, he still argues that there are certain traits that run through all mystical writing. However, these characteristics do not relate to the initial experience, but to the way in which language is used within the texts. He argues that the language that we find within mystical texts performs a variety of functions. He believes that one of the main functions of paradoxical statements, for example, is to prepare the practitioner's mind so that it can enter a new state of consciousness that is not governed by the rules of logic. However, he does not think that Christian mystics use paradox in this way, since he believes that Christian mysticism is always centred on a transcendent reality; although he holds

---

[23]   S.T. Katz, 'Language, Epistemology and Mysticism', in *Mysticism and Philosophical Analysis*, pp. 27–74, at p. 26.

[24]   Objections have been raised to Katz's understanding of perennial philosophy. See, for example, H. Smith, 'Is there a Perennial Philosophy?' *Journal of the American Academy of Religion*, 55:3 (1987), 553–68.

that Christian mystics do sometimes use paradox to try to talk of that which cannot be spoken, as in the case of Meister Eckhart.[25]

Katz's analysis has led some critics to reinvest value in the theology recounted in mystical texts. Taking a similar approach, Ninian Smart, while holding that the experiences encountered by the *Cloud*-Author and Buddhaghosa (a fifth-century Buddhist scholar) may have been similar, stresses the importance of reading any account of such experiences in relation to the doctrinal beliefs held by the writer.[26] Nicholas Watson is likewise deeply critical of the way in which perennialist readings of the Middle English mystics have led to their relationship to other literature of the period being largely overlooked.[27] As with James's perennialist position, there are many scholars who both expand and challenge Katz's contextualist stance.

Bernard McGinn, undoubtedly one of the most famous scholars of mysticism in the twenty-first century, can perhaps also be associated with this category to some extent. McGinn too believes that the context and theological statements made by the mystics cannot be separated from their experiences and should not simply be dismissed as unimportant or incidental.[28] Yet, as we will see over the course of this book, McGinn, following the philosopher Bernard Lonergan, argues for a very nuanced reading of mysticism which also accepts the possibility of pre-linguistic experience of God, or what he terms 'mediated immediacy'.[29] Taking a position that in fact straddles not only the perennialist and contextualist positions, but also contains elements that are resonant of the performative language position discussed below, he is less critical of James.[30] We will further explore the contextualism of

---

[25] S.T. Katz, 'Mysticism and the Interpretation of Sacred Scripture', in *Mysticism and Sacred Scripture*, pp. 7–67, at p. 43.

[26] N. Smart 'What would the Buddhaghosa Have Made of The Cloud of Unknowing', in Katz, *Mysticism and Language*, pp. 103–22, esp. p. 121.

[27] For example, see N. Watson, 'The Middle English Mystics', in D. Wallace (ed.), *The Cambridge History of Medieval English Literature* (Cambridge: Cambridge University Press, 1999), pp. 539–65, at p. 539. Watson's view is further discussed in Chapter 9, pp. 195–6.

[28] McGinn, *The Foundations of Mysticism*, pp. xvi–xvii and 265–343. Also see J.E. Smith, 'In What Sense Can We Speak of Experiencing God?', *Journal of Religion*, 50 (1978), 229–444.

[29] Bernard McGinn, ed. and trans., *The Essential Writings of Christian Mysticism* (Modern Library Classics; New York: Random House, 2006), pp. xvi–xvii. McGinn adopts the phrase "mediated immediacy" from Bernard Lonergan; see for example, *Method in Theology* (New York: Herder & Herder, 1972), p. 77. For a discussion of McGinn's use of this term, see E. Howells, 'Relationality and Difference in the Mysticism of Pierre de Bérulle', *Harvard Theological Review*, 102/2 (2009), 225–43.

[30] Likewise, George Pattison is critical of the trajectory that he sees in Katz and Turner that prioritises language over experience. Instead he argues that both work together, allowing access to that which lies beyond language. In this sense he argues for a slight return to William James's reading of experience, although not one that considers it apart

Katz and others, as well as those, such as McGinn, who somewhat critique this position, in relation to the various aspects of Christian mystical literature examined in this book.

Performative Language Readings

Denys Turner and Michael Sells have independently developed approaches to Christian mystical literature that, even more than contextualism, move away from seeing experience as central to the production of Christian mystical texts. Both focus on the performative element of mystical language, particularly on the negative statements that characterise many accounts of Christian mysticism.

Denys Turner

Denys Turner has written a number of books in which he discusses the notion of mysticism.[31] Rather than considering this idea across a range of faiths like James and Katz, Turner confines his analysis of it to accounts of mysticism by Early Church and medieval writers. His reading of these texts has led Turner to question whether the Christian writings which are commonly viewed as accounts of 'mysticism' should, in fact, be described in this way. He does not consider the main concerns of these texts to be the same as the main concerns that underlie the modern study of mysticism.

Turner views the modern term 'mysticism' as so bound up with the idea of experience that the terms 'mysticism' and 'experience' cannot be separated. He argues that one cannot refer to a text as 'mystical' without it being assumed that one is referring to a text which talks about some kind of experience (ineffable or otherwise). Looking almost exclusively at male Christian contemplative writing, Turner argues that, rather than being concerned with *experiences*, Christian contemplative literature, at least within the Latin West, attempts to tell its readers something about the *nature* of God.[32] Turner identifies what he sees as two strands within medieval mystical literature: one that chiefly makes use of contradictory and

---

from context. See G. Pattison, 'What to Say: Reflection on Mysticism after Modernity', in K. Vanhoozer and M. Warner (eds), *Transcending Boundaries in Philosophy and Theology: Reason, Meaning and Experience* (Aldershot: Ashgate, 2007), pp. 191–205.

[31]   Turner has, to date, produced three books in which he examines medieval accounts of mysticism: *The Darkness of God: Negativity in Christian Mysticism* (Cambridge: Cambridge University Press 1995), *Eros and Allegory: Medieval Exegesis of the Song of Songs* (Kalamazoo: Cistercian Publications, 1995) and *Faith Reason and the Existence of God* (Cambridge: Cambridge University Press, 2004). A further work, *The Dark Vision of God: Denys the Carthusian and Contemplative Wisdom* is due to be published by Brepols in the near future.

[32]   Turner, *The Darkness of God*, pp. 4–8 and 252–73.

paradoxical statements and the other that engages in erotic dialogue. However, he argues that, regardless of the strategy, the aim is the same. Its objective is, through a clever use of literary devices and word play, to communicate an epistemological message (that is, knowledge about God) rather than an experiential message (that is, an experience of God).

Michael Sells

Michael Sells's approach is similar. He focuses exclusively on the role of negative or apophatic language, or as he calls it 'languages of unsaying'. He too suggests that its purpose is more epistemological than experiential. He argues that in mystical texts negative and positive statements are brought together in such a way that the language is deliberately destabilised. Like Turner, he sees this as an attempt to communicate to the reader something of the *nature* of God, that is, that God cannot be encapsulated in language. However, unlike Turner, Sells's work is interdisciplinary, examining not only Christian but also Neoplatonic, Jewish and Islamic mystical texts. Sells argues that there are texts in many religions that are 'mystical' in this epistemological sense. In fact he argues that there are writers who are not normally classified as 'mystics' but whose texts contain languages of unsaying. Sells argues for a reconfiguration of the taxonomy of mysticism based around this idea of apophasis. Some texts currently viewed as mystical would end up being excluded, others not seen as mystical (because they do not appear to report mystical experiences) would end up being included. Sells's fullest exploration of this idea is found in his *Mystical Languages of Unsaying*.[33]

Although both arguing that an event occurs that allows the reader to somehow grasp that which is beyond language, Turner and Sells differ in that Turner maintains that this brings the reader to a point of silence, as language collapses. Sells, however, critiques this position, asserting that the event is so momentary and language so inexhaustible that the process never ends. The reader quickly slips from the dialectic tension engendered by 'languages of unsaying' to a more binary understanding of God's nature, therefore needing a further negation to return to mystical knowledge. What is important for both writers is that choice of style in the form of literary devices such as paradox is determined by a theology (rather than an experience) that accepts the absolute otherness of the divine and is the outworking of that *belief* in language, the one reinforcing the other.

A few scholars have followed Turner and Sells in rejecting the belief that experience is the essence of medieval contemplative writing. Mark McIntosh, for instance, argues that much modern interpretation of mystical texts results from conditioning, in which the preconception that these works describe experiences

---

[33] M. Sells, *Mystical Languages of Unsaying* (Chicago: Chicago University Press, 1994). Much of Sells's other work focuses particularly on Islam.

is simply accepted. He suggests that when more closely analysed it emerges that medieval Christian mystics, in fact, encouraged their readers to let go of all experiences, even those which seemed most pure.[34] Rebecca Stephens has also applied Turner's and Sells's analyses to her own evaluation of the writings of Marguerite Porete. She, like Sells, argues that Marguerite's text is better understood if not read primarily in terms of mystical experience or for that matter with reference to female bodily spirituality.[35]

A writer who can perhaps also be classified as offering a form of performative language approach is Michael de Certeau. His work pre-dates that of Turner and Sells, but he also concentrates on linguistic representation, linking it with social subjectivity and the reinterpretation of fables. His approach is also closely related to the feminist approaches to mysticism of Julia Kristeva and Luce Irigaray since this leads him to stress the socially disruptive nature of mysticism. The sense in which his account echoes performative language readings lies in its emphasis on semiotics and the stress he places on the relationship between the word 'mystical' and allegorical exegesis of the Bible, an issue that we discuss in Chapter 6. De Certeau's approach has exerted great influence on late twentieth- and twenty-first-century discussions of mysticism. It is therefore with great regret that we have not been able to widely consider his thought in this volume. His important work on mysticism draws heavily on writers like John of the Cross and Teresa of Avila whose later developments of mysticism are not explored in this book. To do so lies beyond the scope of this short introduction. His marginalisation is in no way intended as a reflection of his importance in this field. By stressing the contribution of performative language readings and feminist readings we hope to facilitate further consideration of the area in which de Certeau's reading arguably fits, like that of Nancy Caciola, whose work is discussed in Chapter 8. The manner in which she stresses the importance of considering not only the interior value of mysticism, but also its exterior effects, builds on de Certeau's understanding of mysticism.[36] Through such considerations as Caciola's, de Certeau's presence can still be felt in the course of this book.

It is hopefully now clear that both contextualist and performative language reading are responding to the perennialist position, in that both pose criticisms of its rather static emphasis on ineffable experience. We can get some idea how these different interpretations work in practice if we look at the opening prayer from Pseudo-Denys's *Mystical Theology*:

---

[34]   McIntosh, *Mystical Theology*, pp. 136–7 and 142.

[35]   R.A. Stephens, 'Orthodoxy and Liminality in Marguerite Porete's Mirror of Simple Souls' (unpublished doctoral dissertation, University of Birmingham, England, 1999).

[36]   M. de Certeau, *The Mystic Fable: Volume One, The Sixteenth and Seventeenth Centuries*, trans. M.B. Smith (Chicago: University of Chicago Press, 1986), esp. pp. 94–7. For a clear summary of de Certeau's position, see P. Sheldrake, 'Unending desire: De Certeau's "mystics"', *The Way Supplement*, 102 (2001), 38–48.

Trinity!! Higher than any being,
              any divinity, any goodness!
    Guide of Christians
              in the wisdom of the heaven!
Lead us up beyond unknowing and light,
    up to the farthest, highest peak
              of mystic scripture,
    where the mysteries of God's Word
              lie simple, absolute and unchangeable
              in the brilliant darkness of a hidden silence.
    Amid the deepest shadow
              they pour overwhelming light
              on what is most manifest.
Amid the whole unsensed and unseen
              they completely fill our sightless minds
              with treasures beyond all beauty.[37]

We can see that Pseudo-Denys uses a number of interesting literary devices and images in this passage. First, we find the images of light, darkness and height. Secondly, we note that the language is deliberately paradoxical – the meaning is not immediately clear. How can you have a brilliant darkness? How can a silence be hidden?

- For James, Pseudo-Denys is using language to illustrate that mystical consciousness transcends conceptualisation in the sense that it is imageless and ineffable.
- For Katz, Pseudo-Denys is claiming that his experience was ineffable, but no experience can be truly ineffable, so we can ignore this trope. (Although Katz elsewhere argues that Eckhart uses similar language to try to talk about the nature of God who exceeds all language.)
- For Turner and Sells, Pseudo-Denys is bringing positive and negative statements together to show the inadequacy of both as a means of describing God, since it is God's nature, as opposed to our experience of God, that exceeds description.

The relative merits of these readings of Pseudo-Denys are discussed in more detail in Chapter 2. Here the passage hopefully serves as a useful illustration of the types of reading that one can expect if scholars strictly adhere to these three categories. Although far from entirely divorced from perennialist, contextualist and performative language approaches, feminist readings critique all three approaches in so far as they fail to make room for feminine spiritual self-expression within mysticism.

---

[37] Pseudo-Denys, *Pseudo-Dionysius: The Complete Works*, p. 135.

Feminist Readings

Feminist readings suggest that the boundaries of perennialist taxonomy, in particular, are too narrow to incorporate the female struggle for self-awareness found in the many accounts of contemplation composed by women. We will consider a number of feminist readings of mysticism, including those of Julie Kristeva, Luce Irigaray and Amy Hollywood. However more than any other feminist critique, Caroline Walker Bynum's extensive writings have provided the impetus for a significant renewal of interest in women mystics.[38] Bynum identifies a distinctive form of female mysticism in the later Middle Ages through which she sees women empowering themselves and finding a distinctively feminine spiritual voice.

Caroline Walker Bynum

Caroline Walker Bynum's work is not limited to mystics. However, in seeking to recover the female voice and redress a tendency of history to be an account by men of men's deeds, Bynum turns to a number of mystical texts written by women, approaching them from an openly feminist perspective. She argues that we find a distinctive form of female Christian mysticism and spirituality emerging particularly between the twelfth and fifteenth centuries. Rather than being concerned, like the male spirituality of the period, with transcending the body, Bynum argues that women's spiritual writings use bodily and homely imagery to move to the spiritual heights that men pursued in a more intellectual fashion. She draws attention to the way that feminine spirituality in this period is characterised by an almost obsessive fascination with food, suffering and fertility, for example. By understanding women's spiritual writing from a feminist perspective, her analysis creates a space for an embodied form of mysticism that is distinctively feminine. Bynum's account of female mysticism is now, without doubt, the predominant reading of Christian female mystical writing within a medieval context. Her approach has been adopted and developed by numerous scholars. The importance of the idea that mysticism is gendered is such that it warrants an entire chapter. The inclusion of a specific chapter on gendered mysticism is also an attempt to redress the balance of our book, which could otherwise be accused

---

[38] We discuss this issue in Chapter 7. Bynum's main works are: *Jesus as Mother: Studies in the Spirituality of the High Middle Ages* (Berkeley: University of California Press, 1982); *Holy Feast, Holy Fast: The Religious Significance of Food to Medieval Women* (Berkeley: University of California Press, 1987); *Fragmentation and Redemption: Essays on Gender and the Human Body in Medieval Religion* (New York: Zone Books, 1991); *The Resurrection of the Body in Western Christianity, 200–1336* (New York: Columbia University Press, 1995); *Metamorphosis and Identity* (New York: Zone Books, 2001); *Wonderful Blood: Theology and Practice in the Late Medieval Northern Germany and Beyond* (Philadephia: University of Pennsylvania Press, 2007).

of being a rather male-centric treatment of contemporary theoretical readings of Christian mysticism.

Postmodern Re-readings

In addition to these four readings, another approach to the Christian mystics has also begun to appear in the last two decades – these are postmodern re-readings. Most focus on the writings of Augustine and Pseudo-Denys. These readings cannot easily be incorporated into Chapters 2 and 3 of this book, this despite the fact that some scholars make use of a more postmodern approach to critique the four categories of interpretation outlined above. However, they are too important to ignore. Two parallel chapters (Chapter 11 and 12) therefore explore the postmodern approaches to the mysticism of Pseudo-Denys and Augustine, concentrating on three prominent writers: Jacques Derrida, Jean-Luc Marion and Jean-François Lyotard. Authors such as Kevin Hart and Mark Burrows, who draw on both modern and postmodern readings, are briefly referred to in both parts of the book.[39]

Conclusion

These then are the different approaches that we will be considering over the course of this book. Each chapter explores a different theme, motif or idea considered definitive of Christian mysticism. The chapters begin with a brief outline of the theme or motif, focusing on the way it is used in the writings of Christian mystics whose ideas have proved particularly influential. Augustine and Pseudo-Denys therefore figure highly. Once the idea and its importance have been clearly explicated, we turn to a discussion of different theoretical responses to it. Each chapter refers to a range of scholarly treatments of the theme. From these discussions it will be apparent that some scholars legitimately straddle the different approaches to mysticism outlined above. From this it should become clear that modern scholarly discussions of mysticism are often highly nuanced, with a subtly which is sometimes missed. It is, however, important that we take note of this if we are to seriously consider what we mean by Christian mysticism.

Despite our best efforts, in such a short book there will, inevitably, be gaps. Not all scholars who have written on the mystics can be included. Our intention

---

[39]   See, for example, K. Hart, 'The Experience of Nonexperience', in M. Kessler and C. Sheppard (eds), *Mystics: Presence and Aporia*, Religion and Postmodernism Series (Chicago and London: University of Chicago Press, 2003), pp. 188–206. This entire volume, in fact, contains essays that explore the interplay between modern and postmodern readings of mysticism. Also see M.S. Burrows, 'Raiding the Inarticulate: Mysticism, Poetics and the Unlanguageable', *Spiritus*, 4 (2004), 173–94.

was not to offer a comprehensive summary of *all* those who have *ever* written on Christian mysticism, but simply to provide an outline of the main contemporary theoretical approaches to Christian mysticism that readers are likely to encounter in the literature and to indicate the parameters of these approaches by showing how they fall within the work of key scholars. As we will discuss in the conclusion to the book, we believe that this approach offers us the best possible chance of gaining insight into the question 'What is mysticism?', and the extent to which an answer to this question is really possible.

Part I
Key Themes and Motifs

The six chapters in this section of the book look at themes and motifs that are often considered definitive of Christian mysticism. They explore the relationship between Christianity and various forms of Platonism, the use of negative statements about God and of erotic imagery, the idea that the spiritual journey is a movement within the soul, the role performed by hierarchy and the connection between symbolism and the mystical interpretation of scripture. Through our discussion of these themes we aim to reflect on the various theoretical approaches to Christian mysticism outlined in the introductory chapter.

Chapter 1
Platonism and Christian Mysticism

It is widely recognised that there is a relationship between Platonism in its various forms and the Christian mystical tradition.[1] The chapter begins with an introduction to Plato and two ideas which had important implications for Christian mysticism: his theory of knowledge as exemplified in his famous cave analogy and his theory of the love of beauty. It then considers how Plato's ideas were developed by three Neoplatonists: Plotinus, Iamblichus and Proclus.

Platonism

Platonism is a philosophical system attributed to Plato (428–347 BC), who is perhaps the best known of the ancient Greek philosophers, and arguably the most important philosopher of all time. He was the first Western philosopher to put his thinking into writing, and much, if not all, of his output has survived. He presented his thought in the form of philosophical dialogues between his teacher Socrates and various other parties. He also established his Academy (so called because of its location at a site sacred to the hero Academus) in Athens, the place of his birth.

Plato's Theory of Knowledge

Plato's early dialogues focus on the Socratic method of revealing moral insights through a process of self-discovery. Being virtuous was not a question of finding a missing piece of information. Rather it is about coming to understand that we already possess knowledge of virtue. In Andrew Louth's words, our understanding needs to be '*awakened*'.[2] This principle of knowledge, that we already possess but have managed to obscure, is central to Plato's philosophy. Even more important is Plato's belief that the soul, or inner part of a person, is more important and more real that the outer physical part.

According to Plato, the soul originally contemplated the truth or true reality, that is the 'Forms' or 'Ideas'. Access to true reality was, however, obscured when the soul was born into a body. The embodied soul forgot its vision of Truth and Beauty and instead accepted the changeable world of the senses – a world of

---

[1]   See, for example, the important work of A. Louth, *The Origins of the Christian Mystical Tradition: From Plato to Denys* (Oxford: Oxford University Press, 1981).

[2]   Ibid., p.1.

illusion in which nothing stays the same – as the only reality there is. The world we experience on a day-to-day basis is, according to Plato, a world in which real knowledge is impossible since real knowledge cannot be based on that which is changeable and corruptible. For knowledge to be certain it must be based on that which is eternal and unchangeable. To reacquire such knowledge the soul – the eternal and unchangeable element in the human being – must leave this world and remember what it once knew. According to Plato, this act of remembering or *awakening* is the object of philosophy. At the end of Book 5 of *The Republic*, Plato discusses perception, distinguishing between knowledge, ignorance and an intermediate state called 'opinion'. He refers to these 'states' as forms of awareness or acquaintance. Knowledge, he says, is awareness of that which has being; ignorance is awareness of that which does not have being; and opinion is awareness of something that is between being and non-being. Knowledge or apprehension of the Good is free from error, whereas opinion is prone to error. These distinctions have a specific function in Plato's famous cave analogy, through which he tries to explain his theory of knowledge.

Plato's Cave Analogy Plato discusses the cave analogy in Book 7 of *The Republic*. He describes a cave that is connected to the outside world by a long passage. Sitting deep in the passage are a row of prisoners facing the cave's end wall. There is no natural light where they sit, they are chained to the spot and their necks are clamped to prevent them seeing anyone else – all they can do is look forward at the cave wall. Plato's asks us to imagine that this has always been the case for these prisoners; their reality is the reality of the cave.

Unknown to the prisoners, behind them a fire burns and their captors use the firelight to cast the shadows of objects onto the cave wall. Having no experiences to the contrary, the prisoners accept these shadows to be all the reality there is. But what would happen if a prisoner wrestled free from his chains, turned around and started to walk towards the cave's entrance? The experience would surely be physically painful, at first sight the fire would be dazzling and the experiences beyond the shadows would be incomprehensible. There would be a strong temptation, Plato thinks, for the prisoner to return to the comforting deception of the shadow world. Outside the cave, Plato says, the experience would be totally blinding. As the prisoner became accustomed to natural sunlight, he would begin to make out those objects he had previously experienced only as shadows. Eventually, Plato thinks, the prisoner would become accustomed to the brilliance of the sun and the 'truth' of its revealing rays.

The cave analogy illustrates the progress of the soul, drawn up by its schooling in philosophy, to knowledge of reality, 'the Good', which is free from opinion. Plato is clear that contemplation of the Good is not a static goal. The progress of the soul, as an education from opinion to knowledge, must be made available to those still living amongst the cave's shadows. In this relation it is important to recognise that Plato's *Republic* is a treatise concerning, amongst other things, who or what a philosopher ruler should be. According to Plato, a philosopher ruler is one who has been educated in the philosophical method that his cave analogy outlines. He will therefore judge by what is ultimately good and true, and not rely on mere opinion. However, the philosopher ruler must not only become accustomed to the light of the Good, he must reacquaint himself with the darkness of the cave. He must be aware of the deceptions of those only acquainted with shadows. In Plato's words, addressing would-be philosopher rulers:

> You must therefore each descend in turn and live with your fellows in the cave and get used to seeing in the dark; once you get used to it you will see a thousand times better than they do and will distinguish the various shadows, and know what they are shadows of, because you have seen the truth about things admirable and just and good.[3]

This idea of a second descent after ascent is also found in Christian mysticism.[4]

Plato's Theory of the Love of Beauty

True knowledge in a Platonic sense also means union with and participation in the objects of true knowledge: Truth, Beauty and Goodness. How such participation works is clearly illustrated by Plato's theory of Beauty. Plato outlines his understanding of Beauty most clearly in *The Symposium*. The setting for the dialogue is a banquet at which certain guests make speeches in praise of the god of love, Eros. Socrates makes a speech in which he sets out a progressive ascent to the love of beauty. Socrates asks his audience to consider concrete manifestations of beauty. He moves them beyond these to beauty in its universal form as illustrated in these many objects. Finally he leads them to Beauty itself. Andrew Louth has described this process of ascent as the soul's 'intellectual purification', since it is a movement away from the senses.[5] Yet all things are beautiful through participation in Beauty itself. Diotima's speech makes this clear: 'When anyone, ascending from a correct system of Love, begins to contemplate this supreme beauty, he already touches the consummation of his labour.'[6] The Form of Beauty is the spark perceived in a beautiful face but it can never be limited to a corruptible material object.

Love (*Eros*) intensifies as the soul approaches the final rapturous vision of Beauty. Contemplating Beauty, like the contemplation of the Good in the cave

---

[3]   Plato, The *Republic*, trans. D. Lee, (London: Penguin Classics, 2nd revised edn, 2003), p. 247.

[4]   See, for example, the writings of Richard of St Victor, who stresses that the mystic has a moral duty not to simply remain in the mystical heights. Writers like Marguerite Porete and Meister Eckhart do not seem so clear on this point, however. It is one area of their thought that interestingly becomes linked to heresy, as we discuss in Chapter 10.

[5]   Louth, *The Origins of the Christian Mystical Tradition*, p. 10.

[6]   Quoted in ibid., p. 11.

analogy, transcends all that the soul previously remembers understanding and knowing. Love also becomes purified as it moves away from carnal attachments. What is revealed is eternal, it cannot be defined nor can it be represented in an image – it is unique. Here knowledge is not so much 'knowing' in a human sense, 'participation'. Everything that the soul previously thought it knew and all embodied means of knowing are transcended. To know what is unknowable the soul must transcend the normal limits of knowledge and encounter it in ecstasy – literally *ekstasis*: 'out of one's senses'.

All of these ideas were important for later medieval writers. As we will see in subsequent chapters, the idea that one is both ascending but also journeying within becomes a central theme in Christian mysticism. The relation of image to eternal knowledge and the relatively lowly status of imagination are also important features, as is the idea of not-knowing and ecstasy. Many of these ideas are passed to later Christian mystics through the writings of Augustine and Pseudo-Denys. Rather than being influenced by Plato directly, these two authors were influenced by the writings of two important NeoPlatonists: Plotinus and Proclus.

Neoplatonism

After Plato's death, the Academy was headed by a series of distinguished pupils, each of whom claimed to be preserving the authentic teaching of Plato. A variety of slightly divergent schools of thought emerged. The result is what experts now identify as 'Middle Platonism' and 'Neoplatonism'. The greatest Middle Platonists lived in Alexandria in Egypt: Philo (25 BC–AD 50) who synthesised Judaism with Platonism; and Clement (150–215) and Origen (185–254) who combined Christianity with Platonic concepts. Neoplatonists who headed the Academy and were particularly important for Christian mysticism were Plotinus (*c*.204–270) whose ideas influenced Augustine, and Iamblichus (*c*.240–325). The most famous proponent of Iamblichus's approach was Proclus, who was a major influence on Pseudo-Denys.[7]

Plotinus and the Theory of Emanation

At the core of his philosophical system, Plotinus describes different levels of being, of which the head is the One. The One is not simply numerical unity, it is an all-embracing unity in which everything is related to everything else. But just as the One is not to be thought of exclusively as numerically one, so it is not simply the unity of all things. The One is the author of all things, not as a creator external to creation, but in the sense that all that exists has emanated from the One and

---

[7]   Pseudo-Denys's account of mysticism is fully considered in Chapters 2 and 5.

therefore shares its substance with the author of creation. Emanation is the One's simplicity unfolding into what we understand as reality.

As well as emanation out from the One there is a process of return. For Plotinus, emanation and return establish a perfect balance in the cosmos. E.R. Dodds explains this dual movement through the analogy of the ripples caused by a stone breaking the calm surface of water. He writes:

> We may think of the continuously expanding and continuously weakening circle of ripples that you get when you throw a stone into still water – save that here there is no stone-thrower and no water either: reality *is the ripples* and there is nothing else.[8]

The overflowing of the One into diversity is counterbalanced by the One's longing to return to perfect simplicity by drawing everything back to itself. There is the corresponding desire of multiplicity to become simple again. However, care must be taken when using a word like 'longing' in reference to the One. The One is a generative unity that has no time or place, quality or quantity – it has no personal investment in the way reality is constructed. In fact, Plotinus's One is totally unknowable and nameless, and could not be identified with any personal qualities of relatedness. The One's relationship with the created order is dialectical only; it is a philosophical structure that explains a mid-point between undifferentiated unity and unrelated multiplicity. However, this does not mean that all that is not undifferentiated unity is an illusion. For Plotinus, the emanations from the One are real, including matter, though their reality is of a lower order to that of the One.[9] While there is a soul and mind within each human, for Plotinus these also exist on a cosmic level. At a cosmic level they are in fact the two highest emanations of the one: Mind (*nous*) and Soul (*psyche*). They are divine and together with the One constitute a Triad. In the emanation of the Mind the undifferentiated state of the One is made intelligible. Soul is inferior to Mind and grasps things discursively by moving from one thing to another. Like everything else, human beings come forth from the One. Their highest aim is to return to the One. This must be done by rising above material and sensible reality first to the Mind and from there, by an ecstatic leap, to the One.

Introspection   For Plotinus this process is achievable because, while most of the soul becomes embodied, a bit of the soul remains connected to Mind. Therefore, for the soul to make progress towards to the One, it must turn inwards not outwards. As the soul journeys within, it becomes purified and comes to realise the existence of this intelligible realm beyond the material world. By entering deeply into itself

---

[8]   E.R. Dodds, *The Ancient Concept of Progress and Other Essays on Greek Literature and Belief* (Oxford: Oxford University Press, 1985), p. 130; quoted in Louth, *The Origins of the Christian Mystical Tradition*, p. 39.

[9]   For this reason it would be wrong to think of Plotinus as a monist.

the soul is seeking to know itself better. Here, ultimately, self-knowledge and knowledge of the One are undifferentiated – the soul's withdrawal into itself is simultaneously the ascent to the One. Plotinus describes the process as follows:

> 'Let us flee to the beloved Fatherland' … The Fatherland to us is There whence we have come, and There is the Father. What then is our course, what the manner of our flight? This is not a journey for the feet; the feet bring us only from land to land … all this order of things you must set aside and refuse to see: you must close the eyes and call instead upon another vision which is to be waked within you, a vision, the birth-right of all, which few turn to use.[10]

Plotinus goes on to recommend that the soul learn to sculpt itself into that which is recognisably beautiful. The result of this labour is that virtue shines out of it in 'godlike splendour'. Plotinus refers to this newly sculpted soul as a unity that cannot be broken. The considerable effort needed to put aside the distractions of the outer world and undertake a profound moral purification is repaid by the discovery of a selfhood that is the soul's true nature and its realisation of its relation to true reality.

With outward distractions negated, the soul advances beyond having to know through the painstaking process of linking together disparate pieces of information. To use Plotinus's phrase, when the soul is thinking intuitively it 'thinks reality'.[11] This knowledge is considered a possession of the soul and it cannot be wrong. The state of intuitive knowing is, however, not the summit of the soul's ascent. For this highest unity, Plotinus abandons talk of the soul's serene flight inwards. The soul's final stage is achieved abruptly as it is swept out of itself and into an ecstatic union with the One. The One or the Father does not, however, actively draw out the soul; it is unaware of anything below itself. This is a genuine case of ecstasy. In the moment of ecstasy the soul is no longer itself and passes into unity. Plotinus describes his own moments of ecstasy thus: 'Many times it has happened: lifted out of my body into myself; becoming external to all other things and self-centred; beholding a marvellous beauty'.[12] His understanding of the One was particularly important for Augustine's understanding of mysticism, as we will see in Chapter 3.

Iamblichus and Religious Ritual or Theurgy

As we noted above, another form of Neoplatonism centres on the thought of Iamblichus. Iamblichus (240–325) placed particular emphasis on religious ritual, a feature not found in Plotinus's Neoplatonism. Iamblichus claims that religious ritual or 'theurgy' has the power to effect change within the universe. Translating 'theurgy' (erroneously) as 'magic' rather than 'divine action', many modern critics

---

[10]   Quoted in Louth, *The Origins of the Christian Mystical Tradition*, pp. 40–41.
[11]   Ibid., p. 46.
[12]   Ibid., p. 48.

dismissed Iamblichus's approach as a corruption of Neoplatonism. Recent research by Gregory Shaw, however, suggests that this is a misunderstanding of Iamblichian theurgy. This in turn affects a misunderstanding of Proclus's understanding of hierarchy, and makes confusing the references to theurgy in Pseudo-Denys's writings (as we shall see in Chapter 5).

Unlike Plotinus, who argued that a connection remained between the soul and the world soul (*nous*), which simply had to be awakened, Iamblichus held a far gloomier picture of the soul's relation to the Absolute or One. He believed (contra Plotinus) that the *whole* human soul descended into the body; no connection remained between it and the world soul. Introspection (the inward journey suggested by Plotinus), therefore could not be used as a method for the soul to rise back up to the One. Yet, despite this lack of connectivity, the soul still had a higher faculty, which meant that it longed (had an erotic desire) to ascend. However, all was not lost. Iamblichus maintained that rituals had been revealed by the gods for the purpose of allowing the human soul to reunite with the One. These rituals, when properly performed (using theurgy), enabled the soul to travel back to the One. Liturgical-type rituals or theurgy, consisting of audible and visible symbols (meant to encompass all aspects of human nature – material, rational and intellectual), were used to mediate between the material world of the human and the immaterial world of the gods. The gods in turn mediated (were illuminated by) that which was above them. Rather than being 'magic' or a way of 'manipulating the gods' and forcing them to descend to a human level, Iamblichian theurgy was a subtle and intellectual practice. It was a way of allowing the gods, divine creations of the lowest kind, to illuminate the soul so that it could rise up to a higher level. As Gregory Shaw puts it, 'Iamblichus developed a soteriological practice that by its very name, *theourgia*, defines not what the soul does, but what the gods do through the soul'.[13]

This was Iamblichus's method of explaining humanity's being in the world yet still desiring transcendence and a way to the divine. It was also a means of coming to terms with the One's need to love itself. Iamblichus held that the Absolute needed embodiment to enable it to both overflow in erotic yearning and receive erotic love. The fall into embodiment for Iamblichus was not therefore a mistake. Theurgy was the preordained means that facilitated the process of emanation and return. As Shaw puts it:

> Thus, theurgy saved the soul and the cosmos, for without the embodiment of the soul and its inversion (*anatrope*), the divine could never yearn for itself, *Eros* could never arise as 'the first born god,' and the cosmos could never come to exist.[14]

---

[13]   G. Shaw, *Theurgy and the Soul: The Neoplatonism of Iamblichus* (University Park: The Pennsylvania State University Press, 1995), p. 72.

[14]   Ibid., p. 124.

Theurgy was no peripheral superstitious activity. It was central to Iamblichus's entire understanding of Neoplatonism.

Proclus and the Importance of Triads

Another important Neoplatonist from a Christian mystical perspective was Proclus (410–85). His thinking greatly influenced Pseudo-Denys, whom we discuss in detail in Chapters 2 and 5. Although Proclus followed Iamblichus in accepting that the soul descends in its entirety when it is embodied, he could not accept that the highest part of the soul was changed in its substance. To accommodate this difference of belief, Proclus created a triadic systemisation of Neoplatonism in which the human soul stood in-between eternal substance and temporal activity. The soul therefore had both an eternal and temporal dimension and oscillated between them. Shaw points out that in suggesting this Proclus is actually closer to Plotinus than Iamblichus, since he is suggesting that there is still something in the soul that is eternal.[15] Despite this, Proclus also maintained the importance of theurgy, which is central to his understanding of how hierarchy works.[16]

Following Iamblichus, Proclus maintained that material things were analogously related to particular gods. It was therefore necessary to identify the material things that acted as symbols through which, via theurgy, one could ascend. Thus the usefulness of a symbol depended not on how physically powerful it was, but on how much it participated in the god that ruled it. Participation was the key, and as one came to participate in the gods and be illuminated by them, so one moved closer to the One, as through a kind of hierarchy. Each god therefore served a particular function in the chain of being. At the same time, however, every god contained everything directly because all were connected to the One via emanation.

Proclus also claimed that from each aspect of the divine triad – One, Mind and Soul – particular related emanations occurred: gods emanated from the One, angels or daemons from Mind, and souls from Soul. These emanations were themselves triadic, like the gods who emanate from the One, who were Goodness, Wisdom and Beauty.[17] As Andrew Louth notes, in this way Proclus created a complex system of relations between the various triads that occurred, creating an intricate system of hierarchical relationships through which the soul could ascend to the One:

---

[15]   Ibid., p. 102.

[16]   Shaw points out that, since Proclus suggests that there is something eternal in the soul, it is unclear whether what he means by theurgy differs from Iamblichus's understanding, or whether this is just an inconsistency in Proclus's thought. See Shaw, *Theurgy and the Soul: The Neoplatonism of Iamblichus*, p. 105.

[17]   See B. McGinn, *The Foundations of Mysticism: Origins to the Fifth Century*, The Presence of God: A History of Western Christian Mysticism, Vol. 1 (SCM: London, 1991), pp. 57–61.

by bringing into play the various triads a complicated set of interrelations is constructed and we have a sort of cosmic minuet, proceeding from rest, out through procession, and back again by reversion. The whole of reality is structured and everything has the right degree of being consistent with its own level of reality: 'all things are in all things, but in each according to its proper nature'.[18]

Beyond all these emanations stands an undifferentiated unity, a deity beyond being, towards which the soul progresses.[19]

It is this system of progression through hierarchy and ritual that lies at the heart of Pseudo-Denys's understanding of mysticism. As we will see in Chapter 5, Pseudo-Denys complicates this system still further adding additional triads to those suggested by Proclus, all of which he then reinterpreted within the framework of Christian liturgy and sacrament. It is largely as a result of his thinking that this view of cosmology comes to dominate the medieval world.[20] The influence of these ideas on Christian mysticism is hard to overestimate. As Andrew Louth has convincingly shown, Christian mysticism cannot be understood without reference to Platonism in its various forms.[21]

CONTEMPORARY APPROACHES TO MYSTICISM

In order to gain a sense of how the relationship between Platonism and mysticism has been understood within contemporary scholarship, we will begin with the perennialist position, highlighting its strengths and weaknesses, before moving on to contextualist, performative language and, finally, feminist readings. It will, however, quickly become apparent that, while such distinctions are helpful, many scholars straddle these categories as they attempt to account for the weaknesses of the approach with which they can be most closely aligned. Two main issues are discussed in the scholarly literature: the mystical status of Christian mystics who show great reliance on Platonic sources; and whether the Platonic writers were themselves mystics who, like Christian mystics, had mystical experiences, whether ineffable or not.

---

[18]   Louth, *The Origins of the Christian Mystical Tradition*, p. 163; quoting Proclus, proposition 13, in *The Elements of Theology: A Revised Text with Translation, Introduction and Commentary*, ed. and trans. E.R. Dodds (Clarendon Press: Oxford, 1933; revised 2nd edn, 1969), p. 93.

[19]   McGinn, *The Foundations of Christian Mysticism*, p.60.

[20]   Medieval conceptions of sign and symbol are also briefly discussed in Chapter 6.

[21]   Louth, *The Origins of the Christian Mystical Tradition*, p. xiii.

Perennialist Readings

Perennialists are most concerned with the issue of ineffable experience. This is evident, for example, in Evelyn Underhill's response to the relationship between Christian mystics and Platonism. Evelyn Underhill begins by famously arguing that there is an enormous difference between a mystic and a philosopher. On the one side are the mystics, those who experience, while philosophers stand on the other side, being those who reflect on the nature of these experiences. She regards the two activities as different as chalk and cheese, or as she puts it – philosophers 'are no more mystics than the milestones on the Dover Road are travellers to Calais'.[22] Yet where experience seems present in Platonic writing, Underhill argues that we see a movement from philosophy into mysticism. She views Plotinus as 'the most characteristic example – of Platonic philosophers who have passed far beyond the limits of their own philosophy'.[23] On these grounds André Jean Festugière argues that Plato himself was a mystic.[24] For Underhill, the distinction lies between theory and practice, not with profession. The personal experiential encounter, wherever it is found, is mystical.

> The difference between such devout philosophers and the true mystics, is the difference which the late Father Tyrrell defined as separating theology from revelation. Mysticism, like revelation, is final and personal. It is not merely a beautiful and suggestive diagram of experience, but is the very stuff of life. In the superb words of Plotinus, it is the soul's solitary adventure: 'the flight of the Alone to the Alone.'[25]

Those who philosophise about mysticism – 'mystical philosophers' – provide the 'stepping stones' for non-mystics to arrive at some understanding of the truth that mystics encounter, so that it is possible to be both mystic and philosopher. Both Plotinus and Meister Eckhart were, she argues, not only mystics but also philosophised about their mysticism in this way.[26]

Yet, for perennialists, the issue of philosophy remains problematic. Writers like Origen, Pseudo-Denys and Augustine have had their mystical credentials severely criticised by perennialists. The close verbal parallels between Augustine's famous vision at Ostia and Plotinus's description of the soul's flight to the One in Enneads 5 lead perennialists to question whether Augustine's account records a personal

---

[22]   E. Underhill, *Mysticism: A Study of the Nature and Development of Man's Spiritual Consciousness*, 4th edn (London: Methuen and Co., 1912), p. 98. This passage is also quoted in McGinn, *The Foundations of Mysticism*, p. xiii.

[23]   Underhill, *Mysticism*, p. 98.

[24]   Bernard McGinn draws attention to the debate which has surrounded whether or not Plato was a mystic; see *The Foundations of Mysticism* , p. 5.

[25]   Underhill, *Mysticism*, p. 98.

[26]   Ibid., p. 98.

experience or a philosophical discussion.[27] The problem is even more pronounced for a writer like Pseudo-Denys, whose debt to Proclus is widely acknowledged as a shaping force behind his thinking, since it is not clear that there is anything experiential at all underlying what he writes. This focused emphasis on experience within perennialist accounts makes it difficult for them to take context seriously.

A.H. Armstrong presents a particularly sophisticated account of Plotinus's mysticism, which attempts to get round this problem. He argues that there are two main ineffability claims in Plotinus's writing. The first is a mathematic claim that the One exceeds limit – that is, is 'beyond being' – and is therefore ineffable. This claim relates to the ontological unity of all things. He argues that such discussions of the One have little to do with 'religious feeling'.[28] However, he claims that there is another sense of ineffability expressed in Plotinus's thought that is much more devotional. When the One is spoken of as 'beyond being' and in terms of negative language, Armstrong finds a sense that experience of the One exceeds our capacity to describe it. He suggests that, much in the same way that *The Cloud*-Author describes himself as nothing in relation to God, so the soul in Plotinus's flight into the Alone sees itself as nothing before the One.

> There is, however, a real difference of emphasis, according to whether the main stress is laid on the underlying, pre-existing unity and on the unifying element in the experience or on the 'shock', the 'sentiment d'une présence' (Bréhier), the intense perception at once of the Supreme as wholly other and yet of being united with that other, which is also a most vital element of the experience.[29]

In this way Armstrong is able to accommodate a close relationship between philosophy and experience in a way that other perennialist accounts cannot.

Related to such perennialist readings is the notion, popularised by Anders Nygren, that Neoplatonic philosophy, particularly the Neoplatonic notion of love as *Eros*, corrupts a prior Christian ideal of love as *Agape*.[30] Although approaching the issue from a slightly different angle, Nygren's criticisms, along with those of Adolf Von Harnack, exerted enormous influence on twentieth-century Protestant attitudes towards mysticism, most notably the views of Karl Barth. Since, according to Nygren, *Agape* and *Eros* are not equivalent, mysticism therefore

---

[27]   Andrew Louth has shown the depth of similarity between the two accounts; see his *The Origins of the Christian Mystical Tradition*, pp. 138–40. Louth's discussion of this is considered below under 'Contextualist Readings'.

[28]   A.H. Armstrong, *The Architecture of the Intelligible Universe in the Philosophy of Plotinus: An Analytical and Historical Study* (facsimile of 1940 Cambridge University Press edn, Hakkert: Amsterdam, 1967), pp. 29–30.

[29]   Armstrong, *The Architecture of the Intelligible Universe*, pp. 31–2.

[30]   A. Nygren, *Eros and Agape*, trans. P.S. Watson (London: Westminster Press, 1953).

represents a perversion of Christianity proper.[31] While this is not the place for a detailed consideration of modern theological approach to mysticism per se, this reading is again one that dismisses context, overlooking it in favour of beliefs and practices that are seen as perennial. As with perennialist readings of mysticism that focus on the issue of ineffable experience, these perennial readings of mysticism detach faith from context, an approach which does not easily allow them to account for variation based on setting. It also runs the risk of promoting one contextual approach to faith (if contextualists are right that no view of faith can be detached from context) as the one true understanding.[32]

In viewing context as an inescapable element of human interaction, including religion, contextualist approaches are far less dependent on the experiential aspects of mystical texts, and therefore can more easily accommodate the undeniable relationship between Neoplatonic thought and Christian mysticism. This would seem to be a strength of the latter approach.

Contextualist Readings

Contextualist readings emphasise the relationship between Christian mysticism and Neoplatonism as part of the context in which Christianity developed. As such, they see it as an inescapable influence on Christian mysticism. However, unlike Perennialist accounts, for them the Neoplatonic influence does not lessen the value of the experience. Steven T. Katz, who we noted epitomises a strict contextualist position, suggests that in the Early Church Neoplatonic writing was treated as part of Christian canonical literature. As such he suggests that mystics approached it in the same way that they did Biblical texts; viewing it as part of the sacred writings from which they sought to draw secrets. He is not surprised to find ideas from Neoplatonic texts embedded in Christian mystical ones.[33] For him this does not lessen the experiences of God that they report, since he holds that no experience of God can ever be truly ineffable. Other scholars who take a positive stance towards context do not however go as far as Katz, trying instead to incorporate both context and unmediated experience into their readings of Christian mysticism.

---

[31]   We will briefly consider Nygren's argument in Chapter 3, pp. 96–7, since Denys Turner's approach to mysticism seeks to defend the Christian mystics against this accusation.

[32]   The problems caused by perennialist understandings of Christianity are widely discussed within missiology. See, for example, S.B. Bevans and R.P. Shroeder, *Constants in Context: A Theology of Mission for Today* (Maryknoll, NY: Orbis Books, 2004).

[33]   S.T. Katz, 'The "Conservative" Character of Mysticism', in S.T. Katz (ed.), *Mysticism and Religious Traditions* (Oxford: Oxford Uiversity Press, 1983), pp. 3–60, at p. 13.

Andrew Louth

Andrew Louth has offered one of the most detailed discussions of the relationship between Christian mysticism and the various forms of Platonism. In his book *The Origins of the Christian Mystical Tradition*, Louth traces what he sees as a historical lineage of mystical thinking from Platonism to the writings of the Church Fathers. In this regard, Louth argues that Augustine is not just influenced by Plotinus, but that his thinking is so infused with Plotinus's thought as to make any absolute separation of the two mystical visions nonsensical. To take but one very striking example, Louth shows how Augustine's vision at Ostia, which he describes in *Confessions*, is not merely Plotinian in flavour, it is actually recounted in words that have close verbal parallels to Plotinus's flight to the One described in *Enneads*. Louth argues that it is clear from this that Augustine grafts his own experience of the soul's journey to the God into Plotinus's account of mystical experience:

> in Augustine's account of his (and his mother's) vision at Ostia, we have close parallels with passages in one of Plotinus' *Enneads*. And they are not simply verbal parallels: there is a fundamental sympathy. Augustine has learnt from Plotinus ... drunk deep from Plotinus ... what he takes from Plotinus is not the odd idea, but much of the same spirit: there is a deep sympathy between them ... as he read Plotinus he found a movement of thought that echoed in his own soul.[34]

The closeness of Augustine's mysticism to Plotinus's flight to the One leads Louth to suggest that this is a particularly clear example of the dynamics of this relationship at work. The fact that Augustine's earliest Christian mystical experience was not solitary, but encountered *with* his mother is odd. Louth suggests it reveals a tension within Augustine's thinking between the mystical journey being an interior quest and the need for companionship along the way, something which he finds in Christianity but which sits uneasily with the rest of Augustine's more Plotinian account of mysticism. This trait, which admittedly only appears in early texts, is, however, but one of the changes that he makes as a result of beliefs, such as creation *ex nihilo* (out of nothing). As such, this leads Louth to conclude that beliefs too are more than simply interpretative add-ons, post-experience; rather they also form the fundamental ground out of which mystical understanding or experience springs. As he says of Augustine's belief in creation *ex nihilo* and the eschatological processes underpinning bodily resurrection, 'in his understanding of mysticism he goes beyond Plotinus, and does so by gradually deepening his understanding of Christian interpretation of eschatology'.[35]

---

[34] Louth, *The Origins of the Christian Mystical Tradition*, pp. 139–40.
[35] Ibid., p. 141.

Yet Louth also believes that profound experiences occur and are central to the accounts of mystics like Augustine. In fact, he maintains that an experiential element is already integrated into the writings of the Platonists, being, for example, a central element in Plato's whole philosophical enterprise:

> It could be argued that mystical theology, or perhaps better, a doctrine of contemplation, is not simply an element in Plato's philosophy, but something that penetrates and informs his whole understanding of the world.[36]

He presents strong historical evidence to suggest that the theological/philosophical discussions that we find in Christian mystical texts cannot be separated from the experiential aspect; the two seeming fundamentally embedded in one another. Like McGinn, whose thought is discussed below, Louth holds that there is a nuanced relationship between context, belief and ineffable experience, all of which are integrated and cannot really be understood without reference to one another. This position is contextualized, not strictly contextualist.

Bernard McGinn

Bernard McGinn likewise stresses the importance of reading mysticism in a historical manner, emphasising the need for a more contextual understanding of it than perennialist accounts provide. He is critical of scholars who question the mystical credentials of Pseudo-Denys and Augustine: for example, citing, in Augustine's case, dependence on prior literary sources (Plotinus's *Enneads*) or, in Pseudo-Denys's case, the lack of any clear experiential discussion of mysticism. McGinn suggests that such approaches are problematic because they detach Christian mysticism from the historical development of Christianity per se, which results in a distortion of it. He argues that we need to look at Christian mystical writers not as timeless examples of ineffable experience, but as authors whose writings were shaped by the ecclesial and societal developments of their time.

McGinn also believes that Christianity has always had a mystical element in it from its origins, such that the Early Church Fathers developed an inherent aspect of Christianity by means of the cultural and philosophical resources they found in the writings of the Greek philosophers (many of whom McGinn also considers to be mystics in their own right). He does not accept, as Anders Nygren posits, that the Early Church Fathers inserted an alien element into Christianity. McGinn suggests that we need to see the changes made to Platonic systems in this light, as part of Christian truth expressed through context, from which he argues it is in any case inseparable. Thus Proclus, an anti-Christian philosopher born into a society

---

[36]　Louth, *The Origins of the Christian Mystical Tradition*, p. 1. John Macquarrie also maintains that Plato had 'mystical tendencies': J. Macquarrie, *Two Worlds are Ours: An Introduction to Christian Mysticism* (London: SCM, 2004) p. 65.

that had become Christian in its worldview, had his ideas altered and used by Pseudo-Denys as a vehicle to express the latter's own Christian mysticism.[37]

McGinn, perhaps even more than Louth, is deeply invested in the notion of unmediated experience. As we will discuss in subsequent chapters, he believes that an unmediated experience of God is certainly possible. However, at the same time he wants to nuance perennialist views of how such experiences are understood. He believes that it is only when a mystic is read against his or her contextual background that an understanding of their mysticism is possible. Like Louth, McGinn believes that experience cannot be prised apart from philosophical and societal influences as though they were some independent entity. Mysticism is much more than this, it is an original part of the Christian religion, a way of life and an attempt to express direct consciousness of God, all at the same time.

Performative Language Readings

Performative language readings also set out to critique perennialist readings of mysticism. However, unlike contextualist accounts they are particularly interested in how language functions in a given text, regardless of what its origins are. This emphasis on language rather than experience reflects the view that mystical texts primarily set out to convey beliefs not experiences. As such, Christian mysticism's relationship to Neoplatonism (or any other contextual system) does not pose a particular problem. Rather, performative language readings delight in the way that Neoplatonism provides Christian mystics with a resource to explain the unknowability of God.

Michael Sells

Michael Sells argues that the same principle of unsaying language is found in both Christian mystical texts and the Neoplatonic writings which precede them.[38] In particular he draws attention to the 'referential regress' that lies at the heart of Plotinus's understanding of the One. By 'referential regress' Sells means that Plotinus stresses that the One cannot be named, since no name is sufficient for 'the One', 'the unlimited', or 'the beyond-being'. Sells argues that Plotinus's writings are filled with a continuous desire to negate what is being said even as it is spoken. 'Plotinus frequently acknowledges that the terms used in reference to the unlimited are incorrect and should not be taken referentially.'[39] Sells warns us that we therefore need to be very careful not to make Plotinus's ideas much more static

---

[37]   McGinn, *The Foundations of Mysticism*, p. 61.

[38]   M. Sells, *Mystical Languages of Unsaying* (Chicago: Chicago University Press, 1994), p. 15.

[39]   Ibid., p. 16.

than they were intended to be. He urges us to enter into this 'referential regress' in an attempt to really understand what is involved in a language of unsaying.

Sells views Plotinus as the father of Western mystical tradition. He sees him as the one who first drew together the mystical quality of Neoplatonic thought by creating a language of unsaying. Sells argues that Pseudo-Denys took up this tradition (via Proclus), and drew together the kataphatic (saying) elements with the apophatic (unsaying) elements – although for Sells it was the unsaying elements which both Pseudo-Denys and Plotinus view as most important:

> An overview of Western apophasis would begin with Plotinus (d. 270 C.E.). Though elements of apophasis existed earlier, it was Plotinus who wove these elements and his own original and mystical insights into a discourse of sustained apophatic intensity … It was Dionysius [Pseudo-Denys] who wrote most specifically of the twin elements of kataphasis (saying) and apophasis (unsaying) in 'mystical theology' (a term Dionysius coined), with the apophatic element being the 'higher' or more accurate.[40]

According to Sells, within Christianity this tradition flows from Pseudo-Denys into the writings of John Scotus Erigena and from there into other Christian mystical texts such as the anonymous *Cloud of Unknowing*.[41] However, for Sells there is nothing specifically Christian about mysticism or languages of unsaying.

Denys Turner

Denys Turner also paints a positive portrayal of the relationship between Christian Mysticism and Neoplatonism. However, unlike Sells, he suggests that the language of unsaying, or what he calls 'apophasis', is distinctively Christian in origin. For Turner it was Pseudo-Denys, not Plotinus, who first realised the apophatic potential of Neoplatonic theories of knowledge, by drawing together the kataphatic and the apophatic (as we discuss in Chapter 2). Turner argues that metaphors of ascent, descent, darkness and light used in Christian mystical theology start with a synthesis of two stories – one Greek and the other Hebraic. The Greek influence comes in the form of Plato's famous cave analogy found in Book 7 of *The Republic*. The Hebraic flavour is added by the Exodus account of Moses's encounter with Yahweh on Mount Sinai. The Exodus story describes Moses being summoned to ascend Mount Sinai where he encounters Yahweh in thick cloud accompanied by thunder and lightening.[42] At the trumpet call, Moses and the Israelites stand at the foot of the mountain not daring to go any higher. Eventually, as the trumpet call gets louder, Moses ascends to the mountaintop where he enters the cloud and he speaks to Yahweh, who answers through thunder.

---

[40]   Ibid., p. 5.
[41]   Ibid., p. 5.
[42]   Exodus 19: 9.

Although not the first to draw these ideas together, Turner views Pseudo-Denys as the most influential exponent of this tradition.[43] Turner is categorical that 'mystical theology' is unintelligible in the West unless it is viewed against the backdrop of Pseudo-Denys's writing. The conflation of these two ideas is perhaps nowhere more apparent than in the passage we considered on the opening pages of the introductory chapter.

> When every purification is complete, he [Moses] hears the many-voiced trumpets. He sees the many lights, pure and with rays streaming abundantly. Then, standing apart from the crowds and accompanied by chosen priests, he pushes ahead to the summit of the divine ascents. And yet he does not meet God himself, but contemplates, not him who is invisible, but rather where he dwells. But then he breaks free of them, away from what sees and is seen, and he plunges into the truly mysterious darkness of unknowing.[44]

Here we see Pseudo-Denys building an apophatic discourse that mirrors the philosophical notion of the otherness of God expressed in both Jewish and Neoplatonic traditions. In Turner's words, this is 'the vocabulary of our mysticism: historically we owe it to Denys; and he owed it, as he saw it, to Plato and Moses'.[45]

The strengths of the performative language position in terms of a reading of Pseudo-Denys are apparent (as we will further discuss in Chapter 2), since Pseudo-Denys is a writer who does not explicitly discuss experience – which poses a problem for the perennialist readings. Within a performative language context, Pseudo-Denys is no less mystical for this, since he is able to communicate the ineffability of God to his readers. Yet, while this approach stresses language use as an integral and central aspects of culture (as we will see in subsequent chapters), a strict performative language reading struggles to accommodate more overtly experiential accounts of mysticism, such as those produced by Bernard of Clairvaux and Richard Rolle (and Turner arguably overlooks the liturgical elements of Pseudo-Denys's thought as a result, as we discuss in Chapter 5).

---

[43]   In the fourth century, Gregory of Nyssa provides a distinctively Platonic reading of the Exodus account in his *Life of Moses*. This account influenced Pseudo-Denys, although medieval readers, who thought that Pseudo-Denys was an ancient authority, believed that the influence went from Pseudo-Denys to Gregory. (See Chapter 2 for more discussion of who Pseudo-Denys was.)

[44]   Pseudo-Denys, 'The Mystical Theology', in *Pseudo-Dionysius: The Complete Works*, p. 137. (See Chapters 2 and 3 for further discussion of this passage, pp. 38–9, 46, 52, 74.)

[45]   D. Turner, *The Darkness of God: Negativity in Christian Mysticism* (Cambridge: Cambridge University Press, 1995), p. 13.

Feminist Readings

Finally, we come to feminist responses to this Neoplatonic heritage. As we noted in the previous chapter, feminist readings of mysticism criticise the way in which feminine spirituality is often considered less elevated than male spirituality because it contains less of an intellectual dimension. Many blame Platonism for this trajectory. Grace Jantzen argues that Platonism's impact on Christian mysticism was also to women's spiritual detriment.

Grace Jantzen

While far from the only scholar to critique Platonism from a feminist perspective, Grace Jantzen focuses her criticism on its effect on Christian mysticism. In her study *Power, Gender and Christian Mysticism*, Jantzen draws attention to the gender-related issues in Plato's philosophy – issues that she argues are frequently ignored by academics. Jantzen is concerned by Plato's account of who is best equipped to follow the spiritual life and why. She believes that many of the gender assumptions made by Plato are carried over into the Christian mystical tradition. She sees a strong tendency in Plato's *Symposium* to associate women with the body and men with the intellect. Those in whom the fleshly instinct is strong 'turn to a woman as the object of their love'.[46] Jantzen argues that not only are women excluded as agents of their own intellectual advancement (they are objects of men's desire instead), they are even excluded on a physical level, since she reads this text as portraying homosexuality as the better fleshly relationship for men to enjoy. She points out that in *The Symposium* Plato argues that this is the case because homosexual love 'creates something lovelier and less mortal than human seed'.[47] Jantzen is not suggesting that Plato is advocating the physical consummation of an all-male relationship; the spiritual consummation of minds is clearly the goal. However, for her the important point is that for men in relationship with other men this spiritual advancement is possible, whereas it appears implicit that women cannot enjoy similar spiritual fulfilment in relationships because their primary role is child rearing. In Greek philosophical thinking, the male was the active principle and the female the passive. The problem for the female soul was its battle with what inherently made it female – the very bodily activity of having children. It is not therefore clear whether it was possible in practice for a woman, bodily by nature and function, to follow the spiritual life.

Given Plato's neat division of the body and the soul, particularly in his early writings, it may seem confusing that Jantzen should attach such importance to

---

[46]   Plato, *The Symposium and Other Dialogues*, trans. J. Warrington (New York: Dent, 1964), p. 43; quoted in G. Jantzen, *Power, Gender and Christian Mysticism* (Cambridge: Cambridge University Press, 1995), p. 35.

[47]   Plato, *The Symposium and Other Dialogues*, p. 44; quoted in Jantzen, *Power, Gender and Christian Mysticism*, p. 36.

gender. After all, it is the soul's progress in the spiritual life that is most important. The problem, as Jantzen sees it, is one that replicates itself throughout the history of Christian mysticism. The issue is not the division of soul and body as such (women, like men, have a soul) but the primary identification of maleness with the intellect and femaleness with the body. This is an issue which many medievalists have also discussed from a feminist perspective. Both Elizabeth Robertson and Dyan Elliott comment on the crippling effect of such beliefs for female spirituality.[48] Nonetheless, as we will discuss subsequently (particularly in Chapter 7), it is also argued that it was partly because of the restrictions placed on women that new forms of female devotional activity flourished in the later Middle Ages, including visions, bodily mortification and erotic encounters with Christ. With no alternative, women identified the body as a means of spiritual progression – particularly in relation to a very human, suffering Christ.

Conclusion

This chapter has drawn attention to the different ways in which contemporary theorists have understood the impact of Platonism on Christian mysticism. For some, like Grace Jantzen, its influence was almost wholly negative. For those who assume a performative language position the reverse is true. Many contextualists take a more neutral standpoint, regarding Neoplatonism as the seedbed in which Christian mysticism nurtured its understanding of mysticism, because this was the context in which the Christian mystics of the day found themselves. All these readings challenge a narrow perennialist reading of mysticism which struggles to account for the relationship between Platonism and Christian mysticism.

The next chapter turns to a theme considered definitive of Christian mystical literature, the use of negative or apophatic language in Christian mystical texts. Again the merits of the various philosophical approaches will be outlined.

---

[48] See, for example, E. Robertson, *Early English Devotional Prose and the Female Audience* (Knoxville, TN: University of Tennessee Press, 1990), and D. Elliott, *Spiritual Marriage: Sexual Abstinence in Medieval Wedlock* (Princeton, NJ: University of Princeton Press, 1993).

Chapter 2
Negative or Apophatic Language

In this chapter we consider the role that negative or apophatic language plays in Christian mystical texts. We focus mainly on how Pseudo-Denys uses such language in his *Mystical Theology*. As in the previous chapter, having looked briefly at the use of negative language in mystical texts, we will turn to consider how modern scholars have understood this language and some of the challenges that their discussions pose to a strict perennialist reading of mysticism.

Who Was Pseudo-Denys?

Pseudo-Denys (also known as Pseudo-Dionysius or Dionysius the Areopagite) was the first to coin the phrase 'mystical theology'. He is also usually considered the Founding Father of the use of negative/apophatic language in Christian mystical texts. Yet his identity is shrouded in mystery. Like classical writers before them, antique and medieval authors often used pseudonyms as a way of gaining greater spiritual authority. Pseudo-Denys writes as though he was the Denys or Dionysius the Areopagite, who is only named in Acts 17: 34. Dionysius the Areopagite was the only convert when St Paul preached in Athens, and is later recorded by the historian Eusebius (263–339) to have become the first bishop of Athens. Yet, even though he does not reveal his true identity, there are clues as to who Pseudo-Denys was. His work *Ecclesial Hierarchy* (a text that we discuss in more detail in Chapter 5) refers to a liturgy that was used within the Eastern wing of the church, from the sixth century BCE. Based on this, and other remarks found within his writings, it is usually assumed that Pseudo-Denys was a Syrian Monk from the early sixth century.[1] Yet in the medieval period after the sixth century few, with the possible

---

[1] Louth, *The Origins of the Christian Mystical Tradition*, pp. 160–61; P. Rorem, *Biblical and Liturgical Symbols within the Pseudo-Dionysian Synthesis* (Toronto: Pontifical Institute of Medieval Studies, 1984), p. 4. There are elements within Pseudo-Denys's writing, especially the very infrequent and underdeveloped nature of his references to Jesus, which have caused modern scholars to debate whether Pseudo-Denys was really an orthodox Christian. For a discussion of the Monophysite controversy, see H. Chadwick, *The Early Church* (Grand Rapids, MI: Eerdman's 1968), ch. 14; W.H.C. Frend, *The Rise of Christianity* (Philadelphia: Fortress Press, 1984), ch. 21 and pp. 873–7.

exception of Thomas Aquinas (1225–74), questioned that he was the Dionysius mentioned in Acts 17.[2]

His choice of pseudonym is interesting. Andrew Louth suggests that it was perhaps not chosen primarily for its obscurity, but because Dionysius the Areopagite was a believer who identified the unknown God worshipped in Athens as the Abrahamic creator of the world. Louth argues that this self-description as Denys the Areopagite therefore fits the character of Pseudo-Denys's project, since he takes Athenian philosophy (Proclus) to create an Athenian theology that explains how God is unknown, but still the creator of everything.[3]

Pseudo-Denys's Mystical Theology

Pseudo-Denys's develops his use of negative language in *The Mystical Theology*, a short work that forms the pinnacle of his corpus. The main thrust of his argument is that there are many different ways that we can talk about or name God. Firstly, we can use what he calls 'perceptual' or 'symbolic' names. These names compare God in some way to things we see. We use them symbolically to refer to God.[4] Then, there are conceptual names. These are concepts that we apply to God, like 'goodness', 'holiness' or 'beauty'. In *Mystical Theology* he focuses on just five conceptual names: 'existence', 'goodness', 'life', 'wisdom' and 'power'. He argues that conceptual names can be used in two ways. Firstly, they can affirm things that are true of God – this use of them is kataphatic (cataphatic) theology.[5] Secondly, they can be used to express how God transcends even conceptual naming – this use of them is negative or apophatic theology; and it is this second method that particularly interests Pseudo-Denys in this text. In this work he sets out to show how no name adequately describes God.

Mystical Theology begins with the prayer that we considered in the introductory chapter:

---

[2]   J. Pelikan, 'The Odyssey of Dionysian Spirituality', in *Pseudo-Dionysius: The Complete Works*, pp. 11–24; also Sells, *Mystical Languages of Unsaying*, p. 34. Sells notes that when Pseudo-Denys's texts were translated into Latin by Hilduin, he conflated the other identities of the anonymous author with St Denis, bishop of Paris. This further increased the sense of authority that was attributed to Pseudo-Denys's texts in the medieval period.

[3]   A. Louth, 'Dionysios the Areopagite', in A. Louth et al., *The Christian and the Mystical*, The Way Supplement 102 (2001), pp. 7–14, at p. 7.

[4]   Pseudo-Denys states that he explains exactly what he means by these in a work called *The Symbolic Theology*. This work no longer exists and was possibly fictitious.

[5]   This is what most interests Pseudo-Denys in *Divine Names*, even though he stresses in this work that God cannot be *fully* encapsulated by such conceptual names.

Trinity!! Higher than any being,
> any divinity, any goodness!
Guide of Christians
> in the wisdom of the heaven!
Lead us up beyond unknowing and light,
> up to the farthest, highest peak
>> of mystic scripture,
where the mysteries of God's Word
> lie simple, absolute and unchangeable
> in the brilliant darkness of a hidden silence.
Amid the deepest shadow
> they pour overwhelming light
> on what is most manifest.
Amid the whole unsensed and unseen
> they completely fill our sightless minds
> with treasures beyond all beauty.[6]

This prayer sets the tone for the rest of the work by offering a balance between positive and negative names, which work together. In his *Mystical Theology*, Pseudo-Denys argues that, to show the inadequacy of naming God, both kataphatic and apophatic theology is needed; he pictures them working in symbiosis. He begins with the oneness of God, naming him conceptually. Gradually he moves downwards to creation, noticing that all physical things (even the lowliest worm as mentioned in his *Divine Names*) can be used to talk about God, since everything points towards its cause, God. Yet he also asks the reader to notice that none fully discloses God's nature. It is easy to see this when he considers a worm, for example. No one would normally say that the name 'worm' fully encapsulates God. However, it is less clear when he initially considers names like 'goodness' or 'existence'. What Pseudo-Denys is keen to show is that even these names do not provide sufficient descriptions of God.

In order to do this, he takes us back from perceptible names to conceptual ones. He starts by negating names like 'worm', and 'drunken soldier', both images used of God in the Bible. Slowly he moves towards conceptual terms like 'goodness', helping the reader to see that nothing we say can capture God's essence. Once the reader begins to realise this, Pseudo-Denys argues, talking about God becomes more and more difficult:

> the more it climbs, the more language falters, and when it has passed up and beyond the ascent, it will turn silent completely, since it will finally be at one with him who is indescribable.[7]

---

6   Pseudo-Denys, *Pseudo-Dionysius: The Complete Works*, p. 135.
7   Pseudo-Denys, 'Mystical Theology', in *Pseudo-Dionysius: The Complete Works*, pp. 133–42, at p. 139.

Thus he tries finally to move us beyond thinking of God conceptually. He writes that God is 'beyond every affirmation and every negation'.[8] Pseudo-Denys, does not see negation as merely the opposite of affirmation: in saying that God is not good, he is not saying that God is evil. Rather he uses negation to stress that even conceptual names, like 'goodness', cannot hope to encapsulate the nature of God because God is greater than any human concept. Even if there is some sense in which God is good, it is not a sense that we can comprehend through our concept of goodness. In the final chapter he brings the reader to the end of this journey of naming and unnaming God where he negates the negation, arguing for example that God is neither similarity nor dissimilarity, neither light nor darkness. In this way he reaches a point where language, having proved insufficient, falls silent. 'There is no speaking of it [God] ... it is beyond every assertion and denial.'[9] For Pseudo-Denys, God is beyond any name that we apply, even the name God, since God is prior to language.

When the soul arrives at this point of silence, Pseudo-Denys holds that its knowledge is left behind. Instead it knows by 'knowing nothing'.[10] It is here that, like Moses, the mind or soul moves 'away from what sees and is seen, and ... plunges into the mysterious darkness of unknowing'.[11] For Pseudo-Denys, this is the fulfilment of all erotic longing.[12] It is the soul's response to the fact that the act of creation is God's erotic overflow, which plants in it a desire for union with that from which it came.[13] In this way Pseudo-Denys moves the reader in a kind of circle, starting from the unity of God, moving them towards a sense of muliplicity, and finally pushing them back up to the unity or oneness of God. This structure is clearly influenced by Neoplatonism and the idea of emanation, even if Pseudo-Denys believes in creation *ex nihilo*.[14]

Later Developments of Negative or Apophatic Language

The Mystical Theology had a huge impact on subsequent Christian mystical literature, increasingly so in the late medieval period after its translation into Latin in the ninth century. Many writers quote from it; Bonaventure, in the thirteenth century, for example, is happy to end his own mystical text with extended quotations from it. Later mystics also develop complex literary strategies of their own that employ negative stylistic devices. Take, for example, the writings of

---

[8]   Ibid., p. 141.

[9]   Ibid., p. 141.

[10]   Ibid., p. 137.

[11]   Ibid., p. 137.

[12]   A central motif in *Divine Names*.

[13]   We will talk more about the role of *Eros* and erotic language in Christian mystical texts in Chapter 4.

[14]   See n. 39.

Meister Eckhart (born *c.*1260), whom we will consider in Chapter 10. Here is a passage from one of his Latin sermons in which he discusses how St Paul was blinded on the Damascus road after his conversion to Christianity:

> In this enveloping illumination he was thrown to the ground, and his eyes were
> opened for him so that with eyes open he saw all things as nothing. And when he
> saw all things as nothing, he saw God.[15]

This passage is just one of many that shows the central role that paradox plays in many of Eckhart's discussions of God. The effect is even more pronounced in Eckhart's vernacular sermons. He develops a whole range of paradoxical stylistic devices. Take, for example, the passage from Sermon 18 on which Oliver Davies comments:

> If the content of Eckhart's writings is often searchingly paradoxical, then this
> is a characteristic which is sustained and strengthened by his use of a number
> of purely stylistic devices. We find many instances of chiasmus, for instance
> (a form of inverted repetition: a+b, b+a), as in Eckhart's comment on the
> transcendence/immanence dialectic of God and the world: 'The more he is in
> things, the more he is out of things: the more in, the more out, and the more out,
> the more in …'[16]

This passage contains a clear example of negation of negation; however, it is also clear that Eckhart extends the concept as it appears in Pseudo-Denys thought. Although Caroline Walker Bynum argues that, for the most part, women tended to favour rather different literary devices and images (see Chapter 7), some female mystics do negate language. The following passage is taken from the writings of the fourteenth-century beguine Marguerite Porete.[17] Here Porete uses language in a profoundly paradoxical manner as she describes the efficacy of willing nothing:

> Lover, you have grasped me in your love,
> To give me your great treasure,
> That is, the gift of your own self,
> Which is divine goodness.
> Heart cannot express this,
> But willing pure nothingness purifies [the heart],
> Which makes me climb so high,

---

[15]   Meister Eckhart, 'Sermon 71', in B. McGinn (ed.), *Meister Eckhart: Teacher and Preacher*, trans. B. McGinn, F. Tobin and E. Borgstädt (New York: Paulist Press, 1986), p. 321.

[16]   O. Davies, *Meister Eckhart: Mystical Theologian*, p. 187.

[17]   We will consider Marguerite Porete more carefully in Chapter 10.

> By union in concordance,
> Which I ought never to reveal.[18]

Such use of negative language in Christian mystical writing clearly demands an explanation.

CONTEMPORARY THEORETICAL READINGS

In turning to consider contemporary theoretical readings we will see that the issue of negative language is particularly problematic from a perennialist perspective. We begin by considering a strict perennialist position, and then explore the responses to it of, firstly, Katz's strict contextual reading and then the performative language readings of Sells and Turner. Two important responses to both positions are then examined. The first is Robert Forman's defense of a neo-perennialist reading, the second is Thomas Knepper's development of Katz's contextualist position, which moves it in a more linguistically sensitive direction, resonant of Sells' reading. However, as we have stated in previous chapters, most scholars who discuss mysticism do so in complex ways which move between these categories. This said, most scholars do not, however, consider language and its importance in the way that Sells and Turner do and from the chapter it is clear that both scholars make an important contribution to the study of mysticism.

Perennialist Readings

William James

We noted in the introduction that William James offers a perennialist reading of Pseudo-Denys's use of contradictory and negative language. James asserts that Pseudo-Denys's negative language is a way of explaining that his description of his experience exceeds a single frame of reference. It cannot be limited in this way or any other. James sees the use of paradox in Pseudo-Denys's writing, and in other mystical texts, as a means of passing beyond the limits of either the positive or the negative description to what he calls 'a higher kind of affirmation'.[19] By this James means mystical consciousness is experienced as neither a 'this' nor a 'that', but something that transcends such conceptulisation. W.T. Stace also believes that negative statements relate directly to ineffable experiences. Yet, for him, they are wholly referentially such that the mystic feels embarrassed by the paradoxical

---

[18]   Marguerite Porete, *Marguerite Porete: The Mirror of Simple Souls*, trans. with intro. and preface by E.L. Babinsky (New York: Paulist Press, 1993), pp. 199–200.

[19]   W. James, The Varieties of Religious Experience: A Study in Human Nature (London: Burns and Oates, 1952), p. 321.

nature of language that they are forced to employ.[20] This reading of negative language has led some scholars to argue that such a use of language is nonsensical and illogical. Both contextualist and performative language readings attempt to defend paradoxical language against this accusation. Both approaches reject the idea that negative language is wholly referential in the sense that it is simply an attempt to describe an ineffable experience. They consider the texts of mystics to serve a more purposeful function. They do so, however, in rather different ways.

Contextualist Readings

Steven T. Katz

As we noted, Steven T. Katz's understanding of mysticism is based on the idea that context is unescapable, such that there are no imageless experiences. This belief underpins his understanding of the language of mystical texts. As Sallie King notes, Katz's understanding of mysticism depends on his belief that there is no such thing as a private language or a private experience. For him, everything is connected to the public sphere:

> [He] ultimately derives [his approach] from a post-Wittgensteinian epistemological model that holds that there are 'no private languages, no purely private experiences and no purely "private" realm at all because all our experience derives its meaningfulness from the public realm of culture and language.'[21]

As such, this means that Katz attributes very purposeful roles to the language that he finds in mystical texts. We will consider some possible criticisms of this position below. However, first we will examine the functions that Katz believes mystical language has, focusing particularly on his beliefs about the language used in Christian texts.

Katz argues that the language that we find in mystical texts performs a variety of functions. Particularly relevant to our discussion of negative language in this chapter is the role of Katz ascribes to this type of language. One of the main functions of paradoxical statements in his opinion is to prepare the practitioner's mind to enter a new state of consciousness, one that is not governed by the rules of logic. He illustrates this by examining the role that *kōans* play in Buddhist meditation, arguing that 'the sounds of one hand clapping' is not meant to be

---

[20] J.J. Murphy, 'Meister Eckhart and the Via Negativa: Epistemology and Mystical Language', *New Blackfriars*, 77/908 (2007), 458–72, at p. 460.

[21] S.B. King, 'Interpretation of Mysticism', *Journal of the American Academy of Religion*, 56/2 (1988), 257–79, at p. 259.

understood as a description. Rather its disrupted semantics are intended to lead the reader away from an ordinary mode of thinking. [22]

> It is the ability of language to induce 'breakthroughs' of consciousness by being employed 'nonsensically', literally non-sense-ically, that is fundamental to the traversal of the mystical path, to the movement from consciousness A to consciousness B. [23]

Katz sees such language as an 'essential epistemic channel' to such modes of consciousness. [24] This argument deliberately challenges the position of scholars like A.J. Ayer, who argue that paradoxical statements are meaningless because they are inherently contradictory. [25]

However, Katz does not believe that Christian texts use negative and paradoxical statements in this way. Certainly in his earlier writings he asserted that the paradoxical claims that he found in Christian mystical writings were too unsophisticated to operate as a disruptive discourse. Instead he simply dismisses this mode of language as part of the mystic's mistaken belief that their mystical experience was ineffable:

> Christian mysticism has a much less well-developed tradition of such linguistically induced techniques. This is due largely to the very different status of scripture and the strong apophatic influence drawn from Neoplatonism in Christian spirituality. Yet while lacking a tradition of anything like the Zen *kōans*, in the 'Jesus prayer' and other motifs, such techniques are to be found in segments of the Christian world as well. That is to say, in all the major mystical traditions, recognizing their real and undeniable phenomenological diversity, language as a psychospiritual means of radical reorientation and purification is present. [26]

What Katz is most keen to emphasise is that Pseudo-Denys's talk about nothingness should not be taken out of its context. He stresses that the idea of 'nothing' which Pseudo-Denys mentions cannot be taken to be the same as the idea of 'emptiness' expressed in Mahayana Buddhism, for example.

> Again, it is often, but in my view erroneously, argued that the Christian mystical tradition of Dionysius the Areopagite and his heirs which talks of the

---

[22] S.T. Katz, 'Mystical Speech and Mystical Meaning', in S.T. Katz (ed.), *Mysticism and Language* (New York: Oxford University Press, 1992), pp. 3–41, at pp. 6–7.

[23] Ibid., p. 7.

[24] Ibid., p. 8.

[25] See C. Barrett, 'The Logic of Mysticism', in M. Warner (ed.) *Religion and Philosophy* (Cambridge: Cambridge University Press, 1992), pp. 61–71, at p. 61.

[26] Ibid., p. 15.

'nothingness', as *nichts* in Eckhart's language, is the same as Buddhist *Mu*, for the Christian mystic such as Eckhart seeks the re-birth of this soul now purified through its immersion in the *Gottheit* [Godhead], whereas the Buddhist seeks *sunyata* [emptiness] as the transcendence of liberation from all selfhood.[27]

For Katz, everything derives from and is situated within a context, and must be read first and foremost in the light of it. This said, Katz is still fascinated by the inherent contradiction that he sees in a writer like Pseudo-Denys, who claims he can ultimately say nothing about God, but still writes a text.

In his more recent writings Katz has qualified his position in relation to the paradoxical discourse that he notes in the writings of Meister Eckhart. He stresses that, while Meister Eckhart's paradoxical language cannot be taken to be doing the same thing as Buddhist *kōans*, this is not because it is unsophisticated. It is rather because he believes that *kōans* 'push language to such an extreme that it ceases to operate altogether'. However, in Eckhart's case he argues that language still serves a purpose, to signify the transcendental reality that cannot be signified. 'Instead, Eckhart utilized language to indicate something of the transcendental reality – of God's nature and speech – that must be "known" but cannot be known, that must be expressed but cannot be expressed in ordinary language, that *is* but whose "isness" is unlike that of any other reality.'[28] Katz also admits that this use of language has its root in the writings of Pseudo-Denys and Neoplatonism. Where Katz's position does not change is in his view that the use of such language is be determined by context. It cannot simply be presumed that its use is the same across all religions. In the Christian context it is always governed by a metaphysical God.

Sallie King, however, disputes this aspect of Katz anti-perennial understanding of language, arguing that it is possible to distinguish between perennial experiences, such as pain, and subsequent cultural explanations. In fact, a serious criticism of this element of Katz approach (sometimes referred to as hard constructivism) is that, if meaningful conversation is possible between two people who witness the same event but interpret it differently, it is also true that mystics could have a kind of perennial experience that they then interpret differently in accordance with their traditions, such that meaningful dialogue between mystics from completely different religious traditions is not inconceivable.[29]

In addition to paradox, Katz also ascribes a number of other functions to the language of mystical texts. He argues that many religious traditions treat the language of these texts as sacred and ascribe to it an almost magical power,

---

[27]   S.T. Katz, 'The Diversity and Study of Mysticism', in S. Jakelic and L. Pearson (eds), *The Future of the Study of Religion: Proceedings of Congress 2000* (Boston, Brill, 2004), pp. 189–210 at p. 203.

[28]   S.T. Katz, 'Mysticism and the Interpretation of Sacred Scripture', in Katz, *Mysticism and Sacred Scripture*, pp. 7–67, at p. 43.

[29]   For a detailed discussion of this issue, see the *Stanford Encyclopedia of Philosophy*, online at www.plato.stanford.edu/entries/mysticism

which provides access to the transcendent realm. He notes too the use that is
sometimes made of special alphabets in Jewish mystical writing, for example.
Again, however, Katz does not ascribe this linguistic function to the language he
finds in Christian mystical texts – this despite the importance of symbolism, as
we will discuss in Chapter 6. Such an omission seems odd considering that Katz
ascribes this function to Neoplatonic texts and also notes the close relationship
between Christian mystical texts and Neoplatonic writing. Related to both these
two functions of language, Katz also suggests that the language of mystical texts
has 'locomotive power': that is, it helps the mystic to ascend to 'other worlds
and realms of being'.[30] Again Katz offers no Christian examples of this use of
language. Other scholars, who support strict contextualist readings, have, however,
developed an approach to Christian mysticism along similar lines. Nelson Pike,
although positing a rather different approach to mysticism, which suggests that
experience of God can be known phenomenologically in a manner analogous
to sense experience, nonetheless credits Katz with moving some way towards
establishing a phenomenological reading of mysticism through his emphasis
on the locomotive power of language.[31] Although taking a much more nuanced
approach to mysticism (as we will discuss in Chapter 4), Bernard McGinn also
believes that the language of Christian mystical writing has a kind of locomotive
power in that, he argues, it is intended to be transformative. Like Katz, he holds
that such language relates to the ineffability of God rather than the experience,
particularly in the case of Meister Eckhart.[32]

Although extremely supportive of the contextualist position, Ewert Cousins
diverges from Katz's understanding of Pseudo-Denys's use of negative language.
He argues that the negative statements and images we find in Pseudo-Denys's
writing *are* a type of disruptive discourse, like those that Katz believes prepare
the mind for entry into another mode of consciousness. For Cousins, these
literary devices help suppress the mind, allowing the practitioner to move beyond
intellectual activity and so receive an apophatic, seemingly ineffable, experience.
This, for him, explains Pseudo-Denys's description of Moses's ascent of Mount
Sinai: 'The pseudo-Dionysius presents the narrative of Moses ascent of Mount
Sinai as a path to apophatic mystical experience'.[33] Cousins's position is more

[30]   Katz, 'Mystical Speech and Mystical Meaning', p. 20.

[31]   Pike comments that Katz's approach goes some way towards establishing a
phenomenological approach to mysticism. See, N. Pike, 'Steven Katz on Christian
Mysticism', in *Mystic Union: An Essay in the Phenomenology of Mysticism* (Ithaca, NY:
Cornell University Press, 1992), pp. 194-213.

[32]   See, B. McGinn, 'The Language of Love in Christian and Jewish Mysticism',
in S.T. Katz (ed.), *Mysticism and Language* (Oxford: Oxford University Press, 1992),
pp. 202–35.

[33]   E. Cousins, 'The Fourfold Sense of Scripture in Christian Mysticism', in S.T.
Katz (ed.), *Mysticism and Sacred Scripture*, (New York: Oxford University Press, 2000),
pp. 118–37, at p. 121.

sympathetic to the perennialist one than Katz's because he believes that such language prepares the mind of the reader for the receipt of an ineffable experience, rather than just moving the reader into a new mode of consciousness that is not governed by rules of logic. Yet it is also slightly unclear what Katz means by such a mode of consciousness and the extent to which this does not to some extent undermine the hard contextualist position that we find within his writing. It is important to note that Cousins is not, however, supporting a strict perennialist reading of mysticism since for him negative language has more than a descriptive function, and as such his reading of it differs from that of the perennialists, for whom such language is wholly referential. The same, as we noted above, is true of McGinn.

Performative Language Readings

We turn now to consider performative language readings, which also disagree with the perennialist view that negative language serves a purely descriptive function. However, unlike Katz's contextualist reading, the performative language readings of Sells and Turner do not primarily connect the use of this language to experience or to preparation for new modes of consciousness, rather they argue that it is serves a much more theological function. Turner in particular, reacting strongly against the perennialist position, entirely rejects the idea that experience offers us any form of starting point from which to assess the negative language that we find in Christian mystical texts.

Michael Sells

Michael Sells's account of mysticism is based on the linguistic strategies that he finds in a number of religious traditions. He views the naming and unnaming of God as a deliberate epistemological strategy of 'referential regress' that he terms a 'language of unsaying'. As we noted in the previous chapter, he believes these languages of unsaying within the Christian mystical tradition originate with Plotinus.

To explain what he means by a language of unsaying, Sells begins by noting that it is impossible to say that God is transcendent without in some way naming him. 'Any statement of ineffability, "X is beyond names," generates the *aporia* that the subject of the statement must be named (as X) in order for us to affirm that it is beyond names.'[34] He notes that there are at least three possible responses to this dilemma. Firstly, one can be silent. This is an approach that recognises God as unnamable. God's ineffability and transcendence are not affirmed, neither are they contradicted. Secondly, one can contrast 'human' language with 'Godly' language, making a distinction between what Sells describes as 'God-as-he-is-in-himself'

---

[34]   Sells, *Mystical Languages of Unsaying*, p. 2.

and 'God-as-he-is-in-creatures'. He notes that many modern commentators opt for this approach, placing the word 'God' in inverted commas when they find it in mystical texts. Finally, Sells proposes a third response, one that he sees himself adopting, in which the dilemma between naming and unnaming is accepted. He believes doing so leads to the creation of a new kind of language, which he calls 'the language of unsaying'. 'The dilemma is accepted as genuine *aporia*, that is, as unresolvable; but this acceptance, instead of leading to silence, leads to a new mode of discourse.'[35] Sells argues that this mode of discourse is found in negative theology and it is this that he means by apophasis.

Negative theology, for Sells, has to do with the endless denial of attributes to God in the light of God's transcendence. Ultimately the very 'thingness' of God is denied:

> To say 'X is beyond names,' if true, entails that it cannot then be called by the name 'X.' In turn, the statement 'it cannot be then called X' becomes suspect, since the 'it,' as a pronoun, substitutes for a name, but the transcendent is beyond all names.[36]

He argues that this process is one that can never come to an end. One must get caught in 'linguistic regress', if one is to touch this ineffability.[37] While the term 'apophasis' is commonly treated as synonymous with the act of negation, Sells argues that etymologically it means more than this: it is an act of unsaying something. He notes, like Denys Turner, how kataphasis and apophasis are commonly brought together in mystical texts, the former naming, and then the latter unnaming. He too stresses the important relationship that the two have within the writings of Pseudo-Denys:

> Dionysius demonstrates his understanding of theology as a continual interplay between the kataphatic and the apophatic modes of discourse, neither of which can function authentically without the other.[38]

Sells argues that this process reaches a certain intensity, such that even negative statements need to be unsaid. In his opinion, this process ultimately creates a tension where it becomes possible momentarily to stand in the in-between, between saying and unsaying. It is the tension rather than the saying/unsaying which then becomes meaningful. 'It is in the tension between the two propositions that the discourse becomes meaningful.'[39] Such events can necessarily only be brief, however, because Sells believes that the mind cannot stay in the in-between

---

[35]   Ibid., p. 2.
[36]   Ibid., p. 2.
[37]   Ibid., p. 2.
[38]   Ibid., p. 35.
[39]   Ibid., p. 3.

of the language of the unsaying for long.[40] 'That tension is momentary. It must be continually re-earned by ever new linguistic acts of unsaying'[41] – which is why he maintains that silence is an inadequate apophatic response, a position over which he is at odds with Turner.

In relation to this, Sells distinguishes between apophatic discourse and apophatic theory. He argues that the texts that mystical authors produce do not just theorise about apophasis, they actually perform it through the apophatic discourse that they contain. In adhering to the logic of this discourse mystical texts transform the structure of language itself. 'In such discourse, a rigorous adherence to the initial logical impasse of ineffability exerts a force that transforms normal logical and semantic structures.'[42] He argues that the language of these texts is not therefore illogical, but a working within a new objectless mode of logic. This position is not far removed from Katz's view of negative language, yet it is not subject to the same criticisms as those that can be levelled against Katz's position, since Sells does not disregard private language in the same way that Katz does. Also unlike Katz, Sells argues that we find such languages in a number of Christian mystical writings – for example, those of Pseudo-Denys, Meister Eckhart, Marguerite Porete and John Scotus Eriugena (810 BCE). In fact, Sells argues that Eriguena's text, *On the Divine Nature*, typifies what he means by a language of unsaying. He argues that it gives to the Pseudo-Denys's apophatic metaphors a particular intensity that pushes language to its limits. 'By intensity, I mean the ability for a single formula to contain an unusually wide set of semantic transformations.'[43] It does this by destabilising the language at a semantic level.

Turning to the question of experience, Sells argues that mystical literature is *not* primarily forged out of experience. Instead he sees it engendering an experience *in* the reader. However, since the notion of experience is so value-laden within the context of philosophical discussions of mysticism, Sells prefers to talk about 'meaning events'. By this Sells means an event within language when the meaning becomes identical with that which it is trying to describe. Thus, it is the moment in which the idea of transcendence and the meaning of transcendence merge together. Sells has no doubt that a practitioner of mysticism and an academic will understand the significance of such an event differently. What Sells is interested in is not

---

[40]   Sells argues that such apophasis as found within the Western tradition has three main features: a tension between emanation or overflowing and creation; an attempt to stop the transcendent being viewed as a thing; and finally a tension between transcendence and immanence, with the transcendent revealed as immanent. He notes that although mystical union has often been described as 'substantive union', the union of which mystical writers speak is a union in nothing (*ex nihilo*) rather than of substance. Union for Sells is 'the moment in which the boundaries between divine and human, self and other, melt away', Ibid., p. 7.

[41]   Ibid., p. 3.

[42]   Ibid., p. 3.

[43]   Ibid., p. 50.

individual experiences of meaning events but how language manipulation can bring them about and the different kinds of 'performative intensity' found in different texts. He argues that, while some texts simply refer to ineffability, in others even spatial and temporal relationships are subjected to a relentless apophatic treatment – a position which Knepper believes is, in fact, also represented in Pseudo-Denys's *Mystical Theology*, as we will see below.[44]

Denys Turner

Denys Turner also believes that experience is not the key to interpreting the negative language found in Christian mystical texts. Yet rather than Plotinus, he focuses on Pseudo-Denys, since he believes that Pseudo-Denys creates a distinctive epistemological theological strategy that sets out to convey God's ineffability in a way that Plotinus's use of negative language does not.

As we noted in the previous chapter, Turner maintains that Pseudo-Denys turns the philosophical message of Plato's cave analogy into a linguistic strategy by combining it with the biblical motif of Moses's ascent of Mount Sinai, such that it depends on images of light, darkness, ascent and descent.

> He made a theology out of those central metaphors without which there could not have been the mystical tradition that there has been: 'light' and 'darkness', 'ascent' and 'descent', the love of God as *eros*.[45]

Just as the philosopher in Plato's cave analogy is blinded by the light of true understanding when he comes out of the darkness of the cave, for Pseudo-Denys, the theologian is blinded by God's nature when he subjects his intellect to the quest to understand God's ineffability. This quest, according to Turner, makes use of a number of language games that involve both kataphatic and apophatic language.

In *Divine Names*, but also in *Mystical Theology*, Turner notices how Pseudo-Denys stresses that, since God has caused all things, the whole of creation provides potential imagery for the naming of God. In fact, he argues that Pseudo-Denys thinks that it is necessary to talk about God as much as possible. If one wants to know about God who is beyond language, one must, Turner argues, exhaust language, stretch it to its limits until it breaks. Therefore one must babble on and on. It is only once such a naming of God has taken place that the inadequacy of those names can be considered. Turner sees Pseudo-Denys's discussion of God as a worm and a drunken soldier in *Divine Names* in this light:

---

[44]   Mark A. McIntosh follows both Turner and Sells in taking a more performative approach to language. See McIntosh, *Mystical Theology: The Integrity of Theology and Spirituality*.

[45]   Turner, *The Darkness of God*, p. 13.

> Theological adequacy … requires the maximization of our discourses about
> God – and, whatever constraints an apophatic theology may impose, they cannot
> justify the restriction of theological language to just a few, favoured, respectful,
> 'pious', names.[46]

It is only in naming God in as many ways as God can be named that we are brought
to see the inadequacy of all our talk about God, including conceptual names like
'goodness'. It is only by talking ourselves out, as it were, that we can arrive at
'that point of verbal profusion at which we encounter the collapse of language as
such'.[47]

Turner also sees a distinction within Pseudo-Denys's descriptive discourse
about God between what he calls 'similar and dissimilar similarities'. He argues
that these correspond to a distinction that Pseudo-Denys makes between conceptual
and symbolic or perceptual names. Turner argues that this distinction is based on
ideas of created distance between God and ourselves. Those things we perceive
(in terms of their existence – ontology) are further away from God than concepts.[48]
Turner argues that this is why Pseudo-Denys starts with the names closest to God
(like goodness) and moves from there to explore names that are derived from the
causal link between creation and God, coming eventually to the lowly worm.

Turner thus argues that, together, affirmative and negative language forms a
kind of apophatic linguistic strategy that allows the reader to know God who lies
beyond language. It is in the naming and the unnaming together that apophasis
(that is, negative theology) is born. As a result Turner argues that the negative
imagery that we find in mystical texts still belongs to kataphatic, affirmative
discourse.[49] The apophatic or negative language that Turner identifies in Pseudo-
Denys's *Mystical Theology* involves a further final step:

> It is of the greatest consequence to see that negative language about God is
> no more apophatic in itself than is affirmative language. The apophatic is the
> linguistic strategy of somehow showing by means of language that which lies
> beyond language.[50]

Apophasis is the point at which we realise that God is so different from creation that
we cannot differentiate God from creation – this is why we fall silent – language
fails us. For Turner, this is a movement towards unity which only comes about

---

[46]   Ibid., p. 24.

[47]   Ibid., p. 25.

[48]   This idea is further discussed in Chapter 5, pp. 115–16.

[49]   While perceptual names are metaphorical, conceptual names are not necessarily so,
since 'there is nothing in the *logic* of existence, of goodness, of truth or of oneness, which
limits their attributions to created things'. That is, there may be notions of goodness and so
on which far exceed human concepts of it (Turner, *The Darkness of God*, p. 41).

[50]   Ibid., p. 34.

when we negate 'the last negation of all: *the difference itself between similarity and difference*'.[51] He regards this as *true* apophasis – 'speech about God that is the failure of speech'.[52] As he states:

> the negation of the negation is not a *third* utterance, additional to the affirmative and negative, in good linguistic order; it is not some intelligible *synthesis* of affirmation and negation; it is rather the collapse of our affirmation and denials into disorder.[53]

He understands the oxymorons in the opening prayer – like 'brilliant darkness' and 'hidden silence' – as examples of this 'negating the negation'. Unlike Sells, who draws on Plotinus and so slightly privileges negative discourse, Turner concentrates on Pseudo-Denys and therefore focuses on the interplay between the negative and positive language. For him, this is the key to understanding negative discourse in Christian mysticism.

Turner's strongly anti-experiential approach results from the fact that he considers the contradictory language that he finds in mystical texts to operate primarily on an intellectual level. He also appears to be echoing a Wittgenstinian understanding of how language functions in terms of the idea that we cannot of speak of that which cannot be spoken of. For Turner, this language conveys knowledge of God that exceeds both language *and* experience. Therefore, despite being very similar to Sells's, Turner's approach leads ultimately to silence, while Sells's analysis lead to 'referential regress', This lack of emphasis on experience is perhaps a weakness of Turner's approach, one that leads him to seemingly confuse all notions of experience with the experientialism that he associates with a Jamesian perennialism. Kevin Hart, from a more postmodern perspective, has argued Turner confuses two notions of experience represented by the German *Erlebnis* and *Erfahrung*. Hart believes that, although mystics reject *Erlebnis*, they still encounter *Erfahrung* when they enter into a process of continued apophasis in which 'the apophatic and cataphatic engage each other without ceasing'.[54] In his defence, Turner is very wary of any emphasis on personal experience in scholarly discussions of mystical texts since he sees this as a distinctly modern/post-modern preoccupation. When applied to medieval mystical writing, in his opinion it leads to a non-contextual reading, that thereby misconstrues the nature of negative language and the nature of mystical writing per se. Like Katz therefore, Turner is uncomfortable with the idea of private personal experience being read into mystical texts. However, as noted in the previous chapter, as a result Turner's approach has

---

[51]   Ibid., p. 45.

[52]   Ibid., p. 20.

[53]   Ibid., p. 22.

[54]   K. Hart, 'The Experience of Nonexperience', in M. Kessler and C. Sheppard (eds), *Mystics: Presence and Aporia*, Religion and Postmodernism Series (Chicago and London: University of Chicago Press, 2003), pp. 188–206 at p. 201.

difficulties accommodating the experiential aspects of mystical literature, such as that of Bernard of Clairvaux, despite his acknowledging Bernard as an important mystic. It is an aspect of his approach for which Turner seems to have been fairly criticised.[55]

A Perennialist Defence

Some scholars believe that a perennalist reading of mysticism is still possible, despite the criticisms that Katz and Turner level against it. They defend the existence of Pure Consciousness Experiences (PCEs). This idea heralds from the thought of Robert Forman.

Robert Forman

Robert Forman's discussion focuses particularly on the contextualist positions of scholars like Katz. However, Peter Kügler has argued that Forman's view also presents a challenge to Turner's performative language reading of Pseudo-Denys, since it suggests that a totally acontextual experience *is* possible.[56]

Robert Forman's discussion focuses particularly on the contextualise positions of scholars like Katz. In *The Problem of Pure Consciousness*, Robert Forman and his contributors argue that there is at least one type of experience, a mystical experience, which is free from all mediating influences. Forman calls this type of experience a Pure Consciousness Event, (which he refers to as a PCE for short). When experiencing a Pure Consciousness Event, Forman argues that the mystic is enabled, through the practice of specified spiritual techniques, to nullify the role concepts play in shaping experience.[57]

In his essay 'Mysticism, Constructivism and Forgetting', Forman identifies three characteristics for which perennialist accounts of mysticism have been criticized. Firstly, they have been accused of having an unsound methodology – in that they take material out of context. Secondly, they have based their assumption of the homogeneity of mystical experience on similar sounding reports, often dismissing the need to investigate religious and cultural contexts. Thirdly, they have blindly assumed that a similarity of experience lies behind the diverse reports of religious texts. However, adopting Ninian Smart's definition of mysticism as 'a set of experiences or … conscious events, which are not described in terms of

---

[55] M.S. Burrows, 'Raiding the Inarticulate: Mysticism, Poetics and the Unlanguageable', 173–94.

[56] P. Kügler, 'Denys Turner's Anti-Mystical Mystical Theology', *Ars Disputandi*, 4 (2004), at www.ArsDisputandi.org.

[57] R.K.C. Forman, 'Mysticism, Constructivism, and Forgetting', in R.K.C. Forman (ed.), *The Problem of Pure Consciousness: Mysticism and Philosophy* (New York: Oxford University Press, 1990), pp. 3–52.

sensory experience or mental images', Forman sees himself coming close to what he believes Pseudo-Denys intended by the idea of ecstasy:

> In restricting the term 'mysticism' to experience not described with sensory language, I believe I am in accord with its original meaning of 'too close' and to the overtones of the term as it was employed by Pseudo Dionysius, that is, separate from the sensory ('rapt out of himself').[58]

Rather than *always* mediated through religious and cultural contexts, Forman argues that a Pure Consciousness Event is a contentless form of consciousness in which no mediating factors contribute to the content of the experience. Against Katz, for whom the concept of a pure experience is an epistemological impossibility, Forman argues that mediating factors cannot be applied to non-sensory mystical consciousness. Associated with this purity of experience is what Forman calls 'novelty'. In such cases, the mystic's experience acts as a disconfirmation of expectations and previously acquired concepts. Forman argues that cases of novelty expose a problem with what Katz and other contextualists regard as the clearly causal connection between a mystic's beliefs and their expectations and experiences. Lay people and trained mystics alike, he claims, report experiences that they cannot account for in terms of their cultural/religious contexts.

To demonstrate this theory, Forman focuses on spiritual techniques of 'forgetting' – a type of negation process. For him, the forgetting technique enables the mystic to progress along the mystical path, holding images, symbols, desires, hopes and fears in abeyance. He believes that this is what Pseudo-Denys means by 'unknowing', and as such is a technique to bring about a Pure Consciousness Event:

> [This is t]he key technique by means of which Eckhart ... instructs his listeners to bring about the experience [that] he advocates is a turning away from ideas and conceptual forms, a *gelazen* – letting them go. It denotes a retreat from thought; a coming to forget all things in what Pseudo-Dionyius called an 'unknowing'.[59]

To illustrate his point, Forman turns to another mystical work, the fourteenth-century Christian contemplative text *The Cloud of Unknowing* (which we consider in Chapter 9). He draws attention to the *Cloud*'s description of a 'cloud of forgetting', under which all sensorial imagery must be trampled. Forman likens the *Cloud*'s forgetting technique to the absence of sensory data during the Pure Consciousness Event. This type of forgetting is not, Forman tells us, unique to Christian mystical writers. Meditation practice in orthodox Theravadin Buddhism teaches a progression through ascending states of consciousness. At each stage the mediator is instructed to eliminate or 'forget' the content of the previous stage

---

[58]   N. Smart, 'Interpretation and Mystical Experience', *Religious Studies*, 1 (1980), 75–87, at p. 7.

[59]   R. Forman 'Mysticism, Constructivism and Forgetting', p. 31.

until the meditation becomes abstracted from empirical content. The technique of forgetting requires a high level of repetitive, focused mental activity such as that practised during short prayers, mantras and visual meditation on a sacred picture or object. Forman argues that this mental routine acts as a catalyst to enable the mind to forget all thought and sensation. In the Pure Consciousness Event, the subject not only ceases to construct sensually, but ceases constructing altogether. Therefore, Forman argues, 'If to think is to construct thoughts, and to construct is to think, to cease thinking is to cease constructing.'[60] He believes that it is such Pure Consciousness Events that the paradoxical language of the *Mystical Theology* sets out to convey.

Forman's analysis has the benefit of pointing out that, since neither Katz nor Turner can demonstrate that no perennial experiences exist – as noted above, pain is possibly such an experience – neither proves the absolute impossibility of imageless experiences. However, a weakness of Formans' position, particularly when applied to a write like Pseudo-Denys, is that it is far from clear that there is anything experiential about Pseudo-Denys's writing. In fact, it is when applied to a writer like Pseudo-Denys that Turner's position appears most convincing.

A Contextualist Defence

However, against the type of performative language reading offered by Turner, which leaves little room for experience, other scholars who take a contextual approach to mysticism believe that it is possible to make greater room for experience without adopting the position advocated by Forman et al. One scholar who does this in a particularly sophisticated manner, building his argument around the negative language used in mystical texts, is Thomas Knepper, who, like Turner, focuses on the writings of Pseudo-Denys.

Thomas Knepper

Against the perennialist defence noted above, and as an important development of Katz's position, Thomas Knepper offers a slightly different reading of Pseudo-Denys. Knepper sees himself as a post-Wittgenstinian in the contextualist tradition and consciously sets out to extend Katz's approach. Knepper points out that negation for Pseudo-Denys does not normally involve a simple turning away of property after property from God. Rather, it is more often expressed in terms of hyper-predication. He notes that Pseudo-Denys's use of the term 'hyper' has two possible meanings. It 'can be translated in two ways, either as "above and beyond", or as "above and over" (that is to have something in excessive measure)'.[61] He

---

[60] Forman, 'Mysticism, Constructivism and Forgetting', p. 38.

[61] T. Knepper, 'Investigating Ineffability: What the Later Wittengstein has to offer to the Study of Ineffability', *International Journal for Philosophy of Religion*, online June

stresses that both meanings convey the ineffability of God, yet do so differently: 'the overall meaning is in both cases the same: God cannot be spoken of since God is on the one hand beyond effability, on the other hand preeminently ineffable'.[62] According to Knepper, when Pseudo-Denys speaks of 'brilliant darkness' he is talking of an excess which blinds. In addition to these conflicting visual metaphors, Knepper notes that Pseudo-Denys makes use of conflicting spatial metaphors – arguing that God dwells everywhere, on high and nowhere – to which Knepper equally applies the notion of excess as a kind of privation, noting that spatiality also needs to be negated when applied to God.

Yet Knepper also argues that Pseudo-Denys uses the term 'hyper' to go beyond negation, claiming that God is *both* identifiable, effable and symbolisable *and* not even unidentifiable, ineffable and unsymbolisable. Rather, God exceeds, is hyper, the opposition between indentifiable and unidentifiable. This leads to an ever increasing awareness of God's transcendence. Thus far, Knepper, despite building on Katz, appears to arrive at a position close to Turner's. However, rather than suggesting that one is led to a position in which language collapses, Knepper argues that one gets caught in this conversation. Every time we say something of God – for example, that God is beyond similarity and difference – we get caught by something else that needs to be negated. Knepper argues that we cannot exit this language game – it is never-ending – it cannot be won and it cannot be lost.

> This is a process that can never really end, a game that can never finally be won, for it is technically impossible to say what can't be said. But it is also a game that is never really lost since the ineffability of God does get conveyed by this relentless ratcheting.[63]

As such, his understanding of negative language comes close to that of Michael Sells discussed above. Yet, unlike either Sells's or Turner's performative language readings, Knepper maintains that mystics talk about experiences that they believed were ineffable.

In trying to understand how such mystical ineffability discourse functions, Knepper again draws on Wittgenstein. He argues that all language, even that within mystical texts, is essentially rule-based. He suggests that even Pseudo-Denys makes use of three basic rules:

- He identifies God as that which cannot be identified.
- He speaks of God as that which cannot be spoken.
- He symbolises God as that which cannot be symoblised.

2008 at www.springerlink.com/content/u1k2754gw61p11q7/fulltext.pdf.
[62] Ibid.
[63] Ibid.

Knepper argues that such rules help us to consider whether or not mystical texts are really describing ineffable experiences. Following Katz, he notes that we do not have access to the psychological content of mystical encounters – what we have is access to a language of ineffability. By exploring Pseudo-Denys's use of ineffability discourse and seeing that it leaves us with a game that we cannot get out of – that we are unable to transcend the bounds of language – he argues that we become aware of a difference between absolute ineffability and relative ineffability. Absolute ineffability is that which is totally other, that which we cannot talk about – in speech we always reduce it to something other than itself. However, relative ineffability is part of everyday language. For example, we often say 'I can't tell you how happy I am'. Knepper argues that in *Mystical Theology* Pseudo-Denys does not prove that God is absolutely ineffable, but only relatively so:

> Dionysius' claim that God is *hyper* ineffable should be read as something like the attempt to indicate the divine transcendence through creative linguistic hyperbole.[64]

Thus, ultimately, Knepper sides with Katz and contextualism, not with the performative language readings discussed above, albeit he does so in a way which advances (or perhaps softens) Katz's hard contextualist argument significantly by highlighting the difference between relative and absolute ineffability.[65]

Impact on Other Scholarly Readings

The belief that medieval contemplative literature uses negative language to convey the ineffable nature of mystical experiences still colours much contemporary interpretation of Christian mystical writing, as the following two examples indicate.[66] Emily Zum Brunn and Georgette Epiney-Burgard adopt a reading of Hadewijch's use of this language that still sees it as largely descriptive, although it is not clear that they view it as wholly referential. They argue that Hadewijch uses images of light, darkness and abyss, as well as paradox, as a means of conveying the transcendent nature of her experiences to her readers:

---

[64]   Ibid.

[65]   As we will see in Chapter 11, there are interesting parallels between Knepper's and Marion's readings of Pseudo-Denys. Please see especially, pp. 234–5.

[66]   Also see, for example, J.B. Hollenback, *Mysticism: Experience, Response and Empowerment* (University Park, PA: Pennsylvania State University Press, 1996); W. Teasdale, *Essays in Mysticism* (Lake Worth, FL: Sunday Publications, 1985); M. Cox, *A Handbook of Christian Mysticism* (Wellingborough: Aquarian, 1948; repr. 1986), esp. pp. 19ff; E. Underhill, *Practical Mysticism* (New York: E.P. Dutton and Co., 1915), esp. pp. 1-8.

In Hadewijch's poetry, metaphors can be interpreted at several levels, as can be seen in *Poem XVI* of the *Mengeldichten* in which love is successively called Bond, Light, Charcoal, Fire, Dew, Living Source, Hell. Her songs express an experience which allows Hadewijch to give enthusiasm and enlightenment to those who wish to follow her along the path of her spiritual 'adventure.' This adventure leads to something beyond the poem, in a transcendence experienced as a loss, darkness, abyss, as expressed in these admirable lines:

> Her deepest abyss is her highest form ..

followed by the image of silence as the end of the experience:

> Her deepest abyss is her highest song.[67]

For them, Hadewijch's transcendence is *experienced* as a kind of negative encounter, as a loss, darkness and abyss. Taking a more obviously nuanced understanding of how mystics use language, Oliver Davies, however, suggests that, failing such a clever use of language, it would be impossible to glean anything about the nature of a mystical encounter with God, unless we were able to share in the experience ourselves:

> Questions of imagery and style are fundamental to the nature of mystical writing. It is these which give life, and form, to intuitive experience which is otherwise locked away in individual subjectivity, and cannot be shared, except, of course, by direct personal contact. The use of the written word allows some gifted individuals from the past to speak to us today with an undiminished clarity and vigor. The particular use which a mystic makes of words will express and convey the particular quality of their vision. In this sense, close linguistic analysis of a mystic's work reveals the wealth of their inner world.[68]

For Davies, style and imagery matter, but also work as a means of conveying unmediated experiences to the reader. Thus he sees language as integrated with belief and experience in a way that is resonant of McGinn's approach to mysticism. As we will discuss in more detail in Chapters 4 and 10, McGinn asserts that the language used within medieval contemplative texts is intended to be transformative rather than purely descriptive. For him, it has a connection to experience, but also relates to the ineffability of God.[69] This said, McGinn does not really develop a discussion of the language of these texts in the way that Sells, Turner or Knepper do. The work of these three writers is an important contribution

---

[67]   G. Epiney-Burgard and E. Zum Brunn, *Women Mystics in Medieval Europe*, trans. S. Hughes (New York: Paragon House, 1989), p. 102.

[68]   Davies, *Meister Eckhart: Mystical Theologian*, pp. 191–2.

[69]   See, McGinn, 'The Language of Love in Christian and Jewish Mysticism'.

to the study of these texts but the readings they provide have yet to fully filter into most contemporary discussions of mysticism.

Conclusion

In this chapter we have considered a number of different explanations for the use of negative language in Christian mysticism. Perennalists treat it as wholly descriptive, in the sense that they believe it refers directly to an ineffable experience that defies linguistic analysis. Both contextualists and performative language advocates disagree. Contextualists, like Katz, argue that the language found in mystical writing is more purposeful than this. They treat negative language as a strategy to destabilise ordinary modes of thought, thereby preparing the mystic to enter into a new mode of consciousness. Performative language readings too reject the idea that negative language found within mystical texts should be approached as a description of a type of experience. They consider it instead to be first and foremost an epistemological strategy that attempts to convey the inadequacy of all language as a descriptor of the divine, even if, some like Sells, allow that this creates a space for experience of a certain type.

It is worth noting that postmodern re-readings offer yet another slant on the negative language of Pseudo-Denys. Such re-readings, because of their complexity, are considered separately in Chapter 12. The next chapter turns not to these accounts, but to another theme considered definitive of Christian mystical writing, the idea that mysticism is an interior journey into one's own soul.

Chapter 3
Selfhood and Interiority

In this chapter we consider the idea that the mystical journey is an interior journey into one's soul, mind or self. We focus particularly on Augustine's discussions of this idea in his works *The Confessions* and *On the Trinity*.

Augustine's Interior Journey

Born in Alexandria around 354, Augustine became Bishop of Hippo in 396. He wrote numerous works on Christian spirituality and belief. Alongside Pseudo-Denys, he is considered one of the Founding Fathers of Christian mysticism.

The Confessions

Augustine's work, *The Confessions* is often regarded as the first ever spiritual autobiography. The first eight chapters describe events in his life prior to his conversion. Here we learn of the importance of his mother Monica, herself a Christian, and discover the important role she plays in Augustine's own spiritual journey. This is nowhere more apparent than in chapter 9, where Augustine records a turning point in his life, a vision of God which he shares with Monica while they converse in a garden in Ostia. Both find that through their conversation they embark on a journey that takes them through and beyond the various aspects of the Created Order until finally they enter their own souls, where they briefly encounter God. As Augustine writes in this famous passage:

> Our minds were lifted up by an ardent affection towards eternal being itself. Step by step we climbed beyond all corporeal objects and the heaven itself, where sun, moon and stars shed light on earth. We ascended even further by internal reflection and dialogue and wonder at your works, and we entered into our own minds. We moved up beyond them so as to attain to the region of inexhaustible abundance where you feed Israel eternally with truth for food. There life is the wisdom by which all creatures come into being.[1]

---

[1]   Augustine, *Confessions* 9.x.25, in *St Augustine's Confessions*, trans. H. Chadwick, Oxford World's Classics (Oxford: Oxford University Press, 1998), p. 171. (All quotations are taken from this edition.) Andrew Louth has convincingly shown that, although Augustine owes a tremendous debt to Plotinus in this passage, the changes he makes illustrate that he

From this point onwards the focus of *The Confessions* shifts away from external events in Augustine's life to those which take place within his soul.

Mapping out this turn towards interiority, and with it the discovery of true selfhood, Augustine begins with an interrogation of creation. He asks each element if it is God. It replies that it is not, but that it points beyond itself to its Creator. Having exhausted everything in the external creation, Augustine finally turns to interrogate himself.

> And what is the object of my love? I asked the earth and it said: 'It is not I.' I asked all that is in it: they made the same confessions. I asked the sea, the deeps, the living creatures that creep, they responded: 'We are not your God, look beyond us.' ... I asked the heaven, sun, moon and stars; they said: 'Nor are we the God whom you seek.' And I said to all these things in my external environment: 'Tell me of my God who you are not, tell me something about him.' And with a great voice they cried out: 'He made us' ... Then I turned towards myself ...[2]

Augustine now reflects on the different aspects that constitute his created being. He has a body, senses, an imagination, an intellect and desires. Through introspective reflection Augustine arrives at the conclusion that thinking or intellect and desire or will constitute the most spiritual parts of his being because they are the least connected to the material world.[3] Reflecting now on these various elements of his soul, he eventually comes to 'the fields and vast palaces of memory'. He is struck by the memory's capacity to contain images of past events, people, things and emotions, all of which can be recalled without the soul being fully transported back to the moment in question. He can, he realises, be happy, yet still remember a sad event. Augustine marvels at the memory, which he distinguishes from the conscious mind (*mens*). Memory (*memoria*) is unconscious and full of things that have been forgotten; although the notion of forgetting itself can never be entirely forgotten, otherwise the mind would not know what it means either to forget or to remember!

> What we remember we retain by memory. But unless we could recall forgetfulness, we could never hear the word and recognise the thing which the word signifies. Therefore memory retains forgetfulness.[4]

---

is staking out a different and importantly a Christian account of spiritual ascent. See Louth, *The Origins of the Christian Mystical Tradition*, pp. 134–141.

 [2]   *Confessions* 10.vi.9, p. 183.

 [3]   We will discuss this in greater detail in Chapter 8 when we consider the relationship between visions and mysticism.

 [4]   *Confessions* 10.xvi.24, p. 193.

Augustine journeys further into his memory and notes that, as well as images (which enter the soul via the senses), there are also 'things' housed within it. He finds things like numbers, questions of logic and geometry, which he argues could not simply have entered the mind through the senses. A question like 'does this exist?' is not, he reasons, founded on our sense experience of the outside world. Rather such questions just make sense to us when we hear them. So, Augustine argues that principles of logic, mathematics and numbers already exist in our memories, waiting to be recalled or remembered by us.

> How they came to me let me explain if I can ... The answer must be that they were already in the memory but so remote and pushed into the background, as if in most secret caverns ... we find that the process of learning is simply this: by thinking we ... gather together ideas which the memory contains in a dispersed and disordered way ...[5]

This conclusion betrays the influence of Plotinian Neoplatonism on Augustine's thought, since, as we noted in Chapter 1, remembering is central to the soul's return the One for Plotinus. Augustine's attitude to remembering changes throughout his life – he eventually rejects the idea of the pre-existence of souls – thus his views are not exactly the same as Plotinus's. However it is not entirely clear what he believed about the pre-existence of souls at the time he wrote *The Confessions*.[6]

Yet Augustine argues that there is something even deeper within memory than numbers or geometry: joy or happiness (*eudaemonia*). Augustine holds

---

[5]   *Confessions* 10.x.17–10.xi.18, pp. 188–9.

[6]   Ronald Teske notes that we know that earlier in his career Augustine accepted the Platonic idea of reminiscence or recollection (*anamnesis*). This involves the belief that we pre-existed as souls before our earthly existence, and thus retained knowledge which had been forgotten by us at birth. However, much later in life Augustine plainly rejects this idea. What he believed at the time of writings *Confessions* is not clear. As the passages quoted above indicate, Augustine seems to be deliberately ambiguous about what he thinks. Modern scholarship remains divided on the issue. Denys Turner suggests that while it is unclear we can at least see residues of this platonic idea within *Confessions* (Turner, *The Darkness of God*, p. 58). Teske takes a similar line, noting that, although 'Augustine rejected the Platonic view that learning is recollection, he does not necessarily abandon all thought of the pre-existence of the soul' (R. Teske, 'Augustine's Philosophy of Memory', in E. Stump and N. Kretzmann (eds), *The Cambridge Companion to Augustine* (Cambridge: Cambridge University Press, 2006), pp. 148–58, at p. 150. He notes that, even in the later work *On the Trinity*, Augustine still argues that we were all present in Adam in his first sin, even though our lives had not yet properly begun. Teske outlines the different approaches to what Augustine believes about recollection or reminiscence taken by some of the most prominent Augustine scholars (ibid., pp. 150–51). Teske himself believes that this idea, of us all being joined to God through Adam, makes best sense of Augustine's comment 'I found nothing coming from you which I have not stored in my memory since the first time I learnt of you' (*Confessions* 10.xxiv.35, p. 200).

that happiness is retained by the memory in a unique manner. Happiness is not remembered in the way that the city of Carthage is, for example. Nor is it an image, even though the memory contains images of happy moments. It is not even there in the same way that numbers are: we do not desire numbers and principles of logic in the same way that we desire happiness! All this leads Augustine to conclude that happiness is, in fact, our deepest and so most fundamental desire:

> There is one goal which all are striving to attain, namely to experience joy. Since no one can say that this is a matter outside experience, the happy life is found in the memory.[7]

Augustine asks himself, what then is this happiness that he so longs for? Although he sees that people try to find happiness in other things, he concludes that it must consist of finding God, for it is only when he journeys within himself to his deepest point that he is able to find this happiness. This leads Augustine to conclude that God also exists within his memory. For all these reasons, Augustine suggests that the memory is so vast, as to be ungraspable. '[Memory] is a vast and infinite profundity. What has plumbed its bottom?'[8]

Augustine is clear that the inner journey he embarks on is the culmination of a life of searching in dissatisfaction for the true source of happiness – a searching that led Augustine in many directions before he found the Christian God. Augustine's mystical journey is dominated by an overwhelming sense that he is and always has been longing to find God, although he didn't realise it.[9] In encountering God in Ostia within his own soul, he finally finds what he has been endlessly searching for, as he recalls in this famous passage:

> Late have I loved you, beauty so old and so new: late have I loved you. And see, you were within and I was in the external world and sought you there … you called and cried out loud and shattered my deafness. You were radiant and resplendent, you put to flight my blindness. You were fragrant, and I drew in my breath and now pant after you. I taste you, and I feel but hunger and thirst for you. You touched me, and I am set on fire to attain the peace which is yours.[10]

At the very moment when Augustine reaches the point within his soul where he finds God, God then reaches down and raises Augustine above memory, just momentarily, 'in the flash of a trembling glance'[11]:

---

[7]   *Confessions* 10.xxi.31, p. 198.

[8]   *Confessions* 10.viii.15, p. 187.

[9]   The erotic nature of the Christian mystical journey is considered in Chapter 4.

[10] *Confessions* 10.xxvi.37, p. 201.

[11] *Confessions* 7.xvi.23, p. 127.

Surely my memory is where you dwell, because I remember you since I first learnt of you ... Where then did I find you so that I could learn of you if not in the fact that you transcend me? There is no place, whether we go backwards or forwards; there can be no question of place.[12]

It is at this point that he does not merely *see* the light of God in his soul, but he also *enters* this light and *sees by it*. This is the moment, Augustine says, when he also finally finds himself. 'So in the flash of a trembling glance it attained to all that is. At that moment I saw your "invisible nature understood through the things which are made." (Rom. 1:20)'[13] It is therefore the most significant event in his autobiography, the culminating moment to which all the events have been leading.

However, in *Confessions* the realisation of God and of selfhood is only momentary. In later works Augustine comes to suggest that this experience of God and self which he records in *The Confessions* is just the starting point of his spiritual journey of self-discovery.

On the Trinity

In *On the Trinity*, Augustine rejects his original belief that Christ is the image of God. He reasons that to believe this subordinates Christ to a level that is less than fully divine. Instead he argues that it is actually the soul that is the image of God.[14] In true Neoplatonic fashion being an image entails participation. In *On the Trinity* he explores what this means for his understanding of the interior journey and the way in which the soul comes to find God within it.

Augustine pictures the image of God within the soul as a trinity of primary functions: to know, to love and to remember. These three functions belong respectively to three aspects of the soul: the intellect, the memory and the will – the three highest elements of the mind that he discussed in *The Confessions*. Just as God the Trinity has three persons who are all interrelated within one another, so the soul, who is God's image, has three interrelated aspects. For Augustine, intellect, memory and will mirror God the Trinity both by their triune nature and through the interrelatedness of their functionality:

---

[12]   *Confessions* 10.xxv.36–10.xxvi.37, pp. 200–201.

[13]   *Confessions* 7.xvi.23, p. 127. This is the first of two occasions in *Confessions* where Augustine describes a moment of encounter with God.

[14]   Andrew Louth notes that in *Confessions* Augustine claims there was an intermediary who mediated between the soul and God. This was Christ, the image of God (*imago dei*), who came down to us, and called us back. In this text the soul is a copy of this image (*ad imaginem deum*). However, the later Augustine rejected this idea. He argued that Christ, the word of God, is co-equal with the Father; and was not therefore an image or a copy. In *On the Trinity*, he argues that consequently the soul is the image of God (*imago dei*) (Louth, *The Origins of the Christian Mystical Tradition*, pp. 146–7).

These three, the memory, the understanding, and the will, are ... not three lives
but one life ... For I remember that I have memory, understanding and will;
and I understand that I understand, will, and remember; and I will that I will,
remember and understand.[15]

What is more, he reasons that as an image of God they cannot be three separate
activities or faculties. They must, like God, be mutually dependent on each other.
As Robert Teske notes, 'whatever is said of each of them is said of the three
together in the singular, just as the three Persons [of the Trinity] are not three gods,
but one God'.[16]

Yet Augustine is not satisfied that this truly makes the soul the image of God.
He believes that to truly be an image of something, the image must also participate
in that which it was the image of:

This Trinity of the mind is not on that account the image of God because the
mind remembers itself, understands itself, and loves itself, but because it can
also remember, understand and love Him by whom it was made.[17]

We will explore this complex idea of image and participation further in chapter 8.
For now it suffices to say that, as such an image of God, Augustine holds that the
soul has a deep and special relationship with God that enables it to journey to God
through introspection, which at the same time reveals to the soul its true nature.

This journey into his soul moves Augustine beyond earthly knowledge
(*scientia*) to true knowledge, which Augustine calls wisdom (*sapientia*). Here he
finds Christ, the Wisdom of God, whose light it is that shines within the soul. This
light transforms the soul when it participates in it, changing its perception of all
that it sees. Andrew Louth notes that this belief requires Augustine to argue that
there is something eternal within the soul, a place of overlap with God. Augustine
calls this point the soul's highest pinnacle (*acies mentis*) or its spark (*scintilla*).
Entry into this light is participation in God, and as such it is the end of the mystical
journey begun in *The Confessions*. There can be no doubt that his discovery of
God and his discovery of self are one and the same.

Later Medieval Development of the Interior Journey

The notion that the soul is made up of different aspects is a fundamental element
of later accounts of mysticism. We noted that Augustine did not see intellect,
will and memory as separate faculties but interrelated aspects that are only truly

---

[15]   Augustine, *On the Trinity* X.xviii.11, pp. 311–12. All translations are taken from
Saint Augustine: The Trinity trans. S. McKenna (Washington: CUPA, 1962).

[16]   Teske, 'Augustine's Philosophy of Memory', p. 155.

[17]   Augustine, *On the Trinity*, XIV.xii.15, pp. 432–3.

the image of God through their participation in God. Yet as the Middle Ages progressed something of the subtly of Augustine's argument appears to be lost as intellect, memory and will are increasingly treated as a mimetic, rather than a participatory, image of the Trinity. Although the soul's participation in God is far from unimportant, attention shifts to consideration of the spark of the soul within the conscience. Later writers increasingly come to view intellect and will as separate faculties, with defined relationships to lower faculties, such as sensation and imagination.[18]

William of St Thierry

William of St Thierry, who wrote in the eleventh and twelfth centuries, is deeply influenced by Augustine.[19] However, while in his account of mysticism William is careful to describes the role played by intellect and will, he seems to neglect memory, which, as we noted above, was the central element in Augustine's account of mysticism. Unlike Augustine, William argues that the memory is insufficient to order or retain the wisdom that results from the mystical quest. Instead he argues that wisdom is held in the conscience. Subsequent mystical writers follow him and argue that God and the soul overlap in the conscience, where they believe the spark of the soul is to be found. William also stresses the functions of intellect and will relative to memory in his own journey of introspection. He argues that the spiritual journey is orchestrated by these *two* aspects of the soul, when they proceed together, hand in hand, as it were. As they cooperate with one another, he argues, they move the soul towards God, until both are suddenly raised up to and subsumed in the wisdom of God.

> Contemplation has two eyes, reason and love ... one of these eyes searches the things of men, according to knowledge [*scientia*]; but the other searches divine things, according to wisdom [sapientia] ... when they are illuminated by grace, they are of great mutual assistance, because love gives life to reason and reason gives light to love ... often when these two eyes faithfully cooperate, they become one; in the contemplation of God, where love is chiefly operative, reason passes into love and love is transformed into a certain spiritual and divine understanding which transcends and absorbs all reason.[20]

As this passage suggests, William believes that eventually these two aspects of the soul become united. They become a single eye as their functions amalgamate.

---

[18] See Chapter 9 for a discussion of these ideas in English Mysticism.

[19] D.N. Bell, *The Image and Likeness: The Augustinian Spirituality of William of Saint-Thierry*, CS 78 (Kalamazoo: Cisterician Publications, 1984).

[20] William of St Thierry, Song 1, stanza 8.92, in *Exposition on the Song of Songs: The Works of William of St Thierry, Volume 2*, trans. Mother C. Hart OSB, with intro. by J.M. Decharet OSB, Cisterian Fathers 6 (Shannon: Ciscercian Publications, 1970), p. 74.

When this happens they gain wisdom that totally transcends human knowledge. William says that this knowledge is of its own type (*sui generis*). There is a fair amount of debate as to exactly what William meant by this. However, it is clear that he believes that it entails a union of these two elements, as love becomes a type of knowing (*amor ispse intellectus est*). While all this may take place within memory, the lack of emphasis on memory's role is important in the light of later medieval developments.

Thomas Gallus

Thomas Gallus, builds on William's account, but interestingly argues that there comes a point beyond which intellect cannot progress. After intellect and will are joined together, Gallus posits a further level of knowing in which the intellect is left behind.

> Intellect and desire, as it were walk hand in hand [until] intellect finally fails
> ... and intellect, though drawn up ... can go no further but there achieves the
> fulfillment of its knowledge and its light.[21]

Gallus, as well as being influenced by Augustine's account of mysticism, was also deeply influenced by Pseudo-Denys, whom we considered in the previous chapter. Gallus offers an alternative interpretation of Pseudo-Denys's *Mystical Theology*. In particular, he focuses on Moses's plunge into the darkness of unknowing that we considered in the introductory chapter. Gallus interprets Moses's final move into the darkness of unknowing as a sign that intellect ultimately gets left behind in the mystical journey. When this happens, the will, through its love for God, has to reach out alone to God. Gallus argues that this is why *The Mystical Theology* ends in silence. There is nothing that can be thought or said because intellect is not involved. All that the soul can do is to enter into a kind of blind love of God. As Bernard McGinn wryly remarks, 'For Gallus and his followers, the affective union no longer seems as interested in subsuming the lower forms of intellectual activity as it is in kicking them downstairs'.[22]

Denys Turner argues that Gallus's interpretation of Pseudo-Denys constitutes a turn towards a more affective (or what Turner calls 'affectivist') understanding of contemplation. He notes that both Bonaventure (1221–74) and *The Cloud*-Author (later fourteenth century) follow Gallus's interpretation. Like William of St Thierry, Bonaventure stresses the activities of intellect and will over and above that of memory. In fact, Étienne Gilson notes that Bonaventure regards memory and intelligence as

---

21   William of St Thierry, 'Preface to the Song of Songs', in D. Turner, *Eros and Allegory: Medieval Exegesis on the Song of Songs*, CS 156 (Kalamazoo: Cistercian Publications, 1995), pp. 332–3.

22   B. McGinn, 'Love, Knowledge and Mystical Union in Western Christianity: Twelfth to Sixteenth Centuries', *Church History*, 56 (1987), 7–24, at p. 13.

functions of the same faculty.[23] Following Gallus, Bonaventure ultimately believes that intellect is left behind in the process of introspection and self-discovery. The importance of this affectivist turn impacts on later understandings of mysticism, especially in terms of the role experience comes to play within them, as will be considered in Chapter 9.

In addition, many texts from the eleventh and twelfth centuries exhibit a growing self-referentiality which, when coupled with a shift from Latin to vernacular textual production and a more visually-orientated culture, has led scholars like John Burrows, Peter Dronke and Sarah Spence to argue that a more distinctive sense of self begins to emerge in the twelfth century.[24] Caroline Walker Bynum argues that this is not really the case. Although she notes that Bernard of Clairvaux stresses self-love as the first step towards loving God, she questions whether this can really be said to demonstrate the emergence of the 'individual' in anything like a twenty-first century understanding of the word. Rather, she argues that twelfth-century mystics were doing as Augustine before them, discovering within themselves a self that was made in the image of God:

> One might say, to simplify it a little, that … to the twelfth century the goal of development is likeness to God, but on the image of God found in 'the inner man'; to the twentieth century the goal is the process itself.[25]

However, Mark McIntosh is not so sure that the self is really central to Bernard's mysticism in the same way that it is to Augustine's.

McIntosh suggests that, judging by the imagery Bernard uses as well as the emphasis that he places on experience, Bernard is doing something slightly different. McIntosh argues that in Bernard we see a more modern sense of self that actively seeks out and experiences God at all stages of the journey, rather than emerging in its final apophatic step:

> But the language of experience does not stop there for Bernard … Bernard's language also points to experience as a new kind of spiritual tool, a guide by which one begins to chart one's inner spiritual journey … Are we moving in imagery at least, if not intent, from the common public realm of salvation history to the inner private realm of emotions?'[26]

---

[23]   É. Gilson, *The Philosophy of St. Bonaventure*, trans. I. Trethowan and F.J. Sheed (London, Sheed & Ward, 1940), pp. 341–403, esp. 344. As Gilson explains, the real distinction for Bonaventure lies between intellect and will.

[24]   See, S. Spence, *Texts and the Self in the Twelfth Century* (Cambridge: Cambridge University Press, 2006).

[25]   C.W. Bynum, *Jesus as Mother: Studies in the Spirituality of the High Middle Ages*, p. 87.

[26]   McIntosh, *Mystical Theology*, pp. 66–7.

Yet, regardless of the interior mechanics of mysticism, post-Augustine, it is clear that introspection, interiority and selfhood are inextricably interlinked and as such form a fundamental aspect of Christian mysticism. This is perhaps nowhere more apparent than the writings of the sixteenth-century Spanish mystics Teresa of Avila and John of the Cross. Teresa pictures her mysticism as an interior movement within her soul, which is an interior castle that she has to penetrate. For John, his dark nights of the soul betray this same tension between finding God and finding self, for it is only as he loses self on one level that he comes to find both self and God on another.[27] Clearly this complex relationship between self, God and introspection demands explanation, as does the developing role of experience.

CONTEMPORARY THEORETICAL APPROACHES

We will begin by first considering scholarly responses to Augustine, before turning in the final section of the chapter to briefly reflect on some of the complex developments in selfhood and experience that appear in later Christian mystical texts.

Perennialist Readings

Augustine's mysticism has not always been favourably received by perennialists. Some distrust his reliance on Neoplatonism, as we noted in Chapter 1. Others have criticised him for not clearly focusing on mystical union, which many perennialists believe is an essential trait of a 'mystical' experience. Ephraem Hendrikx also suggests that Augustine's experiences are too fleeting to count as mystical.[28] Cuthbert Butler famously attempted to justify Augustine's account of mysticism from a perennialist perspective. Describing him as the 'Prince of Mystics',[29] he marries Augustine's interior journey with the notion of 'union with God', which Butler claims it entails. Butler argues that when read in this way Augustine's interior journey can legitimately be understood as an account of an ineffable experience.[30] The dificulties that arise for strict perennialist readings, which struggle to deal with the complex interplay of human experience, philosophy, belief and introspection that Augustine presents, suggest the limitations of this position.

---

[27]   See, for example, E. Howells, *John of the Cross and Teresa of Avila: Mystical Knowing and Selfhood* and Turner, *The Darkness of God*.

[28]   E. Hendrikx, 'Augustins Verhältness zur Mystik: Ein Rückblick', in C.P Mayer and W. Eckermann (eds), *Scientia Augustiniana*, (Würzburg: Augustinus-Verlag, 1975), pp. 107–11. This article is unfortunately only available in German.

[29]   See McGinn, *The Foundations of Mysticism*, pp. 276–7.

[30]   Ibid., p. 231.

Contextualist Approaches

Those scholars who take a more contextualist approach to Augustine argue that perennialist readings fail to fully account for the depth of relationship, particularly that between Augustine's interior journey and Plotinus's flight of the soul to the Alone. They suggest that this can only be done by taking a more contextual approach which does not demand that Augustine's interior journey is read merely as an account of ineffable experience. The shared nature of Augustine's experience at Ostia is also more explicable when considered from a contextualist position.

Andrew Louth and James O'Donnell

Despite holding that the vision at Ostia is characterised by features that suggest it was a transcendent experience, as noted in the previous chapter, Andrew Louth stresses the extent and depth of Augustine's relationship with Plotinus. He notes, for example, how the vision in chapter 9 culminates in 'a transitory experience of rapture or ecstasy', which entails the mind being totally withdrawn from bodily sensation. This understanding of the relationship between body and soul is one that owes a great deal to Neoplatonic ideas of reality. Louth notes too that this understanding of vision mirrors the most transcendent form of knowing, 'intellectual vision', that Augustine describes elsewhere in his *Literal Commentary on Genesis* – meaning that there was nothing physical about it.[31] Louth also comments on the shared nature of Augustine's vision at Ostia. He suggests that Monica's role highlights the importance of friendship and communication, thereby bringing into question the extent to which Augustine's Christian vision of God is really the same as Plotinus's vision, which is characterised as a flight of the lonely soul into the Alone, even though we should note that this is not a feature that appears in Augustine's later writings.

> It is at once an account of a personal experience, and yet not a purely solitary one. The experience grows out of his conversation with his mother. This makes one wonder to what extent friendship, companionship, communion with other human beings, is important for Augustine in his ascent to God.[32]

To be fair to Louth, he is concerned not so much with this experience as with context and the need to consider this alongside mystical experience. It is this that he stresses as invaluable for understanding Augustine.

In his commentary on *Confessions*, James O'Donnell likewise queries the value of reading Augustine's inner journey in terms of a perennialist understanding of mysticism. Commenting on the vision at Ostia in book 9, he argues that we

---

[31]   See Chapter 8 for further discussion on vision and ideas about seeing in Christian mystical texts.

[32]   Louth, *The Origins of the Christian Mystical Tradition*, p. 136.

cannot access Augustine's 'experience', nor determine the extent to which it can be classified as either Christian or Neoplatonic. Thus he says we cannot judge its 'mystical' worth in a perennialist sense. What most concerns him is that such questions obscure the real purpose behind the mystical experiences recounted in books 7 and 9, which he believes intentionally indicate that, while the Plotinian quest for the One is valuable, the quest for God through Christ is better.[33] O'Donnell notes that, rather than using the verb 'to see' as he does of his Plotinian vision in book 7, Augustine describes the encounter at Ostia as an '"audition" rather than a "vision"'.[34] To O'Donnell, this implies that the Christian vision is of a higher kind, despite the Plotinian thinking that still underpins it.[35] O'Donnell's aim is not to deny the possibility that these texts are mystical, that is experiential, in the sense McGinn or Louth, for example, suggest, but to caution against reading Augustine's *Confessions* as only descriptive of experiences, since this is to miss much of the richness of the text.

John Kenney

An even more explicitly anti-perennialist reading of Augustine's interior journey is offered by John Kenney in *The Mysticism of St Augustine: Rereading the Confessions*. Kenney argues that a perennialist reading, particularly a Jamesian one, demands a dislocation of the mystical experience from its surrounding religious culture. As a result, he notes that a Jamesian reading fails to give an adequate explanation for how Augustine's inner journey can depend on both Plotinian and Christian influences:

> The problem with [a perennialist] approach is that it cuts the mystic off from the surrounding religious culture, offering an atomistic view of human experience. It also ignores the social and cultural components of any conceptualization employed to describe the experience.[36]

He argues too that the transitory nature of the vision at Ostia has less to do with its being a mystical encounter than with the emphasis that Augustine places on the soul's sinfulness, which cannot sustain a full vision of God.

---

[33]   'The difficulties of modern scholars with the passage arise from the need to decide what *really* happened, and the desire to put the correct label upon it. These exercises in fruitless zeal give to much scholarship on this passage an air of special pleading that often obscures both evidence and argument' (*The Confessions of St Augustine*, ed. J.J. Odonnell, 3 vols (Oxford: Oxford University Press 1992), vol. 3, pp. 127–8).

[34]   Ibid., vol. 3, p. 128.

[35]   Ibid., vol. 3, p. 128.

[36]   J.P. Kenney, *The Mysticism of St Augustine: Rereading the Confessions* (Oxford: Routledge, 2005), p. 67.

Augustine's concern is to underscore the soul's moral imperfection, something that the brevity of its attention exhibits. Augustine's soul suffers not from the transiency of mystical experience but from its moral insufficiency. The defining axis of this episode is not temporal but ethical.[37]

He notes too that a specifically Jamesian reading cannot really account for the shared nature of Augustine's experience at Ostia:

> It would be a stretch to describe the vision at Ostia as two parallel mystical experiences, given the level of mutuality articulated in the passage. So the atomism of the psychological model is another point of friction with the Augustinian text.[38]

Kenney therefore concludes that the characteristics of Augustine's mysticism do not sit well with perennialist ideas of mystical experience, indicating the strength of a more contextualist approach[39]

Performative Language Readings

In his performative language readings of Augustine's interior journey, Denys Turner does not deny that there is an experiential element to Augustine's account of mysticism. However, as with his readings of Pseudo-Denys, he questions the validity of reading Augustine's account of selfhood in terms of modern subjectivism. Instead he draws attention to the way in which Augustine's various accounts of the self interact with and negate one another as they seek to find an idea of selfhood that is synonymous with God.

Denys Turner

In *The Darkness of God*, Turner argues that Cuthbert Butler's perennialist reading totally misconstrues Augustine's understanding of contemplation:

> There is hardly any proposition which could be more disruptive of an adequate understanding of the subtleties of Augustine's thought – or even, if it comes to that, of Christian Platonism generally – than the sort of dichotomizing of 'experience' and 'speculation' which Butler engages in.[40]

---

[37] Ibid., p. 67.

[38] Ibid., p. 141.

[39] Ibid., p. 142.

[40] Turner, *Darkness of God*, p. 262.

According to Turner, the value of Augustine's mysticism does not hinge on whether Augustine encountered mystical experiences. However, this does not mean that Turner is not interested in the question of experience – far from it. The pivotal question in Turner's reading is what Augustine *means* by experience?

In *Confessions*, Turner notes that Augustine seems to merge genres in a bewildering way. He asks how Augustine can have written an autobiography, which in our understanding of the term means 'a life story', through a philosophical exploration of what it means to know God? Are not experience and inference (I must have knowledge of God *because* I long to find him) two separate things? Not, Turner argues, for Augustine. Turner believes Augustine manages to hold together both the experiencing self and a philosophical understanding of what a self is, in a way that baffles modern readers. Turner argues that this occurs precisely because Augustine comes to understand his experiencing self as inextricably bound to his philosophical self. Before this occurred, Turner argues, Augustine did not have a self to write about. For Turner, experience, philosophy, selfhood and knowledge of God are therefore all bound together. It is this that he believes makes the idea of Augustine having mystical experiences in a perennialist sense untenable. 'The true excitement to be gained from Augustine's story of his life lies in following through the subtle interplay of the conceptual and the experiential language in which he tells it,'[41] rather than in separating these out from one another.

Turner argues that this is especially apparent in book 10 of *The Confessions*, where Augustine reveals his search for God to be a search for himself and vice versa. As we noted above, Augustine comes to realise that, in finding God in himself, he finds himself in God, who is both within him *and* transcends him. Turner stresses the paradoxical nature of this idea:

> The paradox, then, is that there, where God is most intimately and 'subjectively' interior to us, our inwardness turns out beyond itself towards the eternal and boundless objectivity of Truth.[42]

Turner points out that both in *The Confessions* and *On the Trinity* Augustine's mystical journey is characterised by metaphors of interiority and ascension. He suggests that this language is 'self-subverting' – Augustine is not talking of some psychological inner journey, rather he is speaking of a journey beyond and above himself. He criticises perennialist readings for not understanding this:

> It would ... be the ultimate irony if that metaphor of interiority which shapes Augustine's critique of a materialist psychology of 'selfhood' should after all be pressed back into the service of just that same semi-materialism ... a 'quasi-

---

[41] Ibid., p. 54.

[42] Ibid., p. 69.

physical' psychological act of 'turning of the mind inward' towards its own mental contents.[43]

The key to all of this, for Turner, is memory, through which Augustine both recalls his self, who he is (knowledge that was forgotten), but at the same time reconfigures his self – understanding his past in terms of the God who he finds now within his memory.[44] The complex interplay of past and present, and of experience and philosophy, leads Turner to feel perplexed by modern readers who ask if experience takes precedence over philosophy or vice versa.[45] Turner argues that our concern with personal subjective experience is a decidedly modern one which Augustine would not have understood. This is not, Turner argues, what Augustine means by either self or experience.

Turner argues that his reading of the interrelationship between experience and self-discovery first voiced in *Confessions*, is confirmed in *On the Trinity*, as Augustine develops his thinking on the soul as the image of God. Here it becomes even clearer that, for Augustine, the true self is interior, not because the inner man is psychologically better than the outer man – Turner points out that imagination and the memory of images are also part of the outer man for Augustine – but because in the innermost part of the soul, the soul discovers itself: that is, that who it really is, is who it is *in God*. As such, the mind is brought to the paradoxical place that is both most deeply within itself and totally beyond itself. At its highest deepest point, its spark, God and the soul overlap. Turner argues that this paradoxical anthropology moves the soul beyond itself to knowledge of God who transcends it:

> Here, where time intersects with eternity, the mind's most intimate interiority is also its 'highest' point, a point which Augustine calls the *acies mentis*, the 'cutting edge' of the mind, the place 'in' it which overlaps with the eternal Light it is in.[46]

Turner holds therefore, that Augustine's account is 'implied apophasis', because the metaphors of selfhood and interiority that Augustine uses lead the soul beyond language, conceptions and metaphors. The God that Augustine finds within himself as he finds himself necessarily transcends himself, even while he and God are one. This apophasis is revealed at that moment of transcendence in which true knowledge of God (wisdom) becomes possible.[47] Turner therefore argues that, while Pseudo-Denys's strategy is built on apophatic language about God, Augustine's rests on apophatic language about the self. This idea of mystical anthropology becomes

---

[43] Ibid., p. 88.
[44] Ibid., p. 69.
[45] Ibid., p. 69.
[46] Ibid., p. 99.
[47] Ibid., p. 265.

even more pronounced in later writers like Eckhart and *The Cloud*-Author, whose mystical strategies Turner describes as 'apophatic anthropology'.[48]

For all these reasons, Turner argues that it simply does not make sense to apply a perennialist reading to Augustine's account of experience. Nor does it seem adequate to suggest that ineffable experience is the primary driving force behind texts like *The Confessions* or *On the Trinity*. For Turner, this is to misconstrue the nature of Augustine's mystical journey in terms of modern psychology. The inclusion of experience undoubtedly nuances Turner's position as discussed in the previous chapter. From this we can see that Turner does not wish, at least in the case of a writer like Augustine, to dismiss the value of all experience in an absolute sense. He merely wishes to caution against a Jamesian treatment of mysticism that privileges subjective experience, and posits the underlying goal of Christian mysticism as an ineffable encounter, thereby omitting the relationality of the experience of God that he finds in Augustine.

Mark McIntosh

Following Turner, Mark McIntosh argues that, far from instigating a more individualistic and subjective understanding of spirituality, Augustine envisaged a complete overlap between God and the soul. For God to look for Augustine was the same thing as for Augustine to look for God: 'For God to seek out Augustine through all eternity takes the form, in time, of Augustine seeking out God.'[49] McIntosh argues that this non-privatised sense of what it means to know God is also found in later writers, even in Bernard of Clairvaux (1090–1153), whose discussions of mysticism are replete with references to experience. For example:

> while all individuals need to have their own experiences of the reality Bernard describes, these experiences do *not* isolate them from each other in private selves but rather draw them together in the common journey into deeper relationship with the one God.[50]

However, McIntosh also believes that a more modern sense of selfhood appears in Bernard's writings, one that brings into question the limited role that Turner ascribes to experience in his discussions of mysticism. While Turner admits that there is a human element to Bernard's understanding of experience, for Turner, as we will see in the next chapter, the unitive nature of love in Bernard's mysticism leads Bernard to an apophatic rather than an experiential understanding of mysticism. Since he takes the goal of mystical writing to be the communication of apophasis, for Turner, experience, even when acknowledged, is always peripheral.

---

[48]   E. Babinsky, *Church History*, 66/4 (1997), 821–22, at 822. See Turner, *Darkness of God*, p. 6.

[49]   McIntosh, *Mystical Theology*, p. 222.

[50]   Ibid., p. 66.

This seems a limitation of Turner's model, particularly when faced with more experiential accounts of mysticism, such as those that develop in the later Middles Ages, as we will discuss in Part II.

A final aspect of McIntosh's readings of mysticism also seems worth mentioning, since it draws attention to the development of more affective forms of mysticism in the later Middle Ages, which build on the thought of Gallus. Reflecting on the role that mystical anthropology plays within mystical writing, McIntosh argues that it is possible to divide mystics into two categories depending on whether their understanding of mystical anthropology is predominantly one of sameness or one of difference. He argues, for example, that Bernard offers a positive mystical anthropology based on sameness, since it is through the soul's positive relationship to God, which gradually becomes more apparent, that the soul finds God. On the opposite side of the coin, as it were, McIntosh identifies mystics whose mystical anthropology is decidedly negative. Following Turner, he argues that writers like Eckhart and Porete develop an 'apophatic anthropology' in which the sense of their own self is totally negated when faced with the presence of God. In relation to God it is as though they were nothing.

> So one might begin to argue that the distinction of the creaturely self is not an ontological distinction at all, that at its ground (as Eckhart says) the soul's being and God's being are one being, or alternatively, that the being of the creature is literally no-thing, nothingness, in the sense that the divine existence is not an *item* of reality.[51]

In suggesting this division based on mystical anthropology McIntosh stresses that he is not advocating that we differentiate between affective mysticism and intellectual mysticism in the crude terms. Despite this, McIntosh's reading is clearly a simplification of Turner's approach which advocates a complex apophatic strategy in all mystical texts whether using anthropology or not. In this vein, it is important to note that McIntosh's position is also at odds with that of Bernard McGinn. Keen to stress the relatedness between God and mystics, McGinn cautions against dividing mystics into two types: that is, those who see human and divine relations as positively defined in terms of similarity, and those who see it negatively defined in terms of difference. He believes that these differences ultimately collapse, because love and intellect always create a tension within the mystic, even in those mystics who seem to reject intellect to some extent.[52] This end point is also where McIntosh wants to arrive. For McIntosh argues that the final result of both these two mystical anthropologies is the same. In both cases the difference between the self and God is ultimately collapsed, on the one hand for positive and on the other hand for negative reasons. Whether exhibiting a positive

---

[51]   Ibid., p. 223.

[52]   See B. McGinn, 'Mystical Consciousness: A Modest Proposal', *Spiritus: A Journal of Christian Spirituality*, 8/1 (2008), 44–63.

or negative anthropology, he holds that all mystics stress a relatedness between God and the soul that is therefore difficult for modern readers to grasp. Like Turner, McIntosh therefore cautions against overly psychological or subjective readings of selfhood and interiority such as those found in perennialist accounts. However, in simplifying Turner's model in this way, he, in fact, inadvertently mitigates against some of the complex interrelatedness that Turner highlights as part of his rebuttal of a perennialist position.

Conclusion

This chapter has discussed various contemporary readings of the ideas of selfhood and interiority that underpin Augustine's account of mysticism. Perennialist accounts treat Augustine's mystical selfhood as an account of mystical union. Contextualist approaches focus on the relationship between experience, Plotinian philosophy and Christianity, suggesting that a much more nuanced readings is needed. Denys Turner's performative language reading likewise focuses on a complex web of relationships between experience, philosophy and selfhood in Augustine's account of mysticism and later medieval understandings of selfhood. All suggest weaknesses in the perennialist reading.

In addition to these approaches there are also postmodern re-readings of Augustine; these are considered separately in Chapter 12. The next chapter of the book turns not to these but to another important motif in Christian mystical literature, its use of erotic language.

Chapter 4
Erotic Imagery

Two things are immediately noticeable when we look at many Christian mystical texts. Firstly they are filled with erotic imagery, and secondly they often refer to the biblical book, The Song of Songs, a deeply erotic text. In fact, many Song of Songs commentaries double up as accounts of mysticism. This chapter explores the connection between mysticism, erotic imagery and The Song of Songs.

The Use of Erotic Imagery

Erotic imagery takes different forms in different accounts of Christian mysticism. We will briefly consider seven mystics – Pseudo-Denys, Origen, Bernard of Claivaux, Hadewijch, Marguerite Porete, Gertrude of Helfta and Margery Kempe – who use erotic imagery in four slightly different, but overlapping, ways.

Erotic Imagery and the Creation

Erotic imagery is often used in Christian mystical text when referring to creation and its relationship to salvation. This use of erotic imagery has a strong connection to the Neoplatonic idea of emanation.

Pseudo-Denys   Erotic imagery first entered into Christian mysticism through the writings of Origen and Gregory of Nyssa. One particular use of it present in their thought is also developed the writings of Pseudo-Denys, whom we considered in Chapter 2. It is most apparent in his book *Divine Names*, in which erotic longing is a central motif. We already noted that Pseudo-Denys portrays the point at which the soul plunges into the darkness of unknowing as the fulfilment of all erotic longing. For him this is the soul's response to the act of creation. Consider, for example, the following passage from *Divine Names*:

> The divine yearning brings ecstasy so that the lover belongs not to self but to the beloved … it must be said too that the very cause of the universe in the beautiful, good superabundance of his benign yearning for all is also carried outside of himself in the loving care he has for everything. He is, as it were, beguiled by goodness, by love, and by yearning and is enticed away from his

transcendent dwelling place and comes to abide with all things, and he does so by his supernatural and ecstatic capacity to remain, nevertheless, within himself.[1]

At the centre of Pseudo-Denys's understanding of creation is the idea of fall and return, an idea which he derives from Neoplatonism. Pseudo-Denys describes creation as the boiling over of God. For him, love (*Eros*) leads God to move outside of God's self, without any lessening to God. As a result, all of creation longs erotically to return to God. *Eros* therefore becomes a unifying force within creation, with God moving out of himself in ecstasy, while everything yearns ecstatically to return to God. When Pseudo-Denys speaks of love, he therefore means such an erotic yearning.[2] As McGinn succinctly puts it, '[i]n the circle of love that forms the Dionysian universe we have a God who becomes ecstatic in procession and a universe whose ecstasy is realised in reversion'.[3] Many other mystics likewise use erotic imagery in this way. Meister Eckhart too likens creation to God's boiling over in erotic love, extending Pseudo-Denys's imagery.

Erotic Imagery and Union: Commentary on The Song of Songs

The importance of *eros* in Neoplatonic thought also influenced medieval attitudes to The Song of Songs. As we will further discuss in Chapter 6, in the medieval period this was the most exegeted book of the Bible. To modern readers this will seem strange, since The Song of Songs is an illicit love story with no mention of God. One reason for its popularity seems to have been the acceptance of Origen's understanding of this biblical text.

Origen   No discussion of erotic imagery within mystical texts would be complete without reference to Origen (185–254), from whom as we noted the use of erotic language in Christian mysticism chiefly originates. He produced two exegeses of The Song of Songs: a commentary and a collection of homilies. They were translated into Latin by Rufinus and Jerome respectively and passed in translation to medieval readers. In the prologue to his *Commentary on The Song of Songs*, intended for a more scholarly audience, Origen outlines his understanding of erotic imagery, and why The Song of Songs is, in fact, the most spiritually profound book of the Bible.

From this prologue it is clear that Origen understands *eros* as the key to participation in God. He models his understanding of Christian love for God on the Platonic idea of the love of beauty, arguing that human erotic desire is a poor shadow of true erotic desire for God. We noted in Chapter 1 that Plato asserts,

---

[1]   Pseudo-Denys, '*Divine Names*', in *Pseudo-Dionysius: The Complete Works*, pp. 47–132, at p. 82.

[2]   For a fuller discussion of eroticism in Pseudo-Denys, see Louth, *The Origins of the Christian Mystical Tradition*, p. 176.

[3]   McGinn, *The Foundations of Mysticism*, p. 168.

through Diotima's speech, that everything that we love contains the spark of the Form of Love. Origen held that this was especially true of the accounts of love found in The Song of Songs. In the same way that Socrates attempted to lead his audience from concrete manifestations of beauty, to its universal Form as illustrated in them, and finally to Beauty itself, Origen argues that God provides a book in the Bible, The Song of Songs, that can to lead its readers from a description of illicit sex to union with God.

More than other books of scripture, Origen therefore believed that The Song of Songs contained spiritual secrets of great mystical significance. He held that it was possible to find a deep 'mystical' message in this text.[4] However, he also held that it was possible to misunderstand it. Great danger awaited readers who were not spiritually advanced enough to realise that this was not just an illicit love story:

> But if anyone approaches who is a grown man according to the flesh, no little danger arises for such a person from this book of Scripture. For if he does not know how to listen to the name of love purely and with chaste ears, he may twist everything he has heard from the inner man to the outer and fleshly man …[5]

Origen therefore cautions that The Song of Songs should only be read by those who understand the need to pass beyond the sexual images it contains to the universal love of God, which the images are intended reveal.

Like other exegetes before him, Origen regarded The Song of Songs as an allegory detailing the love possible between God and his church. Origen's belief that the spiritually advanced could use the words of The Song of Songs to help their souls rise back up to God added a further individualised reading of the text that was universally accepted in the Middle Ages as an appropriate additional understanding of this work. In relation to his individualised reading of The Song of Songs Origen contributed several erotic images that were taken up by later mystics. He was the first to talk of the Word of God being born within the soul, an image that becomes important for Meister Eckhart. Henri Crouzel notes that Origen was also the first to conflate Isaiah 49:2 to Song of Songs 2:5 and describe God as wounding the soul with the arrow of his love, another important erotic image found within later accounts of mysticism.[6] Andrew Louth has shown that Origen's view of erotic imagery was instrumental in leading later mystics to associate erotic love with advanced spirituality and mysticism.[7] He is therefore

---

[4]   This very early use of the term 'mystical' is carefully discussed in Chapter 6.

[5]   Origen, 'Prologue to the Song of Songs', in *Origen: An Exhortation to Martydom, Prayer, First Principles: Book IV, Prologue to the Commentary on the Song of Songs, Homily XXVII on Numbers*, trans. R.A. Greer, Classics of Western Spirituality (New York: Paulist Press, 1979), pp. 217–44, at p. 218.

[6]   H. Crouzel, *Origen*, trans. A.S. Worrall (Edinburgh: T. & T. Clark, 1989), pp. 123–5.

[7]   Louth, *The Origins of The Christian Mystical Tradition*, and A. Louth, *Eros and Mysticism: Early Christian Interpretations of the Song of Songs*, Guild Lecture 241

also a key source for the union language and talk of 'marriage' to God that we find in many later mystics and which is an important way in which the erotic manifests itself in mystical texts.

Bernard of Clairvaux

If Origen is the undisputed founder of this exegetical tradition, most scholars agree that Bernard of Clairvaux is its champion. Born in 1090, Bernard was a Cistercian monk who, at age 26, was appointed Abbot of the Cistercian Abbey at Clairvaux. His accounts of mysticism stress the centrality of love as the force through which one arrives at perfection.[8] At the heart of Bernard's understanding of the spiritual journey is a movement of love in which one progresses from carnal attraction to pure spiritual erotic love for God. In his mystical discussions of The Song of Songs, Christ's Incarnation becomes the bridge between these realms of physical and spiritual erotic desire:

> I think this is the principal reason why the invisible God willed to be seen in the flesh and to converse with men as a man. He wanted to recapture the affections of carnal men who were unable to love in any other way, by first drawing them to the salutary love of his own humanity, and then gradually to raise them to a spiritual love.[9]

Christ acts as the focal point through which transcendence from one level to another occurs. This is apparent from a particularly famous discussion of love in his Song of Songs *Commentary* where he describes love's journey as three kisses.[10] The first, the kiss of Christ's feet, is a beginner's love, and signifies forgiveness from sins. The second, the kiss of Christ's hand, indicates spiritual progression through the receipt of God's grace. Finally, there is the kiss of Christ's mouth, a perfect love. Most of Bernard's writings focus on this relationship between physical and spiritual desire. In *On Loving God*, he describes this perfect love as a selfless love, a love of God for God's own sake. He also describes such love as a kind of deification of the soul.

In describing how the soul moves from carnal to pure spiritual love, Bernard sometimes talks of four types or levels of erotic desire but at other times only three. Yet, regardless of the particular permutation of love through which the soul moves or how he categorises it, the process is the same. The person begins with

---

(London: The Guild of Pastoral Psychology, 1992).

   [8] Bernard's ideas about mysticism come from the writings of Origen and Augustine. He does not seem to have read Pseudo-Denys. See Bell, *The Image and Likeness: the Augustinian Spirituality of William of Saint-Thierry*.

   [9] Bernard of Clairvaux, *On the Song of Songs I*, trans. K Walsh, Cistercian Fathers Series 4 (Shannon: Cistercian Publications, 1971), Sermon 20, p. 152.

   [10] Ibid., Sermon 3, pp. 3–4.

carnal desire and moves towards a spiritual form of erotic desire. As Denys Turner points out, Bernard moves between different levels of love with great fluidity. For Turner, this indicates that Bernard is in love with God at every level, not only spiritually, but also in a physical sense, making Bernard's mysticism deeply erotic.[11] J.R. Sommerfeldt sees this as a deliberate strategy intended to exemplify the unending nature of mystical love. He believes that Bernard is fascinated by the eroticism of this text because it provides him with an endless repository of metaphors for the incomprehensibility of spiritual love; something accentuated and highlighted by his refusal to systematise the different levels of love.[12] Although undertaking exegesis, Bernard's approach to The Song of Songs is therefore more literary than Origen's.

Erotic Love as Courtly Love

The literary quality of Bernard's erotic exegesis is extended by writers who mix imagery from The Song of Songs with courtly love literature – a treatment of love within secular literature that focuses both on the illicit nature of erotic love and its morally elevating characteristics.[13] Many of those who used erotic imagery in this way were women.

Hadewijch and Marguerite Porete   Such an intermingling of biblical exegetical motifs and secular love poetry is apparent in the writings of two fourteenth-century itinerant beguines (lay religious women), Hadewijch and Marguerite Porete, both of whom are considered mystics. Erotic imagery lies at the heart of their accounts of mysticism. Consider, for example, the following excerpt from one of Hadewijch's letters:

> O beloved, why has not Love sufficiently overwhelmed you and engulfed you in her abyss. Alas! When Love is so sweet, why do you not fall deep into her? And why do you not touch God deeply in the abyss of his Nature, which is so unfathomable? Sweet love, give yourself for Love's sake fully to God in love.[14]

---

[11]   Turner, *Eros and Allegory*, pp. 165–8.

[12]   J.R. Sommerfeldt, *The Spiritual Teachings of Bernard of Clairvaux: An Intellectual History of the Early Cistercian Order*, Cistercian Fathers Series 125 (Kalamazoo: Cistercian Publications, 1991), p. 98.

[13]   See S. Kay, 'Courts, Clerks and Courtly Love', in R.L. Krueger (ed.), *The Cambridge Companion to Medieval Romance* (Cambridge: Cambridge University Press, 2000), pp. 81–96.

[14]   Hadewijch, Letter 5.28, in *Hadewijch: The Complete Works*, trans. Mother Columbia Hart OSB, Classics of Western Spirituality (New York: Paulist Press, 1989), p. 56.

Here Hadewijch plays with the idea of commitment to God the allusive lover, who at the same time has the capacity to overwhelm the soul with a love that she cannot comprehend.

Marguerite Porete combines courtly love motifs with the linguistic devices associated with negative theology. She offers a particularly sophisticated account of the apophatic qualities of such erotic desire, as, for example, in the following passage about Mary Magdalene:

> But when she [Mary Magdalene] was in the desert, Love overtook her, which annihilated her, and thus because of this Love worked in her for her sake, and so she lived by divine life which made her have glorious life. Thus she found God in herself, without seeking Him, and she had no why since Love had overtaken her.[15]

Here erotic love overpowers Mary Magdalene and takes away her self, which then allows her to find God.[16]

Erotic Love for the Incarnate Christ

E. Ann Matter notes that by the later Middle Ages the imagery of The Song of Songs had become such a familiar means of discussing spiritual love that it was increasingly found in all manner of spiritual treatises.[17] This period also saw a rise in devotion to the human figure of Christ. Later mystical literature, especially that produced by women, combined all the erotic motifs discussed above with an erotic devotion that focuses almost exclusively on the Incarnate Christ.

Gertrude of Helfta and Margery Kempe   In her *Herald of Divine Love*, Gertrude of Helfa (1256–*c*.1302) listens to the comforting words of a youthful Christ, and feels his tender touch. In her mind's eye, Christ lifts Gertrude over a hedge (representing her sins that separate her from Christ), so that she is able to stand next to him and see his wounded hands. As we will further discuss in chapter 7, she records the following:

> I heard these words: 'I will save you. I will deliver you. Do not fear.' With this, I saw his hand, tender and fine, holding mine ... and he added 'With my enemies you have licked the dust (cf. Ps 71.9) and sucked honey among thorns. Come

---

15   Marguerite Porete, *The Mirror of Simple Souls*, ed. and trans. E.L. Babinsky (New York: Paulist Press, 1993), p. 168. For a discussion of the idea of 'without a why', see Chapter 10.

16   We further discuss Marguerite's account of mysticism in Chapter 10.

17   See E.A. Matter, *The Voice of My Beloved: The Song of Songs in Western Medieval Christianity* (Philadelphia: University of Pennsylvia Press, 1990). Also see A.W. Astell, *The Song of Songs in the Middle Ages* (Ithaca, NY: Cornell University Press, 1990).

back to me now, and I will inebriate you with the torrent of my divine pleasure.'
(Ps. 35.9).[18]

The passage is clearly erotic and displays a love for a sixteen-year-old Christ that incorporates the physical into the idea of spiritual love.

This physical dimension of spiritual love is even more apparent in *The Book* of Margery Kempe. Margery produced her *Book* in the latter half of the fourteenth-century, and is counted as one of the English Mystics. Her mystical writing is deeply erotic, with the eroticism operating on a conspicuously physical level. When she thinks of Christ, she thinks of him incarnate, as is apparent from the passage quoted in the opening pages of the introductory chapter:

> Therefore must I needs be homely with you and lie in your bed with you. Daughter, you desire greatly to see me, and you may boldly, when you are in your bed, take me to you as your wedded husband, as your most worthy darling, and as your sweet son, for I will be loved as a son should be loved by the mother and will that you love me, daughter, as a good wife ought to love her husband. And therefore you may boldly take me in the arms of your soul and kiss my mouth, my head, and my feet as sweetly as you will.[19]

She goes on to write that when she touches Christ's toes, they feel to her just like physical ones. She states that she knows that such visions are not as elevated as visions of the Trinity:

> And then she thanked God for all, for through these ghostly sights her affection was all drawn into the manhood of Christ and into the mind of his passion until that time when it pleased our Lord to give her understanding of his inunderstandable Godhead.[20]

Yet, even when she claims to have a vision of the Trinity, God as appears to her as three cushions. Embodiment therefore permeates her thought at every level.

The extent to which such imaginative carnal devotion counts as mysticism is an issue that we will further reflect on in Chapters 7 and 9. For the purposes of this chapter it is important that we can clearly see that Christian mystical writing is infused with erotic imagery on a number of levels. It is a facet of mystical discourse, which demands some explanation.

---

[18] Gertude of Helfta, *The Herald of Divine Love*, ed. and trans. M. Winkworth (New York: Paulist Press, 1993), p. 95.

[19] *The Book of Margery Kempe: A New Translation, Contexts, Criticism*, ed. and trans. L. Staley (New York: W.W. Norton and Co., 2001), p. 66.

[20] Ibid., p. 152.

CONTEMPORARY THEORETICAL APPROACHES

As in previous chapters, we will begin by considering the perennialist approach, and the limitations of it, before turning to contextualist and performative language readings. We will note how scholars like McGinn offer a reading which blurs the boundaries of these categories, and finally consider feminist responses to the erotic dimension of mystical texts.

Perennialist Approaches

Perennialist approaches to mysticism focus on the use of union imagery in mystical texts in terms of mystical union. As we would expect, they argue that this language is employed in order to explicate a mystical experience of union that defies expression.

William James, William. T. Stace and Robert C. Zaehner

We have already noted that William James holds that mystical experiences are often accompanied by a sense that there is an ultimate oneness in all things; a feeling that seems to remain with the mystic even after the mystical state of consciousness has passed away.[21] Many later perennialist scholars, for example, F.C. Happold, argued that a feeling of oneness is more definitive of a mystical experience than either ineffability or noesis. For Cuthbert Butler, union is *the* defining feature of a mystical experience; which is why he was so keen to associate Augustine's account with this idea, despite the fact that Augustine does not use this terminology. Evelyn Underhill also suggests that mysticism is primarily an experience of union. For her, use of erotic imagery to describe this phenomenon results from its applicability, since, according to Underhill, a mystical experience is 'the perfect consummation of the love of God'. Another prominent perennialist, William T. Stace, likewise argues that an experience of union is the very essence of the mystical experience. Stace presents a complex account of mysticism, dividing mysticism into two closely related types – 'extrovertive' and 'introvertive' – which he says are related to one another like 'two species of one genus'.[22] He lists seven characteristics for each type of mysticism. However, he suggests that union, alongside subjectivity, is its most significant characteristic.

> In this general experience of a unity which the mystic believes to be in some sense ultimate and basic to the world, we have the very inner essence of all mystical experience.[23]

---

21   James, *The Varieties of Religious Experience*, p. 410.
22   W.T. Stace, *Mysticism and Philosophy*, (Los Angeles: J.P. Tarcher, 1987), p. 131.
23   Ibid., p. 132.

Robert Charles Zaehner also places great emphasis on unitive experience. However, he argues that an experience of union is not the ultimate kind of mystical experience in all traditions and religions. Zaehner holds that context cannot in fact be ignored when trying determining why union (and by inference the erotic imagery connected to it) finds its way into the heart of many Christian mystical texts. In suggesting this Zaehner moves close to the contextualist approaches discussed below. One of the problems with the perennialist approach is, as Zaehner points out, that it not only runs into difficulties trying to prove that union holds the same central place in all mystical traditions, but also has difficulty accounting for the multi-faceted nature of Christian mysticism if only one trait, 'experience', is considered its essence.

Contextualist Approaches

Steven Katz is unhappy with the idea that all imagery, including the erotic imagery, that we find in mystical texts is purely descriptive. He argues that the imagery in mystical texts serves a broader purpose than this, although he is somewhat reticent to assign erotic imagery a positive function within Christian mystical writing.

Steven T. Katz

As we have discussed in previous chapters, Steven Katz rejects the idea that mystics have ineffable experiences that they then attempt to define using ordinary language. He asserts that, if we pay careful attention to the literary devices and images that we find used in mystical texts, we see that they are dependent on the sacred texts of the tradition to which the mystic belongs. In Christianity the Bible is considered a form of revelation. Katz points out that Biblical exegesis is not an intellectual exercise, it is meant to reveal God's voice; mystical writings are one attempt to unpack its secrets.

Katz argues that mystics always do this in ways appropriate to the age in which they lived, which for him explains the use of allegorical readings of the Bible in many mystical texts and the importance of Platonic works, which he argues were also often treated as sacred texts. For Katz, mystical texts reveal a process of affirming and negating sacred texts in order to preserve the tradition, thereby making mystics valued members of the religious community.

> Indeed, insofar as … religious communities … are defined by the texts they hold sacred, this process of textual affirmation and negation is one of the essential activities of any such community.[24]

---

[24]   S. Katz, 'Mysticism and the Interpretation of Sacred Scripture', in S. Katz (ed.), *Mysticism and Sacred Scripture* (New York: Oxford University Press, 2000), pp. 7–67, at p. 19.

Overlooking the role which *Eros* plays within Platonic works, Katz explains the prevalence of erotic imagery in mystical texts in relation to what he sees as this revelatory function of mystical writing.

Contra Origen, who argues that The Song of Songs contains a particularly powerful spiritual account of love that mystics attempt to discover, Katz asserts that when we look at how mystics dealt with The Song of Songs we see that the Christian religious tradition to which they belonged saw the eroticism of this text as dangerous. He argues that this is apparent from the way in which mystical texts attempt to nullify the eroticism of The Song of Songs. Katz understands Bernard's discussion of the three kisses in this way. Despite appearances, Katz argues that there is no physical dimension to Bernard's love for God. Rather, he claims that in Bernard's thought 'physical sexuality of the Song is transformed into the spiritual intimacy of Christ and human beings.'[25] He sees in it no 'worldly eroticism'. For him, male and female bodies are replaced by metaphors, and physical intercourse with the flow of God into humanity. Katz is critical of this process of sanitisation which he believes leaves only an 'apotheosis of sanctity, purity and spirituality'. As he writes:

> Repeatedly, like Origen and Augustine before them, medieval mystics expressed their more cherished Christian beliefs through a particular Christian allegorical explication of scripture. Consider as exemplary the esoteric treatment – that is, the transvaluation – of the enormously threatening subject of sexuality as this is represented in the 'pious' renderings given to the Song of Songs.[26]

For Katz, the result of such mystical discourse is a sinless spiritual embrace, which succeeds in domesticating the eroticism of The Song of Songs for the Christian community. It is the concerted attempt of Christian mystics to nullify the sexual potency of this biblical book that Katz believes made The Song of Songs 'the preferred book of the mystical soul'. It is not as Origen claims that this text has inherent spiritual value.[27]

Understanding the eroticism that we find in discussion of The Song of Songs in this way, leads Katz to conclude that it has nothing to do with a personal ecstatic experience. For him, Song of Songs commentary and the use of its imagery are merely the result of a literary-philosophical convention.

> What one has in all of these lofty decipherments of the love poetry of the Song is not a personal description of ecstatic experience – whatever the personal experience of that mystical author may be – but, rather, the repeated application

---

[25] Ibid., p. 26.

[26] Ibid., p. 26.

[27] Ibid., p. 27.

of a literary-philosophical convention, according to which such renderings of
the Song have essentially become standardised.[28]

The erotic imagery that we find within mystical texts is not therefore, according
to Katz, an attempt to describe an a-cultural experience that is unitive in nature.
It belongs to the conscious efforts of mystics to understand, elucidate, and where
necessary tame, the revelatory texts of the religion to which they belong.

It is interesting that Katz should take such a negative view of the way in which
erotic language is used in Christian mystical literature. Firstly his disregard of any
relationship between experience and this language seems odd, given his belief that
language generally performs a number of transformative functions. What is more,
although his contextualising in terms of its Platonic heritage is helpful, his negative
attitude towards the spiritual use of this language seems rather anachronistic.
Why should a medieval writer's use of erotic language, that mirrors that found in
Platonic sources, not be seen as legitimate? It is not apparent why he does not draw
parallels between the role ascribed to *Eros* in Platonic dialogues and Origen's use
of it. It is also not clear what justification Katz has for imposing a rather Freudian
reading onto these texts. All these seem to be significant problems with Katz's
position. Performative language readings take a much more nuanced approach to
the existence of the erotic in mystical texts.

Performative Language Readings

Performative language readings treat the play of absence and presence, especially
the interaction between similarity and difference, as an apophatic realisation of the
unknowability of God. They consider the interplay of opposites that this brings
about to be a reflection of the game of love that The Song of Songs engenders,

Denys Turner

Turner sees the use of erotic language as the perfect expression of the interplay
between positive and negative language that is found is in mystical texts. As we
discussed in Chapter 2, Turner believes that in mystical texts positive and negative
statements are meant to be read together. Negative statements should not be taken
as a negative ascription of God's nature, any more than positive terms should be
thought able to encapsulate the divine. Rather he sees the interaction between
them as negative, that is apophatic, discourse – a process that he calls 'the negation
of the negation'. It is a process he sees mirrored by the language of *Eros*.

On the one hand, Turner notes that the language of union intimates similarity.
Yet on the other, union is still a joining of two distinct parties, who, according
to the medieval conception of marriage, were far from equal. This inequality is

---

[28]   Ibid., p. 27.

even more apparent where the union concerns human beings and God. According to Turner, discussion of erotic union in mystical texts is a means by which the absolute difference between God and humans can be realised. Drawing an analogy from Emily Brontë's *Wuthering Heights*, Turner claims that Cathy's exclamation that she is Heathcliff signals more than a simple assimilation of herself into him. It is rather that there is just no language to describe the difference that exists between them. Thus in the same way that cataphatic and apophatic discourse lead to a true apophasis, as Turner defines this idea, so too erotic imagery leads to the point at which language collapses under the weight of dialectic tension. When this happens, mystics speak of union.

> God is not, therefore, opposed to creatures, cannot displace them, which is why, for pseudo-Denys, the language of the oneness of the soul with God in erotic ecstasy is not, and cannot be, the language of the displacement of the created identity of the mind; nor is Catherine of Genoa's 'the soul becomes God' any more the denial of the soul's identity than is Catherine Earnshaw's 'I am Heathcliff' the denial of her own selfhood. On the contrary, it is for either Catherine the assertion of her identity. These are the paradoxes of *eros*. They are none other than the dionysian paradoxes of God-talk.[29]

Turner believes that the popularity of eroticism within Christian mysticism owes much to Pseudo-Denys, who, as he sees it, creates an erotic metaphysics that is deeply apophatic. Turner argues that eroticism for Pseudo-Denys works in the same way that similar and dissimilar similitudes do. There are things that are like God in some way and things that, clearly, are not like God. An understanding of creation out of erotic love, like that which Pseudo-Denys posits by his idea of boiling over, both indicates human participation in and likeness to God and human difference from God. The otherness of God is revealed in the vast difference between human sexual desire and the pure *Eros* of God, which is at the same time the source of the relationship. As Turner states:

> Human sexuality, which, as the pseudo-Denys says, is a 'partial, physical and divided yearning ... is not true yearning but *an empty image* or, rather, a lapse from real yearning' (DN 709 B-C). It is a vastly 'dissimilar similitude', distanced ontologically from the reality it reflects and to that degree reflecting the divine *eros* in its empty character.[30]

For all these reasons, Turner disagrees with Anders Nygren that the introduction of Platonic and Neoplatonic ideas into Christian discourses on love is a perversion of

---

[29]   Turner, *Eros and Allegory*, p. 64.

[30]   Ibid., p. 143.

true Christian love. Nygren argues that *Eros* is not equivalent to *Agape*.[31] Turner disagrees. He considers it a perfectly appropriate and Christian means of describing interaction between God and human beings. For Turner, erotic language is yet another means of teaching the reader the need to hold similarity and difference in tension. Like apophatic and kataphatic discourse, it too is a means of pushing language (and image) to its limits, so that eventually the reader is brought to the point of silence in terms of union. Erotic language therefore epitomises the underlying purpose of negative language (often known as the *via negativa* or the negative way), as Turner understands this:

> To dissolve the paradoxes ... would entail the possibility of pushing to the limit the language of union with God only at the price of evacuating wholly the language of personal identity, or vice-versa ... to dissolve their [the mystics] thought ... we begin to glimpse what union with God can mean, and equally what true human identity can be, only when the language of both are pushed to the limit and are there *held together* ... There, at the limit of language, we must fall into the silence of the *via negativa*.[32]

Turner argues that the popularity of The Song of Songs is explained when we realise that it is a text that facilitates participation in this apophatic discourse. He suggests that when viewed in this light, 'distanced from the carnal meaning of the Song, its [The Song of Songs'] eroticism could become not only a safe, but even an apt, vehicle for the personal expression of his [the exegete's] love for God'.[33] In suggesting this, Turner admits that there is a sense in which most exegetes, with the possible exception of Bernard of Clairvaux, were somewhat afraid of the carnality of this text, such that they tended to spiritualise it.

> Origen, Gregory, and Denys [the Carthusian], it therefore seems right to say, fear a literalist hermeneutic *because* they fear [that] the text itself ... was a potential temptation to the 'lewdness' which it describes.[34]

However, although agreeing with Katz in this respect, he does not believe that a desire to nullify this text can possibly account for the proliferation of commentaries on it, nor the way in which its language comes to infuse the mystical literature of the later Middle Ages; only the way it engenders apophasis can account for this.

One possible weakness in Turner's argument is its dependence on Pseudo-Denys. As we noted earlier, use of erotic language in Christian mystical texts in the main originates from Origen's writings, being found most markedly in The Song

---

[31]   A. Nygren, *Agape and Eros*, trans. P.S. Watson, revised edn (London: Westminster Press, 1953).

[32]   Turner, *Eros and Allegory*, p. 61.

[33]   Ibid., p. 163.

[34]   Ibid., p. 161.

of Songs' commentarial tradition. To argue that the apophatic strategy adopted by Pseudo-Denys accounts for its popularity appears somewhat dismissive of the role that Origen's Platonic idealisation of the erotic played.

Graham Ward

A similar response to Turner's concerning the proliferation of erotic desire in Christian mysticism is found in Graham Ward's discussions on the idea of touch. Drawing on the French phenomenologist Maurice Merleau-Ponty, Ward offers a reconsideration of what is happening between Cathy and Heathcliff in *Wuthering Heights*. Yet, rather than reading Cathy's statement as her inability linguistically to differentiate herself from Healthcliff, Ward argues that Cathy is expressing the suffering she experiences because she is *not* Heathcliff. Her love and longing causes her to feel torn apart and this fuels her endless desire for him.

> In Emily Brontë's *Wuthering Heights*, at the climax of an argument between Catherine Earnshaw and Nelly Dean concerning Cathy's obsession with Heathcliff, Cathy shouts out, 'I *am* Heathcliff!' (Brontë 1965: 122.) But she is not and that is both her triumph, as a character who especially takes her place at Heathcliff's side, and her tragedy. Intimacy causes tearing apart, to expose the suffering of longing. Distance, difference are figurations of longing (long-ing) – without them there would be stasis.[35]

For Ward, a sense of distance is a necessary feature of contemplation, since it intimates that there is always something else, something that is longed for but not attained. He describes this using Jean-Luc Marion's notion of 'excess'. (Marion's more postmodern approach to Christian mysticism and what he means by 'excess' is discussed in Chapters 11 and 12.) As such, Ward views erotic language in terms of the game of love of which many mystics speak. However, unlike Turner, Ward does not see union as the end of the game, more as its endless starting point, and in this respect his account is closer to the performative language reading of Michael Sells.

Michael Sells

Building on his understanding of the naming and unnaming of God as a deliberate epistemological strategy of 'referential regress', Sells draws attention to what he sees as 'the apophasis of desire' in the writings of the female mystic Marguerite

---

35   G. Ward, 'The *Logos*, the Body and the World: On the Phenomenological Border', in K. Vanhoozer and M. Warner (eds), *Transcending Boundaries in Philosophy and Theology: Reason, Meaning and Experience* (Aldershot: Ashgate, 2007), pp. 105–26, at p. 122.

Porete.[36] He argues that in her book, *The Mirror of Simple Souls*, Porete creates an intense apophatic discourse when she brings together paradoxical linguistic devices, talk of rapture, and courtly love imagery.

> *The Mirror* brings together the apophatic paradoxes of mystical union, the language of courtly love – as it had been transformed in the beguine mystics of the thirteenth century into a mystical language of rapture – and a daring reappropriation of medieval religious themes. The result is an apophasis of desire.[37]

According to Sells, the resulting 'apophasis of desire' totally reconfigures selfless love. Although in the twelfth century Bernard of Clairvaux argued that mystical love was totally selfless – a love in which one loved God for God's own sake – Sells believes that in the fourteenth-century Porete takes this to a new level when she describes the total annihilation of the will. By this she means that the soul has no desires of its own, such that it does not even will what is good. There is nothing that the soul can *do* to bring about its own annihilation. We are all to some extent familiar with the idea of erotic love in an ordinary sense. Sells argues that this makes it difficult for us to grasp the radical force of the apophasis that Porete is suggesting.

> Many of Porete's themes may be difficult to capture in their full force, not because they seem alien, but because they seem familiar … The apophatic placement of the extraordinary within the ordinary recurs with Porete as a confluence of mystical apophasis with the most common vocabulary of erotic love.[38]

The form in which erotic language appears in Porete's *Mirror* is, Sells argues, a 'mystical language of unsaying'.

Sells notes too the images of flowing out and flowing over that appear in relation to the subject of creation.[39]

> When the transcendent realises itself as the immanent, the subject of the act is neither divine nor human, neither self nor other. Conventional logical and semantic structures – the distinction between reflexive and nonreflexive action, the distinction between perfect and imperfect tense, the univocal antecedent of a pronoun – are broken down.[40]

---

[36] See Chapter 10 for a more detailed discussion of Marguerite Porete's approach to mysticism.

[37] Sells, *Mystical Languages of Unsaying*, p. 118.

[38] Ibid., p. 118.

[39] Ibid., p. 6.

[40] Ibid., p. 7.

He argues that by bringing transcendence and immanence together in this way Porete causes the boundaries between these opposites to break down. This, for Sells, is mystical union. Mystical union is effected by the displacement of the grammatical object by means of a 'language of unsaying'. By this he means the perception that there is no real *object* of experience, just a sense that things become as they were before there was anything else. This move beyond subject-object differentiation is for Sells a 'meaning event'. It is a moment when meaning and event are fused together; a moment of realisation when understanding and event become one:

> The meaning event is the semantic analogue to the experience of mystical union. It does not describe or refer to mystical union but effects a semantic union that re-creates or imitates the mystical union.[41]

On the basis of this Sells argues that mystical texts do not describe mystical union, they offer a semantic re-creation of it.

Mark A. McIntosh

In a similar vein, Mark A. McIntosh also argues that the impetus behind Christian mystical writing is not experiential. He stresses, along with Andrew Louth, that Christian mysticism should be viewed as a normal and essential aspect of theology, which as such has both intellectual and spiritual/experiential dimensions. Approaching mysticism from the context of spirituality in general, he argues that mysticism is less individualised and more communal than modern readers realise.[42]

McIntosh argues that we must resist the temptation to reduce apophatic language to something comprehensible. For him mystical texts have a far greater 'theological significance and validity' than this. He suggests that erotic language (like negative language) acts as a discourse that seeks to draw the reader into God's incomprehensibility, thereby facilitating the reader's own mystical encounter. This is far more complex than mere experience. The play of love that he finds within the texts is, he argues, one that seeks to draw the reader into the loving relationality of the Trinity. Focusing specifically on Hadewijch he argues that she invites her

---

[41]   Ibid., p. 9.

[42]   'None of this means that the experience of an individual person was unimportant in this early conception of spirituality. What it means rather is that personal experience is not in itself the goal of spirituality. Individuals are not so much seeking to discover their own feelings as to live into the knowledge and love of God through the hard work of being members one with another of the Body of Christ. Spirituality in this early Christian sense is inherently mutual, communal, practical and oriented towards the God who makes self known precisely in this new pattern of life called church' (McIntosh, *Mystical Theology*, p. 7).

readers into a far deeper and more endless yearning than anything that can be summed up in terms of experience.

> Take for example the ecstatic erotic language of some of the Beguine writers; whatever may have been Hadewijch's experiences, her poetry has consumed those experiences and drawn them into a new polyvalent textuality – and *that* is what she now offers to her fellow Beguines. It is an abyss of meaningfulness in which one cannot simply stop to admire a given feeling or experience as a reified object, but is rather plunged into a new world of yearning which has no name.[43]

As such, he sees mystical writing as performative rather than descriptive or even strictly didactic.

As we noted in the previous chapter, McIntosh also stresses the importance of spiritual anthropology. He argues that, at its heart, spiritual anthropology depends on relationality. He notes that Turner, like Louth, draws attention to the relational dimension of the image of God in Augustine's accounts of mysticism. Yet McIntosh argues that even those writers like Porete and Eckhart, who appear to talk of the soul's annihilation, do not hold the self and God to be ontologically distinct. As such, he suggests that a relationship of unity occurs which mimics that found within the Trinity itself. He suggests that when read in this way Turner presents a more positive spiritual anthropology than at first appears, because Turner too thinks of mysticism in terms of such relationality. This extension of Turner's approach resonates with the understanding of erotic language offered by Bernard McGinn.

Bernard McGinn

Following Bernard Lonergan, McGinn argues that mystical texts are expressions of a form of consciousness that encompasses all aspects of human loving and knowing in a way that exceeds ordinary consciousness. McGinn is, however, also convinced that context informs the experiences that mystics encounter. In this relation, McGinn is deeply concerned with the content of mystical texts. Like Katz, he asserts that it is unsurprising that love plays such a prominent role within mystical texts given its prevalence in Christian scripture. He argues that 'most mystics have accorded some priority to love' simply because the New Testament maintains that God is love.[44] Yet McGinn also suggests that mystical discussions do more than unpack this language. He argues that mystics use love discourse to express their endless yearning for a God who is unknowable, such that their discussions of love are at the same time an expression of this unknowability of God.

---

43   Ibid., p. 125.
44   McGinn, 'Mystical Consciousness: A Modest Proposal', p. 51.

They also argue that the divine infinity is radically unknowable to the limited human mind, but that love involves endless yearning for the enjoyment of the beloved that can never reach fulfillment and therefore shares in infinity.[45]

In this relation he draws careful attention to Origen's development of spiritual sensations, sensations within the soul, which McGinn sees as yet another tool to describe mystical encounters with God.[46] He understands the spiritualising of erotic language within mystical texts as an expression of a deep desire to find God, rather than, as Katz suggests, as an attempt to constrain human sexuality.

McGinn's concern with love and its erotic nature is also connected to the interplay between love and knowledge that we find within mystical texts. McGinn is keen to stress that the love that mystics write about pushes them beyond the bounds of the physical to a spiritual level of consciousness. It is a kind of love that both responds to God and is a gift from God, making this love different from the love which we direct towards ordinary day-to-day objects. In focusing on this aspect of love, McGinn draws attention to an idea found within Gregory of Nyssa, and developed by mystics such as William of St Thierry, Richard of St Victor and Nicholas of Cusa, that true spiritual love is a kind of knowledge (an idea that we briefly discussed in Chapter 3).[47] McGinn holds that mystical discussions of erotic love are related to such knowledge. He argues that a constant dialectic in all mystical writing fluctuates between the unknowability of God on the one hand and the lovability of God on the other. He argues that love, and especially the emphasis on it in certain mystics, indicates that mystics as a whole believed in a deep connectivity between themselves and God, but that such love at the same time draws attention to the mystics' ongoing lack of God:

> The mystic therefore both *loves*, consciously and unrestrictedly, on the basis of the gift of God's direct presence in the ground of awareness, and consciously and unrestrictedly *knows and affirms* the horizon of divine unknowability through the practice of *docta ignorantia*.[48]

By *docta ignorantia* (learned ignorance) McGinn means a special kind of ignorance – the mystic knows there is something to be desired but not what it is and this ignorant knowledge keeps the mystic 'hunting' for God; yearning for and desiring that which they long to know, but are unable to fully grasp. This process, for McGinn, accounts for the erotic nature of mystical texts.

---

45   Ibid., p. 51.

46   B. McGinn, 'The Language of Inner Experience in Christian Mysticism' *Spiritus: A Journal of Christian Spirituality*, 1/2 (2001), 156–71. We discuss spiritual sensations in Chapter 6.

47   For a discussion of William of St Thierry, see Bell, *The Image and Likeness: The Augustinian Spirituality of William of Saint-Thierry*.

48   McGinn, 'Mystical Consciousness: A Modest Proposal', p. 53.

In a sense therefore McGinn comes close to a performative language reading, yet like McIntosh his approach allows him to make greater room for experience than even Sells. In a manner similar to Ward he notes the interplay of absence and presence in erotic language that engenders a longing for that which one already has. However, his discussion of erotic language lacks the detail of either Sells or Turner, particularly their emphasis on what it means for language to result in an encounter with the divine, most clearly envisaged in Sells's notion of a 'meaning event'.

Feminist Readings

There is yet another way of understanding the role of the erotic in mystical texts which further nuances the above readings. This is found in feminist approaches which have also considered the use of erotic imagery in mystical texts, especially those composed by women. Such readings emphasise the role of the body, particularly the female body, in relation to mystical erotic discourse, stressing that the bodily aspect of eroticism cannot be overlooked, even where it is spiritualised.

Simone de Beauvoir

One of the first writers to consider the eroticism of mysticism in this way was Simone de Beauvoir who, in her famous work *The Second Sex*, claims that love is the same whether manifest in romance or in mysticism, for in both a woman's love is directed towards a male human or deity. As such, she argues that women are denied transcendence because men treat women as their 'other'; as a result of which women are always tied to the immanent. Yet, as Amy Hollywood points out, Beauvoir does not want to suggest that the eroticism of women's mystical writings is little more than hysteria. Against some of her earlier thinking, Beauvoir argues that mystical states are more than pathological. In fact, she seems to have had some sympathy with the idea that women use their bodies, and especially erotic mysticism, to attain transcendence in a different but equivalent way to their male counterparts. As Hollywood writes, 'Beauvoir seems to hold open the possibility, against her own earlier claims, that erotic mysticism can be the site through which the body transcends itself and women transcend their sex.'[49] Beauvoir maintains that women, like men, desire to be everything, but in a male-dominated society they have few avenues open to them through which to explore this desire. One means however, does exist – love – which further explains its prevalence in women's spiritual discourse (even if this does not account for the very similar role that it appears to play in some male mystical texts).

---

[49] A. Hollywood, *Sensible Ecstasy: Mysticism, Sexual Difference and the Demands of History* (Chicago: University of Chicago Press, 2002), p. 128.

Caroline Walker Bynum

Feminist readings of the erotic in mysticism are, however, greatly extended by
Caroline Walker Bynum. The idea that women are able to arrive at transcendence
through their bodies, rather than by rejecting them, is central to Caroline Walker
Bynum's re-evaluation of medieval women's spiritual writing, including that
which is classified as mysticism. Bynum argues that from the twelfth century
onwards we see a distinctive form of mysticism emerging which is defined by food
and feeding imagery, suffering and fertility. She too argues that women associated
the male with the deity and the transcendent, and the female with the bodily and
the immanent. However, in the Incarnation, the 'Word made flesh', she argues that
women found God with whom they could identify and through whom they could
transcendent their sexuality. She states:

> Women stressed their humanity and Jesus' because tradition had accustomed
> them to associated humanity with the female. But humanity is not, in the final
> analysis, a gender-related image. Humanity is genderless. To medieval women
> humanity was, most basically, not femaleness, but physicality, the flesh of the
> 'Word made flesh'. It was the ultimate negative – the otherness from God that
> the God-man redeemed by taking it into himself.[50]

For Bynum therefore women were able to cultivate a more fluid movement
between the physical and spiritual than their male mystical counterparts, who
tended, in the main, to separate spiritual and physical love. Bynum argues that
some male writers, like Bernard of Clairvaux, can be said to have taken a more
female approach to the mystical, however, women take the association between
their bodies and spirituality far further than Bernard does.[51] Bynum's general
approach has proved extremely pervasive in recent years.

Amy Hollywood

Amy Hollywood has some sympathy with Beauvoir's and Bynum's accounts, in
that she too thinks that women do use their bodies to attain transcendence. She
also notes the misogynistic dangers inherent in treating women's more embodied
spirituality as merely pathological and hysterical. She is, however, critical of
what she sees as an oversimplification of women's spirituality, which forces all
women's mystical writing and eroticism into this immanence vs. transcendence
model. Hollywood argues that some female mystics in fact use eroticism to do the
reverse, to break down the stereotypes of women as purely embodied. She draws
particular attention to the writings of Marguerite Porete and Hadewijch (whom
we consider in Chapter 10). She argues that both struggle against the patriarchal

---

[50]   Bynum, *Fragmentation and Redemption*, p. 179.
[51]   Ibid., pp. 72 and 145.

models of spirituality into which they are supposed to fit. In this relation she warns against a too hasty glorification of the embodied element within female accounts of mysticism. She notes that women's writing and all it contains cannot be disconnected from issues of authority and power – in relation to which she draws attention to the constant struggles of many female mystics to retain control over the interpretation and recording of their experiences:

> the meaning of woman mystic's experience – in particular her bodily experience – has always been the site of competing interpretations and claims to authority. Angela [of Foligna], like many other medieval and early modern women, actively struggled to maintain interpretative control over her experience against the continual encroachment of male clerical elites.[52]

Hollywood warns that women may have felt compelled to describe their spirituality in embodied terms, whether or not this was the case. She argues that the dangers of not doing so are all too apparent in the case of Porete, who was burnt at the stake for failing to suppress her *Mirror*, which contains a spirituality that is, to Hollywood's mind, anything but embodied. For Hollywood, accounts of erotic desire within women's mystical texts should therefore be approached from a variety of perspectives, not simply read in terms of embodiment.

The feminist perspective adds another important facet to our understanding of the erotic in Christian mysticism. It draws attention to issues of gender and power that cannot be overlooked and are more carefully considered in Part II.

Conclusion

In this chapter we have considered various explanations for the use of erotic imagery in Christian mystical texts. Perennialists argue that it indicates the unitive nature of mystical experiences. However, it is clear that there are problems with the descriptive readings of the erotic that this engenders. Against this Steven Katz suggests that its prevalence results from its prior existence in Christian sacred literature. Katz argues that mystical texts attempt to sanitise the dangers inherent in eroticism, and so preserve the tradition. Performative language readings instead argue that erotic language in mystical texts is an apophatic strategy that stresses the otherness of God. In doing so, Sells and Turner make an important contribution to our understanding of the erotic in mystical texts. Treating experience as a central feature of mystical texts, McGinn suggests this language reveals that mystics long for a form of mystical consciousness in which love and knowledge collide. He also suggests that they use erotic language to express an endless yearning for a

---

[52]   Hollywood, *Sensible Ecstasy*, p. 6.

God who is unknowable, but not unlovable. In this way his understanding of erotic language attempts to brings together both apophatic and experiential readings of this language. Feminist readings add yet another dimension to our understanding of erotic love by focusing particularly on its use within the writings of female mystics. Simone de Beauvoir sees it as a form of human erotic desire, but Carolyn Walker-Bynum argues that it can also act as a means of transcendence. Hollywood cautions against reading all female eroticism in terms of embodiment. She argues that Hadewijch and Porete attempt to transcend the limitations of authorised female spirituality through a clever use of erotic discourse. As such, all these readings clearly advance our understanding of Christian mysticism beyond a strictly perennialist position.

We now turn in the next chapter to another important theme within mysticism: hierarchy. It is a theme that appears to be completely absent from perennialist considerations of Christian mysticism.

Chapter 5

Hierarchy

This chapter examines the concept of hierarchy and its role in Christian mysticism. The idea that hierarchy holds a central place in Christian mysticism may seem strange to modern readers. However, Gregory Shaw, Andrew Louth and Paul Rorem have all convincingly shown how pivotal hierarchy is for Pseudo-Denys's account of mysticism. Pseudo-Denys links hierarchy to liturgical practice in *The Ecclesiastical Hierarchy* and a symbolic understanding of the creation in *The Celestial Hierarchy*. In this chapter we will focus on these two texts, exploring how recognition of the importance of hierarchy within mystical texts impacts on our understanding of what Christian mysticism is in a more general manner.

Pseudo-Denys and Hierarchy

As we discussed in Chapter 2, our knowledge of Pseudo-Denys is limited. Yet his texts on hierarchy give the best clue to his identity. In these texts we clearly see his relationship to both Proclean and Iamblichan Neoplatonism – which shows that he cannot have been the contemporary of St Paul's that he claims to have been. We also find in *The Ecclesial Hierarchy* reflections on a liturgy only used in Syria from around the sixth century. Components such as these have led scholars to place Pseudo-Denys in sixth-century Syria. The distinct lack of any reference to women leads many to suggest that he was a monk.

Pseudo-Denys seems to have been the first to coin the word 'hierarchy', an idea that he bases primarily on a conjunction of two Greek words *hieros* meaning 'sacred' and *archē* meaning 'principle of origin or source'.[1] Yet, as Andrew Louth has noted, this idea is already found in the writings of Proclus and Iamblichus, both of whom used it to try and resolve the problem of embodiment, as we noted in Chapter 1. Both rejected Plotinus's idea that there is a part of the soul that does not become fully embodied, even though Proclus still maintained that the highest part of the soul was not changed in its substance. For Iamblichus in particular this meant that introspection and intellectual endeavour alone could never be enough to enable the soul to rise back up to union with the One from which it had emanated. Greater mediation is needed, something that allows the soul to realise what lies outside itself and so be illuminated by it. For Iamblichus, this mediation occurs through theurgy – that is, ritual practices that allow the soul to become attuned to the divine illumination available to it. While some have accused

---

[1]   A. Louth, *Denys the Areopagite* (Wilton, CT: Morehouse-Barlow, 1989), p. 38.

Iamblichus of incorporating a form of superstitious magic into Neoplatonism, Iamblichus viewed theurgy as the proper means of realising the divinising that is necessary for all things to become part of the creativity that comes from the One. Now, while there are elements within Iamblichus's Neoplatonism that Pseudo-Denys, as a Christian, rejects – such as the idea that there are many routes to the One through a myriad of gods – Pseudo-Denys's notion of hierarchy is built on a similar, albeit Christianised, understanding of cosmology. This means, as Andrew Louth points out, that order and hierarchy are not seen as stifling and unnecessary, far from it, they are the building blocks through which Pseudo-Denys works out his understanding of salvation and so mysticism.

To get a clearer picture of what this means, we need to turn to the two texts in which Pseudo-Denys elaborates his understanding of hierarchy. It is remarkably difficult to talk about these texts without taking sides in a debate about what kind of relationship Pseudo-Denys had with the Athenian Neoplatonists on whom he draws and so how experience fits into Pseudo-Denys's mysticism. We will therefore give only the briefest of outlines before exploring these themes in more detail through contemporary discussion of them.

The Celestial Hierarchy

The Celestial Hierarchy deals with angelology, that is, the various orders and types of angels. Pseudo-Denys suggests that there are nine orders of angels, each belonging to a set of three. As Louth notes, he is not the first to posit this. He is also not always consistent in his ordering of the angels. However, the most dominant hierarchy of angels that he provides, beginning with the highest, is: seraphim, cherubim, thrones, dominions, powers, authorities, principalities, archangels and angels. Within this hierarchy the angels are grouped into triads. The angels in each triad relate hierarchically to one another, and the entire triad relates hierarchically to the other triads in the celestial hierarchy. This notion of triads is something that Pseudo-Denys derives from Proclus but then expands.

Within each triad Pseudo-Denys argues that a process of purgation, illumination and perfection occurs. The members of the triad each have their own function which they must fulfil in order that other members of the triad can be illuminated and gain as perfect a knowledge of God as is possible. Pseudo-Denys states:

> If one talks of a hierarchy, what is meant is a certain perfect arrangement, an image of the beauty of God which sacredly works out the mysteries of its own enlightenment in the orders and levels of understanding of the hierarchy … Indeed for every member of the hierarchy, perfection consists in this, that it is uplifted to imitate God as far as possible.[2]

---

[2]   Pseudo-Denys, 'The Celestial Hierarchy', in *Pseudo-Dionysius: The Complete Works*, pp. 143–92, at p. 154.

Within each triad a relational process exists, whereby some angels are purified while others do the purifying, some are illuminated while others do the illuminating, and some are perfected while others do the perfecting. As Bernard McGinn puts it:

> Each hierarchy comprises a level that perfects, one that enlightens, and one that purifies. And every hierarchy will also contain those who act, those who mediate, and those who are acted upon.[3]

This is the function of hierarchy, not that one should climb up it to God, but that each member should fulfil its role. This means that, although some angels are closer to God in the overall celestial hierarchy than others, all can attain perfection and knowledge of the divine so long as they fulfill the role ascribed to them. While hierarchy is essential for Pseudo-Denys – it is the alternative to chaos – Pseudo-Denys stresses that everything in existence originates in God, such that all existing things also have an immediate relationship to the 'origin or principle' of their creation. Some existing things, like certain orders of angels, are, however, ontologically and epistemologicaly closer to God than other things because of the preordained position that has been ascribed to them.

This sense that everything, including people, is allotted a certain place within creation through which it can reach it own perfection, so long as it remains in right relationship with other things, is also pivotal to understanding Pseudo-Denys's notion of ecclesiastic hierarchy.

The Ecclesiastical Hierarchy

The Ecclesiastical Hierarchy outlines a second hierarchy, this time within the church. As with the celestial hierarchy, the ecclesiastical hierarchy contains three groups of three. Each triad likewise details movement from purgation, through illumination, to perfection. At the bottom are the laity, in the middle the church leaders (or hierarchs), and at the top, the sacraments. It is even clearer from this text than from *The Celestial Hierarchy* that the purpose of hierarchy is not to manipulate God – that is, making either God or the angels do what humans want. Christian theurgy is not a form of magic; it is about preparing the soul for illumination. This is important, as many scholars have considered Iamblichus's notion of theurgy to be a kind of magic through which he tries to manipulate the gods. As we will discuss below, Gregory Shaw disagrees with such a reading of Iamblichus since, unlike magic, theurgy (both Neoplatonic and Christian) respects the created order and the divinely ordained relationship between material and spiritual things. Only by attempting to harness this divinely ordered creation can

---

[3]   McGinn, *The Foundations of Mysticism*, p. 164.

theurgy bring about illumination and make spiritual ascent possible. Magic, on the other hand, tries to harness these powers for unnatural ends.

In Pseudo-Denys's account of ecclesial hierarchy we see this belief particularly in the role that is ascribed to the liturgy and the importance he places on the receptivity of the hierarch or leader to illumination. Pseudo-Denys says that the hierarch stands in a middle position between those who cannot see beyond the material world and those who enter into a totally non-material understanding of God. As such the hierarch acts as a mediator, through which the illumination of God passes to those who are less spiritually inclined. As in Iamblichus's account, there is a matching of ritual with the spiritual capacity of each person. For those who are less spiritually inclined more material rituals are needed, while for the hierarch those that mix both material and spiritual components are appropriate. This is the purpose of hierarchy: that each person, according to their capacity, should receive salvation and share in the divine. As Pseudo-Denys states, God 'has bestowed hierarchy as a gift to ensure the salvation and divinisation of every being endowed with reason and intelligence'.[4] Each soul is lifted up to share in God's perfection in the manner and to the extent that it is able.

Although two separate treatises, *The Celestial Hierarchy* and *The Ecclesiastical Hierarchy* form a unit.[5] The *Ecclesiastical Hierarchy* is the more lowly of the two, describing the created order and how it is can be used to elevate those within it. *The Celestial Hierarchy* stands above it, describing the various ranks of angels which can offer illumination to the soul on its spiritual journey. In some sense the angels replace the daemonic beings or gods described by Iamblichus. However, as Shaw points out, in other ways, Pseudo-Denys's system is rather different. Working within a Christian cosmology there are not many ways to return to the One, but just one way to return to God, that is through Christ. Christ is the supreme sacrament, towards which all sacraments move, and around which they revolve. Although human beings stand below the angels in the hierarchical system and Christ is constrained by human laws whilst embodied, at the same time Christ transcends this by demonstrating the worth of every aspect of the hierarchy. He shows that the point of hierarchy is the mysterious movement from the material to the divine, from the comprehensible to the ineffable, from ignorance to wisdom. In this way Christ supersedes all other elements in the hierarchy, becoming the ultimate analogy for how hierarchy works. Pseudo-Denys sees Christ as the supreme hierarch or leader through whom everything in the hierarchy has to pass on its way back to God. As Pseudo-Denys states, Christ is the 'source and being underlying every hierarchy'.[6]

---

[4]   Pseudo-Denys, 'The Ecclesiastical Hierarchy', in *Pseudo Dionysius: The Complete Works*, pp. 193–260, at p. 198.

[5]   P. Rorem, *Pseudo-Dionysius: A Commentary on the Texts and an Introduction to their Influence* (New York: Oxford University Press, 1993), p. 49.

[6]   Pseudo-Denys, 'Ecclesiastical Hierarchy', pp. 195–6.

Later Medieval Developments

Two subsequent discussions exerted an enormous influence on later accounts of mysticism. These are the accounts of hierarchy found in the writings of Thomas Gallus and Bonaventure.

Thomas Gallus

Thomas Gallus (1200–46) was fascinated by Pseudo-Denys's writings. He produced two commentaries on *Mystical Theology*, one of which, the *Extractio*, became extremely popular in the later Middle Ages and was translated into Middle English by *The Cloud*-Author.[7] Gallus also composed commentaries on *The Celestial Hierarchy* and *The Ecclesiastical Hierarchy*. In addition, Gallus wrote a number of commentaries on The Song of Songs. In these works he produces an internalisation of Pseudo-Denys's celestial hierarchy. While in Pseudo-Denys's writing the celestial hierarchy relates to the soul and its spiritual progress, it is never separate from the cosmological element that makes the soul's journey part of a movement of the whole of creation. Gallus offers a far more individualised, almost subjective, account of the angelic hierarchy, in which its function becomes more analogous than real; the angelic ranks coming to constitute a model for human spiritual progression. This is particularly clear if we reflect on some of the key ideas in his second commentary on The Song of Songs.

In this commentary Gallus explains how the Bride in The Song of Songs progresses through three stages that broadly correspond to the three spiritual possibilities described in Pseudo-Denys's *Ecclesiastical Hierarchy*. First there is the stage in which she knows nothing other than the material – the lowest human spiritual form of knowing, which Pseudo-Denys associates with the laity. Then there is a stage of mixed spiritual and material knowing – which Pseudo-Denys associates with the hierarch. Finally there is the spiritual stage of knowing that exceeds all materiality, which Pseudo-Denys associates with ecstasy and mysticism and the sacraments. Gallus compares these three stages to the three groups of triads that are found in *The Celestial Hierarchy*.

> The lowest hierarchy of mind consists in its very own nature; the middle in what it can do by effort, which incomparably exceeds nature; the highest in ecstasy. At the lowest, only nature is at work; at the highest, only grace; at the middle, both grace and effort work together. The lowest rank of the lowest hierarchy, called the 'angelic', includes the basic and simple natural modes of apprehension both of knowledge and love, without any judgement of the appropriate and inappropriate, which is just like the angels, that is the 'announcers', who, in the simplest sense bring news to the soul.[8]

---

[7] Turner, *Eros and Allegory*, p. 138.

[8] Ibid., p. 321.

Gallus then goes on to explain how the higher ranks of angels correspond to the higher workings of the soul in its journey towards God.

Like Pseudo-Denys, Gallus emphasises the ineffability of God, and therefore argues that the highest form of knowing is an incomprehensible form of understanding that far exceeds human capacities to know. This is the love of the seraphim which, as we already discussed in Chapter 3, is, according to Gallus, a knowledge that can only be attained by love and not intellection. For him it is the fulfilment of all human desiring and longing, a moment of total illumination in which the soul achieves ecstasy and union with God. By suggesting this interpretation, Gallus is attempting to synthesise the different imagery which he has inherited, all of which talks about mystical knowing. He brings it all together in his Song of Songs commentary in his discussion of the most elevated form of love. Here the Bride is illuminated by the light of God, within a hierarchical system that is within the soul:

> This rank embraces God and is wrapped in the embraces of the Bridegroom, this is no knowledge in a mirror, it is Mary's part, which will not be taken away (Lk 10.42). In this order the bed is laid for the Bridegroom and Bride. It is from this order that the torrent of divine light pours down in stages to the lower order.[9]

This is an approach to hierarchy that Bonaventure inherits and extends, internalising it yet further as he tries to bring it into even closer proximity with the tradition of mysticism that he finds in Augustine. Augustine's approach, as we noted in Chapter 3, builds on a more Plotinian foundation than Pseudo-Denys's understanding of mysticism. As such, it carries within it a natural tendency to believe that it is possible for the soul to rise to God through introspection.

Bonaventure

Bonaventure was born in 1221, in Tuscany. He entered the Franciscan order in approximately 1242 and rose to become Minister General and a Cardinal of the Church. He was a master of Theology at the University of Paris, an academic career that was cut short when he took charge of the Order of Friars Minor. He was venerated in his own lifetime and afforded a mention in Dante's *Paradiso*. Bonaventure's theological work centres on the figure of Christ as the true 'hierarch' or teacher who offers knowledge that begins in faith, is developed through reason, and is perfected by mystical union with God.

Bonaventure's key mystical text, *The Soul's Journey into God*, is significantly influenced by Gallus and another Victorine, Hugh of St Victor. Hugh had already begun to synthesise the Neoplatonic traditions of Plotinus and Proclus by drawing the works of Augustine and Pseudo-Denys together. Bonaventure continues this

---

9   Ibid., p. 323.

process. Like Gallus, Bonaventure also internalises the heavenly and earthly hierarchies. He stresses the importance of introspection, introducing a Christ-centred emphasis into his internalised hierarchies that was not nearly so marked in the writings of his predecessors. Bonaventure describes Christ as the ladder and the doorway to mystical knowing.

> And just as, when one has fallen, he must lie where he is unless another is at hand to raise him up, so our soul could not be perfectly lifted up out of these things of sense to see itself and the eternal Truth in itself had not Truth, taking human form in Christ, become a ladder restoring the first ladder that had been broken in Adam.
>
> Thus it is that, no matter how enlightened one may be by the light coming from nature and from acquired knowledge, he cannot enter into himself to delight in the Lord except through the mediation of Christ, Who says, *I am the door. If anyone enter by me he shall be safe, and shall go in and out, and shall find pastures.*[10]

Here Bonaventure picks up on a theme that is also central to Pseudo-Denys's account of hierarchy, albeit in a less communal, liturgical and more individualised manner. Christ, for Bonaventure, is not the focus of communal liturgy, but is an individualised sacrament who helps the soul turn within itself to find God.

This shift requires Bonaventure to provide a slightly different justification for why Christ, the second person of the Trinity, decided to become human. Humanity is a middle-ranking position in terms of hierarchy. Angels stand above humanity and are more expressive of God's majesty; they are therefore more expressive of God than Christ himself. However, Bonaventure argues that because human beings are a mixture of flesh and intellect they are uniquely placed to respond to the symbolic nature of creation that God has made to facilitate salvation. Following Hugh, Bonaventure argues that creation is filled with signs and symbols that facilitate the soul's rise back to God, with Christ drawing the soul eventually into an interior quest, which not only begins with Christ but also ends with him as well. This makes the human soul in effect a microcosm of all things. There is nothing that the soul cannot know and so become; the soul contains within it the microcosm of the whole created universe. The human being, a mixture of soul and body, is a hierarchy of the whole world; from the sentient nature of animals at the bottom to the intellectual capacity of the angelic orders at the top. The microcosm of the human being and the macrocosm of all creation are all reconciled in Christ. It is Christ who reawakens the blind soul to the symbol nature of all creation. He is the supreme sign that God has placed in creation to facilitate the soul's rise back to him, and it is with him, as he dies on the cross, that the soul is finally reunited

---

[10]   Bonaventure, *The Mind's Journey to God*, trans. P. Boehner (New York: Franciscan Institute, 1956; repr. 1990, 1998), p. 73.

with God. As this brief survey indicates, hierarchy is clearly a central theme within Christian mysticism.

CONTEMPORARY THEORETICAL APPROACHES

Unlike the other themes considered in this book, which have captured the attention of scholars of mysticism, the theme of hierarchy is rather neglected. Perennialists do not discuss it; which again highlights the limitations of this approach since it downplays this theme. In fact, most of the readings that do attempt to account for this facet of Christian mysticism are difficult to classify in terms of the four categories outlined in the introductory chapter. All focus on Pseudo-Denys, for whom this is an important theme, as we noted above, but it is a serious lack in the scholarship that little consideration is given to the manner in which the theme of hierarchy is extended by later mystics. We will begin by considering the approach of Paul Rorem, for whom Pseudo-Denys used hierarchy as illustrative of the epistemological nature of his mysticism, in which Rorem finds little room for experience.

Paul Rorem

Paul Rorem has produced a number of important books on Pseudo-Denys in which he stresses the link between Pseudo-Denys's writing and those of the Neoplatonists on which he drew. He argues that the notion of hierarchy, and particularly the idea of progression and return which is so central to Pseudo-Denys's understanding of the created order, is more epistemological than ontological in Pseudo-Denys's thought.[11] By this he means that Pseudo-Denys is more concerned with knowledge about the universe and God than the reality of the universe itself. For Rorem, the key issue is how sacraments work – given that they are at the top of the ecclesiastical hierarchy. Rorem argues that for Pseudo-Denys the sacraments are powerful anagogic symbols; a means through which the soul rises up to a *knowledge* that is mystical. In seeing their function as merely symbolic, rather than effecting any causal change within the soul, he argues that Pseudo-Denys does not use the term theurgy to refer to religious rituals. As such, he detaches Pseudo-Denys's use of theurgy from Iamblichan theurgy. Reading Pseudo-Denys in this way, he suggests that when Pseudo-Denys talks of ecstasy there is nothing experiential about it. Ecstasy is simply a movement outside of the mind and human modes of thinking into a mode of thinking that is outside of oneself. It is akin to being drunk or upset, or when one is said to be beside oneself. As he states:

> The Areopagite himself did not understand the notion of [ecstasy] to mean a private, emotional, and super-rational experience. As usual, the basis for his

---

[11]   See Rorem, *Pseudo-Dionysius: A Commentary*, p. 200.

terminology is a literal definition: standing outside of oneself, as in being drunkenly out of one's wits.[12]

Based on his understanding of hierarchy, Rorem does not think that when Pseudo-Denys talks of ecstasy that he is referring to an experiential event.

Andrew Louth

Andrew Louth, like Rorem, suggests that the angelic and ecclesial hierarchies in Pseudo-Denys's mystical writing serve a mainly symbolic function. He suggests that it is not the symbols themselves so much as human interpretation of them that moves the soul towards union with God. He notes that Pseudo-Denys stresses that angels are not physical beings with, for instance, bestial heads or interlinking wheels (both descriptions found in Ezekiel). He suggests therefore that angels can be viewed simply as perceptible symbols. We noted in Chapter 2 that Pseudo-Denys describes how the soul uses perceptible symbols on its journey towards conceptual understanding and finally a super-conceptual understanding of God. Louth believes that Pseudo-Denys wanted his reader to grasp the meaning of the symbolism contained in these hierarchies, not think of them as ontologically real.

However, Louth also stresses the importance of the liturgy for Pseudo-Denys. In fact, he argues that it is the key to understanding all that Pseudo-Denys writes.[13] Yet, for all this, Louth's view of the function of liturgical rites seems unclear. He suggests that liturgy only works at the level of intellectual understanding. Those participating in the rituals are, according to Louth, led to recall the historical acts of Jesus, which then leads to a form of illumination. As such, this limits the experiential potential that involvement in liturgy can engender and as a result diminishes the role that Jesus plays in the process of illumination via the sacraments. Louth ascribes Christ purely symbolic status, which seems odd given his ontological reality for Christians and the relationship between this and liturgical encounter, particularly within an Eastern Christian context. In doing so, Louth diminishes the possible role experience can have in mystical union, since in this understanding of hierarchy everything operates on an intellectual, rather than an emotional, level. As such, this seems a rather limited reading of liturgy, especially within sixth-century Syria.

Gregory Shaw

Gregory Shaw criticises both Louth and Rorem, suggesting that one of the main problems with both of their approaches is that they are so keen to distinguish

---

[12] Rorem, *Biblical and Liturgical Symbols*, p. 137.
[13] Louth, *Denys the Areopagite*, p. 30.

Pseudo-Denys's approach from a pagan Neoplatonic one that they become blind to the way in which hierarchy for Pseudo-Denys is much more than just an intellectual tool. Shaw suggests Christian theurgy demands far more than a purely conceptual interpretation of hierarchy and liturgy. For him, the result is 'a more direct and performative experience',[14] than either Louth or Rorem suggest, which he believes allows for the possibility that Pseudo-Denys may be describing an ineffable union with God.

Shaw argues that a case for reading Pseudo-Denys's discussions of ecstasy in a more experiential manner can be made if we consider the end point that Pseudo-Denys ascribes to the role of the hierarch. Pseudo-Denys holds that the priest or hierarch experiences deification through the illumination he receives from the liturgy and the ritual practices he performs. Shaw notes that when this happens the priest is transformed in both learning and experience. He becomes Christ, both god and man, and is then in a position to illuminate others, thereby allowing them to share in his perfection or deification. Shaw points particularly to a number of passages in which Pseudo-Denys compares the theurgic process to Paul's vision of God. As we will discuss in Chapter 8, Paul states in 2 Corinthians that he did not know whether he was in or out of his body when he entered into a vision of heaven. As such, this is a kind of ecstasy. Pseudo-Denys writes that a similar experience happened to his teacher, Hierotheus:

> He was so caught up, so taken out of himself experiencing communion with
> the things praised, that everyone who heard him, everyone who saw him ...
> considered him to be inspired, to be speaking divine praises.[15]

As such, Shaw believes that this opens up the possibility of a more experiential reading of what Pseudo-Denys means by ecstasy than Rorem posits. Shaw's is a reading that resonates with McGinn's general understanding of 'mediated immediacy', even though McGinn, like many other scholars, does not focus on the importance of hierarchy in the way that Shaw does.

Denys Turner

Denys Turner, who we have noted in the previous chapter offers a performative language readings of mysticism, also considers the role of hierarchy in Pseudo-Denys's writing. Turner adopts a position that seems close to Louth's, in that he regards the notion of hierarchy for Pseudo-Denys as primarily metaphorical. He argues in a somewhat uncomfortable way that, because creation is actually

---

[14]   G. Shaw, 'Neoplatonic Theurgy and Dionysius the Areopagite', *Journal of Early Christian Studies*, 7/4 (1999), 573–99, at p. 592.

[15]   Pseudo-Denys, *Divine Names*, in *Pseudo-Dionysius: The Complete Works*, pp. 47–132, at p. 70.

(ontologically) hierarchical, hierarchy provides the supreme metaphor for the epistemologic and linguistic process of ascent to God that he considers Pseudo-Denys to be describing. He states:

> there is the problematic question of the role of hierarchy, and so of the metaphor of 'ascent', within the theoretical and metaphorical articulation of Denys' theology. It is because, we saw, the world *is* hierarchical in its ontological structure that the *metaphor* of ascent is constitutive within the dialectical epistemology … In Denys, at least, it is impossible to unpick this complex tissue of imagery and concept, to detach the epistemological from the ontological, the metaphors from their foundations in both or the descriptions of spiritual experience from any of them.[16]

Even though he maintains that it is not possible to prise the ontological, epistemological and metaphorical apart, his approach ends up emphasising the metaphorical and downplaying the other meanings because, unlike Shaw and Louth, Turner does not reflect on the role of liturgy. Yet while Turner does not find expressions of mystical experience in Pseudo-Denys's discussions of hierarchy, he is aware that the internalised discussions of it that appear in Bonaventure and Thomas Gallus open the door for more experiential approaches to mysticism. However, Turner considers this to be a degradation of Christian mysticism proper, which for him is concerned with the epistemological tension between naming and unnaming God.[17] He labels such approaches 'experientialist' to stress that they are not truly apophatic. Turner's failure to account for the liturgical dimension of Pseudo-Denys's thought and its relation to hierarchy (in which room for experience might be found) is surely a weakness of his readings. His focus on the epistemological aspect of Christian mysticism leads him to offer a rather impoverished account of hierarchy's role when compared to that of Shaw. It is a position which belies his general suspicion of approaching mysticism in terms of experience.

While Shaw views hierarchy as a positive element within Pseudo-Denys mysticism, Grace Jantzen takes a rather negative view of the role that hierarchy has performed within Christian mysticism. She blames it for women's forced retreat into more embodied forms of mysticism.

Grace Jantzen

Grace Jantzen offers a feminist critique of many elements Christian mysticism, as we noted briefly in Chapter 1. In this regard, she argues that Pseudo-Denys'

---

[16]   Turner, *The Darkness of God*, p. 48.
[17]   See, ibid., p. 193.

invention of hierarchy establishes the power structures in which the hierarch completely dominates the entire system.[18] In practical terms hierarchy was bishops and clergy, the educated elite who acted as the custodians of God's mysteries revealed in scripture and the sacraments. It might very well be that in abstract theological terms each item of creation is immediately present to God. The mystical path to God, however, is not without its administrators who control entry. In Jantzen's words:

> The mystical theology and ecclesiastical hierarchy are tightly interlocked in Dionysius' thinking: it is by this interlocking that the concept of the mystical is broadened to include not only the hidden or spiritual meaning of scripture, but the whole mystery of God in church and Bible ... It includes all that God has revealed, all that is held in trust by the ecclesiastical authorities who both interpret the scriptures and administer the sacraments, first excluding all who are uninitiated or unworthy.[19]

Jantzen insists that this model of hierarchy was bequeathed to the Middle Ages following the translation and dissemination of Pseudo-Denys's corpus. The mystical path did not recognise all creation's shared immediacy to God. The path was a step-by-step ascent which culminated in ecstasy, which some were better equipped than others to attempt. Jantzen makes clear that women were perhaps considered the least well-equipped to enjoy God's mysteries. Pseudo-Denys does not mention women in his writing and, of course, women would not count amongst the male custodians of God's mysteries for him: bishops, priests and deacons. Furthermore, scholarship required initiation to unlock the mystical meaning of scripture, which was beyond most uneducated women. As Jantzen puts it, 'Such a path required the best of minds, minds at full strength – the minds, therefore of men, not of women.'[20] Jantzen acknowledges that Pseudo-Denys probably did not intend his mystical theology to be gender constructed. That said, she believes that this model for mysticism, built on the idea of hierarchy as authoritarian, explains much of the gender bias in medieval mystical writing. For her, Pseudo-Denys's mysticism becomes a social construct that favours male power and precludes women from counting as mystics.[21] As such, it is an aspect of mysticism that women were forced to rail against. Her reading highlights one way in which women have had to approach the divine from a different starting point than their male counterparts. It raises important questions about the extent to which men and women do the same thing when they write about mysticism (an issue which we carefully consider in Chapter 7). This subtlety is one which a perennialist account would find difficulty

---

18   See Jantzen, *Power, Gender and Christian Mysticism*, p. 98.
19   Ibid., p. 107.
20   Ibid., p. 108.
21   For a fuller explanation of this point, see ibid., p. 109.

accommodating. The issue is also one which Rorem, Louth, Shaw and Turner do not address in relation to their readings of hierarchy.

Conclusion

This chapter has explored a number of contemporary responses to the role that hierarchy plays in Pseudo-Denys's mysticism. Rorem and Louth argue that it works on a symbolic level. Denys Turner agrees, albeit from a performative language perspective. However, Gregory Shaw argues that, if hierarchy is read both on an ontological and an epistemological level, there is room for an experiential element in Pseudo-Denys's understanding of mysticism. From a feminist perspective Grace Janzten is critical of the way in which hierarchy becomes a social structure in the Middle Ages that often excludes women from intellectual process, forcing them to turn to their own bodies for inspiration.

The next chapter turns to consider a related theme, that of symbolism and Biblical interpretation.

Chapter 6
Symbolism and Scripture's 'Mystical Sense'

This chapter focuses on symbolism and biblical interpretation within Christian mystical texts. In particular it explores what is meant by a 'mystical' sense of scripture. The chapter begins by briefly introducing the allegorical method of interpreting the Bible, which most Christian mystics employ, and then considers how this relates to medieval ideas about sign and symbolism.

Literal and Allegorical Exegesis

It was Beryl Smalley who first realised that in the patristic and medieval periods exegesis was not just a peripheral activity, separate from doing 'real' theology. It does not seem an exaggeration to say that her groundbreaking work opened up a whole new arena of medieval studies, helping scholars to recognise how central medieval exegesis was to medieval theology. Perhaps the idea that the Bible is central to Christian theology does not seem all that surprising. However, the way medieval theologians approached the Bible made it seem fanciful to early twentieth-century scholars, and meant that for a long time it was neglected in favour of theological treatises.[1] Rather than focusing on the literal meaning of the text, or exploring its historical value through methods such as form, redaction, narrative and source criticism (methods developed in the twentieth century that will be familiar to contemporary students of theology), medieval scholars took a largely allegorical approach to reading the Bible. Despite the fact that some postmodern writers have placed renewed emphasis on allegorical readings of scripture, medieval biblical exegesis will still seem unusual to most modern readers, especially those familiar with contemporary exegetical methods.[2]

We have already discussed in Chapter 1 that the Early Church was founded amidst a cultural milieu dominated by Platonism in its various forms. This was a philosophy in which the body and the outer world were less real than the inner mental world. It is perhaps therefore hardly astonishing that this same belief dominates Early Church and medieval hermeneutical strategies. As Beryl Smalley notes, the key to understanding medieval exegesis is the idea found in 2 Corinthians

---

[1]   B. Smalley, *The Study of the Bible in the Middle Ages* (Oxford: Blackwells, 1941; 2nd edn, 1952), pp. xi–xiv.

[2]   For a critical discussion of this issue, see K.J. Vanhoozer, *Is There a Meaning in this Text?: The Bible, the Reader, and the Morality of Literary Knowledge* (Grand Rapids, MI: Zondervan, 1998).

3: 6 that, while 'the letter kills, the spirit gives life'.[3] Medieval writers believed that this distinction between letter or word and spirit paralleled the distinction between body and soul. The body or word was an outer kernel which contained within it an inner spiritual centre. Yet somehow the word or body gave access to the inner. It is this dynamic, the need to get through the outer to access the inner, which underpins medieval approaches to the Bible.

Allegorical Exegesis

It is important to stress at the outset that there is no *one* medieval exegetical method. Firstly, writers employ different terms when they are doing the same thing, or conversely apply the same term when they are actually doing something different! Secondly, allegorical exegesis is divided into different types, only one of which is usually referred to as the 'allegorical' sense. There was no standardised number of levels or senses within allegorical exegesis. Origen, for example, wrote of three senses of scripture: the literal or somatic, the psychic, and the pneumatic or spiritual; yet Augustine speaks of four senses: the literal or historical, the aetiological, the analogical and the allegorical.[4] Despite such important variants, there was a tendency amongst medieval authors (as E. Ann Matter has noted) to follow John Cassian (360-435) in assigning four levels of meaning to scripture.[5] Cassian names these the *historical* sense (also called the *literal* sense), the *tropological* sense (also called the *moral* sense), the *allegorical* sense (also called the *typological* sense), and the *anagogical* sense (also called the *mystical* sense). In his book *Collationes*, focusing on the word 'Jerusalem', he demonstrates how these various senses can all be derived from the same passage. This, he says, is how we are to understand a reference to 'Jerusalem' in the Bible:

> Jerusalem may be understood in four ways: according to history (*secudum historiam*) the city of the Jews, according to allegory (*secundum allegoricam*) the church of Christ, according to anagogy (*secundum anagogem*) the celestial city of God, which is the mother of us all, according to tropology (*secundum tropologiam*) the human soul.[6]

---

[3]   See, for example, Augustine, *The Confessions*, chapter IV. See Smalley, *The Study of the Bible in the Middle Ages*, p. 1-2.

[4]   Smalley discusses how many different levels of exegesis were ascribed to the Bible by various exegetes. She notes, for example, that Angelom of Luxeuil argued that there were seven senses in the Bible. See Smalley, *The Study of the Bible in the Middle* Ages, pp. 23–4.

[5]   E.A. Matter, *The Voice of My Beloved: The Song of Songs in Western Medieval Christianity*, Philadelphia: University of Pennsylvania Press, 1990), p. 54. The discussion that follows draws on her work.

[6]   John Cassian, *Collationes*, quoted in Matter, *The Voice of My Beloved*, p. 54.

As we can see from this passage, there are four senses. The first is connected to history, so on the historical or literal level when the text talks about 'Jerusalem' Cassian says that we should understand it as a reference to a physical city. The other three levels are allegorical readings, although only the second is referred to by this name. On an allegorical level, so named, 'Jerusalem' is a reference to the Church universal. On an anagogical level (also allegory), 'Jerusalem' is a reference to the heavenly city that will be installed after Christ's return and which is called the 'new Jerusalem' in *The Book of Revelation*. The final sense, which Cassian calls tropology, is a moral sense (again allegory). It refers to the operation of the human soul. Cassian states that the rest of the passage helps to determine the moral teaching that a text contained.

Yet, despite speaking of different levels of scripture, there was, in practice, a rather fluid movement between the various levels of meaning. For example, when William of St. Thierry discusses the moral level, he quickly moves onto topics which ought (if the categories were strictly applied) to fall within the anagogical level. He explains that such fluidity is a characteristic of love, which was the driving force behind his hermeneutic. A passage from another of his Song of Songs commentaries clearly indicates that way that spiritual love mirrors his exegetical method.

> But all three loves, or levels of love, often run together and mutually support one another and in a sort of shared and friendly generosity with one another in which they each abound, give to and receive from one another: for the higher often takes pleasure in and enjoys the delights of the lower and sometimes the lower is filled and moved by the joy of the higher, with the middle way running back and forth between either and rejoicing in both.[7]

This fluidity is even more apparent in Bernard of Clairvaux's commentaries on The Song of Songs, where each sense seems to melt in and out of the others.[8]

Understanding of the Literal Level

There was also debate amongst exegetes about how one should understand the literal/historical level.[9] In reflecting on what the literal sense of the Bible was, it is important to be aware that, as in Augustine's *Literal Commentary on Genesis*, discussion of the literal meaning of scripture definitely did not limit itself to the letter of the text. For Augustine, the literal sense was the original meaning intended

---

[7]   William of St Thierry, 'A Brief Commentary on the First Two Chapters of the Song of Songs. Drawn from the Sermons of Saint Bernard, in which an Account is Given of the Threefold Nature of Love', in D. Turner, *Eros and Allegory*, pp. 277–88, at p. 279.

[8]   See Turner, *Eros and Allegory*, pp. 78–9.

[9]   See ibid. Turner gives numerous excerpts in this book to illustrate this debate.

by the author.[10] As such, it could encompass metaphorical interpretations. These were not allegory, which was a different sense. This debate becomes even more pronounced in discussion of The Song of Songs. William of St Thierry is happy to speak of a literal love between Bride and Bridegroom so long as he can take it as a parable, and therefore move immediately to the allegorical message without having to dwell too much on the literal sense![11] When Nicholas of Lyra speaks about the literal sense of The Song of Songs, he argues that the literal sense is not what is symbolised by the words, but what is meant by the things that the words symbolise, therefore allowing him to allegorise the text from the outset (since he is reticent to see it as a human love poem).[12] In suggesting this, Nicholas is close to Hugh of St Victor.

While many exegetes simply equated a particular word with a certain spiritual meaning (as in the case of the word 'Jerusalem' above), Hugh of St Victor argues that the spiritual sense did not lie with the word but in what the word signifies. To illustrate this Hugh discusses the word 'lion', which many exegetes took to signify Christ. He notes that one reason given for this association is that lions were believed to sleep with their eyes open – thus even when sleeping they were awake and so could signify Christ, who died as a human yet lives on in his divine nature. However, in that case Hugh argues it is not the word, so much as the *thing* that the word 'lion' represents – that is, the animal itself – that signifies Christ.

> When saying that a lion signifies Christ, it is not the name of the animal but the animal itself which is meant. It is this which, as is said, sleeps with its eyes open and by virtue of a kind of similarity, is a figure of the one who, in the sleep of death which he accepted, has slept in humanity, while remaining wide awake with his eyes open in divinity.[13]

While it might seem that Hugh's division between word and thing is splitting hairs, his approach reveals the relationship between biblical exegesis and medieval beliefs about sacraments and symbols, which links exegesis closely with mystical discourse.

---

[10] See Augustine, *The Literal Meaning of Genesis*, trans. and with intro. by J.H. Taylor, 2 vols, Ancient Christian Writers 41 and 42 (New York: Newman Press, 1982), vol I, p. 10.

[11] William of St Thierry, 'A Brief Commentary', in Turner, *Eros and Allegory*, pp. 277–88, at p. 281.

[12] See various excerpts from the writings of Nicholas of Lyra in Turner, *Eros and Allegory*, pp. 383–406.

[13] Turner, *Eros and Allegory*, p. 269.

Sacrament, Symbol and Christian Theurgy

Hugh of St Victor

Although Hugh had an approach that placed greater emphasis on the importance of the literal level than that employed by the majority of exegetes, his account of sign and symbol had an important influence on later mystical texts. We saw, for example, in the previous chapter his influence on Bonaventure's mysticism.[14] Hugh explores the issue of symbolism extensively in his commentary on Pseudo-Denys's *Celestial Hierarchy*. He adopts Pseudo-Denys's belief in the importance of hierarchy and theurgy. As a result, he argues that symbols are 'the juxtaposition of visible forms for the demonstration of visible things'. By this, Hugh means that the purpose of creation is to provide human beings with a means to rise up to spiritual knowledge. For Hugh, all created things served this purpose – that is, they act as symbols that can lead the soul to know God. In fact, he claims that it is impossible to talk about invisible things or the ineffable at all, except by means of visible things or the effable:

> It is impossible to represent invisible things except by means of those which are visible. Therefore all theology must have recourse to visible representations in order to make known the invisible.[15]

Hugh viewed creation as a kind of book, in which it was possible to read the physical in a symbolic manner and thereby access spiritual truth. However, he argues that as a result of the Fall (Genesis 3), people are unable to read this book properly, that is symbolically. They are unable to see past the physical (literal) level. A second interpretative book is therefore required – a commentary, if you like, on creation. This second book, according to Hugh, is Christ, the Word of God, through whom the first book of creation was originally made. In his book, *On the Sacraments of the Christian Faith*, Hugh explores this idea further. He notes how all sacraments work in this way. He describes Christ as a book written on two levels, the external and the internal. On the external level Christ has physical form, that is, something that a fallen soul can grasp. Yet internally he is divine and

---

[14]   See B. McGinn, *The Growth of Christian Mysticism: From Gregory the Great Through the 12th Century* (New York: Crossroad, 1992), p. 366, where he notes that the Victorines made 'a special contribution to the history of Western mysticism'. It was also important for Bonaventure, as is clear from *The Souls Journey into God*. See G.A Zinn, 'Book and Word: The Victorine Background of Bonaventure's use of symbols', in J.G. Bougerol (ed.), *S. Bonaventura 1274–1974: Volumen Commemorativum Anni Septies Centenarii a Morte S. Bonaventurae Doctoris Seraphici*, 5 vols (Grottaferrata: Collegio S. Bonaventura: Grottaferrata, 1974), vol. 2, pp.143–69, esp. p. 144.

[15]   Hugh of St Victor, *Commentary on the Celestial Hierarch of Pseudo-Denys*; quoted in Zinn, 'Book and Word', p. 147.

so potentially can help the soul come to a point where it can grasp the symbolic nature of creation. Christ is the supreme sacrament that illuminates the symbolic nature of creation.

All other sacraments work in the same way, although they are less potent than Christ. Sacraments are special signs that, as well as symbolising the spiritual, are established by God and sanctioned by the Church, as a means through which the soul can to rise up to know God. They offer special access to the symbolic potential of creation over and above that naturally found within the created order.

> Now if anyone wishes to define more fully and more perfectly what a sacrament is, he can say: 'A sacrament is a corporal or material element set before the senses without, representing by similitude and signifying by institution and containing by sanctification some invisible and spiritual grace.'[16]

Hugh argues that the relationship between the physical dimension of a sacrament and its spiritual potency is complex. The physical form of the sacrament makes the beholder aware that it is a sacrament. However, access requires more than its physical nature. It occurs through what Hugh calls the 'thing' of the sacrament. This 'thing' is the essence of the sacrament. He explains, the physical form of the sacrament is, in effect, merely the medicine bottle in which the unseen medicine is housed. Now it is the medicine, not the container, that cures illness. Likewise it is the essence of the sacrament, not its physicality, which cures people of their spiritual blindness, even if they need the physical container to realise that a cure is available.

> For the spiritual gifts of grace (that is sacraments) are, as it were, certain invisible antidotes, and since they are offered to man in visible sacraments in certain vessels, what else is shown by the visible species than hidden virtue? For the sick man cannot see the medicine but he can see the vessel in which the medicine is given. And on this account in the species itself of the vessel the virtue of the medicine is expressed that he may recognize what he receives and through this knowledge proceed to love.[17]

Our need for the physical also explains why God becomes incarnate in Christ.

Connected to this understanding of the world, Hugh says the soul had three eyes: a physical eye, an intellectual eye and a contemplative (or mystical) eye.[18] He argues that the Fall blinded the latter two eyes so that the soul could only appreciate things on a physical level. However, as it prayerfully comes to view the world through Christ, the supreme sacrament, it moves to understand that there was a

---

[16]   Hugh of St Victor, *On the Sacraments of the Christian Faith*, trans. R. Deferrari (Cambridge, MA: Medieval Academy of America, 1951), p. 155.

[17]   Ibid., p. 157.

[18]   We will talk about this idea more in Chapter 7 when we look at visions. See pp. 159–62.

spiritual level, and then finally a mystical level, to reality. The mystical level allows direct access to God. While Hugh did not think that it was possible to gain a true mystical understanding of God in this life, spiritual progress could still be made.

In the light of these beliefs we can understand Hugh's approach to the Bible and the three meanings or senses, the literal (physical), the allegorical (spiritual) and the anagogical (contemplative) that he ascribes to it. We can see that there is a direct relationship between Hugh's understanding of symbolism and his approach to exegesis. The soul which is awakened by Christ is able to penetrate the literal/historical story of the Bible and find its mystical meaning. It is in keeping with his general understanding of symbolism and hierarchy that Hugh emphasises that things, rather than words, aid spiritual understanding – thus his problem with people who simply allegorised every mention of lion as a reference to Christ. The Bible is the only book that has this symbolic, theurgeric, dimension, making it a sacred text, preordained, like creation, to help the soul rise up to God.

> Wherefore, it is apparent how much Divine Scripture excels all other writings in subtlety and profundity, not only in its subject matter but also in its method of treatment, since indeed in other writings words alone are found to have meaning, but in it not only words but also things are significant.[19]

Spiritual Sensations

We noted in Chapter 5 that Origen was the first to suggest that The Song of Songs had a tropological or a moral level – that is, one that described the relationship between the soul and God. In exploring the tropological level, Origen also developed the idea of spiritual sensations. For Origen, these were capacities that allowed the soul to realise the symbolic nature of the physical world and look beyond it to knowledge of God. He did not think that spiritual sensations had a direct relationship to their physical counterparts. The only similarity between them was that both physical and spiritual sensations came into direct contact with what they sensed. According to the medieval theory of extromission, a theory held by Augustine amongst others, physical sensations, including sight, worked by means of touch. When one gazed at an object light came from the eye and touched the thing that it saw. A kind of union then takes place so that the thing that is seen is drawn back into the soul through the light of the eyes.[20] Just as the light from the physical eyes brings about union on the physical level, so on a spiritual level love acts as a source of even stronger union. Here a kind of mutual interplay of love

---

[19]   Hugh of St Victor, *On the Sacraments of the Christian Faith*, prologue, v, p. 5.

[20]   The impact of the theory of extromission was also felt at a more popular level in society, as Christopher Joby has noted; see C. Joby, 'The Extent to which the Rise in the Worship of Images in the Late Middle Ages was Influenced by Contemporary Theories of Vision', *Scottish Journal of Theology*, 60/1 (2007), 36–44.

between God and the soul occurs which connects the soul to God. As Margaret Miles writes:

> Just as, in physical vision, the will unifies, in the act of vision, two separate entities – the viewer and the object – so in the vision of God, it is love, 'a stronger form of the will', that, in the activity of loving, connects and unites human longing with God's activity of love.[21]

It was in this way that spiritual sensations were thought to effect union between the soul and God. The idea that the soul could taste, touch, feel, hear and see God became an extremely important feature of later mystical texts.

The Sacred Page

Finally, a few words about the way a Bible would have looked in the twelfth century. Known as the Sacred Page (*Sacra Pagina*), each line of scripture would have been surrounded by numerous lines of commentary or gloss (*glossa ordinaria* or ordinary gloss). This gloss was built up over centuries – its exact origins are unclear.[22] Yet the Bible would scarcely have been read other than in this commentarial form – which stands to reason, since, as Hugh says, one needs help to arrive at secret meanings, whether in scripture or creation. When we think of the Bible in the medieval period it is important that we conceive of it in the commentarial form, realising that the entire Bible would rarely have been bound in one volume – since it would have been unusable, being too heavy to lift. Most Christian mystics thought of the Bible as text plus commentary. Even listening to the Bible would normally have occurred in liturgical contexts, thereby providing an interpretative frame that acted as a commentary.

CONTEMPORARY THEORETICAL APPROACHES

Perennialist Readings

Since perennialists believe that the mystical encounter is an acultural ineffable experience, when mystics refer to the Bible perennialists believe that they are producing an interpretive gloss that tries to explain their experience. Perennialists argue that Christian mystics draw on those biblical images that most resonate with their experience; their use of scripture is therefore wholly referential. This view

---

[21]   Margaret Miles, 'Vision: The Eyes of the Body and the Eye of the Mind in Saint Augustine's *De Trinitate* and *Confessions*', *The Journal of Religion*, 63 (1983), 125–42, at p. 135.

[22]   Smalley, *The Study of the Bible in the Middle Ages* p. 52.

produces a rather detached relationship between religious belief and experience. It is challenged by contextualists and by performative language readings, which both ascribe a much more involved role to exegesis within Christian mystical texts.

Contextualist Readings

Steven T. Katz   Steven T. Katz believes it is apparent that context shapes a mystic's experience from the use of scriptural imagery in mystical texts. He blames our ignorance of this on the perennialist belief that mysticism is 'an essentially individualistic, acultural, ahistorical, asocial, acontextual, anomian (if not primarily antinomian) phenomenon'.[23] He argues that such readings have led to an almost 'uniform neglect' of sacred scriptures in most scholarly literature on mysticism.[24] Arguing that mystical experiences cannot be separated from the theological and philosophical environments in which they develop, Katz asserts that perennialist discussions of mysticism have failed to notice an important dimension of mysticism, namely their relationship to the scriptures 'out of which the mystical personality has emerged'.[25]

Katz argues that we must not forget that mystics across all religious traditions have always seen their scriptures as storehouses of great spiritual truth. He argues that mysticism also depends on scripture as the repository of its revelation:

> The texts taken as sacred – are not just literary compositions but also revelations ... these texts are not merely human accounts ... they and their interpretation ... are authoritative, the very *Urgrund* (source) for all subsequent theological insights and aspirations ... In like manner, the mystical quest is, quite literally, the discovery or rediscovery of the mysteries encoded in scripture, the recovery of the superabundant truth and meaning hidden in these primal documents.[26]

If biblical interpretation underlies the essence of mysticism, Katz reasons that commentary *itself* becomes a spiritual encounter; the way one learns about God:[27]

> The effort to understand scripture is therefore, not merely a literary or intellectual exercise, but also a highly charged spiritual encounter. For to discern the meaning of the sacred text is to come to know something of God ...[28]

---

[23]   Katz, 'Mysticism and the Interpretation of Sacred Scripture', p. 7.

[24]   Ibid., p. 7.

[25]   Ibid., p. 7.

[26]   Ibid., p. 14.

[27]   Katz argues that this is as true of Pseudo-Denys (whom we considered in Chapters 2 and 5) as of anybody else. Also see pp. 34, 49–52.

[28]   Katz, 'Mysticism and the Interpretation of Sacred Scripture', p. 15.

He argues that mystical readings of scripture therefore serve an important function within the religious community. They act as the true readings of the text, those that reveal secrets ordinary people are unable to find:

> Mystics … understand their discrete teaching and goal as *an*, if not *the*, authentic reading of (a particular) scripture … they sincerely believe that the master text that is appealed to has inexhaustible levels of meaning, the innermost layers of which they alone, rather than the 'ordinary' believer or rational exegete, are able to plumb.[29]

Katz argues that allegorical exegesis facilitates such an approach to scripture, allowing it to be viewed as replete with secrets. To him the use of allegorical exegesis in mystical texts is therefore unsurprising. Its exegetical method allows an 'open-endedness' that creates the possibility of inexhaustible meanings. However, Katz does not believe that mystical interpretations are merely arbitrary. Even radical mystical interpretation are, Katz believes, a ways of reinforcing the limits of existing theological tradition.[30] Mystics reveal secrets, but only acceptable secrets.

Katz suggests that mystical orthodoxy is reinforced by the use of religious symbols, which are often the subject of mystical allegorical interpretation. Events like Christ's death have a symbolic meaning that does not operate outside of certain perimeters. Since such symbols act as the foundation of allegory they keep the mystical interpretation within a given interpretive range. For example, sacraments like the Eucharist are symbols that point to a reality that cannot be conceptualised. They allow discussion of what cannot be thought, while at the same time keeping the mystic within a particular theological framework. In this limited sense mystics explore the possibility of reaching the transcendent.

> The 'symbol,' the symbolic modality – and the theurgical and magical possibilities they open up – comprise a fundamental channel of divine teaching through which humankind learns, glimpses, the irreducible Beyond.[31]

While mystics are ultimately interested in levels of meaning beyond the literal level, Katz suggests that they normally affirm the literal level because they want to preserve the truth value of the scripture or symbol, without which no allegorical reading could exist. For Katz, the allegorical exegetical method ultimately reveals that Christian mystics saw their world and their scriptures shaped by transcendental forces, which they believed could be known, at least to some extent, via mysticism. In light of this, Katz criticises many scholars of mysticism for oversimplifying the

---

[29] Ibid., p. 17.

[30] We will comment further on this idea in Chapter 10 when we look at Eckhart and Porete.

[31] Katz, 'Mysticism and the Interpretation of Sacred Scripture', p. 37.

relationship between text and experience. He argues that it is simply not enough to view the use of scriptures as only 'postexperiential' rather than formative of the experience itself.

Ewert Cousins   Ewert Cousins also argues that the Bible acts as the foundation of Christian mystical spirituality. He notes the close relationship between exegesis and theology in the Patristic and Medieval periods, and suggests, particularly in relation to allegorical methods of exegesis, that the Bible constituted a kind of 'spiritual universe' or worldview from which mystics mined the secret meanings that they believed God had implanted there.

Cousins suggests that allegorical exegesis was aided by a practice developed in Christian monastic communities known as *lectio divina*, (divine reading). He argues that the practice of *lectio divina* is closely connected to mysticism, as the monks were encouraged to use it to progress from 'meditation', to 'prayer' and finally to 'contemplation', a term often treated as synonymous with mysticism. This practice involved the slow prayerful reading of texts over several hours, a method that did not focus on the literal meaning of the text, but on multiple layers of interpretation:

> [The] goal was not to finish a passage, but to enter prayerfully into its depths by dwelling on a sentence, a phrase, or even a word – mulling over it, ruminating on it, allowing it to sink into their being and resonate on many levels of meaning.[32]

Cousins highlights the close relationship between this way of reading scripture and symbolism. He also notes the importance of Song of Songs exegesis. Unlike Katz, Cousins does not consider medieval exegesis of this text to be primarily an attempt to contain the dangers of sexuality.[33] Rather he sees it as a resource that Christian mystics used to explore the pinnacle of spiritual love, along with images of ascent and darkness, through which these images come to shape Christian mystical experiences.

In this vein, Cousins makes more room for experience than Katz's hard contextualism allows. Cousins argues that the four levels noted in medieval exegesis mirror four levels of the psyche that have been identified in contemporary research into states of consciousness. Focusing on the work of Robert Masters and Jean Houston, Cousins suggests that interesting parallels can be seen between the levels of consciousness that Masters and Houston identify in people who use psychedelic drugs and the senses described in Christian mystical exegesis.[34]

[32]   Cousins, 'The Fourfold Sense of Scripture in Christian Mysticism', pp. 118–37, at p. 125.

[33]   See the discussion of Steven Katz in Chapter 6, pp. 129–32.

[34]   See R.E.L. Masters and J. Houston, *The Varieties of Psychedelic Experience* (New York: Holt, Rinehart and Winston,1966).

Cousins argues that the highest level of consciousness that Masters and Houston describe, and refer to as the 'mysterium' (using Rudolf Otto's terminology of the *numinous*), comes close to a mystical understanding of scripture. Despite making room for mystical experience, Cousins is nonetheless careful to stress that Christian accounts of mystical consciousness are dependent on scripture. A case in point is that of spiritual sensations. Cousins does not believe that spiritual sensations are superimposed on scripture in relation to experiences received, but that the relationship works the other way round.

> The doctrine of the spiritual senses of the soul in Christianity originated in scripture. If we were to fail to acknowledge it, we would be ignoring one of the major factors in the practice of *lectio divina*, which also functioned significantly in the contemplative interpretation of scripture through the symbolic, spiritual, and mystical senses.[35]

Cousins therefore places great importance on context, albeit while maintaining the possibility of experiencing God in his ineffability through mystical consciousness (something which Katz denies the possibility of – arguing instead that all claims of ineffable experience must be treated as non-literal). For Cousins, mysticism (as exemplified by the mystical level of exegesis) is an experiential encounter; a kind of positive silence arrived at once a person has passed beyond all positive and negative descriptions of God. It is one that is facilitated by spiritual sensations as they are allegorised in relation to key biblical motifs such as darkness and ascent.

> The level we have reached is above and beyond the kataphatic and even the apophatic. I believe that, here on the level of the highest spiritual senses, the negation of a spiritual sense such as hearing, produces another spiritual sense – namely, darkness or silence – which I claim is positive, not negative ... the spiritual senses of the soul ... bring the soul into the immediate experience of God.[36]

Cousin's understanding of mysticism reveals a tension between the idea that all experience is context-bound and the belief that mystical experience is given by God and must necessarily exceed context. Such a tension is also found in Bernard McGinn's account of mysticism as we discussed in Chapter 4 (and will further consider in Chapter 10).

---

[35]   Cousins, *The Fourfold Sense of Scripture in Christian Mysticism*, p. 131.

[36]   Ibid., p. 135.

Performative Language Readings

In contrast, the performative language readings of Sells and, particularly, Turner, while also critiquing a perennialist perspective, make much less room for an experiential encounter of the type that Cousins describes.

Denys Turner

Denys Turner's most careful assessment of the relationship between medieval exegesis and mysticism is found in his book *Eros and Allegory: Medieval Exegesis of the Song of Songs*. Turner sets out to explain why The Song of Songs, a book about premarital sex, was such a popular text in the Middle Ages, a fact which, as we noted in Chapter 4, seems doubly perplexing given that most of the commentaries were written by celibate monks.[37]

Turner notes that, as far as the literal/historical meaning of a text goes, most medieval commentators could not accept that the literal meaning of The Song of Songs was a description of secular love. Even Nicholas of Lyra, who in the fourteenth century defended the importance of the literal sense, did not think that this text was about sexual love.[38] Turner notes too that Origen used his commentary on The Song of Songs to provide a general argument for allegorical exegesis. Building on this, Turner argues that through studying commentaries on The Song of Songs it is possible to understand the general purpose underlying all use of the allegorical method.[39] According to Turner, the aim of such exegesis is not descriptive in the sense that it refers to an experience of God. Its purpose is to talk of the highest form of love, the love of God, a love which exceeds human comprehension. For Turner, it is precisely because such love is so different from human love that medieval exegetes ran into problems trying to talk about it. This is why they found The Song of Songs so appealing: it is precisely the kind of text that easily lends itself to a discussion of love and the problem of differentiating human love from spiritual love. Turner argues that this is why medieval authors related this book to the soul's union with God – not, as Katz suggests, because they found the content of the book dangerous. They saw it as a resource to discuss the otherness of God and the problems posed by trying to relate to that which is completely different from oneself. Turner maintains that this thought process can

---

[37] 'It is, *prima facie*, puzzling that men dedicated to a life of celibacy should find so natural a mode of expression for their spiritual aspirations in the erotic poetry of the Song' (Turner, *Eros and Allegory*, p. 19).

[38] Ibid., p. 37.

[39] 'From Origen to the end of the Middle Ages, then, the Song's overtly sexual eroticism provided a powerful *argument* for the general principle of the allegorical interpretation of the Old Testament as such and not just an instance of its application. For this reason, through the study of mediaeval commentary on the Song it is possible to get at one of the motivating forces of mediaeval biblical hermeneutics' (Turner, *Eros and Allegory*, p. 37).

even be seen in Bernard of Clairvaux's discussions of The Song of Songs, despite the fact that Bernard says that no one can know the true meaning of The Song of Songs except by experience. Although Turner believes that Bernard is in love with God erotically on every level, this does not mean that Bernard is not also driven by a desire to outline theology; it is just that for Bernard experience and theology go hand in hand.

> To say that Bernard's eroticism of language is the language of his experience is not to say that it does not serve any formal, acknowledged theological purpose. The mistake of supposing that Bernard can only write 'expressively' or 'affectively' and that he has nothing to offer by way of a 'systematic' theology was long ago exposed, once and for all, by Gilson ...[40]

Despite this mention of the union of experience and theology in Bernard's account, Turner views allegorical exegesis primarily as an exploration of language that is intended to draw attention to God's transcendence. Whether or not an experiential encounter occurs is not the point for Turner. He does not believe that experience is the driving force behind the creation of Christian mystical literature. For Turner medieval exegesis serves the same purpose as negative language and literary devises such as paradox – it points to the unknowability of God; God who is so different that it is not possible to even distinguish God from ourselves because we just do not know where to begin. For this, Mark S. Burrows has criticsed Turner's approach to mysticism for its lack of openness to the experiential dimension, wryly remarking:

> It may well be, as Denys Turner has argued, that mysticism in the classical sources is essentially an apophatic strategy, and has little if anything to do with the experientialist constructions of modernity with its positivist habits of mind.[41]

Michael Sells

As we have noted, Michael Sells is more open to the possibility of a mystical encounter than Turner. However, although Sells notes that mystics often elucidate their thought through biblical commentaries, he does not ascribe any special status to exegesis or the allegorical method used by Christian mystics. Sells is more interested in the themes that he pre-identifies within mystical texts, such as the tension between emanation and creation. He considers how these are played out in the writings of mystics, including biblical commentaries. He notes, for example, the importance of the idea of boiling over for Eckhart and how this affects his

---

[40]   Ibid., p. 79.

[41]   M.S. Burrows, 'Raiding the Inarticulate: Mysticism, Poetics and the Unlanguageable', 176.

understanding of scripture. In particular, he points to the way that this influences Eckhart's commentaries on Exodus and the gospel of John. Sells views the idea of boiling over as something of a hermeneutic key in each case.[42] However, unlike Turner or Katz, who consider exegesis itself as part of the mystical process, Sells understands exegesis as affected by ideas of apophasis that the mystic already holds. Given Sells's emphasis on language, his failure to engage more thoroughly with exegesis seems odd.

Conclusion

This chapter has explored various contemporary accounts of the way in which mystics used the Bible. Both Katz and Turner make important contributions to our understanding of the role that exegesis plays within Christian mysticism. Cousins's less detailed reading still helps us to see how room can be made for both theological and experiential readings of a theme at the same time. All of the readings above challenge the perennialists' view that the use of biblical imagery and motifs is a means of explicating an experience and nothing more.

This chapter concludes Part I of this book. Part II considers later developments in Christian mysticism, beginning with the notion that mysticism is gender-specific.

---

[42]   Sells, *Mystical Languages of Unsaying*, esp. pp. 151–7.

Part II
Later Developments in Christian Mysticism

The four chapters in this section look at what Bernard McGinn has termed 'new mysticism'. Between the thirteenth and fourteenth centuries the shape of Christian mysticism changed in a number of distinctive ways. Firstly, there was a huge increase in mystical texts written by women, which emphasised different themes and blurred the boundaries between the physical and spiritual in a way not found in earlier mystical texts. Some scholars claim these works are evidence of a distinct form of female mysticism, an issue we touched on in Part I. The period also sees an increase in visionary mysticism, especially amongst women. In addition, as we mentioned in Chapter 3, later Christian mysticism came to debate the soul's relationship to God. Later mystics questioned whether the intellect played a role in the final stages of mystical prayer. Tensions also emerged between mystics and the orthodox structures of the Church. The chapters in this section consider these four important developments in Christian mysticism, beginning with the notion of female mysticism.

As in Part I, we also consider the relative merits of different contemporary understandings of these developments as discussed in the introductory chapter. However, as we saw in the previous section, the more themes we consider, the more difficult it becomes to maintain the strict boundaries of these categories. This is even more apparent when we turn to the scholarly readings of this later material. To reflect this, we soften the rigidity of our categories, moving to talk of 'contextualised' rather than strictly 'contextualist' reading, which better seems to encapsulate the majority of scholars who place emphasis on context. This shift also allows us to focus in greater detail on the nuances of different scholarly readings.

Chapter 7
Female Mysticism

This chapter explores the idea that women's mysticism constitutes a particular type of mysticism that, while different from that produced by men, is no less a form of mysticism.

The Gendering of Mysticism

The thirteenth and fourteenth centuries saw a huge increase in mystical texts produced by or on behalf of women. These texts are, as Bernard McGinn notes, multiform. It is almost impossible to offer just one or two examples as an illustration of the richness and the difference that marks this proliferation in female spirituality. McGinn argues that they are characterised by five nebulous themes or motifs: an emphasis on human experience that challenges more doctrinal modes of authority; greater use of visions and images; more concrete discussions of sexuality and physical eroticism; a closer relationship between mysticism and madness, coupled with a stress on longing and desire as well as annihilation and, linked to the latter, new forms of apophatic language which mix biblical imagery with secular motifs, such as those drawn from courtly love literature. McGinn suggests that two problems arise when we try to discuss this development. Firstly, it is hard to know where to begin. As he states, 'Attempting to classify the women mystics of the period ca 1200–1350 is difficult and will always be a bit artificial'.[1] Secondly, many of the motifs that we find, although more prevalent in women's mysticism, are not exclusively female. Men in this period also take them up and develop them. 'In the case of each of these five aspects of new mysticism – the problem of authority, the role of visions, totalising embodied consciousness, excess, and annihilating indistinction – we find evidence for the creative, even initiatory, role of women. We do not, however, discern themes that can be restricted *only* to women.'[2]

The argument that there is something distinctively feminine in such developments is a theory of mysticism that was first popularised by Caroline Walker Bynum. Before considering examples of women's mystical writing from this period that are illustrative of some of these themes, we need first to outline Bynum's argument that we have in them a distinctively feminine form of mysticism.

---

[1]   B. McGinn, *The Flowering of Mysticism: Men and Women in the New Mysticism, 1200–1350* (New York: Crossroad, 1998), p. 157.

[2]   Ibid., p. 157.

Caroline Walker Bynum

Caroline Walker Bynum draws attention to the bodily nature of spirituality that
emerges in the later Middle Ages:

> Compared to other periods of Christian history and other world religions,
> medieval spirituality – especially female spirituality – was peculiarly bodily;
> this was so not only because medieval assumptions associated female with flesh
> but also because theology and natural philosophy saw persons as, in some real
> sense, body as well as soul.[3]

She argues that the psychosomatic unity of the person as body and soul, spirit and
flesh, was the platform from which religious women began to reach out to God
through tears, bleeding, fasting and flagellation. Women came to realise that they
were not distanced from God by their body; the body was intimately connected to
the spiritual. Likewise God's gifts came to be written into the woman's bodies as
stigmata, spiritual pregnancy and bodily visions.

For Bynum, an awareness of the possibility of a relationship with God through
Christ developed particularly amongst women because they were excluded, both
through lack of education and in terms of societal norms, from more intellectual
consideration of God. Drawing attention to the importance of devotion to the
Incarnate Christ in women's writing, she notes that emphasis is placed on his
sufferings, which in turn engenders Eucharistic devotion. Women came to
associate the Eucharist with mystical union, linking Christ's body with feeding
and food imagery – motifs which she argues come to dominate female mystical
discourse in this period.

> The point of Christ's humanity is that Christ *is* what we are: our humanity is in
> him and in him it is joined with divinity. We encounter this humanity-divinity
> of Christ in the Eucharist and in mystical union, each of which is an analogue
> for the other.[4]

While not emphasising suffering, Bynum notes, for example, how Christ feeds
Gertrude of Helfta through his blood in her intimate union with him.[5] In terms of
fertility imagery, another motif that she identifies as central to female mysticism,
Bynum notes that the wound in Christ's side resonates amongst many female
mystics as a vaginal point of entry, which leads to a spiritual gestation and a

---

[3]   C.W. Bynum, 'The Female Body and Religious Practice in the Later Middle Ages'
in *Fragmentation and Redemption: Essays on Gender and the Human Body in Medieval
Religion* (New York: Zone Books, 1991), pp. 181–238, at p. 183.

[4]   Bynum, *Jesus as Mother*, p. 191.

[5]   Ibid., p. 192.

final transformative rebirth.[6] She argues that Julian of Norwich's motherhood of Jesus theology transcends mere simile in this respect. Rather than dismissing any phenomena, including strict enclosure, extreme fasting, illness or self-mortification, as by-products of psychological frailty, she locates them in a devotional framework where the female body is considered an instrument for growing closer to God.[7] Emphasising Christ's humanity in the devotional activity of religious women, she rejects the assumption that acts of bodily mortification were expressions of body hatred, shaped by ideas of the female body as lustful, emotional and disorderly.[8]

Bynum argues that the integration of the physical and spiritual is perfectly illustrated in the erotic poetry of the mid-thirteenth-century beguine Hadewijch.[9] Hadewijch describes the visions she received as 'tokens of love'.[10] The closeness that Hadewijch speaks of between herself and God, her lover, culminates in mutual consumption, 'each one as it were tasting all, eating all, drinking all, consuming all the other'.[11] The interaction of the physical and spiritual was repeated in the visions shown to many religious women.[12] In a vivid example Bynum describes a vision received by the French Carthusian Marguerite of Oingt (d. 1310). Marguerite sees herself as a withered tree irrigated by a torrent of water that represents Christ. Once nourished by Christ, Marguerite is able to read the names of the five senses (sight, hearing, taste, smell and touch) on her flowering branches.[13] As Bynum observes, 'It is hard to imagine a more pointed way of indicating that the effect of experiencing Christ is to "turn on" so to speak, the bodily senses of the receiving mystic'.[14] Bynum argues that women who receive such experiences have a tendency to 'somatize' them. She acknowledges that somatic language is not the exclusive property of medieval women. Men also talk about their experiences and use the kinds of images that she identifies with female mysticism. Her argument is that, whereas male writers use imagery and language to describe the state of

---

[6]   For a vivid representation of the wound in Christ's side as vaginal, see J.F. Hamburger, *The Visual and the Visionary: Art and Female Spirituality in Late Medieval Germany* (New York: Zone Books, 1998), p. 142.

[7]   This section focuses on three essays found in Caroline Walker Bynum's book *Fragmentation and Redemption: Essays on Gender and the Human Body in Medieval Religion*: 'The Body of Christ in the Later Middle Ages: A Reply to Leo Steinberg', pp. 79–118; '"... And Woman His Humanity": Female Imagery in Religious Writing of the Later Middle Ages', pp. 151–79; and 'The Female Body and Religious Practice in the Later Middle Ages', pp. 181–238.

[8]   Bynum, '"... And Woman His Humanity"', p. 152.

[9]   Bynum, 'The Body of Christ', p. 86.

[10]   E.A. Petroff (ed.), *Medieval Women's Visionary Literature* (New York and Oxford: Oxford University Press, 1986), pp. 189–200.

[11]   Ibid., p. 194.

[12]   Bynum, 'The Female Body', p. 191.

[13]   Ibid., p. 192.

[14]   Ibid., p. 192.

a mystical encounter with God or Christ, women describe their encounters as 'my experience'. Women internalised language and imagery in a way not commonly found in men. They also show a much greater usage of feeding and fertility imagery than their male counterparts. This is accompanied by a graphic devotion to Christ's sufferings in which women often link the very personal nature of their experiences to the suffering body of Christ as a female body.[15]

Bynum thus draws attention to the Middle Ages as a special case that illustrates the unique struggle of women to give voice to their spiritual desires. Her analysis seeks to allow that voice to be heard more clearly and suggests that female spirituality needs to be read on its own terms. She stresses that future historians need to pay attention to all that seems weird and wonderful in the writings of female spirituality, and not judge it by categories that are either too modern or misogynistic to appreciate its worth.

> The task for future historians of women's piety is not only to devote more detailed study to texts by women but also to pay attention to the full range of phenomena in these texts, no matter how masochistic or altruistic, unattractive or heroic, peculiar, amusing, or charming such phenomena may seem, either by modern standards or by those of medieval men.[16]

In this complex way, Bynum seeks to explain the more embodied forms of mysticism that she finds in the writings of many female mystics.

Embodied Mysticism in the Writings of Female Mysticism

We will consider three examples of the forms of embodied mysticism that Bynum's reading seeks to defend as mysticism.

Mechtild of Magdeburg (1210–82)

Mechtild of Magdeburg's writing exhibits a number of features that are considered distinctively feminine. Margot Schmit refers to the way in which Mechtild merges themes such as Christ the physician with love for God. This brings a distinctly human element into the motif of erotic love. Not only does God's love for Mechtild change and transform her; her erotic love for God is able to lay hold of Christ and force him into a place of intimacy. *Eros* is all powerful because the action takes place at an embodied level. Schmit quotes the following passage from *The Flowing Light of the Godhead* where the soul and God enter into dialogue:

---

[15]   Ibid., pp. 93–102.

[16]   C.W. Bynum, 'Religious Women in the Later Middle Ages, in J. Raitt (ed.) *Christian Spirituality: High Middle Ages and Reformation* (New York: Crossroad, 1988), pp. 121–39, at p. 137; quoted in McGinn, *The Flowering of Mysticism*, p. 16.

Soul: 'Lord, you are constantly love sick for me
    That you have clearly shown personally.
    You have written me into your book of the Godhead;
    You have painted me in your humanity;
    You have buried me in your heart …
    Ah, allow me, my dear One, to pour balsam upon you.'
God: 'Oh, One dear to my heart, where shall you find the balm?'
Soul: 'Oh Lord, I was going to tear the heart of my soul in two and intended
    to put you in it.'

The love between the soul and God is both mutual and homely. Mechtild speaks of a relationship between God and the soul where 'hand touches hand' and 'mouth speaks to mouth'. The embodied dimension of her understanding of union is apparent. This is a feature echoed in the writings of other female mystics, such as Gertrude of Helfta and Margery Kempe.

Gertrude of Helfta

In her early twenties, Gertrude of Helfta (1256–*c*.1302) was consumed by a deep melancholy after she lost interest in intellectual pursuit of God. On 27 January 1281, Gertrude was saved from this by a vision of Christ who appeared to her as a handsome 16-sixteen year old. Christ speaks to Gertrude and tells her, in affectionate terms, that he is her salvation. Consider the following passage from her *Herald of Divine Love*:

> I heard these words: 'I will save you. I will deliver you. Do not fear.' With this, I saw his hand, tender and fine, holding mine ... and he added 'With my enemies you have licked the dust (cf. Ps 71.9) and sucked honey among thorns. Come back to me now, and I will inebriate you with the torrent of my divine pleasure.' (Ps. 35.9).[17]

As Gertrude listens to the comforting words of this youthful Christ, and feels his tender touch, she comes to visualise a thorny hedge representing her faults and crimes. These separate her from Christ, her lover. However, in an instant, Christ lifts Gertrude over the hedge and places her by his side. When she is offered Christ's hand Gertrude notices his wounds. These come to mark her permanent detachment from the vanities of her intellectual life. In gender terms it is interesting that Gertrude should so dramatically abandon her intellectual self-improvement in favour of this deeply erotic and homely relationship with Christ.

---

[17]   Gertude of Helfta, *The Herald of Divine Love*, trans. and ed. M. Winkworth (New York: Paulist Press, 1993), p. 95.

Margery Kempe

Another example of embodied mysticism is found in the *Book* of Margery Kempe (1373–1439). Margery was a complex individual, prone to bouts of hysteria and weeping. She describes her relationship with Jesus in very intimate and erotic language. In a passage already referred to in Part I of this book, Christ plays the seducer:

> Therefore must I needs be homely with you and lie in your bed with you. Daughter, you desire greatly to see me, and you may boldly, when you are in your bed, take me to you as your wedded husband, as your most worthy darling, and as your sweet son, for I will be loved as a son should be loved by the mother and will that you love me, daughter, as a good wife ought to love her husband. And therefore you may boldly take me in the arms of your soul and kiss my mouth, my head, and my feet as sweetly as you will.[18]

Margery's relationship with Christ is remarkably homely. There is a complex admixture of images in the passage. Christ is Margery's lover, husband and son. These tangible characteristics are offset by Margery's instruction to hold and kiss Christ in the arms of her soul. As we noted earlier, even where Margery discusses the Trinity she does so in very embodied terms – picturing each person of the Trinity as a different cushion.

Margery was also well known amongst contemporaries for her weeping and hysterical behaviour. The habit started when she arrived in the Netherlands on her way to the Holy Land. Margery's tears continue throughout her pilgrimage, much to the annoyance of her fellow pilgrims, and when she reaches Jerusalem 'roaring' is added to weeping. At one point a friar asks for Margery to be ejected from church because her weeping was disrupting his sermon. Margery herself believes that her tears are a gift from God. Another example of such 'holy tears' is found in the writings of St Umiltà of Faenza who says that her tears resulted from being elevated to heaven and then returned to the darkness of earth:

> From my eyes there came one stream only, that was for me a sweet bath in which I continually delighted, overcoming all weakness. My face that was luminous is now dark. O unhappy me![19]

Marie of Oignies and St Bridget of Sweden also described having such holy tears.

---

18 Kempe, *The Book of Margery Kempe*, p. 66.
19 Quoted in Petroff, *Medieval Women's Visionary* Literature, p. 248.

By and large Bynum's theory of the gendering of mysticism has been widely accepted. Most consider it a reasonable challenge to earlier perennialist readings of female mysticism. These we will now briefly consider, along with a number of more contextualised responses, although most are not contextualist in the strict sense discussed in Part I. After this we will turn to consider several important feminist responses that themselves either contextualise or challenge Bynum's approach.

Perennialist Readings

Perennialists such as William James dismiss the more embodied and hysterical forms of women's mysticism as less than mystical. For James, these women are not describing ineffable experiences, so their writings are not mystical. Bynum notes that he describes such writings as 'theopathic, absurd and puerile'.[20] Other perennialist scholars who have followed James in taking this line include William R. Inge, who describes Gertrude of Helfta's *Herald of Divine Love* as 'a paltry record of sickly compliments and semi-erotic endearments'.[21] As such, he sees it as anything but mystical. David Knowles has been kinder to female mystics like Julian of Norwich, who produces a more ecstatic form of visionary mysticism, which can more easily be read as an attempt to describe an experience which cannot be conveyed. However, the embodied form of spiritual sensation and physical eroticism that Knowles finds in Margery Kempe's *Book* is bluntly condemned.

> With Margery Kempe … though visions and revelations make up a considerable part of the story from start to finish, they do not … deepen the writer's spiritual insight … Margery Kempe is, in fact, a figure of a different kind [to Julian of Norwich], more homely, perhaps, and even more comprehensible, but of an altogether coarser mould … the numerous marvels and visions and locutions, though never repellent and rarely silly, are the least striking part of her book; they give something of the same impression as do a series of banal conversations in an otherwise well-written novel of adventure.[22]

Knowles thus argues that Margery's *Book* is only worth reading as an example of mercantile life in later medieval England, its mystical aspects are of little value, and can largely be ignored.

---

[20]   James, *The Varieties of Religious Experience*, p. 275; quoted in Bynum, *Jesus as Mother*, p. 171.

[21]   W.R. Inge, *Studies in English Mystics: St. Margaret's Lectures 1905* (London: John Murray, 1906), p. 52; quoted in Bynum, *Jesus as Mother*, p. 171.

[22]   D. Knowles, *The English Mystical Tradition*, (London: Burns and Oates, 1961), pp.143–4.

Writing more recently, and therefore responding to contextualist developments, Peter Dinzelbacher is critical of the tendency he sees in modern scholarship to reduce mystical texts to little more than a collection of images and metaphors, thereby forgetting that the essence of this literature is an ineffable experience of the divine:

> I feel that paradoxically the mystagogic and mystographic aspects have been studied much more intensively by modern scholars than the records of mystical experience, notwithstanding that very experience being the explicit intention of all mystology, nay, the *raison d'être* of this genre literary … there also exists a tendency … to interpret records of charismatic events … not as evidence of mysticism experienced but as mere metaphorical expressions and genre-inherent topoi … reducing them to mystology.[23]

For Dinzelbacher, what actually makes visions, trances, tears and all manner of other physical phenomena mystical is the relationship to Jesus that is expressed in and through them, where they are then part of a mystical journey that culminates in mystical union. As such, he is himself critical of perennialists like Cuthbert Butler and W.T. Stace, who exclusively privilege the notion of union:

> I think it is quite unsuitable to restrict a definition of mysticism experienced … in this period … to the soul's union with the Lord itself. All the varied phenomenon and sensations which prepare and accompany this experience should be regarded as truly mystical …[24]

As such, Dinzelbacher is willing to expand a perennialist taxonomy of mysticism. He warns, however, that most physical experiences of this nature are not mystical precisely because they are not associated with mystical union. 'Most visions, apparitions, audition etc. of other contents have nothing to do with mysticism.'[25] Yet Dinzelbacher's discussion of mysticism in his essay 'The Beginnings of Mysticism Experienced in Twelfth-Century England' suggests that the type of physical spirituality that has come to be associated by Bynum with women has, in fact, a much less gender-specific heritage. He notes how men engage in holy weeping and visions alongside women. What concerns him is that when connected to union, this more practical physical mysticism cannot be accounted for purely in terms of culture. He believes that its origins are both 'social and psychic'.[26] Yet in

---

[23]   P. Dinzelbacher, 'The Beginnings of Mysticism Experienced in Twelfth-Century England', in M. Glasscoe (ed.) *The Medieval Mystical Tradition in England IV: The Exeter Symposium IV: Papers read at Dartington Hall, July 1987* (Cambridge: D.S. Brewer, 1987), pp. 111–31, at p. 111.

[24]   Ibid., p. 112.

[25]   Ibid., p. 112.

[26]   Ibid., p. 127.

accepting that context may have some impact on the shape of new mysticism he moves towards a more contextualised position.

Contextualised Readings

Those who take a more contextualised approach challenge perennialist readings of female mysticism on a number of grounds. They argue that when read in relation to their historical context we see that women were constrained both by beliefs about female spirituality and by, in many cases, not being able to write down their own accounts of mysticism. The arguments presented by contextualised readings fall roughly into two categories: those that relate to issues of authority and authorship, and those that discuss taxonomy. The number of scholars who write on these issues is vast. We will draw attention to only a few of them.

Context and Taxonomy

David Wallace One issue that concerns those who seek to offer more contextualised readings of the mystics is what they see as a general inadequacy of the perennialist taxonomy. David Wallace, for example, notes the problems that arise when modern scholars try to fit a character like Margery Kempe into a perennialist understanding of mysticism. He suggests that what this indicates it not that there is something wrong with Margery's *Book*, which claims to be an account of contemplation, but with the categories that we are using: 'Much of the abuse that has been lavished on Margery reflects critical frustration: her *Book* refuses to adapt itself to the critical categories that have been prepared for it.'[27] Wallace warns of the dangers of reading accounts of mystics at 'a remove from the secular world', as though untouched by society and context. He sets out to show how not even mystics can escape culture and that to truly understand mystical writers we need to look at the cultural practices that surrounded them and reflect on how these have shaped their writings. He notes that certain aspects of Margery Kempe's devotion seem less unusual when we consider them in relation to the spirituality of her time. For example, imaginative meditation on the life of Jesus became extremely popular in the later Middle Ages. There are many elements within her *Book* that suggest that Margery was influenced by this spiritual practice. Wallace suggests that what we find in Margery is actually a woman steeped in the spirituality of the later Middle Ages, who used the devotions available to her try to transgress (albeit it unsuccessfully) the models of female spirituality into which she was supposed to fit.

---

[27] D. Wallace, 'Mystic and Followers in Siena and East Anglia: A Study of Taxonomy. Class and Cultural Mediation', in M. Glasscoe (ed.), *The Medieval Mystical Tradition in England: Papers read at Dartington Hall, July 1984* (Cambridge: D.S. Brewer, 1984), pp. 169–91, at p. 169.

Authorship and Authority in Female Mystical Texts

As in the case of Margery Kempe, opportunities for women to receive a good education were few and far between. Rather than writing their texts themselves, they commonly used the services of a male scribe to record the detailed descriptions of their visions and spiritual encounters. The scribe was often also the spiritual confessor and director of the mystic. This complex relationship makes it unclear how much authorial control women had over the production of their texts. For example, while most scholars assume that Julian of Norwich can be treated as the author of her text, the case is less clear with writers like Margery Kempe and Marie d'Oignies.

Another related issue, which Bernard McGinn draws attention to, is the extent to which women were able to relay the actual content of their mysticism given the constraints of the misogynistic society in which they lived. While men were able to claim the direct influence of the divine, this was more difficult for women, who were considered less spirituality capable than men and so more prone to the deceptions of Satan. As McGinn comments:

> It is important to remember at the outset that women mystics had to face problems and issues that most male mystics did not. Foremost among these was the issue of what authority the mystic claimed for her writings … The teachings and life stories of the mystics … both men and women … usually involving the possession of special graces and the call to present a message about attaining God … it was relatively easy for most male mystics, because of their theological education and clerical status to make such claims … the difficulties were far greater for women.[28]

As we noted in Chapter 4, women found themselves in a difficult position. They might face a struggle if they wanted to retain control of their texts, as in the case of Angela of Foligno.[29] However, to retain control could also be dangerous – as we will discuss in Chapter 10, Marguerite Porete was burnt at the stake for failing to suppress her book. There was also great pressure to conform, either to shape texts so that they reflected accepted 'female' models of spirituality, or to practise such modes of spirituality in the first place. Amy Hollywood therefore cautions against reading accounts of female spirituality without embedding them carefully in the social context of the time. Even if male scribes did not alter women's accounts to make them fit with gender-appropriate spiritual conventions, Hollywood stresses that we cannot simply read embodied mysticism as a liberating form of female spirituality.

According to Hollywood, studies of mysticism and gender take a wrong turn when they look for something deeply subjective in the spiritual life of women and

---

[28]   McGinn, *The Flowering of Mysticism*, p. 154.
[29]   For a discussion of this, see ibid, pp. 149–50.

identify it as essentially feminine. The reality of why female mysticism appears in the form it does is more complex. It is tied to social norms, to expectations and authoritative conventions that are quite possibly anything but feminine. She therefore offers a warning against an easy association of the body and women that in the end only serves to reinforce the male gender-stereotypes that medieval women were fighting against. For Hollywood, such a reading misses the full disruptive potential of the female mystic who cannot easily be contained within established, male-prescribed categories of the feminine. In suggesting this Hollywood takes a stance towards female mysticism more akin to that of earlier feminists such as Irigaray, Kristeva and Beauvoir (whose accounts of female mysticism are discussed below). She values mysticism precisely because the male oppressiveness of religion is threatened by the mystic and the hysteric. It is this which she sees the gendering of embodied mysticism in Bynum's approach threatening to nullify despite its attempt to do the opposite.

Feminist Readings

Earlier Feminist Discussion of Women's Mysticism

Feminists pre-Bynum were interested in women's mystical writings because they saw them as potentially disruptive of misogyny. They argue that mysticism has the potential to liberate femininity specifically because of its emphasis on the body. For these writers, the female body acts as a discursive site through which transcendence takes place. They regard the mystic's disruptive tendencies as a positive means of connectivity with the divine. Also of interest for our general discussion of mysticism is the idea that experience is privileged over language, not from a perennialist perspective but because it overcomes the patriarchal nature of language. The five feminist scholars considered below discuss mysticism in relation to a far larger discussion of society and religion. Here we highlight only those ideas that are particularly pertinent to their discussions of mysticism.

Simone de Beauvoir   Simone de Beauvoir discusses mysticism in her book *The Second Sex*, in relation to her belief that being a 'woman' is a social category constructed by dominant males. 'One is not born a woman, but rather becomes a woman.'[30] In her own life, Beauvoir shifted between infatuations with men of influence and intellectual stature, and a strong desire for the infinite. Yet, whether it was love of men or love of God, Beauvoir thought that women limited themselves whenever they utilised love to justify their existence through another. She believed that female mysticism (the possibility of transcending male-defined norms) was an extension of women's limited gender identity. Amy Hollywood

---

[30]   S. de Beauvoir, *The Second Sex*, trans. H.M. Prashley (Harmondsworth: Penguin, 1972), p. 267.

explains, Beauvoir believed that 'since women are deemed incapable of achieving transcendence except through men, in men's absence, they turn to the male God'.[31] Beauvoir thought that neither human nor divine love ultimately afforded women the opportunity to transcend their sex. Even in its mystical mode, where women were said to love men and the male God in a divine way, women were committing themselves to an imminent relationship to maleness – either directly or in its absence.

However, Beauvoir insisted that some women mystics, principally Teresa of Avila, loved God with a control that did not reduce that love to physiological expressions. Teresa, Beauvoir claims, is not hysterical, nor was she the slave of her hormones, nor did the value of Teresa's mystical experience lie in any subjective pleasure she experienced; it rested on its objective outcomes. In this respect, Teresa is, in Beauvoir's estimation, different to her fellow Carmelite sisters. For whereas Teresa sought out questions of universal significance and in so doing affected a transcendence of her sexual nature, the so-called 'lesser women' wished only to achieve an ultimate form of feminine experience.

Beauvoir also argues that women mystics needed to immerse themselves in the body in order to own it as something irreducibly female. In Christian terms salvation was made possible by the suffering body of Christ – a mirror image of the suffering female body: 'the Man-God has assumed her role. It is she who is hanging on the tree, promised the splendour of Resurrection.'[32] As the site of salvation for the female mystic the body causes an unresolved tension in Beauvoir's thinking. On the one hand she insists that mystics like Teresa reach beyond the body to the universal, yet, on the other hand, she is certain that anything imminent such as the body cannot successfully achieve transcendence.

Luce Irigaray Luce Irigaray believed that, if subjectivity is achieved through entry into language and language is masculine, it follows that women can only achieve subjectivity by becoming masculine themselves. The consequence is that femininity falls silent and the powerful masculine discourses of politics, law, science and religion ensure women's marginal existence. Irigaray's unique contribution to gender studies is her insistence that the normative male symbolic, particularly the religious, must be disrupted so that women's voices can be heard. Female mystical texts provided Irigaray with some insight into how a disruption of the masculine religion can be achieved, and a site for the feminine recovered.

Irigaray connected mysticism with the body and, because the body is intrinsically linked to sexual difference, she felt that mysticism disrupted the masculine, firmly establishing women's *différence*. Irigaray's reading of mystical texts focused on aspects of bodily experience that challenged the objective nature of language. For her, the body is the site of femininity – femininity is not, as Lacan would have it, a matter of discourse. This is because she sees the body as

---

31   Hollywood, *Sensible Ecstasy* p. 127.
32   Quoted in Hollywood, *Sensible Ecstasy*, p. 130.

closer to the more fluid, tactile world. 'Touch' therefore becomes, for Irigaray, a feature of feminine subjectivity. She holds that touch confuses the language-defined differences between self and other, subject and object, and so language itself begins to falter in its attempts to describe bodily experience. For Irigaray, the female body's ability to unsettle language is comparable to the mystic's ineffable encounter with God. As such, the mystical text is less important to Irigaray than the female body. Hollywood explains that, 'Irigaray reduces mystical language to pure affect – a barely articulated song that conveys emotion with little if any signifying power'.[33] The female body replaces the textual world as the point of inscription. It is a safe place where both the feminine and God are liberated from the restraints of patriarchal discourse.

Irigaray was, however, suspicious of extreme forms of bodily asceticism. Instead she emphasised a deeply inward change in the female body and as such was fascinated by metaphors that challenged straightforward categorisation of inward and outward and masculine and feminine. In her later work, she referred to this inward change, anchored in the body, as a 'sensible transcendental' – a transcendence rooted in immanence.[34] Like Christ's sacrificial body, Irigaray sees the female body as wounded and broken. It is therefore a perfect site for overturning the objective neatness of male discourse through the chaos of inarticulate, fluid, inward metaphors for bodily experience. It is this which, for her, female mysticism attempts to harness.

Julia Kristeva   Julia Kristeva is also concerned with the relationship between immanence and transcendence. In *The Feminine and the Sacred*, Kristeva considers Angela of Foligno's erotic encounter with God. Kristeva interprets Angela's writing as an attempt to represent an immanent, bodily experience of a God that cannot be represented in concrete terms. Kristeva is impressed that Angela does not let go of her primal bodily experience, but neither does she conflate the transcendental quality of the experience with the material world. Rather, Angela affirms the transcendental potential of the immanent body, specifically the maternal body. For Kristeva, transcendence is not what lies beyond the immanent body, it is access to the immanent body – to its very beginnings. Kristeva's use of mystical texts is an attempt to liberate the sacred from its repression in religion and belief. In particular, Kristeva was keen to free the sexual potential of the sacred, which she described as 'unconscious recognition of an unsustainable eroticism'.[35] The physicality of language is therefore a theme that dominates her work. Whether it is spoken or written, in the first instance, language requires a body to produce sounds and to make the marks on a page we recognise as writing.

---

[33]   Ibid., p. 197.

[34]   L. Irigaray, *Ethique de la différence sexuelle* (Paris: Gallimard, 1960), p. 111.

[35]   From Kristeva's *Le féminin et le sacré*, quoted in A. Bradley, '"Mystic Atheism": Julia Kristeva's Negative Theology', *Theology and* Sexuality, 14/3 (2008), 279–92, at p. 283.

While the physical basis of language precedes the symbolic where it is given order and logic, without the symbolic world, for Kristeva, there would be no language or culture. Kristeva uses Plato's term '*chora*' from *The Timaeus*, a maternal receptacle of disorder and nourishment, to illustrate the shift from an unstable, formless semiotic world of primal drives to the order that is imposed in the symbolic. According to Plato, it is only when a deity intervenes that the *chora* can become ordered. Kristeva likens this intervention to Lacan's 'Name of the Father', the prescriptive male discourse that determines the ordered symbolic world and the subject who occupies it. As such, female mysticism illustrates an important transition to psychoanalysis. Female mystics move beyond theology to what Kristeva terms 'mystic atheism' – where the idea of otherness is found within the mystic rather than in some external deity. In doing so, male language is superseded by female experience. Thus, she is less interested in the standard psychoanalytic study of speech development than the *chora*, the emotional drive and flow of language that precedes rationalisation. She describes the *chora* as 'prior to the One, the father, even the syllable, metaphorically suggesting something nourishing and maternal'.[36] For Kristeva, the *chora* is more than a mere metaphor. She makes the connection between the maternal body and the child's earliest language development in pregnancy. The bodily basis of language is therefore inseparable from the mother's body – it is the possibility for any speaking subject at all. Kristeva's writing on religion and mysticism reflects this commitment to psychoanalysis. She thought that the female body was in a unique position to experience the sacred, positioned as it is between women's biological nature and the symbolic value attached to the biological. She does not hold that the sacred can show itself in the symbolic; rather, Kristeva saw the sacred as the resistance to the symbolic order of the religious that she associates with maleness. She believes that female mysticism exemplifies this resistance. Two important ideas for the subsequent study of mysticism are 'the abject' and '*jouissance*'. For Kristeva, the abject is the otherness on which identity is built but which always threatens its stability. We can know it only through *jouissance*, in a manner that it both painful and violent, since it transcends both knowledge and desire.

Catherine Clément and Hélène Cixous   Hélène Cixous and Catherine Clément also discuss the disruptive function of female mysticism. Yet they disagree over the hysterical behaviour often associated with female mystics such as self-mortification, bouts of screaming and intense visions. Clément argues that hysteria is contained within the oppressive structures of male-dominated society. The hysteric may cause mild alarm or embarrassment, a fact that for her only serves to reinforce the rigid norms of a more rational and measured patriarchy. Cixous, however, insists that the female's hysteria is a liberating and creative force that is seated in desire. Desire, according to Cixous, can be suppressed but

---

[36]   G.M. Jantzen, *Becoming Divine: Towards a Feminist Philospohy of Religion* (Manchester: Manchester University Press, 1998), p. 195.

it can never die. Both Clément and Cixous agree that the hysterical phenomena reported by female mystics and ascribed to them is straightforwardly pathological. But far from diminishing its religious value, in Cixous's writing the value of the pathological is increased precisely because it is aligned with mysticism and not religion. The pathological appearance of some forms of mystical phenomena was therefore generally accepted as a good cause for rejecting its religious value, as we will further discuss in Chapter 8. As such, for Cixous, women's mysticism serves an important disruptive function, one that helps liberate women from male religion.

Developments in Understanding Women's Mysticism Post-Bynum

A large number of scholars have commented on and critiqued earlier feminist discussions of mysticism.[37] These discussions have then found there way into expositions of the type of female mysticism with which this chapter is concerned. We have already considered Amy Hollywood above. Susannah Chewning has likewise argued that we see an awareness in female mystical texts, and even in devotional material composed for women by men, that women need to move beyond the categories by which they are defined in language if they are to connect with that which lies beyond. Drawing on Lacan, she notes a conflict between the female Imaginary (the world as perceived by women), the Symbolic (which appears in the language of patriarchy) and the Real (that which lies beyond). She notes that Kristeva holds that to operate within the Symbolic women must deny their own Imaginaries. Following Kristeva she holds that in desiring mystical union women seek a return to their own Imaginary: 'The mystic's desire for union with the Divine, for a return to what Kristeva, borrowing from Plato, refers to as the *chora*, is part of the Imaginary. But the location of that state of being is the Real.'[38] Just as in the *chora*, the mystic loses her self–identity in mystical union as she enters into the Real. In this sense experience overthrows language. Chewning cannot be accused of anthropomorphising otherness in the same way

---

[37]   For a discussion of body theology, see, for example, J. Butler, *Bodies that Matter: On the Discursive Limits of 'Sex'* (London: Routledge, 1993), p. ix; See J. Nelson *Body Theology* (Louisville: Westminster/John Knox, 1992), a study of 'body theology' that discusses the notion of illness in relation to HIV and AIDS, embryo development in the context of personhood, and the ethical complexity of couples making 'reproductive choices'; L. Sullivan, 'Body Works: Knowledge of the Body in the Study of Religion', *History of Religions*, 30 (1990), 86–99.

[38]   S.M. Chewning, '"Mi bodi henge / wið þi bodi': The Paradox of Sensuality in þe Wohunge of Ure Lauerd", in S.M. Chewning (ed.), Intersections of Sexuality and the Divine in Medieval Culture: The Word Made Flesh (Aldershot: Ashgate, 2005), pp. 183–96, at p. 190; Also see her 'Mysticism and the Anchoritic Community: "A Time of Veiled Infinity"', in D. Watt (ed.), Medieval Women in their Communities (Cardiff: University of Wales Press, 1997), pp. 116–37.

that Kristeva can, however, since Chewning connects the experience of otherness with an experience beyond the self that is in some sense ineffable.[39]

Beverly Lanzetta has argued for the idea of the *via feminina* or 'the feminine way'. *Via feminina* is a conspicuously feminist contemplative path that emancipates women from the oppression of religious traditions defined in male terms. Lanzetta employs the dialectic of apophasis to shift women's spiritual experience away from patriarchal norms by 'unsaying' the limiting, abusive nature of these norms. The apophatic process that Lanzetta prescribes however does not stay in a constant state of 'unsaying' in the way that it does for Sells. Instead she believes that the female mystic is able to return to language and express herself in accordance with a new self-understanding and a new vision of the sacred.[40]

Numerous scholars of mysticism have also followed and extended Bynum's reading of female mysticism seeing her approach too as exemplifying female empowerment.[41] Lynn Staley, for example, asks us to recognise Margery Kempe not as a 'female hysteric', but as a writer who employed the fiction of the holy woman as a persona to subvert accounts of medieval religious life, from the relative safety of a gender with no social status or influence.[42] Denis Renevey, who combines this type of reading with that suggested by earlier feminists, argues that Margery Kempe's body becomes the site in which she performs her mysticism, so elevating the body as a place of divine interface. Thus, while Bynum's theory has become the accepted reading of embodied female mysticism, a number of scholars have critiqued and nuanced her general approach in a variety of ways.

---

[39]   For a critique of Kristeva's 'mystic atheism' for anthropomorphising otherness, see Bradley, '"Mystic Atheism"'. In taking this approach Chewning reconfigures the erotic as the means of transcendence, arguing that its potential to allow women to transcend societal descriptions is a possible reason for its prevalence in women's mystical writing.

[40]   B.J. Lanzetta, *The Other Side of Nothingness: Toward A Theology of Radical Openness* (Albany: State University of New York, 2001); *Radical Wisdom: A Feminist Mystical Theology* (Minneapolis: Fortress Press, 2005).

[41]   See, for example, K. Lochrie, *Margery Kempe and the Translations of the Flesh* (Philadelphia: University of Pennsylvania Press, 1991); S. Beckwith, 'A Very Material Mysticism: The Medieval Mysticism of Margery Kempe', in D. Aers (ed.), *Medieval Literature: Criticism, Ideology and History* (Brighton: Harvester Press, 1986), pp. 34–57. For a useful overview, see S. Coakley, 'Introduction', in S. Coakley (ed.), *Religion and the Body* (Cambridge: Cambridge University Press, 1997), pp. 1–12.

[42]   L.S. Johnson, 'The Trope of the Scribe and the Question of Literary Authority in the Works of Julian of Norwich and Margery Kempe', *Speculum*, 66 (1991), 820–38, and D. Aers and L. Staley (eds), *The Powers of the Holy: Religion, Politics, and Gender in Late Medieval English Culture* (University Park, PA: Pennsylvania State University Press, 1996). D. Renevey, 'Margery Kempe's Performing Body: The Translation of Late Medieval Discursive Religious Practices' in D. Renevey and C. Whitehead (eds), *Writing Religious Women: Female Spirituality and Textual Practices in Late Medieval England* (Toronto: University of Toronto Press, 2000), pp. 197–216. Although Renevey comments that Margery is unable to translate her performances outside of her *Book* (p. 208).

Before we conclude this chapter we need to consider two other approaches to the issue of female mysticism, a rather more sceptical feminist critique offered by Patricia Ranft, who questions the extent to which female mysticism should be distinguished from its male counterpart, and the performative language readings of Sells and Turner.

Patricia Ranft   Contradicting earlier feminist readings of female mysticism, in her book *Women and Spiritual Equality in Christian Tradition*, Patricia Ranft disputes the idea that misogyny pervades every aspect of Christianity.[43] She draws attention to the influence of sainted women in Christian communities, and argues that these offered a paradigm of perfection to which women could aspire. She does not see how an analysis of such women can succeed using universal or 'essentialist' concepts of gender, biological sex and symbol, and asks the readers to picture the following scene:

> A medieval peasant woman going to Notre Dame cathedral at Chartres to celebrate the Annunciation gazed at Mary in the centre of an exquisite rose window dedicated to Mary, while she sang the *Ave Maria*, listened to a sermon on Mary's role in redemption, and prayed the Hail Mary. Everything around her focussed on the spiritual perfection of one creature, Mary.[44]

Ranft is confident that this exact scenario would have been enacted many times throughout Christian history. She sees it as a positive expression of women's spiritual equality, and a celebration, in spiritual terms, of the feminine. Thus in Ranft's work one cannot detect the hermeneutic of suspicion that pervades many feminist studies of female spirituality. When considering the mystical tradition, for example, she rejects the idea that the Flemish mystic Ruusbroec used bridal mysticism, the bridegroom being Christ and the bride being humanity, as a humility topos that reinforced the female stereotype as one of domestic inferior status.[45] Ranft argues that no medieval person would consider an intimate relationship with Christ as one of inferiority. She adds that nowhere in Ruusbroec's work is there 'a sense of his adoption of the female persona of bride as being an exercise in humility, a ritual of renunciation, or a demeaning role reversal'.[46] Instead, Ranft thinks that Ruusbroec's use of bridal language and the feminising of humanity picks out the crucial, democratising potential of mysticism. Ranft is therefore reticent to accept that women needed embodied mysticism to engage with the transcendent. In turn, however, she can be criticised for failing to fully recognise that women, as Grace Jantzen points out, begin from a different spiritual starting

---

[43]   Patricia Ranft, *Women and Spiritual Equality in Christian Tradition* (New York: St Martin's Press, 1998).

[44]   Ibid., p. xi.

[45]   Ibid., p. 183.

[46]   Ibid., p. 183.

point to men, and that this must be taken into account if we are not to confuse similarity with sameness. She also ignores Turner's readings of the erotic in which he stresses the inferiority of the soul in mystical marriage as an essential aspect of spiritual love.

Denys Turner and Michael Sells   Finally, both Denys Turner and Michael Sells consider that the writings of some female mystics contain examples of apophasis in the same sense that male accounts do. We noted, for example, in Chapter 4, how Sells argues that Marguerite Porete's account of mysticism constitutes a language of unsaying by creating what he terms 'an apophasis of desire'. Amy Hollywood agrees. In Chapter 8 we will discuss Turner's understanding of Julian of Norwich, whose writing he considers apophatic in the sense that image operates within it in such a way that it points beyond experience to the ineffability of God. However, neither comments on those female writers who offer more embodied forms of mysticism. Their performative language readings find no room for such discussions as accounts of apophasis; their strong linguistic emphasis seeming to precludes a female counter-experience through which male language is overcome. This experiential paucity seems a weakness of their both theories of mysticism.

Conclusion

In this chapter we have reflected on the idea, popularised by Caroline Walker Bynum, that women's mysticism is distinctively feminine. Bynum argues that women used their bodies to find a spiritual voice within the constraints of a male-dominated society and a patriarchal view of religion. For perennialists, however, these more embodied forms of mysticism are less than mystical because the experience that they describe is not ineffable. More contextualised readings present a challenge to perennialists and even Bynum. David Wallace argues that embodied forms of mysticism were influenced by other devotions of the time and that even mystics cannot be read apart from their context. As such, he argues that we need to alter our taxonomies of mysticism. Other contextualised readings have drawn attention to the complex interplay of social and cultural forces within the medieval period. Hollywood warns against a too simplistic reading of embodied spirituality that fails to take into account the social norms to which women were expected to conform. She argues that to ignore this could lead to a glorification of embodiment that merely reinforces misogyny. Like early feminist readings of mysticism, she and others have stressed the disruptive potential of female embodiment, seeing embodied mysticism as a challenge to patriarchy. Against this Patricia Ranft suggests that mysticism in general contains sufficient female imagery to allow a more gender-neutral understanding of mysticism, although she can herself be accused of overlooking important differences between male and female mysticism which previous feminist accounts highlight. Both Michael Sells and Denys Turner point out that some women produced forms of mysticism that were anything but embodied. However, their inability to accommodate the wider movement of female mysticism seems a weakness of both Sells's and Turner's positions.

The next chapter builds on the issues discussed here by turning to the related theme of visionary mysticism, a form of mysticism that was most prevalent amongst women.

Chapter 8
Visionary Mysticism

We noted in the previous chapter that visions were a particular feature of women's mystical writings. This chapter considers the issue of visions and their complex relationship to mysticism. Focusing on female visionary mysticism, we explore the sense in which visions can be regarded as the same thing as mysticism.

Medieval Theories of Vision

Medieval theories of vision ask a fundamental question – how is it possible for a human being to see God and in what sense is this the same as attaining knowledge of God? For most female mystics, writing in the later Middle Ages, the main theory with which their visionary mysticism had to contend was one proposed by Augustine.

Augustine's Three Types of Vision

In his *Literal Commentary on Genesis* Augustine distinguishes between three types of vision: bodily, spiritual and intellectual. Bodily vision is seeing with the eyes of the physical body – a process in which errors are possible. For example, when we are ill we sometimes see things that are not there. Spiritual vision is the exercise of the imagination, picturing physical things in the mind's eye as if they were present. Again, we can make mistakes. We can create fantastical images and misremember things. As we noted in Chapter 4, Augustine considered imagination to belong to the external part of a person since imagination depended on images that were connected to physical sight. Intellectual vision is the soul's inner mode of seeing. It does not depend on anything outside of the soul.

John Hammond Taylor notes that Augustine in fact distinguishes between two types of intellectual vision.[1] The first consists in understanding concepts. Drawing on Platonic beliefs about truth, Augustine reasons that real knowledge of concepts cannot depend on what is changeable and corruptible. It can only result from a vision of the unchangeable light of God, which exists within the soul. Only such a vision allows the soul to understand and pass judgements on concepts like love

---

[1] See his edition of Augustine, *The Literal Meaning of Genesis*, p. 316, n. 155. While corporeal and spiritual vision both also have two parts, Taylor notes that the difference between the levels here is nothing compared to the one that Augustine makes between the two types of intellectual vision, in which the distinction is absolute.

and beauty. However, the second kind of intellectual vision is a *direct* sight of God's illumination in the soul. This second type of intellectual vision is a form of ecstasy or rapture. Étienne Gilson refers to it as 'mystical knowledge'. Gilson clarifies the difference between these two forms of intellectual vision thus: 'when he [Augustine] speaks of knowledge by or in the eternal reason, he speaks of natural knowledge, but when he speaks of knowing or of seeing the eternal reasons and the divine light, he speaks of mystical knowledge'.[2]

Augustine clearly explains that this light within the soul is the source from which all understanding comes. Both bodily and spiritual vision rely on the higher parts of the soul to help them understand what they see. However, the higher parts of the soul do not need the lower parts, all they need to gain understanding is the light of God. Yet to catch a glimpse of God, to attain revelation from God, actually involves seeing this light. When this happens Augustine states that the soul is withdrawn from all bodily sensation. No part of its knowledge depends on anything changeable or that could be in error. Its knowledge comes directly from this infallible light which *is* God:

> But distinct from objects is the Light by which the soul is illumined, in order that it may see and truly understand everything, either in itself or in the light. For the Light is God Himself, whereas the soul is a creature; yet since it is rational and intellectual, it is made in His image. And when it tries to behold the Light, it trembles in its weakness and finds itself unable to do so. Yet from this source comes all the understanding it is able to attain. When, therefore, it is thus carried off, and being withdrawn from the senses of the body, is made present to this vision in a more perfect manner (not by a spatial relation, but in a way proper to its being), it also sees above itself that Light in whose illumination it is enabled to see all the objects that it sees and understands in itself.[3]

Augustine stresses the difference between such intellectual vision of God and more image-based visions by comparing the visions of St Paul in 2 Corinthians 12:2-4 and St John in The Book of Revelation. Augustine argues that Paul's vision is the superior because when Paul is caught up to the third heaven he is unsure whether his soul is still connected to his body. John's visions, on the other hand, depend on physical imagery.

Augustine further clarifies the difference between bodily, spiritual and intellectual sight in his short letter *On Seeing God*. He argues that, even though God assumed human nature in the Incarnation, looking at Christ's corporeal body cannot provide true knowledge of God since the physical eyes do not have the

[2]   É. Gilson, *The Christian Philosophy of St Augustine*, trans. L.E.M. Lynch (London: Victor Gollancz, 1961), p. 92.

[3]   Augustine, *The Literal Meaning of Genesis*, trans. J.H. Taylor, bk 12, xxxi.59, p. 222

capacity to see the light of God. Only after the resurrection, when the soul has a new resurrection body, will the physical eyes be able to function in this way:

> He [the Father] is not sought by bodily eyes, nor confined by our sight, nor held by touch, nor heard by His speaking, nor perceived in His approach. But the only-begotten Son who is in the bosom of the Father (Jn 1.18) soundlessly declares the nature and substance of the Godhead, and hence to eyes worthy and apt for such appearance He shows it invisibly ... Therefore whoever can see God invisibly can be united to God spiritually.[4]

Since true knowledge of God cannot be uncertain, this is why, when experiencing advanced ecstasy, St Paul was unsure what relationship, if any, his mind had to his corruptible body,

> He who heard 'secret words which it is not granted to man to utter' (2 Cor12:2–4) was so enraptured that a certain withdrawal of his consciousness from the senses of this life occurred, and he said that he did not know 'whether he was in the body or out of the body,' that is, as usually occurs in advanced ecstasy, when the mind is withdrawn from this life unto that life without loosing the tie of the body, or whether there is a complete separation as occurs in death.[5]

Augustine's understanding of vision was extremely pervasive and influenced the way that most theologians in the Middle Ages understood visions. His account influenced Boethius, whose understanding of cognition was also important in the Medieval Period.

Boethius's Modes of Cognition

Boethius (*c*.475–525), argues that there are four faculties through which cognition can occur: the senses, imagination, reason and intelligence. As in Augustine's model, he believes that lower modes of cognition get incorporated into the higher modes of cognition, but the higher modes do not need the lower ones. So, for example, reason can abstract ideas from the imagination, but the imagination cannot abstract ideas from reason. In his *Consolations of Philosophy*, Boethius clarifies this relationship through the character 'Philosophy', who explains that, while the higher faculties have access to the knowledge of lower faculties, they are actually able to attain such knowledge without recourse to them. As John Marenbon explains:

---

[4]   Augustine, 'On Seeing God', in *Augustine of Hippo: Selected Writings*, trans. M.T. Clark (New York: Paulist Press, 1984), pp. 365–402, at pp. 389–90.

[5]   Ibid., p. 385.

Yet Philosophy wishes to say that the cognitions of the thing, the image, the abstracted form and the Form (God himself) are all ways of cognizing the same thing, which is known in different ways – more perfectly by higher faculties, less perfectly by lower ones: 'the higher power of understanding', she explains, 'includes the lower one, but the lower one does not at all rise up to the higher one' ... So, for instance, the intelligence knows 'reason's universal and imagination's shape and the sensibly-perceptible matter, not by using reason or the imagination or the senses, but Formally in that one stroke of the mind, as I might put it, surveying all things'.[6]

For Boethius, human intelligence is the mode of cognition through which certain knowledge of God is possible. It is the closest mode to divine intelligence, which is the highest of all the modes of cognition. Like Augustine's therefore, Boethius's discussion of cognition depends on the Platonic concern with certainty of knowledge. For Boethius, while all modes of knowledge strive to know God, only intelligence is able to attain sure and perfect knowledge of God. Even though his discussions of the various modes of cognition do not focus on vision per se, they still influenced medieval thinking about what knowledge of God can and cannot consist in and so the relative value of visions.[7] Boethius's view reinforced Augustine's general understanding of visions as it had passed down to medieval readers: that infallible knowledge, that is, knowledge of God, cannot be based on the senses or the imagination.

The Challenge of Female Visionary Mysticism

As we discussed in the previous chapter, Bernard McGinn argues that one facet of the new mysticism that emerged in the later Middle Ages was that it took Christian mysticism in new directions. One such element of change related to the value of visions as sources of revelatory knowledge of God. It is perhaps worth repeating the passage from McGinn's *The Flowering of Mysticism* in which he claims that female visionary mysticism, in particular, blurred the delineation between types of vision as Augustine understood them:

> Many of the visions found in late medieval mystical texts, especially by women, tend to collapse the Augustinian hierarchy, not only by merging the spiritual and intellectual visions ... but also in ways that meld all three modes of vision into

---

[6]   J. Marebon, *Boethius* (Oxford: Oxford University Press, 2003), p. 133.

[7]   See V.A. Kolve *Chaucer and the Imagery of Narrative: The First Five Canterbury Tales* (Stanford: Stanford University Press, 1984); H.R. Patch, *The Tradition of Boethius: A Study of His Importance in Medieval Culture* (New York: Oxford University Press, 1935); P. Courcelle, *La Consolation de Philosophie dans la tradition littéraire: Antécédents et postérité. de Boèce* (Paris: Études Augustiniennes, 1967).

a direct form of 'total' conscious experience of God realised as much in and through the body as in a purely spiritual way.[8]

Female visionaries initiated this collapse of categories in two ways. Many demonstrated that their bodies were in effect dead during their visionary encounters, while others, in a more intellectual way, actively and consciously transgressed Augustine's visual categories.

Dead in Body, Alive in Spirit

Dyan Elliott notes that there are several examples of women whose revelatory experiences leave their bodies apparently dead. Vanna of Orvieto (d. 1306), would sit so still that flies settled on her half-open eyes. Vanna contested the suspicions of male clerics with further exhibitions of bodily rapture that demonstrated that the senses of her body had become totally disassociated from her soul. Such demonstrations allowed the strange physiological effects of Vanna's visions to be treated as a genuine aspect of her encounter with God; for example, Vanna sweated so much she could not wear clothes. Margaret of Cortona (d. 1297) also claimed to experience rapture. During one of her experiences, the community of Franciscans took the opportunity to throw her body about to satisfy themselves that she was totally desensitised.[9] Likewise Christina the Astonishing was said to be so withdrawn from the body that during her raptures she would curl up into a ball and whirl around the room.

> Sometimes when she was sitting with them [the nuns of St Catherine], she would speak of Christ and suddenly and unexpectedly she would be ravished in the spirit and her body would roll and whirl around like a hoop played with by boys. She whirled around with such extreme violence that the individual limbs of her body could not be distinguished. When she had whirled around for a long time in this manner ... all her limbs grew quiet. Then a wondrous harmony sounded from between her throat and her breast which no mortal man could understand, nor could it be imitated by any artificial instrument ... The voice or spiritual breath ... did not come out of her mouth or nose, but a harmony of the angelic voice resounded only from between her breath and throat.[10]

---

[8]   McGinn, *The Flowering of Mysticism*, p. 155.

[9]   D. Elliott, 'The Physiology of Rapture and Female Spirituality', in P. Biller and A. Minnis (eds), *Medieval Theology and the Natural Body* (Woodbridge: York Medieval Press), pp. 141–73, at p. 164.

[10]   Thomas Cantimpre, *The Life of Christina the Astonishing*, trans. M.H. King (Toronto: Peregrina, 1999); quoted in B.W. Holsinger, *Music, Body and Desire in Medieval Culture: Hildegard of Bingen to Chaucer* (Stanford: Stanford University Press, 2001), pp. 223–4.

In addition to these revelations of Christ, Christina claimed that during her initial experience of death she was able to lead souls out of hell. Afterwards she was acutely aware of the smell of sin carried by all humans. As the passage above illustrates, Christina's strange behaviour is explained by the author of her life, Thomas Cantimpre, in terms of a separation of body and soul. Yet in his discussion of Christina's rapture it is also apparent that, as indicated by her whirling limbs, there is a far greater integration of bodily, spiritual and intellectual vision than occurs in Augustine's categories. Various levels of integration are also a feature of the visual experiences of other female mystics. On her deathbed Bridget of Sweden had a vision of Christ using her bodily eyes. Alphonse of Jaén (d. 1388), who wrote the preface to her Life, argues that this is a true intellectual vision because it anticipated the vision she would enjoy in her resurrected body.[11] Yet other mystics, such as Julian of Norwich and Hildegard of Bingen, play with this relationship between death or illness and the possibility of a closer integration of intellectual, spiritual and physical sight in even more sophisticated ways.

Transgressing the Bounds of Intellectual Vision

Hildegard of Bingen   The theological writing of Hildegard of Bingen (1098–1179) comprises three large books *Scivias* (short for 'scito vias domini' meaning 'know the ways of the Lord'), *The Book of Life's Merits* and *The Book of Divine Works*. Each book is based on a series of visions that follows a similar pattern. This can be illustrated from her second vision in book II of her *Scivias*. First she describes what she saw; in this case a splendid light burning the most beautiful fire in which the figure of a man, sapphire in colour, stands. Then Hildegard records word for word what was said to her by a heavenly voice. After this, she offers her own tentative interpretation of the vision. Here she explains that this is a vision of the Trinity and its relationship to the Incarnation. The splendid light represents the Father, the fire the Holy Spirit and the figure of a sapphire-coloured man the Son. She then explores the dynamics of the Trinity in relation to the characteristics of a gemstone, explaining that, like the Trinity, three characteristics make up its essential unity – moisture, palpability and fire. The Trinity can furthermore be likened to such a gemstone. Like moisture, the Father is never exhausted, the Son is present in palpable flesh and the Holy Spirit is the kindler of human hearts.[12] As this illustrates, her vision plays with the categories of intellectual, spiritual and physical understanding, moving somewhat fluidly between them. This relationship is further reinforced by the illustrations that she commissioned to accompany her written account of her visions in *Scivias*, which were intended as meditative aids for those who read her work.

This fluid relationship between the physical and the spiritual is also reinforced by the fact that Hildegard's visions were often accompanied by intense physical

11   Elliott, 'The Physiology of Rapture', p. 164.
12   See Petroff, *Medieval Women's Visionary Literature*, p. 140.

pain and illness. It is in relation to this pain that she sees a light. She calls this light the 'reflection of the living light', and states that it is constantly with her. However, sometimes she sees another light within this 'reflection of the living light', which she describes as 'the living light'. She does not define the relationship between the two. However, the second light causes all pain and sorrow to vanish. Likewise, when she is receiving a vision, the pain that she feels is forgotten by the transformation that she undergoes as she tastes and sees within her soul. Yet while there are similarities with Augustine's account of light, Hildegard's discussion blurs the boundaries of Augustine's hierarchy of vision. On the one hand, in true Augustinian fashion, she reports a light within her soul and speaks of seeing a living light within it. Yet she transgresses the absoluteness of Augustine's understanding of intellectual vision. Any reader of Hildegard's *Scivias* also cannot help but be struck by the careful descriptions of vivid colours and familiar objects, and the illustrations of the visions made by her nuns. Thus while she claims to 'see' her visions spiritually not bodily and stresses too that she was not dreaming, for all this, Hildegard's discussion of intellectual vision does not stand apart from the other modes of seeing she discusses in the way that Augustine suggests it ought. Instead each mode of vision depends on the others, such that it is not clear that she really seeks to move beyond bodily and spiritual modes of vision to a pure imageless form of knowing.

Julian of Norwich   Another female mystic who similarly flouts the strong delineation between bodily, spiritual and intellectual vision is Julian of Norwich (*c.*1342–1413). One of the 'English Mystics', Julian wrote down her visions in her *Showings* or *Revelations of Divine Love*. The book appears in two versions, the first she wrote immediately after receiving the visions and the second after years of reflection.[13] Neither account simply records her visions, since the later version contains things she claims she 'saw' that are not included in the earlier text. When we look at the accounts it quickly becomes apparent that in both versions of her text, Julian has a very complex understanding of 'seeing'.

As with Hildegard, Julian's receipt of her initial visions is connected with illness. She asks God to allow her to share in Christ's suffering through illness and grant her a bodily vision of Christ's death, so that she may be a real witness to the event: 'for I would have been one of them and have suffered with them'.[14] She thus wanted a bodily vision that replicated active involvement in the crucifixion scene. She then states that God sent her an illness which caused her to remain bedridden for three days and three nights. On the fourth night, believing she would not last until morning, she received the last rites of the Church. In what she believed to be

---

[13]   Julian did not write the book herself. It was written down for her by an anonymous scribe. Nonetheless, most scholars believe that the content of the book is Julian's not her scribe's.

[14]   Julian of Norwich *Showings*, trans. Edmund Colledge OSA and James Walsh SJ (New York: Paulist Press, 1978), p. 126.

her last moments, Julian asked to be comforted by being lifted up in her bed and supported. The parson placed a crucifix in front of her. Suddenly, much to Julian's astonishment, all her pain vanished. It was then that she saw the blood flowing down Christ's head as he was crucified, as though she were present at his crucifixion.

> Suddenly I saw the red blood trickling down from under the crown, all hot, flowing freely and copiously, a living stream, just as it seemed to me that it was at the time when the crown of thorns was thrust down upon his blessed head. Just so did he, both God and man, suffer for me. I perceived, truly and powerfully, that it was himself who showed this to me, without any intermediary.[15]

The relationship between this bodily vision and spiritual sight is complicated by a second 'spiritual' vision which Julian sees at the same time. This was of an object the size of a hazelnut lying in her palm. The object is so small and fragile Julian says she expected it to 'fall into nothing'. She is shown spiritually that this fragile object is everything that God created and it will never be destroyed because God loves it. Julian intimately connects these two visions. The bodily vision does not simply 'signify' or 'symbolise' the spiritual vision and the abstract teaching that follows from it but, she says, her first vision of the crown of thorns contains all other visions and teachings that she sees. Visionary seeing is an on-going process for Julian in each of her texts and through time. It has no end. When she asks if her vision has an ultimate meaning God shows her that its meaning is simply love – a truth that can never be exhausted.

> And from the time that it was revealed, I desired many times to know in what was our Lord's meaning. And fifteen years after and more, I was answered in spiritual understanding, and it was said: What, do you wish to know your Lord's meaning in this thing? Know it well, love was his meaning. Who reveals it to you? Love. What did he reveal to you? Love. Why does he reveal it to you? For love. Remain in this, and you will know more of the same. But you will never know different, without end.[16]

So it is that in Julian's Long Text that she states that all her discussions of her visions are like an ABC compared with true knowledge of God.[17]

Julian appears to have been directly acquainted with Augustine's three categories of vision. When discussing her vision she divides seeing into three types: 'bodily vision', 'words formed in my understanding' and 'spiritual vision':

> All this blessed teaching was shown to me in three parts, that is by *bodily vision* and by *words formed in my understanding* and by *spiritual vision*. But I may not

---

¹⁵ Ibid., p. 129.
¹⁶ Ibid., p. 342.
¹⁷ Ibid., p. 276.

and cannot show the spiritual visions to you as plainly and fully as I should wish;
but I trust in our Lord God Almighty that he will.[18]

Yet it quickly becomes apparent, as the examples above illustrate, that these
categories are far from clear-cut. Elsewhere she explicitly uses the term 'spiritual
sight' for imaginative visions as well as intellectual understanding. She also adds
additional categories of seeing that further blur the distinction between the main
three. These include 'spiritual into bodily likeness' and 'most spiritual without
bodily likeness', which she uses as a descriptor of a vision she has of the Virgin
Mary. Finally Julian even talks about what she does not see. Nicholas Watson
explains this fluidity by suggesting that Julian employs a 'Trinitarian hermeneutic'
which allows her to override Augustine's categories of vision. By likening her
various modes of seeing to other Augustinian triads, like those of memory, intellect
and will and Father, Son and Holy Spirit, both of which are found in her book,
Watson suggests that Julian feels she can legitimately stretch Augustine's modes of
vision, making them interweave with one another like the persons of the Trinity.

Medieval Theological Response

Despite the complex way in which some women played with categories of vision,
male theologians in the medieval period tended to judge women's visions in relation
to more traditional accounts of seeing, such as those suggested by Augustine and
Boethius, and in relation to what was believed about women and their relationship
with their bodies.

In the Middle Ages the body was thought to be made up of four humours
– heat, dryness, coldness and wetness. Women were associated with the later two
humours. Dyan Elliott points out that this meant that women were considered
softer and more impressionable than men. Thus they were by their very nature less
able to access infallible intellectual knowledge. Thomas Aquinas, for example,
advocated such an understanding of women and their spiritual potential:

> Man is yet further ordered to a still nobler vital action, and that is intellectual
> operation. Therefore there was greater reason for the distinction of these two forces
> in man; so that the female should be produced separately from the male; although
> they are carnally united for generation … As regards the individual nature, woman
> is defective and misbegotten, for the active force in the male seed tends to the
> production of a perfect likeness in the masculine sex; while the production of
> woman comes from defect in the active force or from some material indisposition,
> or even from some external influence; such as that of a south wind, which is moist,
> as the Philosopher [Aristotle] observes (De Gener. Animal. iv, 2).[19]

---

[18] Petroff, *Medieval Women's Visionary Literature*, p. 135.
[19] Thomas Aquinas, *Summa Theologica*, at www.newadvent.org/summa/1092.htm.
Boethius's approach is also influenced by Aristotle as well as Neoplatonic writers.

Elliott notes that their soft nature meant that impressions could be made in a woman's imagination. Women's malleability thus made them potential sites for celestial gifts of a physiological kind, such as illness and visions. However, such visions were fallible and women could easily be tricked by demonic forces since they lacked the intellectual purity demanded for sound judgements of the type that Augustine associates with intellectual vision. The fifteenth-century French theologian Jean Gerson, for example, was also extremely suspicious of women's visions. Gerson had a low opinion of women's ability to receive divine wisdom, claiming that they were not fitting vessels:

> First, every teaching of women, especially that expressed in solemn word or writing, is to be held suspect ... Why? Because women are too easily seduced, because they are too obstinately seducers, because it is not fitting that they should be knowers of divine wisdom.[20]

Even though heavily influenced by Hadewijch, the fourteenth-century Flemish theologian Jan van Ruusbroec was likewise suspicious of visions.[21] He notes that the obvious problem with them is that they can be false and he cautions heretics not to publicise false visions for fear of the punishments that await them in hell.

Women were therefore caught in a double-bind. Though thought prone to visions by reason of their bodily nature, through which they had access to a source of divine revelation, visions were fallible and in order to determine their validity they needed a man to take the steer, since *his* nature gave him access to less fallible and more intellectual knowledge of God. While many of the male confessors and spiritual directors of female visionaries were convinced that the women in their care were mystics of some significance, women mystical visionaries walked a precarious path between sainthood and heresy. With this in mind, we will turn to consider contemporary theoretical responses to the multi-faceted nature of visionary mysticism, particularly female visionary mysticism.

CONTEMPORARY THEORETICAL APPROACHES

While there are perennialist readings of visions, many who have offered responses pertaining to the value of women's visions have done so in terms of a perennial understanding of mental illness. Those who have responded to such readings have more often done so from both contextualised and feminist rather than strictly

---

20   Quoted in R. Voaden, *God's Words, Women's Voices: The Discernment of Spirits in the Writing of Late-Medieval Women Visionaries* (New York: Boydell and Brewer, 1999), p. 7.

21   For a more detailed account, see Jantzen, *Power, Gender and Christian Mysticism*, pp.189–91.

contextualist or performative language positions, although both Katz and Turner offer responses to visionary mysticism, as we shall see.

Perennialist Responses

Perennialist readings are those which tended to consider whether or not visionaries should be differentiated from mystics in relation to the relative ineffability of their experiences.

It is immediately apparent that visions of a non-intellectual variety transgress James's classification of mysticism. Thus, although not herself supporting a strictly perennialist position, Barbara Newman argues that, despite the fact we can understand Hildegard's experience of the living light as a direct experience of God, this does not mean that Hildegard is best classified as a mystic. Hildegard does not have ecstatic encounters, but offers visions that teach about theology. Newman therefore argues that Hildegard is a prophetic visionary, not a mystic.[22] Rosalynn Voaden likewise argues that the expectations of medieval women led them to express their spirituality in visionary mysticism. According to Voaden, mystical experience has no sensory content and is characterised by an inward knowledge of God's presence. She argues that mysticism was mainly a male preserve: 'it was predominantly men who embraced mysticism and, for the most part, women who had visions'.[23] For her, visionaries, in contrast to mystics, see and hear things with the physical senses, thereby conforming to Augustine's second level of vision – spiritual or imaginative. Surprisingly, despite the bodily nature of some of Julian of Norwich's visions, few perennialists have cast doubt on her credentials as a mystic. Her experience is viewed as mystical by a number of perennialist scholars such as David Knowles, William R. Inge, Evelyn Underhill, Edmund Colledge and James Walsh. However, we can see from the approaches taken by scholars like Voaden and Newman that women's visions transgress contemporary understandings of mysticism in a manner that perennialist readings find hard to accommodate.

The Issue of Illness

Early readings of the visionary mysticism tended to approach them in a perennial rather than perennailist manner, arguing that they could be explained in terms of mental health problems.

---

[22]   B. Newman, *Sister of Wisdom: Hildegard's Theology of the Feminine* (Berkley: University of California Press, 1987).

[23]   Voaden, *God's Words, Women's Voices*, p. 9.

Perennial Readings

Women who reported visions often suffered from symptoms of illness, malnutrition or self-mortification. We noted above that female visionaries, in particular, write about these extreme episodes as the very thing that initiates a visionary experience. Some scholars have therefore argued that if these visionaries were alive today we would simply think of them as unwell. Charles Singer suspects Hildegard of migraines. Rudolf M. Bell famously refers to some of the more extreme accounts of malnutrition as 'holy anorexia' and suggests that some of the 'visionaries' experiences can be accounted for as the psychological effects of starvation.[24] There are, as Elizabeth Petroff argues, examples of women hating their bodies to such an extent that they cut themselves. Marie d'Oignies is reported to have accidentally cut off such a large piece of her flesh that she hid it by burying it.[25] Eric Colledge,[26] classifies Margery Kempe's religious experiences (considered in the Chapter 7) as the result of either hysteria or epilepsy.[27] Conrad Pepler dismisses Julian of Norwich's visionary experiences as the result of her being mentally unwell.[28] He suggests that she was suffering from 'an acute neurosis, induced by an over-enthusiastic life of penance and solitude'.[29]

Contextualised Responses

Frank Tobin is, however, suspicious of readings that simply reduce visions to accounts of ill-health. He argues that 'Medieval visionaries are admittedly unusual people, but it is unfair and "unscientific" to approach them with the assumption that they can best or only be approached through modern psychology.'[30] Tobin

---

[24]   R.M. Bell, *Holy Anorexia* (Chicago: Chicago University Press, 1985), pp. 14–15.

[25]   Petroff, *Medieval Women's Visionary Literature*, p. 7.

[26]   Eric Colledge started using the religious name 'Edmund' later on in life.

[27]   E. Colledge, 'Margery Kempe', *The Month*, 28 (1962), 16–29, at p. 28. Thurston also argued that Margery had 'terrible hysteria': see S.B Meech and H.E. Allen (eds), *The Book of Margery Kempe: The Text From the Unique Ms. Owned by Colonel W. Butler-Bowdon Vol. 1*, Early English Text Society, OS 212 (London: Oxford University Press, 1940), p. ixv. David Knowles likewise criticises Margery for being less than a mystic: see Knowles, *The English Mystical Tradition*, p. 142. Also see Chapter 7, p. 145. A range of other diagnoses have been placed on Margery. For a discussion of them, see P.R. Freeman, C.R Bogarad and D.E. Sholomskas, 'Margery Kempe, a New Theory: The Inadequacy of Hysteria and Postpartum Psychosis as Diagnostic Categories', *History of Psychiatry*, 1 (1990), 169–90, at 173–4.

[28]   R. Lawes, 'Psychological disorder and the autobiographical impulse in Julian of Norwich, Margery Kempe and Thomas Hoccleve', in D. Renevey and C.A.R. Whitehead (eds), *Writing Religious Women: Female Spiritual and Textual Practices in Late Medieval England* (Cardiff: University of Wales Press, 2000), pp. 217–43, at p. 234.

[29]   C. Pepler, *The English Religious Heritage* (London: Blackfriars, 1958), p. 312.

[30]   F. Tobin, 'Medieval Thought on Visions and Its Resonance in Mechthild von Magdeburg's *Flowing Light of the Godhead*, in A.C. Bartlett et al. (eds), *Vox Mystica:*

points out that medieval audiences were extremely receptive to the occurrence of visions. He argues that mystical visions should not therefore be analysed in isolation, but should instead be viewed against their full cultural, intellectual and religious background. Even if a vision occurred at the same time as a severe illness, it cannot be counted as spiritually insignificant when set in its medieval context.

A number of psychologists and psychiatrists have responded by offering more nuanced positions. Focusing on Margery Kempe, Phyllis R. Freeman, Carley Rees Bogarad and Diane E. Sholmskas agree that it is wrong to try to read her behaviour as a form of hysteria or postpartum depression when these diagnoses would not have been applied to her at the time. Yet, taking into account medieval diagnoses and the way that her contemporaries reacted to her, they suggest that it does seem likely that Margery suffered from a type of bi-polar disorder. They argue that holding this belief does not negate the value of her experiences or make them less than mystical. While some of her contemporaries suggested that she was ill, others accepted her as a mystic – a fact which affected the course of her life to such an extent that it is not possible to prise sickness and mysticism apart.[31] They argue, however, that psychological analysis adds another layer to our understanding of Margery and her *Book*, without which she is less well understood.

Richard Lawes agrees but argues that it is possible to apply modern psychiatric categories to medieval mystics without being reductionist since mental illness is a constant that cuts across cultural categories, being in this sense perennial.[32] He sees nothing wrong with applying diagnoses to mystics based on symptoms that seem to be described in their writings, so long as one is careful not to confuse religious experience with illness per se. Examining the writings of Julian of Norwich, Margery Kempe and the poet Thomas Hoccleave, Lawes offers psychological readings of elements of their writings that he believes refer to illness rather than religious experience. So, in Margery's *Book*, for example, Lawes distinguishes between what he sees as auditory, visual and olfactory hallucinations and Christ's speaking inwardly to her in her ghostly understanding. He views physical experiences, such as the sound of a robin singing in her ear, as evidence of possible temporal lobe or psychomotor epilepsy. The same is not true, he argues, of her inward conversations with Christ, which he believes her *Book* clearly distinguishes from such auditory encounters. Lawes acknowledges that other contextual factors could be cited as explanations for such auditory visions, such as the existence of similar sound events in the writings of Richard Rolle. He is not concerned by this, however, since he is not suggesting that we simply dismiss these experiences as illness. Rather, Lawes wants us to take psychological readings into account in addition to such contextual

---

Essays on Medieval Mysticism in Honour of Professor Valerie M. Lagorio, (Cambridge: Brewer, 1995), pp. 41-53, p. 41.

[31] Freeman, Bogarad and Sholomskas, 'Margery Kempe, a New Theory', 190.

[32] Lawes, 'Psychological Disorder and Autobiographical Impulse', p. 239.

readings. To not do so, simply dismissing the psychological element, is, he argues, to overlook an aspect of context that also needs to be considered:

> To exclude the theological, the artistic or the biological levels of interpretation is to exclude intriguing dimensions of ambiguity in the text and to truncate the fullness of its meaning. This is not only because ... the content of dreams or hallucinations of organic origin usually reflects the subject's waking preoccupations. These texts are not, any more than any other autobiography, or even than any verbally delivered modern psychiatric case history, unmediated realistic description. They are complex and many-layered products of remembering and interpretation.[33]

Lawes' comments seem helpful in that they draw attention to the multifaceted nature of context. However, in a taking a perennial line towards mental health it should be noted that he disagrees with Michel Foucault who argues that madness is entirely a socially construct.

Foucault's contention, outlined in his *History of Madness*, that mental illness is socially constructed, is one of the most famous responses to a perennial reading of mental illness.[34] He suggests that, by making madness a subclass that is excluded from society, and likewise in creating the modern notion of mental illness, contemporary society manages to nullify the disruptive capacities of madness, which would otherwise challenge its conceptions of truth. Foucault points to the topos of madness and Christian mysticism in the fifteenth century, but does not develop this idea in relation to female visionaries specifically.

Nancy Caciola, however, offers a contextualised/feminist response that draws on the work of Foucault, Michel de Certeau and Mary Douglas. She notes that while, following Caroline Walker Bynum, many scholars have considered the 'internal' issues relating to female visionaries and mystics, that is, the supposed relationship between internal spiritual states and outward physical responses, few have reflected on 'external' issues, such as the response of both local and more overarching ecclesial communities. She turns her attention to hagiographical literature through which much visionary writing is reported and asks how this relates to a 'cult' of veneration for female visionaries and mystics in this period. As in her earlier work, Caciola considers this issue in relation to discernment of demonic possession. Although building on medieval responses to women's physiognomy, such as those proposed by Elliott, Caciola is particularly interested in the idea that women mystics were often accused of being possessed and reflects on what it was that made medieval audiences regard them as either spiritually gifted or under demonic influence. Caciola suggests that when we consider communal responses

---

[33] Ibid., p. 238.
[34] M. Foucault, *The History of Madness* (Routledge, 2006).

to these women we find complex ideas of identity-formation, particularly when we apply theories such as those posited by de Certeau and Douglas.

She brings together the more semantic response of de Certeau (which we noted in the introductory chapter acts as something of a forerunner to the readings of mysticism offered by Sells and Turner), with Douglas's discussion of cultural attitudes toward the body in this period. She reads the treatment of women visionaries as a collective evaluation of cultural norms brought into contact with women's 'performances' of their mysticism and audience response. As she states:

> the most elegant solution to theorizing medieval spirit possession will integrate Lewis and de Certeau's experiential individualism with Douglas' sensitivity to cultural attitudes towards the body ... Briefly put, a performative view of spirit possession sees the phenomenon as a particular cultural process of identity-formation that subsists upon three interdependent factors. They are: one, the cultural constructions of particular identity 'roles'; two, the self-representations of the individual as she 'performs' such roles; and three, the collective evaluation of the individual's actions by observers, or the 'audience.' This triad of factors is drawn together by a fourth element: the surface of the body itself, which both contains individual identity and mediates its relationships with outside observers.[35]

This said, Caciola notes that community responses to female mystics and visions cannot be said to dovetail with medieval accounts of societal norms in a comfortable manner. Rather, the latter always pose some form of challenge to the former, creating an epistemological gap between theory and reception. Caciola notes too that, despite medieval theories of bodies and possession, absolute proof of divine or demonic possession depended on observations by communities and male ecclesiastical authorities. Such observation relied on the outward signs of a woman's body – that is, the way in which she performed her mysticism. For Caciola, this shows how the surface of a woman's body brings together inner theory with outer sign.

Caciola's work overlaps with both those who consider the role of religious context over and against more perennial readings, and those who offer feminist critiques of these same readings. We return to her below.

Feminist Readings

The approach that traditionally makes most room for visionary mysticism is the feminist one. Here we consider four such responses.

---

[35] N. Caciola, 'Mystics, Demoniacs, and the Physiology of Spirit Possession in Medieval Europe', *Comparative Studies in Society and History* (2000), 42/2, 268–306, at pp. 287–8. Also see, N. Caciola, *Discerning Spirits: Divine and Demonic Possession in the Middle Ages* (Ithaca: Cornell University Press, 2003).

Hélène Cixous

As we noted in the previous chapter, feminists like Cixous placed value on hysteria for the manner in which it can disrupt the patriarchal constraints of religion, from which Cixous disassociates it. On the one hand she therefore agrees to a pathologising of women mystics and visionaries. She describes Teresa of Avila as a 'madwoman'. Yet in doing so, she is advocating that Teresa is able to access a desire that has been oppressed by religion. As Hollywood states:

> Cixous effects a transvaluation of values, a radical reversal of the medical and psychoanalytical categories against Christian mystics – in particular, women mystics – by means of which their texts and experiences are rendered pathological ... Cixous argues that hysteria – and thence the mystical forms associated with it – marks the return of repressed desire and so unleashes a liberating force that works against the conservative and rigidifying power of religious belief and practice.[36]

Thus while denying mystics a connection with religion in a true sense, she does so not in the reductionist sense found in perennial discussions where hysteria becomes nothing but illness. Instead she believes hysteria illustrative of the transformative value of mysticism, through which women transcend the rigidity of male religious structures.

Elizabeth Petroff

Elizabeth Petroff classifies many of the female visionaries that she studies as mystics. Her discussions of female mysticism range from the bizarre physical behaviour of Christina the Astonishing, to the ecstatic discussions of love found in Hadewijch or the more abstract discussions of the ineffable we see in writers like Marguerite Porete. Although she lists 'seven distinct phases' within female visionary encounters: purgative, psychic, doctrinal, devotional, participatory, unitive or erotic, and cosmic ordering,[37] Petroff sees all female visionary experiences as belonging to a spiritual continuum that drives towards an experience of union with God:

> The experience of union with the divine is one for which the visionary has been yearning since the beginning of her spiritual path; in her earliest devotional visions, it was often she who was the more desirous partner, longing for a

---

[36]   A. Hollywood, 'Mysticism, Death and Desire in the Work of Hélène Cixous and Catherine Clement', in M. Joy, K. O'Grady and J.L. Poxon (eds), *Religion in French Feminist Thought: Critical Perspectives* (New York: Routledge, 2003), pp. 145–61, at p. 146.

[37]   Petroff, *Medieval Women's Visionary Literature*, p. 8.

personal and erotic relationship with Christ the bridegroom and yearning equally for a tender relationship with the Virgin. In ... unitive or erotic visions, the divine figures woo the visionary.[38]

This approach is similar to that of Caroline Walker Bynum in that Petroff values all visionary experiences of women for the way in which they provide insight into women's spiritual worlds. Through them, thirteenth-century women were able to overcome many of the disadvantages of a lesser education and find a mode through which to share something of their own encounters with the divine. She notes that in order to facilitate this women drew on permissible literary genres, such as secular love poetry, a genre through which it was socially acceptable to communicate their feelings.

Petroff is also aware of a need to contextualise medieval women's visionary writing. She notes for example the impact of social context, liturgy and societal norms:

> a woman's experience presents itself to her in two languages, one associated with her daily life and with the unconscious (as Ong suggests) and the other associated with her ritualized religious life, the language of the liturgy.[39]

She also argues that we need to be aware of the interplay between Latin and the vernacular in women's writings if we are to gain 'insight into peculiar or unusual expressions'. Yet, while she also acknowledges that visions gave their recipients authority beyond that normally allowed to women, she in no way believes that this constitutes a total explanation for them. Petroff is certain that, at its heart, mysticism is an experience of the divine. 'Mysticism is the direct experience of the real, unmediated experience of God. Mystical literature is an oxymoronic proposition, for how can we put into words what is beyond language.'[40] The inclusive nature of her own taxonomy, however, stretches the bounds of this definition – well beyond that found within strictly perennialist readings. For Petroff, these women are successful in their attempts to express something of their own spirituality and, ultimately, it appears to be this more than anything else which leads her to view their encounters as mystical.

Dyan Elliott

Dyan Elliott takes a less positive reading of the extent to which visionary mysticism allowed women access to the spiritual heights enjoyed by men. She traces medieval perceptions of embodiment and argues that, despite developing

---

[38]   Ibid., p. 16.

[39]   Ibid., p. 49.

[40]   E.A. Petroff, *Body and Soul: Essays on Medieval Women and Mysticism* (New York: Oxford University Press, 1994), p. 4.

visionary mysticism, there was no way for women to reach the intellectual heights available to men, without them in some way shedding their femininity. Despite the complex way that women like Hildegard and Julian play with categories of vision, Elliott contends that women's spirituality remained second-class.[41] Although women associated their spirituality with rapture and ecstasy in a Pauline sense, Elliott argues that the medieval understanding of rapture was altered to accommodate a less elevated form of knowing.

She suggests that male perceptions about the weakness of the female body and its passive impressionable nature led to a gendering of rapture. This she believes is evidenced by the way that rapture eventually comes to be treated as synonymous with female sanctity. 'In the thirteenth century and the first half of the fourteenth, rapture was frequently so effective a shorthand for denoting sanctity that it was essentially freestanding.'[42] As such, Elliott claims that female rapture came to be seen in highly patriarchal terms, with the connection between women and rapture drawn along explicitly sexual lines, where the dominant male deity ravishes a swooning female in a consensual mystical marriage.[43] The belief that women's bodies compromised the purity of their souls and so their ability to engage in intellectual modes of knowing remains for Elliott the dominant belief. Visionary mysticism thus fails to overcome the patriarchal view of women's spiritual potential.[44] Women achieve rapture, but not in any truly liberating sense.

Nancy Caciola

We return to Caciola whose understanding of the reception of female mysticism, including visionary mysticism, builds on a physiological understanding of discernment like that offered by Elliott. Caciola too sounds a salutary note concerning the eventual treatment of visionary mysticism in the later Middle Ages. As we have already discussed, scholars such as Jean Gerson took a very dim view of some of the more ecstatic and ascetical practices that were at one time associated with female sanctity. For him, only those women who presented a calm exterior should be viewed as saintly; an idea which increasingly held sway in the later Middle Ages. Caciola echoes Elliott's warning that this form of devotion did not in the end achieve its full disruptive potential. She states, 'The ultimate outcome of the process was a devaluation of the kinds of ecstatic trances, somatic miracles, and severe asceticism that were most often ascribed to women mystics.'[45] As attention in discernment shifted towards the body, focusing on outward signs as

---

[41]   See Elliott, 'The Physiology of Rapture and Female Spirituality'.

[42]   Ibid., p. 162.

[43]   Ibid., p. 161.

[44]   The word rapture (*raptus*) comes from the verb *rapire* meaning: to carry off by force, to ravish.

[45]   Caciola, 'Mystics, Demoniacs, and the Physiology of Spirit Possession in Medieval Europe', p. 296.

means of gauging the spiritual validity of an experience, Caciola finds that women's spiritual experiences began to be associated less with the divine and more with the demonic: 'In sum, as the discernment of spirits became a discernment of bodies, the female body increasingly was defined as a habitation for demons, rather than a locus of indwelling divinity. Ultimately, the construction of these social categories fell along gender lines.'[46]

Contextualist and Performative Language Readings

Steven T. Katz

As noted in Part I, Steven T. Katz takes a fairly hard contextualist approach to Christian mysticism. In this relation he highlights the role that images play within mystical texts, suggesting that they illustrate a complex relationship between belief, scripture and tradition. He comments, for example, on the importance of the image of God as lover in Christian mysticism. Firstly, Katz is unsurprised to find this theme in mystical texts because it is a central idea within the Bible, the sacred text on which Christian mystics meditate (an issue we noted in Chapter 4). Secondly, he notes the way in which many Christian mystics seek to identify with the suffering Christ, longing to share in his sufferings. Thirdly, he argues that, unlike Jewish mystics, Christian mystics tend not to see God the Father as their lover, more often Christ appears in this role. He suggests in the light of this that we should not be surprised when mystics experience stigmata (visible signs of the wounds of Christ on their bodies), or see visions of Christ's suffering, experiencing intense pain as they do so. Drawing attention to the writings of Julian of Norwich, Henry Suso, Johannes Tauler, Teresa of Avila, John of the Cross and Lukardis of Oberweimar, Katz argues that the experiential encounters that these mystics report are no less mystical because of their image-based content. They are simply an aspect of 'the conditioning of consciousness produced by the Christian theological context',[47] which for Katz reinforces his argument that mystical texts do not, after all, describe ineffable experiences. Although drawing attention to important elements of mystical texts that are often overlooked by perenialists, one limitation of Katz's view is that he anachronistically plays down a commitment to ineffable experience that he believes he finds in mystical texts.

A rather contrasting defence of the mystical nature of Julian of Norwich's visions is found in the performative language reading offered by Denys Turner and the approach suggested by Nicholas Watson, which also approaches Julian of Norwich's

---

[46]   Ibid., p. 297.

[47]   Katz, 'The "Conservative" Character of Mystical Experience,' p. 16.

vision from what could be classified as a performative language perspective, albeit one that places greater emphasis on experience than Turner does.

Denys Turner

Denys Turner is less interested in Julian's physical visions or her illness than in the way that she stretches linguistic and imaginative categories. Rather than growing less and less verbose, it is the verbosity of her mysticism which Turner believes ultimately brings the reader to realise the limitations of language when faced with God's ineffability. He argues that Julian piles up layer upon layer of imagery, connecting this to a Trinitarian theology, only to conclude that she has produced little more than an ABC. It is such a realisation that all language and reflection can never arrive at knowledge of God that for Turner illustrates that she has a complex apophatic strategy. As Turner clarifies, apophasis is not connected to negative language per se but to what he terms 'the negation of the negation'. This occurs where, by whatever means, a writer leads the reader to see the ultimate difference between themselves and God. While some mystics realise this through negative strategies and the use of negative language, Turner believes that Julian brings about the same effect by continuously reinterpreting her visions. Julian keeps speaking, and so affirms her knowledge of God, but by doing so realises she is as distant as ever from his truth. The dialectic tension that this creates leads to what Turner understand as apophasis. In relation to this, Turner differentiates between first- and second-order negations. The first constitute the method a mystic employs – whether negative language or verbosity – the choice matters little. What is important is the second-order negation, the 'negation of the negation', which he believes Julian's visionary discussions ultimately achieve through her Trinitarian discourse as it breaks its own boundaries:

> In Julian, this same unknowability of God is approached through the 'excessive' variety of our language of the Trinity which bursts its own bounds in a kind of self-negating prolixity. Where, therefore the apophatic is approached in Bonaventure and Julian through the superabundance of affirmations, this same apophatic is approached by Eckhart and the *Cloud* Author through the different route of predominantly negative imagery. But in either case, these qualities of affirmativeness and negativity are first-order qualities, relating to the concrete imagery of a spiritual style and practice of prayer, not to be confused with second-order negations of the negations, which is the truly apophatic dialectic, and is the common possession of them all.[48]

As such, Turner is adamant that mystics should not be divided into apophatic and kataphatic categories. All mystics, regardless of their strategy are precisely mystics because they realise the otherness of God. Experience is not the issue.

---

48   Turner, *The Darkness of God*, p. 257.

Where they have experiences, it is how they use and understand them that count, not that they have them.

Nicholas Watson

Nicholas Watson's understanding of Julian is also best read as a type of performative language reading. As we noted above, Watson believes that Julian of Norwich deliberately stretches the boundaries of language when she transgresses Augustine's three categories of vision. As such, Watson argues, Julian's mystical discussions are a step removed from imagery. He suggests that this becomes apparent when we reflect on her wordplay in using the term 'to see'. Reflecting on the vision of the hazelnut, for example, she moves seamlessly from seeing the Trinity to seeing the object lying in her hand. This is more than theological abstraction from images; for Watson, it is what he describes as 'thinking through image':

> Here Julian claims to 'see' the properties of the Trinity reflected in an image of the creation that is seemingly also 'seen' in a quasi-physical sense, lying in her hand. Evidently the process we are now involved with is not one of abstraction from images but of theological thinking through image ...[49]

Watson goes on to suggest that unlike those of other female visionaries, Julian's visions are not in fact very image-based. They are more disjoined than this, like fragments of sight. As such, Watson suggests that she is not a typical female visionary.

> Julian's revelation has an imagistic sparseness and at least a surface fragmentariness to it that is largely untypical of the experiences of medieval women visionaries.[50]

Her visions and her commentary on them are so indistinguishable from one another that she breaks down the relationship between the experience and the interpretation. Her texts are more than exegesis, Watson contends, there is in fact no primary vision on which to place an interpretation. It is this fluidity that leads Watson to suggest that Julian's texts are ultimately governed by a 'Trinitarian Hermeneutic' in which interpretation and vision weave in and out of one another like the persons of the Trinity. Like Turner, Watson notes that Julian cannot finish the process of describing her visions. Her knowledge will always be incomplete because God is inexhaustible.

---

[49] N. Watson, 'The Trinitarian Hermeneutic in Julian of Norwich's *Revelation of Love*', in S.J. McEntire (ed.) *Julian of Norwich: A Book of Essays* (New York: Garland, 1998), pp. 61–90, at p. 89.

[50] Ibid., p. 85.

Yet, unlike Turner, Watson places greater emphasis on her seeing than language per se, thereby creating greater space for experience than Turner appears to. It is important to note however, that, for both Watson and Turner, Julian is a special case. Neither claims that visions in general, nor for that matter female visionary mysticism in particular, should be read in this apophatic way. However, unlike Turner, Watson's approach to mysticism is first and foremost interested in contextualising mystical writings in relation to literature and devotional material contemporaneous with it. As such, Watson arguably has more room in his taxonomy than Turner for visionary mysticism.

Conclusion

This chapter has considered contemporary understandings of the relationship between visionary mysticism and mysticism in general. Most perennialists dismiss female visionary mysticism as less than mystical. Julian of Norwich, who presents a particularly sophisticated account of vision, is, however, treated as an exception. Related to this there are also those who hold a perennial reading of mental illness, to which state they reduce visionary mysticism. Criticism of this as reductionist has led to more sophisticated contextualised readings of the relationship between illness and mysticism; Richard Lawes, for example, argues that psychological categories should be treated as an added layer of context, rather than used simply to replace all other explanations. Hélène Cixous, however, welcomes the pathologising of female mysticism – not as form of reductionism, but as a feminist critique that undermines patriarchal religion. Nancy Caciola challenges the perennial reading in a different manner by considering medieval responses to visionary mysticism in terms of cultural constructs. Then there are those scholars who challenge a perennialist reading of mysticism from more strictly contextualist, performative language and feminist perspectives (although, as we saw, these categories also break down somewhat in the case of Nicholas Watson). Steven Katz argues that the use of imagery, and particularly the devotion to visions of Christ that we find in visionary mysticism is evidence that mystical experiences are not ineffable, despite what mystics themselves may sometimes claim. Denys Turner argues that the verbosity of Julian of Norwich's mysticism acts as a complex apophatic strategy that leads the reader to realise that one can ultimately say very little about God. Nicholas Watson concurs but stresses that Julian is not a typical female visionary precisely because of the way in which she deconstructs her images. Feminists read visionary mysticism in one of two ways. Elizabeth Petroff argues that it provides women with a voice for their spiritual experiences, and on this ground is rightly defined as mysticism. Dyan Elliott is less certain. She believes that, despite women's attempts to free themselves from the confines of male views about female spirituality, the way in which rapture comes to be redefined as mere saintliness suggests that visionary mysticism fails to give women the spiritual voice that they are craving. Nancy Caciola brings these more contextualised and feminist responses together, but also, like Elliott, feels that women are unfairly treated in this period, noting how ecstatic female visions become increasingly associated with the demonic.

The next chapter turns to look at a development that also impinges on medieval theories of vision – the role that imagination, will and intellect play in the mystical process.

Chapter 9
Imaginative Mysticism, Meditation and Experience

Although related to our discussion of visionary mysticism in the previous chapter, this chapter focuses on a late medieval theological debate by male mystics about the way that imagery can be used in mysticism. It does so by examining the different approaches to the function of imagery and imagination found in the writings of the three male English Mystics: Richard Rolle, Walter Hilton, and *The Cloud*-Author.

Imaginative Devotion and Meditation

In the twelfth century imaginative devotion took on a new importance. The practice of imaginatively meditating on Christ's life and death permeated Christian devotion to such an extent that it came to shape almost every aspect of it.[1] Meditation had always held a place within monastic devotion. It was the second step within the fourfold practice of *lectio divina* (divine readings), which involved reading, meditation, prayer and finally contemplation of the scriptures. What is noticeable in this period is that meditation comes to take on a far greater importance such that the boundaries between these practices become decidedly blurred.

We can see the origins of this shift in the mystical writings of twelfth-century authors such as Anselm of Canterbury and Bernard of Clairvaux. As we noted in Chapter 4, Bernard views devotional response to the Incarnation as a bridge to higher modes of spiritual prayer. This trend is further intensified by the Franciscans. The thirteenth-century Bonaventure, who wrote the life of St Francis, stresses the importance of a relationship between imaginative meditation on Christ's life and a sacramental understanding of creation when he recounts the famous crib scene in Greccio. What is notable about this event is not that Francis creates a live crib scene – he was not the first to do so – but the way in which he allegedly links it to the Eucharist and sacramental theology. As Bernard McGinn comments:

> What is significant about the Greccio incident is … that Francis orchestrated this *tableau vivant* in relation to the celebration of the Eucharist, thus emphasizing

---

[1] E. Cousins, 'The Humanity and the Passion of Christ', in J. Raitt (ed.) *Christian Spirituality, Volume 2: High Middle Ages and Reformation* (London: SCM, 1996), pp. 375–91, at p. 375.

that imaginative recreation of that historical event finds its true meaning in the sacrament in which Jesus, God and man, becomes present to those who recognize him in the Spirit of the Lord.[2]

Bonaventure's mysticism was a driving force behind the Christocentric focus of later medieval devotion.

Bonaventure, like Bernard of Clairvaux before him, places the Incarnate Christ at the centre of his mystical theology. As we noted in Chapter 5, in *the Soul's Journey into God* he argues that without the Incarnation there could be no mystical knowledge, since Christ is the ladder and the doorway to mystical knowing:

> And just as, when one has fallen, he must lie where he is unless another is at hand to raise him up, so our soul could not be perfectly lifted up out of these things of sense to see itself and the eternal Truth in itself had not Truth, taking human form in Christ, become a ladder restoring the first ladder that had been broken in Adam.
>
> Thus it is that, no matter how enlightened one may be by the light coming from nature and from acquired knowledge, he cannot enter into himself to delight in the Lord except through the mediation of Christ, Who says, *I am the door. If anyone enter by me he shall be safe, and shall go in and out, and shall find pastures.*[3]

It is not only at the beginning that Christ is central for Bonaventure, the soul is finally reunited with Christ as it falls alseep at the foot of the cross.

This belief in Christ's centrality depends on the mystical theology of Pseudo-Denys, and also builds on Hugh of St Victor's understanding of sacrament and symbolism, as already noted in Chapter 6.[4] Yet Bonaventure also uses the idea to demonstrate the mutual compatibility of his academic theology with Franciscan spirituality, which as we noted above placed great emphasis on Christ's humanity. His emphasis on Christ's humanity and passion is one reason for the anonymous *Meditations on the Life of Christ* being ascribed to him. This work, together with Bonaventure's writings, had a huge impact on the rise of imaginative devotion, as McGinn comments:

> How much of a development Francis himself made in this tradition is difficult say, though there can be no question that the Franciscans, especially through the writings of Bonaventure and through the pseudo-Bonaventurian *Meditations on the Life of Christ*, were major proponents of this theme in later medieval spirituality.[5]

---

2   McGinn, The Flowering of Mysticism, p. 59.
3   Bonaventure, *The Mind's Journey to God*, p. 73.
4   See Chapter 6, esp. pp. 125–8.
5   McGinn, The Flowering of Mysticism, p. 59.

The Franciscan *Meditations on the Life of Christ*, more than any other text, influenced the shape of popular devotion and artistic representation of Christ in the later Middle Ages.

This text was intended as a devotional manual to help readers enter imaginatively into the scenes of Christ's life and death. As Santha Bhattacharji comments, the text aimed to facilitate new imaginative encounters with Christ. The reader was invited to picture themselves present at the events and let their meditation take whatever imaginative route seemed most beneficial to them:

> One might expect that manuals such as the *Meditationes Vitae Christi* [Meditations on the Life of Christ], which build up each scene in the life of Christ detail by detail, would be particularly prescriptive. In fact, this was not so. First of all, there is a clear understanding that we do know how these scenes actually took place; we are simply imagining them in ways that help to arouse our sympathy ... related to this lack of prescriptiveness is the understanding that each visualised scene, once set in motion, will probably unfold in a way that is personally appropriate to the meditator.[6]

Nicholas Love's English translation, *The Mirror of the Blessed Life of Jesus Christ*, even more than in the original, blurs the distinction between such meditation and contemplation, sometimes using the two terms synonymously. We have already noted the potential impact of this text on the mysticism of Margery Kempe.[7] Likewise it is clear that Julian of Norwich also placed great importance on being a witness at Christ's crucifixion. As we discussed in Chapter 8, she longed for a bodily vision of this event. Her text raises questions about the relationship between meditation and mysticism through the manner in which it plays with different modes of seeing. Yet, while her text explores the mystical possibilities of imaginative devotion in that it blurs boundaries between types of sight, it does not offer a more traditional theological response to the mystical worth of imaginative meditation. This is, however, found in the writings of the male English Mystics, particularly in the writings of Walter Hilton and *The Cloud*-Author, who enter into a debate about the relative value of imaginative meditation.[8] Although they mostly criticise each other, and neither mentions Rolle by name, their discussions more than likely have an eye on his account of mysticism.

---

[6]   S. Bhattacharji, 'Medieval Contemplation and Mystical Experience', in D. Dyas, V. Edden and R. Ellis (eds), *Approaching Medieval English Anchoritic and Mystical Texts* (Cambridge: D.S. Brewer, 2005), pp. 51– 63, at p. 56.

[7]   See Chapter 7. The importance of the text in England is being mapped by a team at Queen's University Belfast and St. Andrew's University: http://www.qub.ac.uk/geographies-of-orthodoxy/discuss/.

[8]   See J.P.H. Clark and R. Dorward, 'Introduction' in *Walter Hilton: The Scale of Perfection*, ed. and trans. J.P.H. Clark and R. Dorward (New York: Paulist Press, 1991), pp. 13–21

Imagination and Affective Response

Imaginative devotion was believed to be particularly effective in altering the spiritual orientation of the will. Vincent Gillespie notes that as intellect and will came to be seen as separate faculties of the soul, rather than merely aspects of it, their operation came to be respectively linked with two lower faculties, imagination and sensation.[9] While it was sensation that was closely associated with the will, imaginative meditation prevented the soul from focusing intellectually on sensual images that would otherwise lead the will to desire carnal rather than spiritual things. The will needed such help, since it was thought to lag behind the intellect, which otherwise aspired to more spiritual ends. As Gillespie notes, these two faculties of the soul were often characterised as two feet, the will constantly trailing behind the intellect and so preventing it from rising up to God.[10]

> A recurring image of this odd relationship between the *affectus* [the desiring part of the will] and the reason takes the image of the soul journeying towards heaven as being like a man walking along a road. One foot is ever ahead, eager to complete the journey and clear about which direction to take, and this is the foot of the intellect (*pes intellectus*); the other foot is always dragging behind and is reluctant to follow its partner, and this is the foot of the affections or the will (*pes affectus*).[11]

Imaginative meditation was thought of as a useful means of rectifying this problem. It was generally agreed that it aided the soul on its spiritual journey. What was less clear is the extent to which imaginative meditation was therefore seen as part of mysticism. An added concern was whether or not the types of experiences that were often associated with imaginative meditation, which included not only visual but also auditory and olfactory sensations, should likewise be seen as part of mysticism.

In this connection it is important to note that the later Middle Ages also saw a shift within mysticism. When reflecting on Augustine's account of mysticism as an interior journey in Chapter 3, we noted that later mystics did not entirely follow Augustine's belief that the soul was the image of God because of the participatory capacity of memory, intellect and will. Writers like William of St Thierry emphasised intellect and will over memory and in so doing facilitated

---

[9]   V. Gillespie, 'Mystic's Foot: Rolle and Affectivity', in M. Glasscoe (ed.), *The Medieval Tradition In England: Papers Read at Dartington Hall, July 1982* (Exeter: Short Run Press, 1982), pp.199–230.

[10]   See ibid.; also see A.J. Minnis, 'Affection and Imagination in *The Cloud of Unknowing* and Hilton's *Scale of Perfection*', *Traditio*, 39 (1983), 323–66.

[11]   Gillespie, 'Mystics Foot: Rolle and Affectivity', p. 203. This paper gives an illuminating discussion of the way that the various faculties of the soul were thought to interact with one another in the later Middle Ages.

a shift towards seeing the tripartite division of the soul as more of mimetic image of the Trinity. William's understanding of the relative importance of intellect and will over memory was extended by Thomas Gallus who, as we noted, argued that intellect was unable to enter into the final stage of mystical prayer. In privileging the will in this way, Gallus created the possibility of a far more affective form of mysticism, which Denys Turner refers to as 'affectivism'.

English Mysticism

The English Mystics in chronological order are: Richard Rolle (b. *c.*1290), Walter Hilton (b. *c.*1349), *The Cloud*-author (later fourteenth-century), Julian of Norwich (b. *c.*1342) and Margery Kempe (b. *c.*1373).[12] However, only the three male writers offer detailed theological discussion on the nature of imaginative devotion and the sense in which it can be viewed as mysticism.

Richard Rolle

Richard Rolle (*c.*1290–1349)[13] composed a large number of mystical texts. In his later writings he stresses that the soul needs to move through three spiritual stages – purgation, illumination and perfection – if it is to arrive at mystical knowledge of God (an idea that, as we noted in Chapter 5, originates in Pseudo-Denys). Rolle argues that the soul's progression through these three stages is facilitated by imaginative meditation. Such meditation takes two forms. The first involves reflecting on the events of Christ's passion. The second uses the name of Jesus as a mnemonic device to prevent the soul's thinking from wandering off onto anything other than Jesus. Through the orchestration of such practices the Incarnate Christ becomes the soul's only desire. When she has no other solace but Jesus the soul's love is described as 'singular'. Such love results in the opening of the eye of heart, as the following passage from *Ego Dormio* (I sleep) demonstrates,

> If you will meditate on this [Jesus] every day, you will be bound to find great sweetness, which will draw your heart upward and make you sink down weeping

---

[12]   For a short introduction to the English mystics, see B. McGinn, 'The English Mystics', in J. Raitt (ed.), *Christian Spirituality, Volume 2: High Middle Ages and Reformation* (London: SCM, 1996), pp. 194–207.

[13]   For a date of 1290, see E. Underhill, 'Introduction', in *The Fire of Love or Melody of Love and the Mending of Life or Rule of Living*, trans. R. Misyn, ed. F.M.M. Comper (London: Methuen, 1914; repr. 1920), p. vii. E.H. Allen, *Writings Ascribed to Richard Rolle Hermit of Hampole, and Materials for his Biography*, The Modern Language Association of America, Monograph Series 3 (New York: D. Heath and Co., 1927), dates Rolle's birth at 1300 and N. Watson, *Richard Rolle and the Invention of Authority* (Cambridge: Cambridge University Press, 1991), re-dates Rolle's corpus, arguing that he was not born until *c.*1310 and that his life was considerably shorter than Allen has posited.

and in deep yearning for Jesus; and your heart will be snatched away above all earthly things, above the sky and the stars, so that the eye of your heart may gaze into heaven.[14]

Rolle states that the eye of the heart is the intellect.[15] He believes that, when this eye is illuminated, the soul enters into mystical prayer. He associates this entry with three experiences that have come to be regarded as the hallmarks of his mysticism: heat, sweetness and song.

Now while there appears to be an integration of intellect and will within Rolle's account of mysticism, in the sense that the intellect is raised up in the final stages rather than being left behind as Gallus suggests, Rolle's account of mysticism does not have an intellectual dimension. In fact, he actively discourages thinking or intellectual questioning of any kind. For example, he writes in *The Fire of Love* that we should not inquire about the nature of God but, instead, accept that God is incomprehensible and with this in mind proceed to love him:

> If you wish to know for yourself, saying, 'What *is* God?' I say that you will never find a solution for this question..... God alone knows Himself, and only He is able to know Himself ... If in truth He could be plainly understood, He would not be incomprehensible! Suffice it for you, therefore, that you recognize *that* God is; it will hinder you if you wish to know *what* God is.
>
> Thus it is praiseworthy to know God perfectly – that He is incomprehensible – by knowing this to love Him, by loving Him to rejoice in Him, by rejoicing to rest in Him, and by internal quiet to come to eternal rest.[16]

Rather than engaging in intellectual pursuits, for Rolle it is actually the curtailment of thinking that leads the eye of the heart to rise upwards. Imaginative devotion and mnemonics quiet the soul by fixing its attention on God and stopping it thinking. As a result, meditation plays a central role in Rolle's account of mysticism.

However, as we noted in the previous chapter it was traditionally believed that mystical prayer transcended imagination and Rolle also claims that his understanding of mysticism is not imaginative. Yet, he argues that his mysticism transcends imagination by moving into the body. It is the physical nature of his three experiences of heat, sweetness and song that proves their mystical validity and thereby demonstrates that his mysticism is more than mere imaginative meditation. He makes this explicit in *The Fire of Love*:

---

[14]   Richard Rolle, 'Ego Dormio', in *Richard Rolle: English Writings*, trans. R.S. Allen (New York: Paulist Press, 1988), p. 139.

[15]   See L. Nelstrop, 'The Merging of Eremitic and "Affectivist" Spirituality in Richard Rolle's Reshaping of Contemplation', *Viator*, 35 (2004), 387–434.

[16]   Richard Rolle, 'The Fire of Love', in *The Fire of Love and the Mending of Life*, trans. M.L. del Mastro (Garden City, NY: Image Books, 1981), pp. 93–264, at pp. 113–14.

I was more astonished that I can put into words than, when, for the first time, I felt my heart glow hot and burn. I experienced the burning not in my imagination but in reality, as it were being done by a physical fire. But I was really amazed by the way the burning heat boiled up in my soul and (because I had never before experienced this abundance), by the unprecedented comfort it bought. In fact, I frequently felt my chest to see if this burning might have some external cause![17]

Here we can see that Rolle thinks that the experience of heat is not imaginary because it is real – he can feel the sensation of heat in his chest.

By moving in the opposite direction to that normally considered spiritual – that is, towards the body, rather than away from it and towards the intellect – Rolle conflates physical and spiritual sensations. Part of his rationale for doing so is that once the soul enters into mystical prayer the body assumes some of the qualities that it will have after the resurrection. While its intellect is still stunted, the body's spiritual capacities for seeing, hearing and so on are restored. To this extent the soul already begins to take its place in heaven and as a result is able to share in angelic song. Despite first appearances, therefore Rolle's account of contemplation can be described as affectivist. Although Rita Copeland argues that in *Ego Dormio* Rolle ultimately moves into a more abstract understanding of God when he talks about the third degree of love, the highest stage of mysticism, his account of mysticism is still image-based.[18]

The elevated function that Rolle ascribes to the imagination is not, however, replicated by either Walter Hilton or *The Cloud*-Author, although they too do not arrive at a consensus about the role that images and imaginative devotion play within mysticism.

Walter Hilton

Walter Hilton (1343–1395/6)[19] composed two books on mysticism which together make up *The Scale of Perfection*. Book II defends Hilton's view of mysticism against criticisms of it found in *The Cloud of Unknowing*.[20]

---

[17]   Ibid., p. 93.

[18]   R. Copeland, 'Richard Rolle and the Rhetorical Theory of the Levels of Style', in M. Glasscoe (ed.), *The Medieval Mystical Tradition in England III, Papers read at Dartington Hall, July 1984* (Cambridge: D.S. Brewer, 1984), pp. 55–80.

[19]   T.H. Bestul, *The Scale of Perfection: Introduction*, online at www.lib.rochester.edu/camelot/teams/hilintro.htm.

[20]   See Clark and Dorward, 'Introduction', in *Walter Hilton: The Scale of Perfection*, pp. 13–21. As Clark and Dorward note, Hilton and *The Cloud*-Author actively debate the nature of mysticism in their writings, each focusing mainly on critiquing the other's

Hilton believes that the eye of the heart is the intellect and that the opening of the eye of the soul leads to a sight of heavenly delight and as such allows the soul to move forward to the final stage of its mystical journey.

> When we are first reformed by virtues to the likeness of God, and the face of our soul is uncovered by the opening of our spiritual eye, we look at heavenly joy as in a mirror; and we are conformed and made one with the image of our Lord, from the brightness of faith into the brightness of understanding, or else from the clarity of desire into the clarity of blessed love. All of this is the work of our Lord's spirit in a person's soul ...[21]

According to Hilton, intellect is not left behind, but both will and intellect are taken up together into mystical knowing. This event restores the true image and likeness of God within the soul.

Yet while Hilton accepts that imaginative devotion serves a purpose in helping to facilitate this process, and believes that those who practise it may experience certain physical sensations, he does not believe that either these physical sensations or the imaginative meditation itself count as mysticism. He suggests that the physical experiences are gifts from God to encourage the practitioner, but this does not mean that either they or imaginative representation can constitute mystical knowledge. Those who are setting out on the mystical journey invariably have imaginative ideas about God. He accepts this and that some people do not even have the capacity to proceed beyond them. However, this does not in any sense justify viewing imaginative meditation as mysticism.

> This way of knowing Jesus, as I understand, is the opening of heaven to the eye of a pure soul, of which holy men speak in their writings. Not as some suppose, that the opening of heaven is as if a soul could see by imagination through the skies above the firmament, how our Lord Jesus sits in his majesty in a bodily light as great as a hundred suns. No, it is not so: and however high he sees in this manner, he does not truly see the spiritual heaven. The higher he climbs above the sun, to see Jesus God thus, by such imagination, the lower he falls beneath the sun. Nevertheless, this kind of sight is tolerable for simple souls, that know no better way to seek him who is invisible.[22]

---

account. In *The Cloud of Unknowing*, *The Cloud*-Author criticises *The Scale of Perfection: Book I*, Hilton replies in *The Scale of Perfection: Book II*, and then *The Cloud*-Author replies in another work, *On Privy Counselling*. As Bhattacharji notes, they are not the only writers to discuss the understanding of imaginative meditation that Rolle espouses. Thomas Basset offers a defence against pointed criticism of Rolle's understanding of imaginative meditation. See Bhattacharji, 'Medieval Contemplation and Mystical Experience', p. 58.

[21]   See Walter Hilton, *Walter Hilton: The Scale of Perfection*, book I, p. 83

[22]   Ibid., book II, p. 261.

As is clear from the above passage, Hilton in fact warns his readers not to confuse imaginative devotions with a true mystical encounter.

In his discussions of mysticism Hilton uses various imagery, including images of light and darkness, which we noted are a feature of Pseudo-Denys negative language. However, as both Alistair Minnis and John Clark point out, when Hilton talks about the mystical encounter as 'luminous darkness' or a 'good night' he is not speaking paradoxically.[23] It is an attempt to convey to his readers that illumination by God involves forgetting and moving beyond earthly things.[24] Thus, while suggesting that mystical knowledge involves leaving behind corporeal understandings of God and being raised up above all imaginative meditations, imagery and physical sensation to a form of knowing that completely exceeds them, he in no sense negates the imagery through which he describes the mystical encounter.

The Cloud-*Author*

The anonymous author of *The Cloud of Unknowing* also lived in the later part of the fourteenth-century.[25] He argues that mystical knowledge only occurs once love is able to reach out to God alone. Like a longing dart it then pierces 'the cloud of unknowing', an image that he uses to symbolise the cloud on Mount Sinai, which Pseudo-Denys recalls Moses entering into to achieve mystical knowledge. It is an image that *The Cloud*-Author uses to represent the mystery and unknowability of God:

> Therefore, it is my wish to leave everything that I can think of and choose for my love the things that I cannot think ... You are to smite upon that thick cloud of unknowing with a sharp dart of longing love. Do not leave that work for anything that may happen.[26]

However, while deeply influenced by Thomas Gallus, *The Cloud*-Author extends Gallus's denigration of the intellect by arguing that reason, thinking and intellection serve no purpose in mysticism. In what is a deeply anti-intellectualist account, while using imagery such as 'the longing dart of love', 'the cloud of unknowing' and 'the cloud of forgetting', *The Cloud*-Author is clear that imagery, which is the

---

[23] See ibid., book I, pp. 234–8.

[24] See, for example, the discussion by Clark and Dorward in the introduction to their translation of Hilton's *Scale of Perfection*, p. 46.

[25] J.P.H. Clark, *The Cloud of Unknowing: An Introduction* (Salzburg: Institut für Anglistik und Amerikanistik, Universität Salzburg, 1994), pp. 13–19.

[26] *The Cloud of Unknowing*, trans. J. Walsh (New York: Paulist Press, 1981), pp. 130–31. The idea is deeply erotic. See Chapter 4 for a discussion of how such erotic language has been understood within the different approaches to mysticism outlined in this book.

product of imagination and so reason, should not be indulged in; it too has to be left behind before the soul can achieve mystical knowledge.

As a result *The Cloud*-Author leads his readers through a process of actively negating the imagery that he uses to describe the contemplative process. Alistair Minnis describes this approach as 'the imaginative denigration of imagination', since, on the one hand, *The Cloud*-Author employs and needs imagery to explain what he means by mysticism.[27] However, on the other hand, he also needs to move beyond such imagery in order for love to enter into the cloud of unknowing. Thus, he is largely suspicious of imaginative meditation, although he accepts that it may serve a very preliminary function for some people. Better, however, than such imaginative meditation is meditating on a concept without breaking it down into its many parts, since this avoids intellectualisation by giving it further imaginative qualities. In order to get to the point where one is able to pierce the cloud of unknowing with love alone, one needs to break free of all such intellectualising, including understanding based on imagery. One needs to 'unknow' all that one knows. Therefore, rather than placing importance on the opening of the eye of the heart, which he, like Rolle and Hilton, understands as the raising up of the intellect, *The Cloud*-Author focuses on this blind stirring of love towards God.

> One thing I must tell you. This blind impulse of love towards God for himself alone, this secret love beating on this cloud of unknowing, is more profitable for the salvation of your soul, more worthy in itself, and more pleasing to God, and to all the saints and angels in heaven; yes and of more use to all your friends both bodily and spiritual, whether they are alive or dead. And it is better for you to experience this spiritually in your affection than it is to have the eye of your soul opened in contemplation either in seeing all the angels and the saints in heaven, or in hearing all the mirth or the melody that is amongst those who are in bliss.[28]

Sights into heaven and hearing angels' songs are tokens of God's grace, yet since they remain bound up with the function of intellect and ultimately need to be rejected, they are potentially distracting. Trying to attain mystical knowledge via imaginative devotion can in fact be positively detrimental to one's spiritual health.

The Cloud-Author argues that, at its best, trying to gain mystical knowledge through imaginative meditation will drive you crazy. You will make a fool of yourself and end up looking like a silly sheep as you strain yourself trying to attain spiritual knowledge from imaginative resources. At its worst, you will open yourself up to the deceptions of the devil, who is apt to convince people that they have gained mystical knowledge, while all along trapping them in human modes of thinking.

---

[27]   Minnis, 'Affection and Imagination', p. 346.

[28]   *The Cloud of Unknowing*, pp. 139–40.

For when they read or hear read or spoken how men should lift up their hearts to God, they look up to the stars as though they would reach above the moon, and cock their ears as though they could hear angels sing out of heaven.[29]

They turn their bodily senses inwards on themselves, physically which is unnatural. They strain themselves, as though they could possibly see inwardly with their bodily eyes and hear inwardly with their ears; and so with all their senses of smell, of taste and of touch ... The result is that the devil has power to fabricate false lights or sounds, sweet smells in their nostrils ...[30]

For *The Cloud*-Author imaginative meditation and the physical sensations that accompany it are far removed from mysticism proper. Thus he warns us to 'take care not to interpret bodily what is meant spiritually'.[31]

From these three accounts of mysticism it is apparent that the relationship between imaginative meditation, experience and new mysticism was extremely complex, not only for female mystics but also for men. Such technical discussion as that detailed in the writings of these three mystics adds another layer to our understanding of new mysticism that also demands explanation.

CONTEMPORARY THEORETICAL APPROACHES

Perennialist Readings

Perennialist readings of the male English Mystics discussed above focus on the differing views that these three writers had about the relative value of physical experience.

David Knowles

Without a doubt David Knowles has offered the most significant perennialist discussion of male English Mysticism. Knowles notes that *The Cloud*-Author condemns the type of physical sensations that Rolle associates with mysticism. He suggests that *The Cloud*-Author does so because Rolle's experiences are not ineffable, which to Knowles's thinking disqualifies Rolle as a mystic:

---

[29]   Ibid., p. 230.
[30]   Ibid., p. 220.
[31]   Ibid., p. 241.

As a mystic, Rolle has little or nothing to teach, and he was soon to be put into the shade, in the eyes of those best able to judge, the author of *The Cloud*, who explicitly distrusted some of his practices and advice .... Rolle ... uses the term 'contemplation' for a kind of prayer and spiritual experience considerably less advanced than that to which the author of *The Cloud* and Hilton, along with later mystical theologians, have rightly restricted it.[32]

The Cloud-Author's discussion of physical experience, like Hilton's, are treated by Knowles as evidence that both Hilton and *The Cloud*-Author understood mysticism as an ineffable encounter with the divine. He views their writing as descriptions of such, and is not interested in their treatment of imaginative meditation per se, since he considers this peripheral to the real concerns of these texts. Much modern scholarly work on English Mysticism assumes such a perennialist reading and this is nowhere more evident than in Rolle scholarship. Firstly, there is very little academic study of Rolle, despite there being more extant manuscripts of Rolle's writings than of any other English Mystic's, with the possible exception of Hilton. The reason for this seems to be that his mystical credentials are doubted. The scholarship that does exist is often preoccupied with defending Rolle against Knowles's criticisms. Margaret Jennings, for example, argues that Rolle's experiences can be viewed as ineffable, since he stresses that they are not merely human experiences, although she admits that such a reading is problematic given some of Rolle's accounts of them.[33] Wolfgang Riehle's reading of the English Mystics also approaches these texts from a similarly perennialist perspective. He argues that in Rolle's case it is the language that he uses to describe his experiences, not the experiences themselves, that lack ineffability. He argues that Rolle's more concrete descriptions, alongside those used by other English Mystics like Margery Kempe, should, in fact, be read as analogies, which safeguards the ineffable experience that underlies them:

> The medieval English mystics, like all other mystics, are faced with the problem of having to express the union with the divine in language that proves to be inadequate because it is limited to earthly things ... Anyone who, like Richard Rolle, is imbued with a very intense mystical experience will wish

---

[32]   Knowles, *The English Mystical Tradition*, p. 54, p. 64. Both William Pollard and Sam Womack have challenged Knowles. However, neither addresses the issue of whether his spiritual sensations can be physical sensations or whether, in order to be a mystic, there has to be a qualitative difference between the two, as Origen seems to suggest. See W. Pollard, 'Richard Rolle and the Eye of the Heart, in W.F. Pollard and R Boenig (eds), *Mysticism and Spirituality in Medieval England* (Cambridge: Boydell and Brewer, 1997), pp. 85–106, and S.J. Womack, 'The Jubilus Theme in the Later Writings of Richard Rolle', (unpublished PhD dissertation, Duke University, 1961).

[33]   For example, see M. Jennings, 'Richard Rolle and the Three Degrees of Love', *Downside Review*, 93 (1975), 193–200.

to communicate it to others ... so that the wish for a similar experience will be awakened in the reader. Here the mystics sometimes fall back on the tried and tested figures of speech of rhetoric, but above all they strive to make their mystical themes clear by means of sensual concrete metaphors and images, and this not infrequently yields certain analogies.[34]

Likewise, we have already noted the perennialist nature of Robert Forman's reading of *The Cloud of Unknowing*. Nelson Pike, following Robert Forman,[35] similarly argues that the English Mystics have Pure Consciousness Events (PCEs).[36] Any theologising that is found in their writing is seen as secondary to the mystical encounter, which is ineffable.

As Rolle's account in particular makes clear, when we consider the multi-faceted nature of male English Mysticism, we can see that it too strains against the confines of a strictly perennialist approach, an issue which more contextualised accounts emphasise.

Contextualised Readings

More contextualised readings reject a perennialist reading of English Mysticism on two counts. Firstly, they stress that these texts need to be read in relation to other vernacular literature of the time, believing that influences that have shaped the mysticism of these writers can be identified. Secondly, they argue that the theology of these texts is fundamental to its form, not peripheral. We will consider each of these aspects in turn.

Relationship to Other Vernacular Literature

Nicholas Watson in particular argues that it is necessary to read English Mysticism in relation to other forms of literature that existed at the time. He is critical both of the term 'mysticism' and of the subcategory 'English mysticism' because the perennialist reading which underlies them results in mystical texts being read a-contextually. He argues that the effect of this in the case of the English Mystics has been to overlook and obscure their relationship to other forms of vernacular literature, resulting in an impoverished understanding of these writings. In this vein he argues that 'both the canon of "Middle English mystics" and the term "mysticism" itself have largely outlived their usefulness to scholars'.[37] He likewise notes that the term 'English mysticism' is a modern construction:

---

[34]   Riehle, *The Middle English Mystics*, pp. 1–2.

[35]   Forman account's of mysticism is discussed in Chapter 2, pp. 59–61.

[36]   Pike, *Mystic Union: An Essay in the Phenomenology of Mysticism*.

[37]   Watson, 'The Middle English Mystics', p. 539.

The terms 'Middle English mystics' and 'fourteenth-century English mystics' have been devised in this century as ways of constituting a heterogeneous club of four or five, writers whose works span the years between c1330 and c1400.[38]

Underlying this taxonomy is the perennialist belief that they each experienced mystical, that is, ineffable, experiences. Watson suggests that this is not enough for these five very different authors to be treated as a homogenous group.

Deny Reveney has also pursued such a contextualised approach in relation to Richard Rolle, arguing that simply defining Rolle as a 'mystical writer' is to ignore the breadth of his spirituality, which runs much wider than mere mysticism: 'the label "mystical writer" [is] much too tight a fit, for his contributions in Latin cover broad religious topics, in the form of pastoral manuals, theological tracts, scriptural commentaries and autobiographical mystical pieces'.[39] The great fluidity with which Rolle moves between genres is, Renevey believes, evidence of a relationship between Rolle's mysticism and other Latinate and vernacular texts of the period.

In highlighting this issue Watson and Reveney draw attention to an important lack within the perennialist position. Another is illustrated by the place held by belief. We will begin by considering Bernard McGinn's approach to mysticism. Undoubtedly one of the foremost scholars of mysticism of the twenty-first century, it is particularly in relation to the interplay of love and intellect that McGinn most clearly outlines his own understanding of mysticism.

The Shaping Power of Interpretation and Theology

Bernard McGinn   Although wary of dismissing a Jamesian reading of mysticism too lightly, Bernard McGinn is critical of the way that James splits feeling or experience from interpretation. In seeking a method of holding in tension ineffable experience on the one hand and interpretation on the other he turns to Bernard Lonergan's analysis of human intentionality.

Lonergan argues that human beings have within them an unrestricted desire to know, which operates even at an ordinary level of consciousness. By this he means that they are always driven by inquisitiveness, wanting to know more than they currently do. He argues that knowledge always precedes desire because, to quote Augustine, you cannot love what you do not know. However, he claims that this dynamic falls apart at the highest level of human consciousness, that is, the level of consciousness that concerns God, since no one can truly know God. Lonergan believes that at this level of consciousness a gift of love is encounter that is not understood, but which nonetheless still forms the basis of faith.

---

[38]   Ibid., p. 539.

[39]   D. Renevey, 'Richard Rolle', in D. Dyas, V. Edden and R. Ellis (eds), *Approaching Medieval English Anchoritic and Mystical Texts* (Cambridge: D.S. Brewer, 2005), pp. 63–74, at p. 63.

McGinn is attracted to Lonergan's idea of human cognition since it posits a relationship between self, learning, communities, rituals and symbols, and whatever is being experienced. However, McGinn rejects the idea that there is no intellectual dimension in the love with which we love God at the highest level of consciousness. Although McGinn acknowledges that there was a certain level of debate in the later Middle Ages about the roles that intellect and will play within the mystical process, and notes that different mystics deal differently with the intellective and affective aspects of mysticism, he is reticent to allow that one can make sense of mysticism outside of a relationship between loving and knowing. Therefore, even though McGinn points out that Nicholas of Cusa, in what has become known as the Tübingen debate, seems to assert that the intellect is left behind in the final stage of mystical knowing, he stresses that Cusa still insists that the intellect serves a vital function within the mystical process at an earlier stage. While mystics therefore talk of God in terms of different aspects (such as memory, intellect and will), according to McGinn these aspects must be fully integrated in God where they are one and the same. Applying this belief to medieval discussions of intellect and will, McGinn remains unconvinced of the value of trying to divide mystics into groups that are 'intellectual' or 'affective', as we noted in Chapter 4:

> Dividing mystics into intellective and affective categories rarely provides much
> insight into their teaching, given the fact that almost all Christian mystics have
> dealt with the roles of both knowing and loving in the encounter with God.[40]

Regardless of how they view the mechanics of mysticism, McGinn maintains that at the level of mystical consciousness mystics hold that God becomes co-present with the self in their souls, such that the mystical consciousness (or 'meta-consciousness') subsumes all lower forms of consciousness. When this happens it transforms even ordinary perception, making it part of a higher way of knowing.

However, far from seeing them as peripheral to the mystical process, he believes that arguments relating to intellect and will bring us to the heart of mystical consciousness. Later interpretations by mystics of their mystical experiences are infused by this 'meta-knowing' and so cannot be distinguished from the initial experience per se. As a result, they reveal that a process of dialogue between intellect and will always lies at the heart of mystical prayer. Viewing medieval mysticism in this way helps us to understand that mysticism is a process which encompasses far more than just one-off experiences. Thus it is that McGinn criticises perennialists who ignore the theology of the texts.

In line with his beliefs about intellect and will, McGinn suggests that imaginative devotion is best understood as a preliminary practice which aids the mystic, although this is not the same as mystical consciousness. Yet at the same time he argues that we need to be flexible and allow that more imaginative forms

---

[40]   McGinn, 'Mystical Consciousness: A Modest Proposal', p. 54.

of mysticism may have existed, like that which Ewert Cousins refers to as 'the mysticism of the historical event':

> The second issue is how far we may wish to speak of much meditative and contemplative practices as mystical. Given the flexible notion of mysticism used in history, I have no difficulty in seeing a 'mysticism of the historical event' as one form of Christian mysticism ... I would suggest, however, that such intense pictorial realizations of the events of Christ's life should be seen as belonging more to the preparation for a direct and often non-pictorial consciousness of identification with Christ, both human and divine, at the summit of the mystical path, than as constituting its core.[41]

This reading accords with McGinn's belief that mystical consciousness is fundamentally an awareness of 'God who always remains unknowable in his infinite mystery'.[42]

Ewert Cousins   However, Ewert Cousins argues that, although imaginative meditation may operate at a very sentimental level, it has the potential to allow the meditator to enter into the revelatory purposes of God that underlie historical events, especially where these are religious. It is possible, Cousin's argues, to 'penetrate to that deeper level of mystical awareness where [one] experiences God himself as he is manifest in the event'.[43] He believes that such a belief underlies the Franciscan emphasis on meditation on the life of Christ, particularly as it is found in Bonaventure's writings. He sees this use of imaginative meditation as a natural development of the monastic practice of *lectio divina* (divine reading) in which an attempt was made to move from the literal level to the hidden mystical level of scipture through a process of reading, prayer and meditation.[44] He argues that this understanding of imaginative devotion explains how it is that Julian of Norwich (whom we discussed in Chapter 8) moves from seeing Christ's blood to an understanding of the Trinity.

Alistair Minnis   Alistair Minnis offers a less theological reading of the role performed by intellect and will than either McGinn or Cousins. It nonetheless appears to be highly contextualised. Minnis, for instance, was the first to notice that Hilton and *The Cloud*-Author engage in a debate about mysticism that centres on the roles of imagination, intellect and will. By looking at the text in this way, Minnis has been able to cogently show that the *The Cloud*-Author's understanding

---

41   McGinn, *The Flowering of Mysticism*, p. 59.

42   McGinn, 'Mystical Consciousness: A Modest Proposal', p. 53.

43   Cousins, 'The Humanity and Passion of Christ', p. 388. Also see E. Cousins, 'Francis of Assisi: Christian Mysticism at the Crossroads', in S.T. Katz (ed.), *Mysticism and Religious Traditions*, pp. 163–91.

44   Cousins's understanding of mystical exegesis is discussed in Chapter 6, pp. 131–2.

of mysticism is a natural extension of Thomas Gallus's approach, such that no further explanation for his account of mysticism is necessary. It was previously assumed the *The Cloud*-Author must have been acquainted with the writings of Hugh of Balma.[45]

Following his analyses of these two writers it is now seems very unlikely that Walter Hilton was the author of the anonymous *Cloud of Unknowing*. Perennialist scholars had previously attributed the text to Hilton because they did not consider the theological differences between the texts to be important. By viewing the theology of these texts as of primary importance, Minnis asserts that reading the theology leads us to a far better understanding of what the texts are about than simply focusing on ineffable experiences. As such, it suggests that discussions of intellect, will and imagination are more than simply add-ons post experience. They pre-shape each of these writers understandings of mysticism and so the sense in which they are then able to accept each other's accounts as mysticism.

Performative Language Readings

A different response to a perennialist position is offered by Denys Turner.

Denys Turner

As we noted in Chapter 3, Denys Turner believes that affectivist accounts undermine mysticism because they replace the dialectic between saying and unsaying with a solely positive outreach of love. As such, for him, they contain no possibility of creating what Turner calls 'the negation of the negation', through which discussion of God is brought to a point of collapse. Rather, he suggests that affectivist accounts tend instead towards experientialism. However, Turner does not believe that *The Cloud*-Author falls into this category. For him, *The Cloud*-Author overcomes the separation between intellect and will by retaining a dialectical process similar to that which Turner identifies in the writings of Pseudo-Denys. He suggests that *The Cloud*-Author does so by means of an active strategy of image negation that leads the soul to 'unknow' – an English verb coined by *The Cloud*-Author in its active form. This process involves both the extensive use of imagery and symbolism, and its self-negation. Turner asserts that images and symbols thus come to perform a similar function to the interplay of cataphatic (kataphatic) and apophatic statements that we find in earlier mystical texts.

---

[45]   Minnis, 'Affection and Imagination in *The Cloud of Unknowing* and Walter Hilton's *Scale of Perfection*', 366–7 n. 54.

We can say that it is a strategy of *opposing oppositions*, and with them of subverting all those pressures, whether secular or spiritual, whether psychological or social, which depend on these oppositions.[46]

Intellect, desire and experience are all negated. He stresses that *The Cloud-Author's* affectivism does not lead him to a false positive in terms of love, because desire is disciplined and negated by imagination, which continually removes its points of attachment.

> In the *Cloud* there is an immanent dialectics of desire which leads to its own *excessus*; if intellect is to be denied in the cloud of unknowing, desire is to be disciplined by means of the dialectic of imagination, for imagination is what lies at the root of false desire for God.[47]

As such, it does not fall into experientialism. Turner notes too that *The Cloud-Author* tries to distance himself as far as possible from the kind of affectivism that is associated with Rolle's reliance of imaginative meditation. Not only does *The Cloud*-Author condemn it, he uses imagery connected with sight, rather than touch – tactile imagery being the type that fills Rolle's mysticism. Yet the manner in which Rolle connects literary device, theological belief and sensation in his discussions of mysticism opens the door for a more sophisticated readings of Rolle's experientialism than Turner allows since touch can operate dialectically when toucher and touch become aware that this sensation both brings a sense of union and distance.[48]

Feminist Readings

Caroline Walker Bynum

Unsurprisingly, feminist writers have not been particularly interested in the three male English Mystics. However, although principally concerned with female accounts of mysticism, in her book *Holy Feast Holy Fast*, Caroline Walker Bynum acknowledges that some male writers also integrate the body into their mysticism. She highlights Francis of Assisi, Jan Van Ruysbroeck, Johannes Tauler, Henry Suso and Richard Rolle. She ascribes a more female form of mysticism to each of these writers, and suggests that it is derived from the close association that each had with female mystics. Yet she also asserts that none of these men integrates the

---

[46]   Turner, *The Darkness of God*, p. 209.

[47]   Ibid., p. 204.

[48]   See L. Nelstrop, 'Richard Rolle and the Apophasis of Touch', unpublished paper delivered at Christian Spirituality Conference, St Mary's University, Twickenham, June 2009.

body and the spiritual to the same extent that female mystics do, a fact evidenced by the lack of food and feeding imagery in their texts.[49] This is perhaps most questionable in the case of Rolle, although it is still important to recognise that as a man Rolle necessarily has a different starting point to female mystics in his approach to the divine.

Conclusion

This chapter has considered the debate about the role of images, meditation and experience within the three male English Mystics. Perennialists dismiss this discussion as secondary to that of ineffable experience. They are interested in the debate only to the extent that *The Cloud*-Author rejects Rolle's mystical experiences for having a physical dimension. Those who take a more contextualised approach, however, stress the need to read the English Mystics both in relation to other vernacular literature and in terms of the theology of their texts. They argue that the author's preconceived beliefs about mysticism shape any subsequent experiences. McGinn in particular attempts to integrate historical movements with an experiential dynamic. However, he is still sceptical about treating imaginative devotions that centre on Christ as mysticism in the manner in which Cousin's posits. In his performative language reading of *The Cloud of Unknowing*, Denys Turner argues that, despite being an affectivist, *The Cloud*-Author still manages to offer an apophatic strategy through his active negation of images. Turner is however less certain that affectivism in general counts as mysticism, since he believes that it opens the door to a form of experientialism that is far from apophatic. In her feminist reappraisal of mysticism, Caroline Walker Bynum argues that authors like Richard Rolle adopt a somewhat feminine approach to mysticism possibly because of their close connection with women mystics. However, she believes that Rolle does not integrate the body into mysticism to the same extent that female mystics do.

The final chapter in this section examines the claims that some new mysticism is also heretical.

---

[49]   Bynum, *Holy Feast Holy Fast*, p. 112.

Chapter 10
Mysticism and Heresy

The final chapter in this section considers the relationship between heresy, orthodoxy and mysticism. It focuses on two notable accounts of mysticism that were accused of being heretical: the mystical writings of Meister Eckhart and Marguerite Porete's *Mirror of Simple Souls*.[1]

Heresy vs. Orthodoxy

Following Herbert Grundmann, Malcolm Lambert argues that in order to understand the nature of heresy it is necessary to understand the trajectories of orthodoxy, its 'short-lived experiments' as well as its general trends.[2] In lieu of this, Lambert argues that medieval heresies fall in into two categories: 'real' and 'artificial'. The former consisted of real groups who contravened orthodox religious beliefs. The latter did not exist, at least in the sense that a body of thinking informed the beliefs and practices of a particular faith community or individual.[3] Artificial heresies were disparate ideas and practices that came to be joined together by the orthodox establishment. The English heresy known as 'Lollardy' is such an artificial heresy.[4] Lambert contends that the Heresy of the Free Spirit is another.

The Heresy of the Free Spirit

Despite such learned scholars as Robert Lerner and Herbert Grundmann insisting on the veracity of the Heresy of the Free Spirit, Lambert is adamant that it was not 'real'.[5] A number of factors lead him to this conclusion. Firstly, research has

---

[1] Eckhart's mysticism has sometimes been referred to as 'speculative mysticism', because of the role which intellect plays within it. McGinn argues that both this title and its counterpart 'affective mysticism' are ultimately unhelpful because of the way in which they can distract attention from the role that both faculties play in the mystical encounter. We noted in the last chapter that Denys Turner does not share McGinn's position here. See Chapter 9 for discussion, pp. 196–8. Also see p. 83.

[2] M.D. Lambert, *Medieval Heresy: Popular Movements from the Gregorian Reform to the Reformation* (Cambridge, MA: Blackwell, 1992) p. 7.

[3] Ibid., p. xii.

[4] For a discussion of Lollardy, see A. Hudson, *The Premature Reformation: Wycliffite Texts and Lollard History* (New York: Oxford University Press, 2002).

[5] Lambert, *Medieval Heresy*, p. 186.

never uncovered an organised sect or programme of teaching that corresponds to this heresy. Secondly, women like beguines, who fell outside the official religious structures of the church, seemed to have been especially prone to it. Lambert stresses that heresy charges levelled against such women need to be treated with extreme caution since it is clear they could be politically or otherwise motivated. As evidence, he notes that, when detached from its author, Porete's *Mirror of Simple Souls* circulated without problem.[6] Finally, the Bull *Ad Nostrum*'s understanding of the Heresy of the Free Spirit appears to be pieced together from disparate, possibly unconnected sources, including several passages from Porete's *Mirror*. Lambert writes:

> Did such a sect ever exist? The surprising answer, after so much research has been carried out on a supposed heresy of the Free Spirit, is that in the medieval inquisitor's usual sense it did not. There was no organised sect at all, with a teaching programme hostile to the Church, like the Cathars or the later Waldensians. All that really existed were individual mystics in communication with like-minded friends and followers on an informal basis, some of whom wrote and said some dangerous or extravagant things. *Ad nostrum* took a set of these statements that looked heretical or immoral when quoted out of context, and wove together a heresy and a sect from them.[7]

According to *Ad Nostrum*, adherents of the Heresy of the Free Spirit placed authority on their own experience and did not recognise that of the Church. They claimed that it is possible to gain perfection in this life. They believed that they could move beyond an ability to sin. Once joined in union with God, they argued, they were also freed from all conventional moral constraints, a belief that led to an association between this heresy and promiscuity or scandalous sexual practices.[8] Yet Lambert contends that this heresy, of which both Eckhart and Porete stand accused, is a creation of the Inquisition. What implications does this have for our understanding of the mystical writings of Porete and Eckhart?

Heretical Mysticism?

The Case of Marguerite Porete

Marguerite's *Mirror of Simple Souls* is structured as a dialogue between key parts of the soul. These are represented as personified characters such as Lady Love, the Annihilated Soul, Reason, NearFar and High Courtesy (all of whom are

---

6   Ibid., p. 184.

7   Ibid., p. 186.

8   For discussion of the heresy of the free spirit, see ibid., esp. pp. 8, 114, 198–207, and N. Cohn, *The Pursuit of the Millenium*, (London: Secker and Warburg, 1957).

female, with the exception of NearFar). Throughout the course of the dialogue, Reason becomes so perplexed by the paradoxes brought forth by Lady Love that she expires (although, as McGinn notes, she is miraculously revived near the end of the book).[9] Marguerite's account of mysticism passes through seven mystical levels of knowing. Stages 4 to 7 were those that were believed to contain heretical teachings.

Beyond the fourth level, Marguerite argues, the soul has no need of reason. It also appears to have no need for good works or virtues. Michael Sells explains that after this point what is important is *how* work is done, not *what* work is done. 'At this point, the issue becomes not whether work is done, but who is the agent of the work.'[10] According to Porete, at this mystical level of existence God works within the soul and the soul does not work in distinction from God. When this occurs the soul's identity apart from God is said to have been annihilated. Porete describes God's working in the soul as a gift that adds nothing additional to the soul. Rather the gift is God, who transforms the soul into God's-self. Such annihilation concerned Porete's inquisitors. They argued that it was heretical to hold that the soul could be united with the Trinity while still attached to the body, as was her claim that the soul could find God without seeking God.[11]

Porete further states that the annihilated soul operates 'without a why', an image also used by Eckhart to describe undifferentiated unity. For Porete, this implies that the soul returns to the state of existence that it knew prior to creation (when it did not exist as a separate entity). It achieves a state of union with God in which it is undifferentiated from God. Marguerite also talks in this relation of a nothingness where the soul both wills and loves nothing. Sells explains that by this she means that the soul is brought to a point where she has 'fallen into the certainty of knowing nothing and willing nothing'.[12] Porete argues that this brings the soul to a place where it can speak of neither its similarity to nor difference from God. In living 'without a why' the soul even declares that she is God. A feature of such annihilation was the abandonment of virtues, which for Porete characterise the active works of the soul. When the soul passed beyond all active willfulness it became passive in its union with God, such that it overcomes all its creatureliness, this despite Porete's assertion that the final removal of creatureliness only occurs at the seventh level, that is, after death. Both these ideas, that of the abandonment of conventional virtue and the notion of the soul's passivity, were condemned by her inquisitors.

---

[9]   McGinn, *The Flowering of Mysticism*, p. 249.

[10]   M. Sells, 'The Pseudo-Woman and the Meister: "Unsaying" and Essentialism', in B. McGinn (ed.) *Meister Eckhart and the Beguine Mystics: Hadewijch of Brabant, Mechthild of Magdeburg, and Marguerite Porete* (New York: Continuum, 1994), pp. 114–46, at p. 117.

[11]   Lambert, *Medieval Heresy*, p. 202–4.

[12]   Sells, 'The Pseudo-Woman and the Meister', p. 123.

In a particularly provocative manner, Porete also talks of two types of church, 'Great church' and 'Lesser church'. She argues that lesser church consists of all ecclesiastical authorities, their rules, rituals and their practices. Yet there is another Church, 'Great church', to which those who love like Porete do belong. Once a member of Great church the authority of Lesser church no longer applies. In what Maria Lichtmann calls a 'subversion of ecclesiastical structure and values',[13] Porete stresses that Lesser church is unable to recognise or understand those individuals who love in this pure way. This was also a belief for which she was condemned.

Also further difficulties arise when we try to make sense of Porete's mysticism because of the paradoxical manner in which she writes; as Maria Litchmann explains, Porete outlined her beliefs using language in such a way that it confounds the meaning:

> Marguerite uses all the linguistic means at her disposal, particularly those of paradox and contradiction to annihilate in language as in reality all understanding, will, love and even the self itself.[14]

Michael Sells notes that Porete even inverts the idea of the Fall, playing with this image so that, having ascended through the first five stages, she falls back into herself at the sixth level, as she becomes truly annihilated.

It is notable that some of her writings had been burnt by the bishop of Cambrai prior to her trial and final condemnation. Despite this, Porete still failed to suppress her supposed heretical beliefs. Between 1307 and 1308 she was therefore arrested and sent to Paris to be tried for heresy.[15] In 1310, she was found guilty and burnt at the stake. Her book, *The Mirror of Simple Souls*, was likewise consigned to the flames. Although as we noted above copies of it still survived, circulating anonymously.

The Case of Meister Eckhart

There are notable similarities between Eckhart's and Porete's accounts of mysticism. This said, it is hard to characterise his mysticism; a fact compounded by the large number of texts he composed, his use of both Latin and vernacular, and the fact that Eckhart is an academic theologian. As Étienne Gilson points out, one of the difficulties in trying to assess Eckhart's thought is that, no matter which aspect we treat as the hermeneutical key, there is always another one that could

---

[13]   M. Lichtmann, 'Marguerite Porete and Meister Eckhart: *The Mirror of Simple Souls* Mirrored', in McGinn, *Meister Eckhart and the Beguine* Mystics, pp. 65–86, at p. 69.

[14]   Ibid., p. 72.

[15]   Lambert, *Medieval Heresy*, p. 202.

equally well have been used.[16] Here we will highlight a number of themes that are stressed in contemporary scholarship for the way that they bear similarities to Porete's thought and/or are related to the heresy charges levelled against him.

The Nothingness of Creatures   Unlike his Dominican confrère Thomas Aquinas, Eckhart held that creatures were analogous to God only in an extremely limited sense.[17] Following Aristotle, Eckhart maintained that knowledge originated from sense experience not from any direct access to the divine. A given characteristic could be applied to creatures *or* to God, but not to both. While it is not false to describe God as good, it was only true in a sense entirely distinct from the way in which a creature can be said to be good. The two notions of goodness were not related. As Frank Tobin explains:

> The core of Eckhart's conception of analogy is that God and creatures, as distinct, are too different to be in any proper sense included in the same term. Whatever goodness or truth creatures possess is nothing compared to the goodness and truth of God.[18]

As such, Eckhart maintained that it was better to state that God was *not* good. Yet, Eckhart still believed that the true definitions of 'goodness', 'truth' and especially 'being' rested with God.[19] Indeed, he often stated that 'God's characteristic or property is being'.[20] If properly understood, the true meaning of these concepts is found in God. He thus referred to creatures as 'nothing' to reflect their relationship to the 'being' of God. However, the way in which Eckhart configured his beliefs meant that he was accused of heresy for claiming that there is no real relationship between the soul and God.

The Unity of God and Undifferentiated Unity   This idea seems to be initially reinforced by the central place in Eckhart's writing given to descriptions of God as '*unum*' or 'one'. Eckhart used this terms as a way of referring to God that avoids, as far as possible, talking of God in terms of human conceptions. For Eckhart, God is utterly indistinct, as opposed to creatures, which are differentiated and distinct

---

[16]   F. Tobin, *Meister Eckhart: Thought and Language* (Philadelphia: University of Pennsylvania Press, 1986), p. 36. This discussion of Eckhart largely follows Tobin's reading of him.

[17]   B. McGinn, 'Introduction', in *Meister Eckhart: Teacher and Preacher*, trans. B. McGinn, F. Tobin and E. Borgstädt (New York: Paulist Press, 1986), p. 25. Here McGinn argues that Eckhart's approach to negation differs from Moses Maimonades in this respect.

[18]   Tobin, *Meister Eckhart: Thought and Language*, p. 72.

[19]   See ibid., pp. 73–4.

[20]   For a discussion of this, see F. Tobin, 'Eckhart's Mystical Use of Language: The Contexts of "eigenschaft"', *A Journal of Germanic Studies*, 8/3 (1972), 160–68.

from one another. By this, Eckhart means that God cannot be distinguished from things, because God is not a thing or one of a type that can be differentiated from others. For this reason, Eckhart even argues that if, in any sense, God is to be 'found', it is necessary to remove the idea of God from talk about God. Translators and commentators often represent this idea by putting the term 'God' in inverted commas. Consider, for example, the following passage:

> When I stood in my first cause, I then had no 'God' ... But when I went out from my own free will and received my created being, then I had a 'God', for before there were any creatures, God was not 'God', but he was what he was. But when creatures came to be and received their created being, then God was not 'God' in himself, but he was 'God' in the creatures.[21]

For Eckhart, the point of mystical prayer is to be rid of God so that the soul returns to a primordial state, the one it had before creation existed, when there was nothing in relation to which God could be called 'God'. Beliefs such as this led Eckhart to emphasise God as *unum* over and against the Trinity, for which he was accused of holding a less than Christian conception of God. It also led him to stress both the eternity and unity of creation. It was in relation to this latter belief that Eckhart claimed there was, in fact, something within the soul that was uncreated. As Bernard McGinn notes, this was considered one of his most dangerous beliefs:

> The most dangerous formulation of this theme in Eckhart's thought was the claim that there was something in the soul that was uncreated – 'Sometimes I have spoken of a light that is uncreated and not capable of creation, and which is within the soul.' One such passage was condemned as heretical in the Avignon Bull ...[22]

This belief extends the idea of 'the spark of the soul' found in Augustine. For Eckhart, what is uncreated in the soul was not the light of God, it is a part of the soul, the intellect, that *is* God. Eckhart held that the soul therefore had within it a light that illuminated itself, a place *within* it where the soul could say that it was uncreated. By viewing the soul in this way, Eckhart suggests (contrary to his belief

---

[21]   Meister Eckhart, *Meister Eckhart: The Essential Sermons, Commentaries, Treatises, and Defense*, trans. and with intro. by E. Colledge and B. McGinn (New York: Paulist Press, 1981), p. 200. Michael Sells objects to the use of inverted commas to distinguish the notion of 'God' as defined by human language from God proper, as it were. He argues that this undermines the way in which Eckhart brings these two ideas together through his use of the same word: God. Sells stresses, as we have discussed in Chapter 3, that it is only by bringing such ideas into conflict with one another that Eckhart is able to create 'a language of unsaying'.

[22]   B. McGinn, 'Theological Summary' in *Meister Eckhart: The Essential Sermons*, p. 42.

that the soul is nothing) that there was a state of total indistinction between the soul and God. This belief is linked to his idea that the ultimate ground of God and the soul is the same.

Once it had returned to its primordial state, Echkart argues that the soul willed God's will, but was unaware that it did so, since God's will was not some 'thing' which could actively be desired. The only sense in which Eckhart allowed that the soul might desire God was from the perspective of mystical understanding, where the soul's love for God is exemplified as non-attachment. Consider, for example, the following passage from Sermon 83:

> You should love him as he is a nonGod, a nonspirit, a nonperson, a nonimage, but as he is a pure, unmixed, bright 'One', separated from all duality; and in that One we should eternally sink down, out of 'something' into 'nothing'.[23]

Prayerful petitions were therefore redundant. The only way in which prayer made sense to Eckhart was in terms of union with God. The emphasis that this placed on individuality in the path to salvation, and the way that it negated the function of the sacraments and the role and practices of the Church, were condemned as heretical.

As we might expect, Eckhart saw the soul's desire for union with God as a desire to return to its primordial state, its ground, in which there was no differentiation between God and the soul. However, for him, arrival at this ground required the negation of union itself, which by definition suggests an original distinction between two objects. In this relation Eckhart speaks of the soul's undifferentiated union with God, an idea for which he was also condemned. It led him to suggest that the soul needed to be detached not only from ideas of difference but also from desires connected to such difference, such that the soul needs to rise above any good desires, including a desire for sanctity. As such, it entails that all of creation should be loved equality – God should not be loved above creatures. These ideas were likewise suggested to be heretical. His belief in the unity of all things led to the additional claim that was also deemed heretical – that evil only existed as a result of what is good, such that even evil gives glory to God.

Other beliefs for which Eckhart was accused of heresy include the idea that the Son is born within the soul. This image is drawn from on from a passage in John 4, where Christ tells the Pharisee that if he wishes to enter heaven he must be born again. Eckhart also uses it to extend the metaphor of the Word being born in the soul which he finds in Origen. Eckhart used this image to represent that idea that, since Christ was human and had redeemed human nature, if a person could strip themselves of everything that individualised their self and realise their pure human nature, then they could become one with the Son. In this way the Son would be born within them, and they would even *be* the Son. This shocking idea again has a close relationship to Eckhart's belief in undifferentiated union.

---

[23] Meister Eckhart, *Meister Eckhart: The Essential Sermons*, p. 208.

In addition, as the extract from Sermon 83 quoted above illustrates, Eckhart employed linguistic strategies that seem to deliberately confound his verbal discussions of mystical theology.[24] His use of paradox, oxymorons, chiasmus, hyperbole, antithesis, accumulation, parallelism and word games is highly sophisticated and deliberately mannered.[25] Take, for example, the following passage from Sermon 52, where his use of paradox is pronounced:

> The more he [God] is in things the more he is outside of things; the more he is within, the more outside, the most outside, the more within.[26]

His meaning is far from clear. Coupled with beliefs that push the bounds of faith, his use for paradox added a further layer of complexity to his mysticism that can only have contributed to the heresy charges levelled against him.

Yet should Eckhart or Porete ever have been condemned for heresy? Are their teachings really heretical, or does the condemnation of Porete and the accusations levelled against Eckhart (he died before he could be properly condemned) demonstrate another way in which new mysticism operated differently from the mystical theology of earlier Christian mystics? Neither Porete nor Eckhart offers any real defence of their beliefs. Porete remains silent during her trial. Eckhart suggests firstly that his accusers read him out of context, secondly that they claim he taught things that he did not teach, and thirdly that heresy is an act of the will – that is, while he may have made intellectual mistakes and so be in error, he cannot be a heretic since it was never his intention to contravene the orthodoxy of the Christian faith. None of these really seems to adequately account for the aspects of his mysticism that were suggested to be heretical.

CONTEMPORARY THEORETICAL APPROACHES

As with the other chapters in Part II, we will begin by considering perennialist discussions of the issue and then turn to consider scholars whose approaches critique this position, examining contextualised readings, performative language readings and various feminist responses to Porete's condemnation.

---

[24]   Tobin, *Meister Eckhart: Thought and Language*, pp. vii–viii, 147–83.

[25]   A. Hollywood, 'Marguerite Porete, Meister Eckhart and the Problem of Women's Spirituality', in McGinn, *Meister Eckhart and the Beguine Mystics*, pp. 87–113.

[26]   Meister Eckhart, *Meister Eckhart, Mystic and Philosopher: Translations with Commentary*, trans. R. Schürmann (Bloomington: Indiana University Press, 1978), p. 9.

Perennialist Approaches

Those who take a perennialist approach to mysticism are not particularly interested in contextual issues such as heresy charges. Robert Forman's discussion of Eckhart is a case in point.

Robert Forman

Robert Forman seems entirely unconcerned by the accusations of heresy levelled against Eckhart. What interests him is the way in which he believes that Eckhart's writings illustrate the existence of altered states of consciousness (ASC), states which come close to his idea of 'Pure Consciousness Events' (PCE).[27] He argues that terms such as 'the birth of the word' and 'detachment' – or, as he translates it, 'the Breakthrough' – are descriptions of such altered states of consciousness.

In fact, Forman identifies three main experiences in Eckhart's writing. The first is linked to Eckhart's use of the Middle High German word '*gezucket*' or rapture. Although Forman argues that Eckhart sometimes seems to denigrate rapture (steering his audiences away from some of the more ecstatic, visionary encounters that are associated with female mysticism, including, Forman thinks Porete's *Mirror*), Forman maintains Eckhart's rejection of rapture does not amount to a denigration of experience per se. It is only attachment to such experiences that Eckhart renounces. This idea accords with a general negation of attachments and image-based knowing in Eckhart's writing. Thus Forman views *gezucket* as a momentary state when all rational and sensory capacities are stilled. The experiencer is experiencing, although not objectifying what he encounters:

> I characterize the pattern of mental functioning denoted by Eckhart's term *gezucket as a mind which is simultaneously wakeful and objectless*. I assume that the mind is awake ... primarily as it would be absurd to suppose that Eckhart would spill such ink over a mere state of sleep or a blackout.[28]

Forman argues that through *gezucket* experiences Eckhart arrives at 'a new State of Consciousness' that is somewhat analogous to being drunk.[29] He asserts that from Eckhart's discussions, we can see that there was an experience that was objectless. Yet, despite the experience of *gezucket* being objectless, Forman holds that it is still possible to speak of such experiences without being self-contradictory as long as they are viewed as 'nothing' experiences. This merely provides 'an analytical,

---

[27] See Chapter 2 for a discussion of Formans's Pure Consciousness states, pp. 59–61.

[28] R.K.C. Forman (ed.), *The Problem of Pure Consciousness: Mysticism and Philosophy* (New York: Oxford University Press, 1990), p. 106.

[29] R.K.C. Forman, *Meister Eckhart: Mystic as Theologian: an Experiment in Methodology* (Rockport, MA: Element, 1991), p. 111.

theological "content" for a phenomenological contentlessness'.[30] For Forman, *gezucket* acts as the initial part of the 'habitual union' that characterises Eckhart's two other, more important, experiences – 'the Birth of the Son in the Soul' and 'the Breakthrough'.

The 'Birth' (*Geburt*), sees the complete abolition of all attachments, such as those to family and friends. In such experiences, Forman argues that one feels no grief in times of sorrow. In trying to assess what kind of experience this is, Forman notes that there is a tension between the divine aspect of the soul, which merges into God, and its human aspect. He postulates that the experience is in some way dualistic. What the soul discovers in this state is a 'ground' that transcends both desire (will) and knowledge (intellect). No matter what one thinks about, a state of stillness exists which constitutes one's primary mode of consciousness.[31] The 'Breakthrough' (*Der Durckbruch*), intensifies the experience of the Birth. It leads Eckhart to a shift in perception in which he comes to see things from the vantage point of God. As such, everything is known from a single point of unity. 'To breakthrough to the Godhead hence carries this weight: one will perceive that things are moved to their ontological core by the Oneness which is both "I" and "God".'[32] Forman argues that such a state of consciousness overcomes all subject–object dichotomy, and therefore the sense of dualism found in the lower experiences.[33]

According to Forman, there are plenty of examples of such states of consciousness in mystical writings that herald from many religious traditions. As such, he sees nothing heterodox about them.[34] Although illustrating that it is possible to read Eckhart from a perennialist perspective, Forman's reading arguably does not seriously engage with the theological issues for which Eckhart was accused of heresy. As such, this reflects a general weakness within the perennialist position that struggles to adequately incorporate elements outside of ineffable experience.

Contextualised Readings

More contextualised readings of Eckhart and Porete do, however, take seriously the heresy charges levelled against them. They try to understand the charges both in relation to the theology of the texts and the relationship of those texts to the Christian religious traditions in which these writers are respectively grounded.

---

[30]   Ibid., p. 111.

[31]   Forman argues that parallels can be drawn with what Eckhart describes in relation to the birth of the Son in the soul and Arnold Ludwig's 'States of Consciousness', particularly altered states of consciousness, to which he ascribes nine different characteristics. See Forman, *Meister Eckhart: Mystic as Theologian*, pp. 151–8.

[32]   Ibid., p. 180.

[33]   Ibid., p. 181.

[34]   Ibid., pp. 188–90.

Malcolm Lambert

While Malcolm Lambert describes Porete as pernicious for remaining silent during her trial, he does not believe that there is anything markedly heretical about her *Mirror*.[35] Instead he views it as an example of how mystics use language to describe states that they at least believe transcend description. He suggests that, like other mystics, she uses shock tactics and paradox to try to convey the otherness of her experience. For Lambert, her condemnation as a heretic resulted from the failure of her accusers to understand the non-literal manner in which this language was intended.

> Mystics, of whom Porete is a fair, although not a distinguished, example, were describing rare states and treating great mysteries, that lay near the limits of ordinary language: they used paradoxical, even shocking phrases in trying to convey their meaning. These were taken up, rawly and literally, by the council and fashioned into a heresy.[36]

In similar vein, Lambert also argues that Eckhart's mysticism was not heretical. However, he does suggest that both these authors can be closely associated with a movement, originating within beguine spirituality, that does push orthodoxy to its limits, certainly in relation to its rejection of the sacraments and need for the Church. Although not 'libertine or immoral ... [it] went at least to the limits of orthodoxy in its views on the possibility of union with God in this life and was indifferent, if not hostile, to the sacraments and to the mediating role of the Church'.[37] While Lambert makes room for the possibility of ineffable experience, Steven Katz assumed a more strictly contextualist position.

Steven T. Katz

Steven T. Katz argues that, despite appearances to the contrary, mysticism is by its nature conservative. Although claiming to reveal secret truths that are not accessible to ordinary believers, Katz holds that mysticism generally operates within the accepted bounds of orthodoxy because the beliefs and experiences of mystics depend on the sacred writings of the religious tradition to which they belong.[38] In the case of Meister Eckhart, Katz draws attention to the close relationship between some of Eckhart's more daring statements and biblical exegesis. He notes, for example, the close relation between John 4 and the birth of the Son within the soul. While he admits that it is legitimate to question whether all of Eckhart's beliefs are orthodox, Katz suggests that their relationship to sacred scripture means that they

---

[35]   Lambert, *Medieval Heresy*, p. 203.

[36]   Ibid., p. 206.

[37]   Ibid., p. 207.

[38]   Katz, 'The "Conservative" Character of Mystical Experience', p. 13.

remain on the bounds of orthodoxy, such that for Eckhart and his supporters they constituted an 'authentic meaning of the Christian faith'.[39] Turning to consider Eckhart's paradoxical use of language, Katz argues that it needs to be seen as an attempt to talk about the Christian God as God who 'must be "known" but cannot be known', a view which also belies Eckhart's Neoplatonism.[40] Katz argues that, as such, this use of paradoxical language differs from paradoxical expressions like Buddhist *kōans* (for example, the sound of one hand clapping), since it does not aim at the collapse of language, but at a description of 'the transcendental reality' that is God, who 'must be expressed but cannot be expressed in ordinary language, that *is* but whose 'isnesss' is unlike that of any other reality'.[41] As such, Katz argues that this is part of a deliberate strategy that plays into Eckhart's relationship with Christianity rather than against it.

Also taking a strongly contextualist postion, Hugh Owen notes that, despite a few exceptions like Eckhart and Porete, the fact that most mystics are not viewed as heretics, seems to confirm that their experiences are not ineffable. One would expect more heresy if that were the case. For Owen, Eckhart is 'the exception that proves the rule',[42] indicating the close relationship between mystics, their experiences and the religious traditions to which they belong. However, like Katz, Owen struggles to make sense of the heresy charges levelled against Porete and Eckhart – again indicating a possible weakness of this approach.

Bernard McGinn

A less strictly contextualist, but still contextualised, defence of Meister Eckhart is presented by Bernard McGinn. McGinn, who as we noted in the previous chapter contends that both indescribable experiences and context can be held together within an interpretation of Christian mysticism, acknowledges that there are difficult sayings within Eckhart's mysticism and that not all the points of theology for which he was condemned can easily be explained. However, he argues that we gain a far greater sense of the orthodoxy underlying Eckhart's claims when we consider them as part of a unified theology. For McGinn, the crux of Eckhart's mysticism is his theological belief that the ground of God and the soul are fundamentally the same:

> Eckhart is pleading for us to open our eyes and to see what has always been
> the case, that God and the soul are truly one in the deepest ground ... In the

---

[39]   Katz, 'Mysticism and the Interpretation of Sacred Scripture', p. 31.

[40]   Ibid., p. 43.

[41]   Ibid., p. 43.

[42]   H.P. Owen, 'Experience and the English Mystics', in S. Katz (ed.), *Mysticism and Religious Tradition* (Oxford: Oxford University Press, 1983), pp. 148–62, at p. 159.

last analysis Eckhart's theology is both theocentric and at the same time fully anthropocentric. God is God and man is man, and yet God's ground and the soul's ground are one ground.[43]

Viewed in this light, he asserts that some of Eckhart's more difficult sayings appear less heterodox. Take, for example, Eckhart's assertion that God is one or *unum*. While the emphasis that Eckhart places on the hidden God as *unum* appears to undermine a belief in the Trinity, McGinn stresses that, in addition to numerous passages that affirm the Trinity, we need to be aware that when Eckhart stresses God's unity he is referring to the priority of God's ground, out of which all that exists arises. His emphasis on oneness therefore needs to be seen as part of an apophatic strategy which Eckhart uses to bring his readers to this essential ground that underlies everything:

> we must again advert to the priority of the apophatic way, bearing in mind that his most intricate arguments and daring assertions are not more than appropriate paradoxes to help us along the path to union with God which is 'one without unity and three without trinity.[44]

McGinn argues that the same is true of other difficult teachings, such as Eckhart's claim that creation has no temporal beginning or that the human soul is nothing compared to God. McGinn suggests that some of these beliefs belie Eckhart's Neoplatonism, which was at odds with the more Aristotelian stance of fourteenth-century Dominican theology. However, he stresses that, in terms of Christian mysticism, Eckhart is far from alone in drawing on Neoplatonism, which of itself makes him no less heterodox than Augustine or Pseudo-Denys.

McGinn also argues that Eckhart often employs the *in quantum* principle – that is, the 'insofar as' principle – within his discussions of difficult mystical ideas. McGinn notes that this qualifying expression is used by Eckhart in the discussion of topics such as 'the just man' who does not feel the need to seek sanctity. McGinn argues that Eckhart's use of 'insofar as' indicates that Eckhart is not referring to a concrete person, but to an abstraction of the just man *insofar as* he is just. It is in this sense that he sees Eckhart's talk of people moving beyond sanctity – on a mystical and idealised level. McGinn states that that lack of distinction between God and man in some of Eckhart's more daring images, such as in the birth of the Son within the soul, must also be viewed in the light of this 'insofar as' principle. In addition to difficult teachings such as these, McGinn notes that Eckhart was accused of ethical errors, such as denigrating the role of good deeds. McGinn merely notes that this is a natural repercussion of the general thrust of Eckhart's mysticism but finds it surprising Eckhart was accused of this given that the Heresy of the Free Spirit was normally associated with salacious external deeds, not a lack

---

[43]   McGinn, *Meister Eckhart: Essential Sermons*, p. 61.

[44]   Ibid., pp. 35–6.

of good ones. Thus, while accepting that there are some difficult teachings within Eckhart's writings, McGinn argues that, when read in the context of Eckhart's deeply apophatic theology, many of the seemingly heretical statements appear more orthodox, and even illustrative of the apophatic impetus that underlies Eckhart's mystical discourse.

Performative Language Readings

Sells's and Turner's defences of Eckhart are connected to their treatment of mystical language as apophatic.

Michael Sells

Michael Sells argues that both Eckhart and Porete create languages of unsaying. As discussed in previous chapters, by this he means their writing constitutes an apophatic discourse that sets out to constantly destabilise language in an attempt to illustrate the ineffability of the divine. In light of this he draws particular attention to what he sees as the deliberate strategies that both authors use to overcome essentialism.

Central to the destabilising of essentialism is the metaphor of emanation.[45] This is an image which Sells argues naturally undoes itself, since the fall or progression of emanation is at the same time its return: 'the paradox of emanation (that the procession *is* the return) is used in a radical way to destabilize the temporal, causal, and spatial structures of language'.[46] Sells notes how Porete combines emanation imagery with another motif, 'without a why'. God is thus portrayed in a series of baffling paradoxes as freely giving the soul free will, while the annihilated soul acts without free will, giving back freely to God the free will that is freely given. As such, the soul is seen to flow out of God, while God flows into the soul. Porete also inverts Fall imagery, having the soul fall both from its pre-created state and then back into it.[47] Eckhart likewise uses the emanation language of boiling over (*bullitio*) and boiling over or out (*ebullitio*) to set up a series of paradoxical relations between God and creation. First, God flows out, but remains within, in the relations of the Trinity. Secondly, God flows out into creation as the first principle or cause, flowing out within himself, and out into the world. Yet God also remains within himself. In addition there is the double paradox within the Trinity, since the Father is the source of the Son, even while the two are identical. Yet there can be no father without a son. Sells maintains that the interdependence of these ideas leads Eckhart to talk of the ground of God, which is beyond Trinitarian

---

[45] We also discussed this idea in Chapter 5, where we explored the theme of hierarchy in Christian mystical texts.

[46] Sells, 'The Pseudo-Woman and the Meister, p. 115.

[47] Ibid., p. 127.

relations, as a means of countering any essentialising of God's nature. Sells also draws attention to what he sees as a countering of gender-essentialism in both writers, as they move the soul beyond any sense of differentiation. Sells sees nothing particularly problematic in the teaching of these writers, which he reads mainly on the semantic level. Although he is not not particularly concerned with the issue of orthodoxy, for Sells, their use of language demonstrates their mystical credentials, which in the end for Sells is what matters.

Denys Turner

Denys Turner focuses more directly on the heresy changes levelled against Eckhart. He dismisses them on two counts. Firstly, he argues that Eckhart is not always concerned with the precision of meaning, such that Eckhart sometimes uses language merely to create a particular effect rather than to impart knowledge. He ascribes this use of language to Eckhart's role a as preacher, suggesting that, as a preacher, he is more concerned with bringing about a transformative effect than a philosophical understanding.[48] Secondly, and more importantly, Turner dismisses the heresy charges as a misrepresentation of Eckhart's thought brought about by a-contextual reading.

Turner argues that in Eckhart we are presented with apophaticism of the most radical kind. By this he means that it belongs to the Western apophatic tradition as Turner understands it:

> we have seen that for the mainstream apophatic tradition in Western Christianity the strategy of the apophatic consisted in a deliberate practice of straining to speak about God, in the purposive stretching of the discourse of theology to those limits at which it snaps, in the contriving of that paradox and contradictoriness on the other side of which there is only silence.[49]

Eckhart's mysticism fits within a broad category of mystical writing that seeks to stretch language to its breaking point when attempting to talk about God. Turner believes that, by reading Eckhart in this way, we gain insight into some of his more difficult sayings, particularly the idea that there is something uncreated in the soul – namely the intellect.

Dismissing other defences, such as McGinn's *in quantum* principle defence, for failing to take seriously the radical nature of Eckhart's claim, Turner stresses that Eckhart really did believe that there was something in the soul that was, in a way not implied by Augustine, uncreated. Yet, at the same time, Turner argues that Eckhart was criticised not so much for believing that the soul was uncreated, as for maintaining that the soul was too distinct from God – that is, that it was nothing in

---

[48]   J. Macquarrie also argues that Eckhart's phrases are at times imprecise – suggesting that this is one factor that led to the heresy accusations levelled against him. J. Macquarrie 'Two Worlds are Ours: An Introduction to Christian Mysticism (London: SCM, 2004), p. 136.

[49]   Turner, *Darkness of God*, p. 150.

relation to him. Turner suggests that this paradox leads us to the heart of Eckhart's apophatic discourse.

He notes that Eckhart claims that there is no distinction between God's uncreated nature and the soul's created nature. He takes it that Eckhart does not mean by this either that the soul is totally distinct from God or that God and the soul are indistinguishable. Rather, he suggests that it entails that they are distinguishable in a manner that defies expression. For Eckhart, the soul is nothing in the sense that it is neither a 'this' nor a 'that', in the same way that God is neither a 'this' nor a 'that'. This brings us to the apophatic realisation which Turner also believes underpins the use of erotic imagery in mystical texts: that is, that we lack the language to distinguish ourselves from God. However, Turner argues that Eckhart takes apophatic discourse to another level. By maintaining that intellect is uncreated, Eckhart moves the dialectic between positive and negative statements into the soul itself. By doing so he creates what Turner calls an 'apophatic anthropology', in which there is no room for dualism. When viewed as such, Turner argues, it is clear that Eckhart's mysticism is not heretical. It is simply a complex theological formula for expressing the ineffability of the divine. It is in this relation that Turner is, however, somewhat critical of Eckhart. He believes that Eckhart sometimes overcomplicates the way that language unsays itself, such that it appears that Eckhart is not satisfied with a linguistic collapse into silence as suggested by Pseudo-Denys:

> Whereas Denys *lets* language collapse into silence and through the cessation of speech express the apophatic, Eckhart wants to force the imagery to *say* the apophatic. Eckhart cannot let the apophatic be … he will use speech, necessarily broken, contradictory, absurd, paradoxical, conceptually hyperbolic speech, to bring to insight the ineffability of God.[50]

Turner is critical of what he identifies as this tendency within Eckhart's writing to try to make language say the ineffable, even though this is not possible. In this respect, Turner's understanding of Eckhart brings him closer to Sell's reading of apophasis in which language constantly needs to unsay itself in order to lead to apophasis.

We have already noted Turner's dependence on Pseudo-Denys as a possible weakness of his approach. This said, Turner's discussion of Eckhart seems extremely illuminating since it moves between the linguistic and the theological in a manner which Sells's focus on semantics does not allow to the same extent. As such, Turner is able to offer a convincing defence of Eckhart's paradoxical use of language without the need to rely on the *in quantum* principle as McGinn does. At the same time, this makes Turner's suggestion that Eckhart may have been careless in his use of language in his sermons seems less convincing. In taking such a theological approach, Turner's account also lacks the emphasis on

---

[50]   Ibid., p. 151.

the role of the Church in determining heresy that we find in Lambert and Katz. It is perhaps worth noting that Julian of Norwich, whose writing reveals an internal dialogue between what she sees and what she knows the Church teaches, is rarely considered heretical. The complex nature of the notion of heresy is illustrative of the benefits of taking a more multi-dimensional approach to understanding Christian mysticism. Thus to conclude our discussion of this topic, we turn finally to feminist readings of Porete's mysticism.

Feminist Readings

Carolyn Walker Bynum interestingly excludes Porete from her analysis of female mysticism on the grounds that she was a 'heretic'. This has not stopped other feminists either including Porete within a Bynum-type model of female mysticism or using her to challenge some of the premises that underlie Bynum's general reading, which seems to inadvertently lessen the disruptive potential ascribed to mysticism by earlier feminists.

Maria Lichtmann

Maria Lichtmann applies Bynum's general model to Porete in that she argues that, although more subtle than writings of other female mystics, Porete's *Mirror* still presents mysticism as a gradual deepening of ordinary, rather than extraordinary, experience. Thus Lichtmann sees it as a typical female account of mysticism through its emphasis on the body. She argues that this differentiates Porete from Eckhart, who maintains an essential body-spirit dualism:

> Marguerite's mysticism is gendered in its body-soul integration, its rejection of the pursuit of 'virtue' over simplicity and nothingness, and its 'theology' of a feminine Divine.[51]

Lichtmann considers Porete's collapse of body–spirit dualism to be an important contributory factor to what her inquisitors found so threatening about her *Mirror*. Other aspects of femininity which characterise this lack of dualism include the feminising of all the characters in her book, even though this involves the re-gendering of love in French. Litchmann does not agree with Sells that Porete unsays gender. She argues that the feminisation of the soul is too integral to be thus abandoned. 'To "unsay" gender to the point where it may unsay nature bespeaks a disregard for materiality and body that Marguerite did not share.'[52] As an example of feminine mysticism, Lichtmann does not accept that Porete's account is heretical; rather she sees it, like other female discussions of mysticism as deeply

---

[51] M. Lichtmann, 'Marguerite Porete and Meister Eckhart', p. 75.

[52] Ibid., p. 75, n. 29.

embodied, drawing on the ordinary that is excluded from male intellectual acounts of mysticism.

Amy Hollywood

Amy Hollywood, however, believes that Porete rejects the female forms of mysticism she finds characterised both in hagiographical traditions associated with women and in female-authored mystical literature. Hollywood argues that Porete's insistence that the soul must return to its pre-creation state goes beyond the ecstatic mysticism commonly associated with female spirituality. Like Eckhart, she argues that Porete arrives at a point where she recognises the limitations of her body and the practices associated with it, such as imaginative devotion and the glorification of suffering, often linked with visionary encounters of God. 'Porete and Eckhart ... are dramatically aware of the limitations of the body and of the imagination, which continually haunt embodied experience thereby engendering further suffering.'[53] In taking such an approach and offering 'subversions of gendered language and image',[54] She sees Porete moving away from accepted female norms. Hollywood believes that this is the underlying reason why the chronicler at her trial called her a 'Pseudo-Woman' and that it contributed to her being accused of heresy. Rather than being a weakness of Porete's mysticism, on the contrary, Hollywood believes it illustrates the limitations of male-dominated Christianity and the authority structures that this reinforces, which seek to contain and tame women by placing their spirituality within its own narrowly defined confines.

Conclusion

This chapter has considered theoretical responses to the heresy charges levelled against Eckhart and Porete. We have noted that Forman is largely disinterested in the charges, viewing them as a secondary issue to that of types of ineffable consciousness events that he believes mystical texts to illustrate. In contrast, more contextualised readings take the heresy charges more seriously. Katz, for example, believes that Eckhart pushes the bounds of orthodoxy, despite being tied to it through scriptural exegesis, Christian theology and tradition. It is this which leads him to assert that, despite such challenges, Eckhart's mysticism never moves far beyond authentic faith positions. McGinn, while recognising that heterodox statements are possibly present in Eckhart's writings, argues that they are considerably softened when viewed in relation to their theological context and the *in quantum* principle. Denys Turner also seeks to defend Eckhart against accusations of heresy. Unlike McGinn, he suggests the best defence is to be found in reading Eckhart's language

---

[53]   Hollywood, 'Marguerite Porete, Meister Eckhart and the Problem of Women's Spirituality', p. 109.

[54]   Ibid., p. 88.

as an apophatic strategy. Finally, several scholars have defended Porete from feminist perspectives, either readings hers as an account of embodied mysticism or suggesting that the accusations of heresy result precisely from her failure to conform to embodied spirituality deemed appropriate for women. All these readings demonstrate the complexity inherent within Christian mysticism.

This chapter concludes our discussion of the four contemporary theoretical approaches with which we began this book. As we moved through the various themes in Part I and II it became increasingly apparent that Christian mysticism is not easily contained with the bounds of any of these positions. Before finally turning in the conclusion to reflect on the implications of this, Part III, the final section of this book, examines postmodern re-readings of Christian mysticism, without which no introduction to Christian mysticism could be considered complete.

Part III
Postmodern Re-Readings of Pseudo-Denys and Augustine

In Part III we examine postmodern re-readings of Christian mysticism. Such re-readings tend to focus on Pseudo-Denys's use of negative or apophatic language and Augustine's account of interiority and selfhood. The two chapters in this section explore these two Christian mystics through the eyes of Jacques Derrida, Jean-Luc Marion and Jean-François Lyotard, who not only offer alternative interpretations of them, but use and critique these Christian mystics as part of their own theoretical agendas.

Chapter 11

Exploring Negative Language through Pseudo-Denys: Derrida and Marion

In Chapter 2 we discussed the use of theological language in mystical texts, using the writings of Pseudo-Denys as our main example. Our discussion focused on Pseudo-Denys's understanding of the relationship between negative (apophatic) and affirmative (kataphatic) theology. Hence, we discussed a number of philosophical interpretations of Pseudo-Denys's theological language that are broadly based around the question of whether or not the main issue in his writings is mystical experience (Katz; Forman) or the knowledge of divine ineffability (Turner; Knepper).

This chapter asks similar questions to those in Chapter 2: 'Is Pseudo-Denys describing an ineffable experience or the ineffability of God?' Is theological language primarily an attempt to recount a mystical experience or to know through unknowing? Yet here we will look through a slightly different lens. Instead of concerning ourselves with modern attempts to interpret Pseudo-Denys's understanding of apophatic language, we will discuss how contemporary thinkers have drawn upon Pseudo-Denys's work as a resource for their own analyses of the relationship between language, transcendence and God. The chapter focuses on a contemporary debate between two highly influential thinkers: Jacques Derrida and Jean-Luc Marion. Derrida and Marion are different and similar in very interesting ways. Both have found Denys's apophatic theology to be important for the development of their respective philosophical projects as thinkers in the phenomenological lineage of Edmund Husserl and Martin Heidegger.[1] Yet Marion is a practising Roman Catholic, while Derrida identified himself as an atheist. Marion began his career as a theologian (who now primarily writes philosophy); Derrida was a radical poststructuralist (who wrote extensively on religion late in his life). This chapter sets out to explore why they converged so closely and so provocatively over the use of theological language within Christian mysticism, and why Pseudo-Denys's mysticism in particular has caused such a stir among two of the most influential thinkers of the last generation.

---

[1]   For a helpful introduction to phenomenology, see D. Moran, *Introduction to Phenomenology* (London: Routledge, 2000).

Postmodernism and Religion

The Debate between Derrida and Marion

The first public debate between Derrida and Marion took place in 1997 at a conference entitled 'Religion and Postmodernism' at Villanova University. In his introduction to the proceedings from this conference, John Caputo noted that the work of Derrida and Marion is so provocative because it makes room for religion, while the authority of modernity – stemming from the Enlightenment – tries to weed it out.[2] According to Caputo, modernity rejects external sources of knowledge, such as divine revelation, in order to pursue knowledge solely through human reason. By making such an exclusionary mandate, the Enlightenment rules out traditionally religious phenomena such as miracles, divine revelation and mystical visions.

The main purpose of the conference, and the main thrust of Derrida's and Marion's work on religion, was to reincorporate trajectories of pre-modern thought (including aspects of medieval mysticism) that have been lost at the hands of modernity, without reverting back to a full-fledged medieval worldview (it is in this sense that they can be understood as postmodern). Both Derrida and Marion hold that formulating philosophical discourse within the boundaries of reason alone does not mean that religion must be edged out. Religion and reason do not have to be understood as opposites, or even worse, as enemies. However, neither wants to abandon the Enlightenment in order to return to a pre-modern form of thinking and faith. As Caputo explains:

> On this telling, the new Enlightenment would constitute a second childhood which is given over to dreaming of the impossible, arising from a deep desire for what, given the constraints and conditions imposed by modernity, is precisely not possible, which for that reason is precisely what we most deeply desire. Let us say that what brought the participants in this conference together is a desire to experience the impossible ... to think the unthinkable ... for the express purpose of restoring the good name of the impossible; to make it respectable, to give it its day in court, to defend it, to produce in short an apology for the impossible.[3]

This desire to readmit the unthinkable and the impossible helps to explain both Derrida's and Marion's interest in Pseudo-Denys. Both thinkers recognise the Christian mystical tradition as a helpful resource for reflecting on language, transcendence and religion within this postmodern context.

---

[2]   J.D. Caputo and M.J. Scanlon, 'Introduction: Apology for the Impossible: Religion and Postmodernism' in J.D. Caputo and M.J. Scanlon (eds), *God, the Gift, and Postmodernism* (Bloomington, IN: Indiana University Press, 1999), pp. 2–3.

[3]   Ibid., p. 2.

The Other, the Impossible and the Gift

Marion and Derrida are descendents of the philosophical lineage known as phenomenology. Some of the philosophical language that they use is derived from this tradition and may be unfamiliar to many readers. We will briefly introduce three central terms: the Other, the impossible and the gift.

First, when Derrida and Marion speak of the Other, they are referring to that which is totally foreign to human thinking and concepts. The Other is capitalised because it is not merely an other, like another person, but an Other that has no representational relationship to existence. As a result, we cannot speak of the Other in a manner that is in any way similar to other things – we cannot say what size it is, what colour, how big, how powerful, or what it looks like. If it had any of these qualities it would cease to be Other. Even if someone speaks of God as all-powerful, all-knowing and completely just, they are not speaking of God as the Other because they are making an analogy between God and existence.

Derrida and Marion also speak of the impossible. The impossible is not merely *an* impossibility – like a square circle. Instead, as Thomas Carlson explains, the impossible would 'engender thought, speech, and desire that remain oriented around a term that thought, speech, or desire cannot finally attain as such'.[4] Thus, the impossible is more than just an *impossibility*, it is that something (or nothing: we do not know) that is beyond thinking and language – which we desire to know, but cannot.

Finally, Derrida and Marion also deal with what they call the gift. Think of the gift as a kind of impossible event of the Other. The gift is how Derrida and Marion refer to the possibility of the Other becoming manifest, or revealing itself within human thinking and language. In a strange way, the gift is the possibility of the impossible taking place – the possible impossibility of encountering the Other. As we shall see, much of their debate centres on the nature of the gift and how it should be understood.

Derrida's Engagement with Apophatic Theology

Deconstruction and Différance

Jacques Derrida is one of the most influential Western thinkers of the last fifty years. His formulation of deconstruction, is a strategy for reading texts. It is allied to the notion of 'différance'. For Derrida, texts are set up in terms of binaries that contain a positive element (presence, God, masculinity, Being) and its opposite (absence, sin, femininity, Non-Being). The positive aspect is a complete, independent, fundamental reality, and it stands in opposition to the incomplete,

---

[4]   T.A. Carlson, *Indiscretion: Finitude and the Naming of God* (Chicago: University of Chicago Press, 1999), p. 250.

dependent, secondary negative term.[5] Derrida says, 'There is not a single signified that escapes, even if recaptured, the play of signifying references that constitute language.'[6] Deconstruction aims to demonstrate the lack of stable meaning within language, speech, and writing. Gary Cutting notes:

> Derrida's readings reveal the dichotomies (binary oppositions) of a text and at the same time show how these divisions collapse as the alleged relations of logical exclusion and hierarchical priority are implicitly undermined by the words deployed to express them.[7]

For Derrida, close readings of any text reveal its complete lack of stable, fixed structure. As William Schroeder states:

> Derrida's 'deconstruction' is an approach to the reading of philosophical texts which shows that they undermine themselves from within. In its strongest form, it demonstrates that – when read closely and attentively – philosophical essays contain realizations that undermine their main assertions.[8]

Thus, deconstruction aims to reveal how the dualism between a stabilising force and its contingent counterpart does not hold; how one text always has an endless array of meanings. Instead of having a stable meaning as part of a structure of language, the meanings of all linguistic references are constantly changing in relationship to one another. Think of a chain comprised of individual links, but instead of a stable, linear chain attached to a solid ground (the signified), in which every link always stays in the same place, the links are always intermingling with one another through perpetual motion. While the links stay separate, there is no fixed structure to the chain – no constituting beginning or end to hold the chain's perpetual motion in place. In echoing such a relationship Derrida's textual approach has been labelled poststructuralism.

Yet deconstruction is only part of the story. Différance describes both the motion of the chain, and the perpetual unstructured intermingling of the links. Différance with an 'a' is a purposeful misspelling of the French word 'différence' with an 'e', meaning 'difference' in English. Derrida uses his misspelling to emphasise the two meanings of his word 'différance', which are 'to defer' and 'to differ'. Différance is used to convey the space (difference) between each linguistic reference and the

---

5   G. Cutting, 'French Philosophy in the Twentieth-Century', in D. Moran (ed.), *The Routledge Companion to Twentieth-Century Philosophy* (London: Routledge, 2008), p. 837.

6   J. Derrida, *Of Grammatology* (Baltimore: The Johns Hopkins University Press, 1976), p. 7.

7   Cutting, 'French Philosophy in the Twentieth-Century', p. 837.

8   W.R. Schroeder, *Continental Philosophy: A Critical Approach* (Oxford: Blackwell, 2004), p. 286.

delay (the deferring) 'in which meaning is deferred until the next element in the series emerges (but the series itself is never-ending)'.[9] In this way, différance bears a trace of the event that set the circle of language and thought in motion – it is what makes it possible.

> Without the possibility of différance, the desire of presence as such would not find its breathing-space. That means by the same token that this desire carries in itself the destiny of its non-satisfaction. Différance produces what it forbids, makes possible the very thing that it makes impossible.[10]

The meaning of every reference is part of a chain of references, each of which differs. However, there is no anchor to the chain to stabilise the space between them. Instead, there is an endless play between the links that make up language.

In contrast to some of his critics, Derrida does not understand the end result of deconstruction's strategy of disclosing the play of différance as crude nihilism, nor as a radical form of relativism. Instead, it reveals the desire – always unfulfilled and deferred – for the appearance of an Other that will provide the presence needed for a stable, fixed meaning for thought and language, and thus, existence. For Derrida, we are always waiting for the perfection of our concepts – for justice, for democracy, for ethics. We have never arrived, but the hope of the appearance of the Other that makes language and thought possible spurs us on to ever improved, refined, and transformed political, ethical and religious forms of human life. In this way, deconstruction's desire for the impossible is a messianic prayer or a dream of the impossible.

Derrida's Re-reading of Pseudo-Denys

Derrida's interest in Pseudo-Denys, and apophatic theology in general, is related to the desire for the impossible. For Derrida, apophatic theology is similar to deconstruction because it desires to move past the binary of affirmation and negation to that which exceeds language. In his most sustained text on apophatic theology, *On the Name*,[11] Derrida begins by noting that all negative theology[12] seems to bear the essential trait of pushing frontiers: 'That is one of the essential traits of all negative theology: passing to the limit, then crossing a frontier.'[13]

---

[9]   Ibid., p. 284.

[10]   Derrida, *Of Grammatology*, p. 143.

[11]   Published in French as *Sauf Le Nom* (Paris: Galilee, 1993) and in English as *On the Name*, ed. T. Dutoit (Stanford: Stanford University Press, 1995).

[12]   In *On the Name*, Derrida uses the phrase 'negative theology' to refer to what he had hitherto referred to as 'apophatic theology'. In this section we shall use 'negative theology' in order to remain close to Derrida's argument.

[13]   Derrida, *On the Name*, p. 36.

Negative theology seeks to go further in speaking about God than all other discourse – theological or not. Derrida believes that it does so out of 'the most insatiable desire for God'.[14] It is this desire for God that characterises negative theology – the desire to go beyond, to transgress, to think, and to experience that which exceeds language. This seems very similar to his textual strategy of deconstruction:

> This thought seems strangely familiar to the experience of what is called deconstruction. Far from being a methodical technique, a possible or necessary procedure unrolling the law of a program and applying rules, that is, unfolding possibilities, deconstruction has often been defined as the very experience of the (impossible) possibility of the impossible, of the most impossible, a condition that deconstruction shares with the gift, the 'yes,' the 'come,' decision, testimony, the secret, etc. And perhaps death.[15]

For Derrida, deconstruction and negative theology share an interest in trying to think the unthinkable and experience the impossible. Both are characterised by an intense desire to move beyond the circle of human concepts, representations and symbols – in short, language. Caputo sums up the comparison:

> Theology and deconstruction share a common passion and desire ... The impossible is what gets both underway, impelling and impassioning them, setting them in motion ... Everything comes down to what is called the impossible, or *tout autre* (wholly Other), under whatever name it goes or comes, God, for example.[16]

Given these substantial similarities, we must ask what the difference is between Derrida's experience of deconstruction and negative theology as set forth by Pseudo-Denys, Meister Eckhart and others.

The difference between the two is revealed in Derrida's simple question: 'How does one leap out of the circle?'[17] How can we possibly know or experience the impossible (the Other that set the circle of language in motion)? Derrida believes language bears the trace of the originary event which put the circle of language in motion; the singular event that makes all language possible; the event which instituted the desire to leap out of the circle: 'the event remains at once in and on language, then, within and at the surface'.[18] For Derrida, the problem with negative theology's answer to the question stems from its determined nature – its claim that

---

14   Ibid., p. 37.

15   Ibid., p. 43.

16   J.D. Caputo, *The Prayers and Tears of Jacques Derrida: Religion without Religion* (Bloomington, IN: Indiana University Press, 1997), p. 51.

17   Derrida, *On the Name*, p. 48.

18   Ibid., p. 58.

the motion of the circle of human language has been instituted by a named event – a God that occupies a place beyond all places:

> This is what God's name always names, before or beyond other names: the trace of the singular event that will have rendered speech possible even before it turns itself back toward – in order to respond to – this first or last reference. This is why apophatic discourse must also open with a prayer that recognizes, assigns, or ensures it destination: the Other as Referent … which is none other than its Cause.[19]

In Derrida's mind, by saving the name 'God' for that which is beyond language, apophatic discourse attempts to retain the resonances of a metaphysical Cause or Referent that makes language possible. This stands in direct opposition to deconstruction's desire to reveal language's lack of stabilising Referent – anything that would give a stable structure to the circular chain of linguistic references.

Thus, for Derrida, even if Pseudo-Denys's God is 'beyond Being'[20] his apophatic discourse retains the echoes of a metaphysical God that acts as the Cause of the circle of language. Pseudo-Denys's emphasis on prayer highlights how this apophatic discourse retains these metaphysical echoes:

> In contrast, at the opening and from the first words of the *Mystical Theology*, Dionysius addresses himself directly to You, to God, from now on determined as 'hyperessential Trinity' in the prayer that prepares the theologemes of the *via negativa* (negative way).[21]

For Derrida, even if apophatic discourse recognises language as inadequate to the task of describing God, Pseudo-Denys's apophatic language is not a pure address or desire for the Other, but is a response directed at a determined Other – the God beyond Being:

> How can one deny that, in this movement of determination (which is no longer the pure address of the prayer to the other), the appointment of the trinitary and hyperessential God distinguishes Dionysius' Christian prayer from all other prayer?[22]

---

[19]   J. Derrida, 'How to Avoid Speaking: Denials', in H. Coward and T. Foshay (eds) *Derrida and Negative Theology* (Albany, NY: State University of New York Press, 1992), p. 98.

[20]   Ibid., p. 90.

[21]   Ibid., p. 116 (emphasis mine).

[22]   Ibid., p. 111.

Thus, for Derrida, the tradition of negative theology tries 'leaping out of the circle' to reach a particular 'named' God that it presupposes to have first set the circle of language in motion.

Dreaming of the Impossible for Derrida

In response, Derrida does not set out to contradict the direction of negative theology, but only to demonstrate how it can and must be uprooted from its determined place in order to be made universal. Derrida's interest in the work of mystics such as Pseudo-Denys and Meister Eckhart is to demonstrate how negative theology paves the way for a general, universal apophaticism. What does this mean? It means recognising that negative theology conducts an 'internal rebellion' that 'radically contests the tradition from which it seems to come'.[23] By moving past predicative statements about God's nature, attributes, and relationship to creation, negative theology uproots itself out of the determined context of its tradition (in this case Christian)[24] and is translated into a universalisable apophatic discourse concerning the impossible – deconstruction.

Thus the name that was saved for the impossible, God, is revealed as unnecessary:

> Then, 'the name is necessary' would mean that the name is lacking: it must be lacking, a name is necessary that is lacking. Thus *managing to efface itself, it itself will be safe, will be, save itself.*[25]

For Derrida, the impossible is preserved by language's refusal to assign it a name. Rather than nominating the impossible as 'God', as is the tendency of negative theology, the impossible remains unnameable. Once it is named, even as the 'God Beyond Being' or as Pseudo-Denys's *hyperousios,* the impossible is lost because it has been brought into the framework of human thinking. As a result, Derrida likens the desire for the Other – that which is beyond language and thinking – to a secret that is sealed by a 'witness without witness'[26] and an 'indecipherable signature'.[27] Our desire for that which exceeds language is a secret that cannot be expressed linguistically. Thus, the paradox shared by negative theology and deconstruction: they share the desire to speak of that which exceeds language, but have only language in which to formulate the desire. By trying to name that which

---

[23]   Derrida, *On the Name,* p. 67.

[24]   Derrida's essay 'How to Avoid Speaking: Denials' was a response given at a colloquium held on his work that dealt with the question of negative theology from Christian, Hindu, and Buddhist perspectives. See the essays collected in Coward and Foshay, *Derrida and Negative Theology.*

[25]   Derrida, *On the Name,* p. 68.

[26]   Ibid., p. 60.

[27]   Ibid., p. 60.

exceeds language, negative theology particularises the impossible within a specific religious-cultural tradition. Deconstruction, on the other hand, seeks a universal apophaticism. It longs to 'leap out of the circle' but knows it is impossible to achieve this through language. As Caputo notes, for Derrida 'the dreaming always arises within language'.[28] It is a primordial desire for the impossible that cannot be spoken of, and thus is a secret signed by an undecipherable Other.

In the end, Derrida wants to translate the apophaticism he admires so much in negative theology into what Caputo calls a general apophatics that concerns all people – whether atheists, religious, Western, or none of the above.[29] He understands this 'religion without religion' to be the way towards a new understanding of the social. It is for him 'the condition for a universal politics, for the possibility of crossing the borders of our common context – European, Jewish, Christian, Muslim, and philosophical … I use the problematic of deconstruction and negative theology as a threshold to the definition of a new politics.'[30]

The Third Way: Jean-Luc Marion and the Discourse of Praise

Jean-Luc Marion began his career writing theology. His early work was concerned with delineating an understanding of God after 'the collapse of metaphysics'. Marion takes seriously Friedrich Nietzsche's declaration of the 'death of God'.[31] Nietzsche stood at the end of a long philosophical and theological tradition in the West that relied upon a transcendent Being of beings to give meaning to the universe. For Nietzsche, this belief in a transcendent, other-worldly God is nothing more than a human projection; what Marion calls an idol – a way of giving meaning to human existence and ensuring that humans have a central place in the universe.

Rejecting Idols

Marion does not treat the death of God as a threat to Christian theology, but sees in it an opportunity to liberate theology from a God imprisoned as an idol

---

[28] J.D. Caputo, 'Apostles of the Impossible: On God and the Gift in Derrida and Marion' in Caputo and Scanlon, *God, the Gift, and Postmodernism*, pp. 185–222, at p. 196.

[29] Caputo, *The Prayers and Tears of Jacques Derrida*, p. 57.

[30] J. Derrida, in 'On the Gift: A Discussion Between Jacques Derrida and Jean-Luc Marion, Moderated by Richard Kearney' in Caputo and Scanlon, *God, the Gift, and Postmodernism*, pp. 54–78, at p. 76.

[31] See, F. Nietzsche, *The Gay Science*, trans. J. Nauckhoff and A. Del Caro (Cambridge: Cambridge University Press, 2001), pp. 119–20.

within human concepts.[32] In his early theological writings Marion argues that God is present through his absence – his uncrossable distance from creation. Robyn Horner summarizes:

> At the most basic level, distance seems to refer to the absolute difference between God and humanity. In other words, distance operates to mark the non-coincidence of God with a concept of God … Where metaphysics often thinks God as the foundation of being and the guarantee of meaning, Marion uses distance as a figure of the interruption of thought, maintaining that it resists recuperation either as a foundation of what can be presented or represented in knowledge.[33]

Thus, instead of making an idol out of God by thinking him within the limits of human concepts, Marion argues that God is the unthinkable, which can neither be thought, nor seen. This generates Marion's interest in Pseudo-Denys, in whom he sees the clearest example of Christian theology's aversion for, rather than reliance upon, metaphysical idols.

Marion's Re-Reading of Pseudo-Denys

In his essay, In the Name: How to Avoid Speaking of 'Negative Theology', Marion begins by criticising Derrida's use of the term negative theology, preferring instead to use 'mystical theology'.[34] Marion claims that neither Pseudo-Denys, nor any of the influential Church Fathers, uses the term negative theology to describe their writings. He argues that Derrida uses this term for a strategic purpose: by labelling the work of Pseudo-Denys and others as negative, Derrida is able to analyse the texts according to a dualistic understanding of language. Marion argues that Pseudo-Denys is actually working within a three-pronged structure of language, rather than the two-pronged approach that Derrida presents: 'The game is therefore not played out between two terms, affirmation and negation, but between three, different from and irreducible to each other.'[35]

Marion labels the third way of language 'praise'. Distinct from the exhaustion of positive and negative statements, he argues that Pseudo-Denys formulated the discourse of praise in order to address the unnameable God:

---

[32]   For a helpful introduction to metaphysics and Marion's postmetaphysical theology and philosophy, see T.A. Carlson, 'Postmetaphysical Theology', in K.J. Vanhoozer (ed.), *The Cambridge Companion to Postmodern Theology* (Cambridge: Cambridge University Press, 2003), pp. 58–75.

[33]   R. Horner, *Jean-Luc Marion: A Theo-Logical Introduction* (London: Ashgate, 2005), p. 51.

[34]   J.-L. Marion, 'In the Name: How to Avoid Speaking of "Negative Theology"', in Caputo and Scanlon, *God, the Gift, and Postmodernism*, pp. 20–41, at p. 1.

[35]   Ibid., p. 24.

It concerns a form of speech which no longer says something about something (or a name of someone), but which denies all relevance to predication, rejects the nominative function of names, and suspends the rule of truth's two values. Dionysius indicates this new pragmatic function of language, aiming at He who surpasses all nomination by giving him the title [*aitia*] – not the metaphysical 'cause,' but what all those who demand demand … when they aim at Him from whom they come and to whom they return.[36]

In this form of speech, praise is directed to the God who surpasses all predication – the unthinkable and unnameable God beyond all Being. In contrast to Derrida, Marion suggests that Pseudo-Denys does not pray to a named God. Rather his understanding of the God who is *hyperousios*, or beyond Being, 're-establishes neither essence nor knowledge, but transgresses them both in view of praising what precedes and makes possible all essence'.[37] The discourse of praise is not exhausted by attempts at predicating attributes, whether negative or positive, because it is not concerned with being true or false. Instead it serves as a perpetual means of aiming praise to that which exceeds all language:

With the third way, not only is it no longer a matter of saying (or denying) something about something, it is also no longer a matter of saying or unsaying, but of referring to Him who is no longer touched by nomination. It is solely a matter of de-nominating.[38]

This brings us back to the concept of distance.

For Marion, distance means God is present to creation only through his absence. He cannot be spoken of through predicative language because there is no coincidence between human thought and God. As Carlson notes, praise, as a purely pragmatic type of language, 'refers endlessly toward God without securing (predicatively) any final meaning for God'.[39] Therefore, according to Marion's reading, Pseudo-Denys has not formulated a theology of presence – one in which a transcendent God is understood as the Cause of all creation – but rather a theology of absence. He explains:

Thus, supposing that praise attributes a name to a possible God, one should conclude that it does not name him properly or essentially, nor that it names him in presence, but that it marks his absence, anonymity, and withdrawal – exactly

---

[36]   Ibid.,p. 27.

[37]   Ibid., p. 28. See also J.-L. Marion, *God without Being: Hors-Texte*, trans. T.A. Carlson (Chicago: University of Chicago Press, 1991).

[38]   Marion, 'In the Name: How to Avoid Speaking of "Negative Theology"', p. 28.

[39]   Carlson, *Indiscretion: Finitude and the Naming of God*, p. 201.

as every name dissimulates every individual, whom it merely indicates without ever manifesting.[40]

The Call of the Impossible for Marion

For Marion, theological language is not primarily a matter of *speaking*, but of *listening* to the call of the One who is beyond all affirmation and negation: 'The theologian's job is to silence the Name and in this way let it give us one.'[41] If Derrida emphasises our ability to think the impossible through a general apophaticism, Marion believes we can experience it through the call of the Other which precedes and exceeds all language.

> This difficulty finds its solution here: the originary word is said, probably (but not necessarily) by an Other who precedes me. I therefore cannot hear it because it speaks an unheard language and sounds in a space whose horizon I cannot fix in advance. In short, the word originarily said holds the status of call – inaugural, it remains inaudible.[42]

Praise aims at the Other we can refer to only by responding to its prior call, and even then, only by aiming our praise in an unknown and anonymous direction.

This last point highlights the second major difference between Derrida and Marion, one which will occupy our attention in the remainder of this chapter: for Derrida negative theology and deconstruction allow us to think the desire for the experience of the impossible, but we can never experience it, because to experience it would be to destroy it. This is what Derrida calls the gift. For Marion, the third way of discourse allows us to imagine a situation in which we could experience the self-giving of the gift – the call of the nameless, anonymous God. This would be a paradox, or what Marion calls a 'counter-experience'. Thus, we are led back to similar positions to those discussed in Chapter 2: is theological language, especially in the writings of Pseudo-Denys, primarily concerned with knowledge or with experience?

The Gift as the Impossible

Derrida

Derrida compares deconstruction and apophatic theology by asking the question: How does one leap out of the circle? The impossible possibility of the Other

---

[40]   Marion, 'In the Name: How to Avoid Speaking of "Negative Theology"', p. 29.

[41]   Ibid., p. 39.

[42]   J.-L. Marion, *Being Given: Toward a Phenomenology of Givenness*, trans. T.A. Carlson (Stanford: Stanford University Press, 2002), p. 288.

appearing within the circle is what Derrida calls the gift. For Derrida, this is not just impossible, but *the* impossible. That means it is not just one impossibility among others. Caputo explains:

> By the impossible Derrida clearly does not mean impossible *stricto sensu*, the simple modal opposite of the possible, but the more-than-possible, the transgression, the chance, the aleatory, the breach, the rupture, the passage to the limits, the *ébranler* and the *solicitation* of the same.[43]

Yet Derrida is clear that the gift is somehow related to the economy of exchange:

> But is not the gift, if there is any, that which interrupts economy? That which, in suspending economic calculation, no longer gives rise to exchange? That which opens the circle so as to defy reciprocity or symmetry, the common measure, and so as to turn aside the return in view of the no-return?[44]

The gift is that which exceeds the economy of language: that which is outside of the circle. Paradoxically, the gift is related to the circle, but at the same time it is not. If it had a representable, thinkable relationship to the circle then it could be apprehended within the circle and thus would no longer be the wholly Other beyond language. Derrida explains:

> It must not circulate, it must not be exchanged, it must not in any case be exhausted, as a gift, by the process of exchange, by the movement of circulation of the circle in the form of return to the point of departure.[45]

Yet how then can the gift be related to the circle? How can deconstruction (and similarly apophatic theology) think that the gift might appear? After all, Derrida himself says that the gift is not foreign to the circle, but 'it must keep a relation of foreignness to the circle, a relation without relation of familiar foreignness'.[46]

In the end, the appearance, and thus the experience, of the gift is the impossible. If it appears within the circle, then it is destroyed as the gift because it becomes circulated within the economy of language. Thus, for Derrida, the impossible – the gift – is a matter of thinking, but not experiencing:

> For finally, if the gift is another name of the impossible, we still think it, we name it, we desire it. We intend it. And this *even if* or *because* or *to the extent that* – we

---

[43]   Caputo, *The Prayers and Tears of Jacques Derrida*, p. 51.

[44]   J. Derrida, *Given Time: I. Counterfeit Money*, trans. P. Kamuf (Chicago: University of Chicago Press, 1994), p. 7.

[45]   Ibid., p. 7.

[46]   Ibid., p. 7.

never encounter it, we never know it, we never verify it, never experience it in its present existence or in its phenomenon.[47]

In terms of the debate in Chapter 2 regarding knowledge and experience, one could say that Derrida believes deconstruction, as a universal apophaticism, is a matter of thinking the impossible, but never encountering it. In a sense, Derrida would side with those who believe Pseudo-Denys's knowledge of the unknowable is a matter concerning the limits of human thinking, rather than an experience Pseudo-Denys himself encountered. It is here that the difference between Marion and Derrida is most acute.

Marion

Contra Derrida, Marion believes the gift is an impossible possibility; possible if the limits of human experience are understood in their broadest sense. He argues that, if we are to think through how the appearance of the Other might take place, we cannot think of it in terms of how we experience ordinary objects: 'I think the difficulty for phenomenology is to become more fair to some phenomena which cannot be described either as object or as being.'[48] Marion suggests that we cannot limit the appearance of the gift to the conditions of finite human experience. If the gift is the wholly Other – that which is outside the circle of exchange and beyond all language – it must be able to appear according to its own logic: 'To the limited possibility of phenomenality, shouldn't we – in certain cases still to be defined – oppose final unconditionally possible phenomenality, whose scope would not be the result of the finitude of the conditions of experience?'[49] In other words, if we are to think the appearance of the gift, would that not imply rethinking the limits and conditions of experience? If the appearance of the gift is the appearance of the wholly Other, which is unlike any other object, or phenomenon, or any sort of being – would this not imply a different kind of experience altogether?

Marion argues that this sort of experience would be a counter-experience, which is not an experience of nothing, but an experience unlike any other. He explains:

> Counter-experience is not equivalent to non-experience, but to the experience of a phenomenon that is neither regardable, nor guarded according to objectness, one that therefore resists the conditions of objectification. Counter-experience offers the experience of what irreducibly contradicts the conditions for the experience of objects.[50]

---

[47] Ibid., p. 29.

[48] J.-L. Marion, in 'On the Gift: A Discussion between Jacques Derrida and Jean-Luc Marion', in Caputo and Scanlon, *God, the Gift, and Postmodernism*, pp. 54–78, at p. 70.

[49] Marion, *Being Given*, p. 197.

[50] Ibid., p. 215.

We see here the contrast between Marion's and Derrida's approaches. Instead of concluding that the experience of the gift is impossible, Marion argues that the conditions for human experience must not be limited by human horizons. According to Marion, this is a permissible move because the gift, or what he calls the 'saturated phenomenon',[51] does not participate within the circle of exchange. The gift cannot be constituted, judged, or defined by human thinking. Language cannot make sense of what appears in the saturated phenomenon, instead, it leaves one with an experience of overwhelming bedazzlement:

> When the gaze cannot bear what it sees, it suffers bedazzlement … It concerns a visible that our gaze cannot sustain. This visible is undergone as unbearable by the gaze, because it fills it without measure … [52]

Thus, the gift is given according to its own logic and cannot be seen by the gaze of the receiver. It is foreign to the senses and must be manifest in another way. How? Marion suggests that the gift can appear only after one has heard it and responded to it. The gift would be akin to the word spoken in silence that we alluded to at the end of the previous section. Marion understands it as a call that appears only through the response of its receiver: 'the call gives itself phenomenologically only by first showing itself in a response'.[53] In sum, the gift would then be given according to its own logic (not constituted by the finite limits of human experience), it would be an experience so different to ordinary experiences that it must be thought of as a counter-experience, and it would be manifest only when its silent call is responded to by a receiver.

Conclusion

This chapter has outlined two rather different readings of Pseudo-Denys's use of negative language to those that we considered in Chapter 2. Derrida views Pseudo-Denys's negative language as a failure, in the sense that Derrida regards it as bound to a metaphysics that Pseudo-Denys is powerless to escape. Yet at the same time, he believes that it points towards the universal apophaticism to which he aspires. Marion, however, believes that Pseudo-Denys does succeed in addressing the transcendent through the vocabulary of praise. Marion argues that the impossible possibility is made possible through an experience that overwhelms us, which he refers to as the saturated phenomenon. For Derrida, such an experience would, however, reduce the impossible to that which is less than impossible. In some ways these two approaches mirror the tension that we noted in earlier parts of our book between those who see negative language as a purely epistemological

---

[51] Ibid., pp. 179–247.

[52] Ibid., pp. 203–4.

[53] Ibid., p. 285.

strategy that attempts to expresses the otherness of God and those who believe that this otherness can in some way be experienced.

In the next chapter we turn to reconsider Augustine's account of selfhood, again through the eyes of postmodern critics, who likewise bring their own concerns to Augustine's ancient text.

Chapter 12

Exploring Selfhood through Augustine: Marion, Derrida and Lyotard

Chapters 3 and 8 explored the themes of interiority and desire in the work of Augustine, mainly in relation to his *Confessions*, *The Literal Commentary on Genesis* and *On the Trinity*. A number of modern philosophical interpretations of Augustine's understanding of selfhood, memory and God were explored. As we discussed, these interpreters disagree over issues such as Augustine's Neoplatonic influences, the genre of his *Confessions*, and his mystical experiences. This chapter will present three more readings of Augustine's *Confessions*. Much like Chapter 11, this chapter explores how three postmodern thinkers – Jean-Luc Marion, Jacques Derrida and Jean-François Lyotard – have produced work that in some way explores Augustine's *Confessions* in order to explicate their own understanding of selfhood. Instead of entering the theoretical debate surrounding Augustine's work, these thinkers have read the *Confessions* as a means of explaining the structure of selfhood in general. As we shall see, all three have embarked on investigations into the nature of the self by taking up, in one way or another, Augustine's famous dictum: 'I have become a question to myself'. Thus, this chapter asks two broad questions: 'How has Augustine's interior quest for selfhood informed each of these scholars's work?' 'How have they patterned their understanding of selfhood after Augustine?'

We are dealing here with a set of thinkers and texts that come from a philosophical trajectory different to that of the other interpretations of Christian mysticism featured in our book. In such a short chapter we cannot hope to give a comprehensive account of their writings, much less of the wider context from which they come. In fact, we cannot even account for the variety of twentieth- and twenty-first-century thinkers who have treated Augustine extensively in their own work, such as the German philosopher Martin Heidegger, the German-Jewish thinker Hannah Arendt and the French existentialist Albert Camus. Thus, the reader should be aware that our accounts of these texts, and their relationships to Augustine, are only provisional summaries. Interested students should follow up this material by reading the texts themselves, along with further secondary material.

Jean-Luc Marion's *The Erotic Phenomenon*

In one of his most recent works, *The Erotic Phenomenon*, Jean-Luc Marion sets out on a personal quest to understand the nature of his self in a manner very similar to that of Augustine in the *Confessions.*[1] Marion is troubled by the fact that if he tries to think of his self according to the means provided by philosophy, Descartes's famous saying 'I think, therefore I am', he can only account for himself as an object. This troubles Marion because it means he has no way to differentiate his self from a rock or a piece of wood: 'Either I am certain of myself, because I think myself; but then I make myself the object of myself and I receive only a certainty of an object. Thus I miss myself as *ego* [I].'[2] For Marion, this method provides certainty that the self exists, but it does not provide an adequate answer to the question of its nature or its reason for existing: 'To produce my certainty myself does not reassure me at all, but rather maddens me in front of vanity in person. What is the good of my certainty, if it still depends on me, if I only am through myself?'[3] Marion wants to know what the *use* of existence really is; he wants to know if there is anything other to being human than being an object that thinks. In sum, he wants to know, 'what is the use?'

While Marion does not refer explicitly to Augustine's *Confessions* in the body of the text, his quest for a stable and fulfilling experience of selfhood was intentionally structured to bear resemblances to Augustine's. In Book 10 of the *Confessions*, Augustine sets forth the structural presupposition which shapes his search for his self:

> What all agree upon is that they want to be happy, just as they would concur, if asked, that they want to experience joy and would call that joy the happy life. Even if one person pursues it in one way, and another in a different way, yet there is one goal which all are striving to attain, namely to experience joy.[4]

This postulate in Book 10 is related to Augustine's experience of self-loss due to the death of his friend during his young adult life. He says, 'I hated everything because they did not have him, nor could they now tell me "look, he is on the way", as used to be the case when he was alive and absent from me. *I had become to myself a vast problem.*'[5] Marion sees here not only sorrow in Augustine, but something deeper: self-questioning. As Marion says in an essay on Augustine, 'this loss of another thus provokes nothing less and nothing other than the loss of self, of my knowledge of myself, which it replaces with my putting myself into question'.[6] This

---

[1]   Marion has recently published a further work on Confessions, J-L. Marion, 'Au lieu de soi l'approche de saint Augustin (Paris: Presses universitaires de France, 2008). This work is not yet available in English and was published to late to be considered in this chapter.

[2]   J.-L. Marion, *The Erotic Phenomenon*, trans. S.E. Lewis (Chicago: Chicago University Press, 2007), p. 15 (interpolation mine).

[3]   Ibid., p. 19.

[4]   Augustine, *Confessions*, p. 198.

[5]   Ibid., p. 57 (emphasis mine).

[6]   J.-L. Marion, 'Mihi magna quaestio factus sum: The Privilege of Unknowing', *The Journal of Religion*, 85/1 (2005), 1–24, at 5.

self-questioning leads Augustine into a discussion of time and death. The theme of temporality comes to the fore as he deliberates on the temporal nature of existence: 'Not everything grows old, but everything dies.'[7] As a result, he concludes that in earthly things 'there is no point of rest' for 'they lack permanence'.[8]

We have here the two elements of Augustine's *Confessions* that inform Marion's own quest for selfhood: the search for the happy life and the theme of temporality. In searching for his self, Augustine is looking not only for happiness, but for a happiness which is permanent. Augustine eventually concludes that, if he was going to experience the sort of eternal rest he desires, his self must be a gift from elsewhere. Eventually, God serves as the anchor of Augustine's self when Augustine recognises that true happiness is found in Him:

> This is the authentic happy life, to set one's joy on you, grounded in you and caused by you. That is the real thing, and there is no other. Those who think that the happy life is found elsewhere, pursue another joy and not the true one.[9]

The answer is not so simple for Marion (of course Augustine would probably say his interior quest for selfhood was not very simple either). If you recall our discussion of his work in Chapter 11, we noted that Marion is a Christian theologian and thinker who understands God to be unthinkable, and thus beyond human concepts.[10] For Marion, God cannot be grasped by human thinking, but instead remains beyond language, and thus beyond comprehension. If Marion is going to find a stable and permanent source for his self he cannot simply turn to the type of metaphysical God which Augustine understood to be the source of his selfhood. Instead of trying to locate the source of his self through an interior quest, Marion asks a follow-up question to 'What is the use?' He asks, 'Does anybody love me?'[11]

Marion claims that, by asking this question, the self can be transported from a vain existence of self-solitude to a place 'where I immediately receive the role of he who can love, and whom one can love, and who believes that someone must love him – *the lover*'.[12] Before we try to explain what he means by this, we need to emphasise that, by structuring the question of selfhood in relationship to love, Marion is emphasising the role of the body in a radical way: 'I do not have flesh, I am my flesh and it coincides absolutely with me – assigns me to myself and delivers me as such in my radically received individuality.'[13] For Marion, there is

---

[7] Augustine, *Confessions*, p. 61.

[8] Ibid., p. 62.

[9] Ibid., pp. 191–2.

[10] For a brief introduction to Marion's thought, see the discussion of Marion's work in Chapter 11.

[11] Marion, *The Erotic Phenomenon*, p. 20.

[12] Ibid., p. 28.

[13] Ibid., p. 112.

no dualism between the mind and the body, or the soul and the body. The body (flesh) is 'me' and 'I' am my body.

By asking, 'Does anyone out there love me?' Marion believes he is on the first step to experiencing a stable and meaningful sense of self. He believes that in order to receive the gift of his true self, the body must be eroticised by the flesh of another: 'I can only free myself and become myself by touching another flesh, as one touches land at a port, because only another flesh can make room for me.'[14] This is a potentially confusing concept. The main point is that, in order to experience the self as being more than an object in the world (like a rock or table), Marion believes it must come into contact with *something that is likewise not an object* – the flesh of another person. Of course one could argue that human beings have the potential to use other human beings as objects, and in some circumstances one person's body is used sexually by another person. But that is not what Marion has in mind here.

Marion is interested in what he calls the eroticisation of the body – the desire aroused in the body to encounter another person who is both immanent (within my field of experience and able to be encountered), and transcendent (one that cannot be fully grasped or comprehended by me – one that is Other). Marion explains:

> And we do this without confusion or mixing, since the two fleshes remain all the more irreducible as they rise up from their respective feelings, and as they give to one another what they do not have.[15]

For Marion, eroticisation is not two fleshes becoming one, or a collapse of one into the other. Just like the relationship between Augustine and God, the other remains transcendent to the self – 'the other stands higher than ever'.[16] This involves a paradox: 'I' give my 'self' over to another person in order to receive from them my true selfhood. In return, 'I' confer upon the other person their true selfhood, even though I do not have my own to give. The self gives what it does not have in order to receive what it does not have – this is the path to experiencing one's true self – one that exceeds the vanity of merely being a thinking object. Eoin Cassidy explains:

> As Marion sees it, I receive the assurance of myself as a love in the very act of making love – I receive the assurance from love itself, which is ultimately received as a gift from the other who accepts my love. In that sense, it is the pledge or the covenant of love or the other who loves me that is closer to me than I am to myself.[17]

---

[14] Ibid., p. 118.

[15] Ibid., p. 127.

[16] Ibid., p. 128.

[17] E. Cassidy, 'Phénomène Erotique: Augustinian Resonances in Marion's Phenomenology of Love', in I. Leask and E. Cassidy (eds), *Givenness and God: Questions*

By receiving another person erotically, the self receives an answer to the question 'Does anyone love me?' At this point, the existence of the self moves past the stage of thinking. Instead of just existing in a mode of 'I think', the self now exists in a mode where it is loved by another – it can say, 'I am loved'. Cassidy is helpful once again: 'Thus Marion's réduction érotique (erotic reduction) situates self-identity under the rubric of love as desire: the gift of erotic love reveals me to myself in my individuality – as a lover.'[18] When someone desires to love the self, they signal it out as a unique, irreplaceable phenomenon in the world. It is more than an object, and more than a face in the crowd. As a result, erotic love gives the self the assurance that its existence is not in vain; it exists to be loved, and in turn, to love the other.

But what about permanence? Can Marion really think that erotic love can provide the same kind of permanent rest for his self that Augustine found in the eternal, unchanging God? Just like Augustine, Marion is seeking not only to be happy, but also to rest in an eternal source. Thus, essential to Marion's concept of the eroticisation of the flesh is the guarantee that the intimacy of the erotic phenomena is pledged forever. Marion calls this the oath: 'The other must not only say to me "Here I am!" in the moment, but she must also promise it for every moment still to come.'[19] In other words, in order to be able to say 'I am loved', the self must rest assured that it is loved for eternity. Love cannot be a temporary experience, or a fleeting desire. If the self is to be experienced as more than mere vanity – as more than just another object in the world – it must be assured that the love it experiences in the eroticisation of the flesh is an eternal love. Obviously, erotic experiences do not last forever (due to physical limitations, among other reasons), and Marion admits that death poses a natural obstacle to eternal love. However, he argues that even if the other is no longer present, one can love without reciprocity.[20] The oath made by the lover within the experience of eroticisation (what Marion calls the erotic reduction) confers upon the self the assurance that it will always exist as more than a vain *thinking* self, or as an object in the world. The oath means that the self has been given itself for all eternity.

Jacques Derrida's *Circumfession*

If Marion's quest for selfhood in *The Erotic Phenomenon* is implicitly patterned after Augustine's *Confessions*, Jacques Derrida's quest for selfhood in *Circumfession* is a direct and deliberate mimicking of the *Confessions*. Derrida wrote *Circumfession* as part of a friendly wager with his friend Geoffrey Bennington, where Derrida bet Geoff that if Geoff wrote a comprehensive book summarising Derrida's thought,

---

of Jean-Luc Marion (New York: Fordham University Press, 2005), p. 208.

[18]   Ibid., p. 208.
[19]   Marion, *The Erotic Phenomenon*, p.104.
[20]   Ibid., pp. 67–88.

Derrida could write something at the same time that would completely surprise Geoff. Consequently, Geoff set out to write a kind of metaphorical computer program, *Derridabase*, that would have absolute knowledge of Derrida's body of work. Imagine a Derridean Encyclopaedia, with an entry relating to every relevant issue, theme, and idea in Derrida's work. In contrast, Derrida set out to produce something that Geoff could not have possibly anticipated to be part of the encyclopaedia – something disruptive and surprising. Thus, the two texts are juxtaposed within a very unorthodox framework. Geoff's text is written on the top of each page like the standard format for any book; Derrida's is written below Geoff's in the bottom third of the page as a separate, smaller subtext. In this way, Geoff, or 'G.' as Derrida refers to him, plays a structurally similar role to God in *Confessions*, since 'G.' hovers above the written confessions as the one with absolute knowledge of the confessor, Derrida. Thus, it is not altogether surprising that throughout *Circumfession* Derrida writes in a non-formal, semi-stream-of-consciousness manner, while inserting long quotations from Augustine relevant to the topics he is addressing.

Moreover, Derrida's *Circumfession* is structurally similar to Augustine's in another very important manner. Augustine's mother Monica played a large role in Augustine's life, writing and conversion to Christianity. The two of them shared a mystical vision at Ostia, which is recounted in Book 9 of the *Confessions,* and Augustine writes intensively about the process he went through while his mother was sick and finally died. Similarly, Derrida wrote *Circumfession* during the year before his mother died. The whole text is haunted by the unknown time when death will finally take Derrida's mother Georgette, whom he calls Geo (another 'G.'). Derrida's own 'confession' to his dying mother is heavily indebted to and informed by Augustine's *Confessions.*

Derrida calls his version of confession *Circumfession* for a very strategic reason. By combining the word confession with the word circumcision, Derrida is able to refer both to Augustine's text and to his own Jewish heritage. Derrida grew up in France as a self-identified 'little black and very Arab Jew'.[21] He uses the idea of circumcision as an avenue for personal revelations about his relationship to Judaism, and to his own personal religion, 'which nobody understands';[22] which surprises 'G.'. Derrida recounts how his mother asked other people if Derrida still believed in God, admitting that he 'rightly passes for an atheist', but also says, somewhat paradoxically, that for him 'God' is present in other names.[23] Thus, the theme of circumcision plays an important role in his version of confession, because, by referring to it, Derrida is referring not only to the Jewish rite, which is literally a cut or 'cision' on an unsuspecting baby boy, but also the primordial 'incision' that has been made in him – the cut within that has produced

---

[21]   J. Derrida, *Circumfession*, in J. Derrida and G. Bennington, *Derrida*, trans. G. Benington (Chicago: University of Chicago Press, 1993), pp. 3–315, at p. 58.

[22]   Ibid., p. 154.

[23]   Ibid., p. 155.

this desire for self-identity through a relationship with the God in whom he does not believe. In both the literal and the figurative cases of circumcision, there is no memory of the cut made to one's self – Derrida cannot remember being circumcised as an eight-day-old baby, nor can he explain from where the desire for God has originated.

The theme of remembering points to another important similarity between Derrida and Augustine. In Book 10 of the *Confessions* Augustine explores the nature of memory at length in order to figure out how he could possibly know about God. Where did his desire for God come from? Where is God present within Augustine? Augustine thinks of his memory as the storehouse of all his experiences – of his very self. Yet he has no memory of God's *incision* into him. Furthermore, he cannot explain how the God who is outside of time might have made contact with him. Derrida has the same problem. There has been an incision within him, one that has left him with the desire to know the impossible – to know the Other, whom Augustine refers to as God. Yet he has no memory of how or when this incision was made. Why then did both Augustine and Derrida turn to the act of confession in order to come to an understanding of the primordial 'incision' that was made in each of them? Why does Augustine, who confessed to a God that he believed already knew everything about him, play such an important part in the quasi-Jewish, quasi-atheist philosopher's personal writing about his mother and his life? And why is Derrida so concerned with confessing something about himself that 'G.' could not have possibly anticipated?

Derrida interprets *Confessions* as Augustine's quest for self-knowledge. In Derrida's mind, Augustine believed that by recounting important instances from his lifetime he could come to some sort of absolute knowledge of himself which would eventually lead to an answer as to where and how God was present within him. Robert Dodaro explains:

> For Augustine can only know God inasmuch as – and in the manner that – he can love God, and he can only know himself insofar as he knows God's knowledge and love for him. In the end this is why Augustine must confess to a God who already knows everything about him. The pretense of the *Confessions* is that God does not need to know Augustine; Augustine needs to know himself. And he can only know himself only by coming to know concretely how, in what manner, God knows him and loves him.[24]

In Derrida's mind, Augustine's confession is a matter of trying to 'collect' his self within the presence of the unchanging God. Augustine is trying to figure out how and where God made his 'cision' in his interior self. If he can do this, Augustine can escape the constant flux of temporal human existence and rest peacefully in the presence of the God who is outside of time. Thus, by confessing, Augustine

---

[24] R. Dodaro, 'Loose Canons: Augustine and Derrida on Their Selves', in Caputo and Scanlon, *God, Gift, and Postmodernism*, pp. 79–111, at p. 82.

is emptying out his interior self with the aim of gaining absolute knowledge of himself. If he succeeds he can locate himself in God, and, in a strange way, find the One who has already found him.

In *Circumfession,* Derrida proceeds in a manner that is both very similar to, but also different from Augustine's. Similar to Augustine, he is confessing things that no one else knows in order to locate his singular, irreplaceable self: 'the inside gives itself up and you can do as you like with it, it's me but I am no longer there'.[25] Derrida likens his pen to a 'word vein'[26] reaching inside of him to draw out his interior self. He talks about wanting a twin or a double of himself that would be a mirror of his self – one that would provide the self with absolute confidence in its identity.[27] He also talks about wanting to be present after he has died – at his funeral when his family and friends mourn his passing. In this way he would be present in a manner that would be unaffected by the flux of time. He would be a self with absolute knowledge of himself – there would be no surprises, or secrets, or hidden things.

However, in contrast to Augustine, Derrida doesn't seem to think that having absolute knowledge of himself is altogether desirable. Despite wanting to be able to rest in himself, he also sighs that if 'G.' really does have absolute knowledge of him, then his future really doesn't matter. In other words, if 'G.' already knows everything there is to know of Derrida, Derrida's future contains no surprises, nothing that cannot be anticipated, and thus in some way he is already dead:

> so that here I am deprived of a future, no more event to come from me, at least insofar as I speak or write, unless I write here … improbable things which destabilize, disconcert, surprise in their turn G.'s program, things that in short he, G. … will not have been able to recognize, name, foresee, produce, predict, *unpredictable things* to survive him, and if something should yet happen, nothing is less certain, it must be *unpredictable*, the salvation of a backfire.[28]

So, Derrida is on a quest for selfhood, but one that has a different goal from Augustine's. As Caputo says, 'Derrida feels obliged to confess that his reading of Augustine is a kind of intentional misreading or mis-leading of Augustine, carrying Augustine down paths that Augustine himself will not travel, all this in the hope that an event would be produced'.[29] Derrida believes that Augustine's quest to rest in God by merging his self into complete unity with God does not

---

[25]   Derrida, *Circumfession*, p. 12.

[26]   Ibid., p. 15.

[27]   Ibid., pp. 138–9.

[28]   Ibid., pp. 30–31.

[29]   J.D. Caputo and M.J. Scanlon, 'Introduction: The Postmodern Augustine', in J.D. Caputo and M.J. Scanlon (eds), *Augustine and Postmodernism: Confession and Circunfession* (Bloomington, IN: Indiana University Press, 2005), pp. 1–16, at p. 4.

result in the revelation of Augustine's true self, but the annihilation of everything that is unique and irreplaceable about him.

Derrida is after something different. He wants to surprise 'G.' with an unforeseeable event in order to demonstrate that absolute knowledge of himself is not possible. If he can disrupt 'G.'s' programme, he will have demonstrated that his past cannot be exhaustibly accounted for – that there are always things about our selves that are not expressed, not understood, and not revealed (even to our own self). If Derrida can show 'G.' that there are things about him that no one could possibly know (not even Derrida himself),[30] Derrida believes he will 'have a future' because it will still be possible for something surprising or unforeseeable to happen. Whether it happens, or what happens, does not matter. What does matter is that his life is open enough not to be encapsulated into a programme. Dodaro is helpful once again:

> Reading *Circumfession*, we are prompted to ask ourselves whether Augustine's sense of self is less absolute, less assured than the surface of his text might suggest. And in tandem with that question, we inquire further whether the self-assurance ... does not at some point deconstruct in the face of self-doubt.[31]

In the end, Derrida's *Circumfession* suggests that, as long as the self continues to be caught in time, it will never experience the kind of stable, permanent rest for which both Augustine and Marion hope. There are always hidden aspects of one's self, which the unforeseeable events of time (like the anticipated death of one's mother), may or may not bring to light: 'I shall never know the whole of me ...'[32] For Derrida, this is always both good and bad news.

Jean-François Lyotard's *Confession of Augustine*

The last text we will consider in this chapter is Jean-François Lyotard's posthumously published work, *The Confession of Augustine*. Lyotard was a contemporary of both Marion and Derrida known for his provocative philosophical writings on

---

[30] This theme of 'non-knowledge' of the self plays an important role in *Circumfession*, one that we do not have space here to explore in full. However, we can point out that the impending death of Derrida's mother helps to make Derrida''s point. Derrida explains that the event of his mother's death is on the horizon, but no one knows when it will happen. He has non-knowledge of an event – he knows it will happen, but has no idea when. The impending coming of this event has a large effect on Derrida—his thoughts, his memories, his confessions. The 'event' conjures up thoughts and memories he did not even know were inside of him. In some sense, the 'event' creates Derrida's 'self' because Derrida has only non-knowledge of it.

[31] Dodaro, "Loose Canons', p. 83.

[32] Derrida, *Circumfession*, p. 217.

postmodernism, ethics, and politics. Somewhat like Derrida's extensive treatment of mystical theology and religion, Lyotard's published notes on Augustine came as a surprise to many readers since Lyotard had not previously published a great deal in the areas of religion or theology. In *The Confession of Augustine* Lyotard uses the saint's quest for selfhood to provide a general commentary on the nature of human selfhood and the theme of temporality. He does not write in a confessional mode like Derrida, nor is he on a personal quest for selfhood like Marion. Instead, Lyotard explains the fragmented, temporal nature of human selfhood by interspersing quotations from Augustine within his own writing so that the two voices (that of Lyotard and that of Augustine) become blurred almost to the point of being indistinguishable.

Consequently, Lyotard's text focuses on some of the same themes as Derrida's. We saw how Derrida confessed that he had experienced a circumcision into himself similar to the one Augustine had undergone. Speaking of Augustine, Lyotard picks up on the same theme:

> Placing your outside within, you converted the most intimate part of him into his outside. And with this exteriority to himself, yours, an incision henceforth from within, you make your saint of saints ...[33]

In Lyotard's mind, Augustine understood himself as having undergone a cut to his inside he knew was there, but that he could not find. He had been transformed from mere 'flesh' into 'soul-flesh'[34] due to God's habitation of his inner self. Yet Augustine was never able to locate how or when God was inside of him. In Book 10, the book Lyotard quotes from most often, Augustine famously tried to locate God in his memory, but in the end concluded that God was not there. For Lyotard, this is the central problem of Augustine's search for selfhood – trying to find the God who is inside him in order to catch-up with his true self. Lyotard says:

> Such is flesh visited, co-penetrated by your space-time, disturbed and confused with this blow, but steeped in infinity, impregnated and pregnant with your overabundant liquid: the waters of the heavens.[35]

Thus, for Lyotard, the central issue of the *Confessions* is the human attempt to attain a stable, permanent self-identity in the Eternal while remaining within the confines of time.

The problem is that time itself can never be represented – it is always only present through its absence. Lyotard explains, 'The past is what is no longer, the future is what is not yet, and the now has no other being than the becoming past of

---

[33]   J.-F. Lyotard, *The Confession of Augustine* (Stanford: Stanford University Press, 2000), p. 3.

[34]   Ibid., p. 9.

[35]   Ibid., p. 11.

the future.'[36] Let us unpack Lyotard's position. There are three temporal instances: the past, present and future. The past is no longer; it is what has already taken place, but is now gone. The future is what is to come – it has not come yet, and thus remains absent as always ahead of the present. But, most importantly, the present itself can never be 'present'. Every time one tries to speak about or write about the present it has already slipped away. The point is that every human response involves a delay:

> For time itself, the time of living creatures, the time that he calls created, is the child of this permanent self-absence. To go blank is what we say for a lapse in memory, but what falls out into the three temporal instances is *the oblivion inherent to existence itself.* Past, present, future – as many modes of presence in which the lack of presence is projected.[37]

For Lyotard, Augustine is confessing the 'sin of time, delay'[38] – his inability to escape the 'oblivion' endemic to temporal existence. Consequently, Lyotard's analysis comes to a similar conclusion to Derrida's. Although Augustine confesses a desire for permanent self-rest in the unchangeable, eternal God, ultimately he cannot escape time.

> Even the shattering visit of the Other, even the incarnation of grace, if it ever truly arrives, from the fact that this visit subverts the space-time of the creature, it does not follow that it removes this creature from the hurried, limp course of regrets, remorse, hope, responsibilities, from the ordinary worries of life.[39]

Thus, for Lyotard, it is no coincidence that at the end of *Confessions* Augustine sighs, 'Is not human life on earth a trial? ... Is not human life on earth a trial in which there is no respite?'[40]

Time and Experience

In the remainder of this chapter we will discuss the respective positions of Marion, Derrida and Lyotard within the framework of Augustine's work on experience (Chapter 3) and in relation to erotic desire (Chapter 4). Despite their differences, the readings of Augustine discussed in this chapter share an affinity for Augustine's quest for his self in something or someone outside of himself. They seem to identify

---

36 Ibid., p. 72.
37 Ibid., p. 17 (emphasis mine).
38 Ibid., p. 27.
39 Ibid., p. 17.
40 Augustine, *Confessions*, p. 202.

with Augustine's experience of himself as lacking the resources to become his true self.

Augustine looked inward to find the place where God resided within him in order to find eternal rest and happiness. Marion's analysis suggests that one must experience not an inward journey, but the eroticisation of the flesh in order to experience one's true self. This other person – or Other – plays a structurally analogous role to Augustine's God in the quest for selfhood – they are a transcendent (outside), yet immanent (interior) Other that provides the gift of the self to the individual. Yet there are important *ironic* differences that should be noted between Augustine's theology and Marion's eroticisation. Augustine is the Father of the Roman Catholic Church who has had the largest theological influence on its teachings. His belief that sex, even within the marriage relationship, was only for procreation, and his influential account of original sin, have led to strict views on sex within Roman Catholic theology. For the most part, sex has been understood as a dangerous force with great potential for leading people into sin. Ironically, as Chapter 4 discusses, mystical writings often deal directly and indirectly with the erotic[41] and erotic desire. Marion, who himself is a Roman Catholic, understands erotic love to hold the potential for a human being to experience a true sense of self. He retains the structure of Augustine's search for selfhood, including the themes of the erotic and of desire, but has transformed them from something to be resisted and even feared, into the mediating locale through which one receives their true self. It comes at no surprise, then, that at the end of *The Erotic Phenomenon* Marion goes on to conclude that God himself is in fact the first lover.

While Derrida and Lyotard are also interested in the theme of the self, their approaches are much more focused on the self's seemingly unavoidable experience of fragmentation at the hands of time. In line with his analysis of Pseudo-Denys (Chapter 11), Derrida's writing on Augustine is largely concerned with the theme of desire. As we discussed above, Derrida shares Augustine's desire for an experience of selfhood that is permanent and stable. Yet Derrida is also concerned that such an experience of selfhood would mean the end of his self. He talks about an inner dialogue with himself where he repeats, 'I want to kill myself.'[42] This is not a suicidal thought; it is the recognition that if one becomes a truly present and stable self everything that is singular or irreplaceable about them is annihilated – the self dies. If God knows everything about me, about my past, my future, and myself, then for Derrida the self has died already. God's absolute knowledge holds it still in eternity, which means there is no possibility for surprise, or disruption, or something totally new to take place. Thus, it seems Derrida's analysis suggests that the desire for union with God that Augustine longed for is akin to the experience of death. Death is the only 'experience' where the self is no longer governed by the

---

[41] See Chapter 4, esp. pp. 92–105.
[42] Derrida, *Circumfession*, p. 38.

throes of time. Yet, paradoxically, death cannot be experienced by the self because once it dies it can no longer experience anything.[43]

Derrida's analysis is thus much closer to Lyotard's than to Marion's. Like Derrida, Lyotard is concerned with the structure of selfhood in relationship to temporality. It seems for Lyotard that the one that Augustine is confessing to is not the transcendent, eternal God, but Time itself. It is time that prevents Augustine from experiencing his true self. He confesses the 'sin of delay' in recognition of the fact that it is only Time that can prevent his self from being fragmented, and because there is nothing he can do to prevent it. As Hent de Vries says of Lyotard's analysis, 'the temporal mode of the confession is not only that of the evanescence of the instant, of presence, of the present instant … Beyond … there lies another time, an immutable time, the Time of all times, the Time of our lives …'[44] Lyotard understands Augustine, and any self, to be caught in the same paradox that Derrida points out. The self is unavoidably fragmented because of its temporal nature. It is unable to catch up with its stable, unchanging self because it is unable to escape time. Therefore, for both Derrida and Lyotard, the experience of selfhood is always one of waiting to become the true self that one can never become. It is hoping for the impossible by remembering or recalling the incision that has already been made – the incision that instilled in the self this hope for God, or for the 'Present,' or for eternal rest. It is the whence of the self's desire for eternal rest and happiness.

Essential to note here is how the two so-called atheist philosophers, Derrida and Lyotard, understand the role of the transcendent/immanent Other to which Augustine (or anyone else) confessed to be almost irrelevant.[45] Yet Marion understands the Other (the one that causes the eroticisation of my flesh) to be essential to the individual's *experience* of their self; Derrida and Lyotard, however, focus more on the elusive chase – *the desire* – for this Other who could possibly provide such an experience. A passage from Thomas Carlson helps to illustrate this point:

> But what remains, radically, at every moment, yet to be thought, spoken, or desired is that possibility which cannot be reduced to actuality – the possibility, precisely, of 'the impossible.' The possibility that ever remains to be thought, spoken, or desired (the possibility of the impossible) indicates what is – irreducibly – not yet thought, spoken, or desired, what still and ever remains outstanding for thought and for language, for desire and the experience it would seek but not attain as such.[46]

---

[43] Thomas A. Carlson has described this 'indiscretion' between naming the unknowable God and death as the 'apophatic analogy'. See Carlson, *Indiscretion: Finitude and the Naming of God*, pp. 190–262.

[44] H. de Vries, 'Instances: Temporal Modes from Augustine to Derrida to Lyotard', in Caputo and Scanlon, *Augustine and Postmodernism*, pp. 68–87, at p. 85.

[45] Ibid., p. 86.

[46] Carlson, *Indiscretion*, p. 250.

Therefore, in some provisional sense, for Marion Augustine's *Confessions* is a matter of the *experience of selfhood* – of the Other giving my self to me for the first time. On the contrary, for Derrida and Lyotard it is about *the desire for the experience of selfhood* apart from the fragmentation of time – a desire that cannot possibly be fulfilled other than by death.

Conclusion

This chapter has examined three postmodern responses to Augustine's *Confessions*. Jean-Luc Marion argues that true selfhood is created by love of another that is pledge for all eternity. Jacques Derrida's parallel question for selfhood leads him to conclude that Augustine is mistaken if he thinks that a stable permanent self can be located without destroying his self. Jean-François Lyotard argues that Augustine is caught in the tension between desiring the eternal while remaining ever temporal, a struggle which epitomises Lyotard's own desire for selfhood. Derrida and Marion also offset their accounts of selfhood in relation to the play of temporality and experience. Both argue that this reinforces their respective re-readings of Augustine's *Confessions*.

The two chapters in this section have sought to introduce some of the ideas that are found in postmodern re-readings of the Christian mystics. Such ideas are becoming extremely pervasive: scholars like Mark Burrows and Kevin Hart use postmodern thinking to challenge various modern readings of Christian mysticism, in particular those that focus on language, such that as that offered by Turner. Such postmodern responses add yet more lenses through which to view Christian mysticism as well as nuancing those that we already have. They highlight further the complexity of Christian mystical texts and the need to be aware what one means if one refers to such writing as 'mystical'.

Conclusion
What is Christian Mysticism?

We began this book by raising a question: 'What is Christian mysticism?' which we then refused to answer. We hope that it is now apparent why this question needed to be held in suspense.

In these pages we set about tracing four main approaches Christian mysticism. There is the perennialist position, which views Christian mysticism as accounts of effable experiences; the contextualist position, which believes that, while Christian mystics discuss experiences, these experiences are not ineffable experiences, because there is no such thing as an ineffable experience; performative language readings, which believe that Christian mystics are writing about God's ineffability not the ineffability of an experience; and feminist readings, which draw a distinction between male and female mystical texts, stressing the integration of body and spirit in female mysticism. Many critics move between the boundaries of these positions. In addition, there are a number of postmodern re-readings which use these mystical texts to reflect on the nature of the self and its relation to otherness. Contemporary theories of mysticism interact with these postmodern approaches in ways that this introduction can only hint at. However, now is the time to return to the question and ask ourselves where this exploration of Christian mysticism has brought us; whether or not it has brought us to an answer?

We have discussed many motifs and themes, each of which is considered to some degree definitive of Christian mysticism – there is negative language, erotic imagery, the interior journey, selfhood, hierarchy, sacramental theology and mystical exegesis. We have noted a complex interplay between body and spirit, visual and intellectual, imaginative and imagelessness, and orthodoxy and heresy. It has become apparent that the perennialist position has many weaknesses. With each theme considered, its insistence that we focus exclusively on ineffable or objectless experiences has been increasingly brought into question. Yet those approaches that critique it – contextualist, performative language and feminist readings – themselves also struggle with different facets of Christian mysticism. By the end of the book the boundaries of each also seem strained to bursting. As the book progressed we also found it increasingly difficult to categorise readings into such tightly delimited taxonomy. This was especially true when we turned in Part II to consider the new mysticism of the Middle Ages. The tensions for each model created by the cumulative effect of the themes discussed ultimately demanded dialogue between models. Yet this did not result in some 'super' taxonomy that straddles them all. It is rather that, like the texts we have considered, we find ourselves holding opposites in tension. Thus, in searching for an answer, it seems that we have also been brought face to face with that which both frustrates and tantalises us within Christian mysticism: that our conversations are not easily brought to a close. We are left to reflect alongside Augustine, who has inspired so much postmodern reflection, that Christian mysticism offers more questions than it does answers.

Yet perhaps this is as it ought to be. Christian mystical texts draw us out of ourselves and point us towards an other/Other. They make for us companions on the way of those we might not naturally turn to, those who approach these texts from almost diametrically opposing perspectives. They engender conversation between practitioners who read them out of deeply personal convictions and academics whose reading is more theoretical. As postmodern readings demonstrate, it is also impossible to escape the religious element within them, even as the texts themselves stress that we must not be limited by it. It is this capacity of Christian mystical texts to take us deeply into the minds of others while at the same time bringing us to an encounter with the deepest part of our own being that makes them truly mystical. These are texts not of the answer, but of the question, and the conversations that they engender are something to delight in. At the end of the day, Christian mysticism is a form of prayer, it is that which cries out of humanities deepest place to the divine. We must never forget that prayer cannot be a solitary activity. It is thus part of the nature of these texts that they continually bring us to dialogue with that which lies outside ourselves, across time and space, and so leads us to return again and again, not to an answer, but to the question 'What is Christian mysticism?'

Bibliography

Aers, D. and Staley, L. (eds), *The Powers of the Holy: Religion, Politics, and Gender in Late Medieval English Culture* (University Park, PA: Pennsylvania State University Press, 1996).

Alexander, G.T., 'Psychological Foundations of William James' Theory of Religious Experience', *Journal of Religion*, 56 (1976), 421–34.

Allen, E.H., *Writings Ascribed to Richard Rolle Hermit of Hampole, and Materials for his Biography*, The Modern Language Association of America, Monograph Series III (New York: D. Heath and Co., 1927).

Aquinas, Thomas, *Summa Theologica*, online at www.newadvent.org/summa/.

Armstrong, A.H., *The Architecture of the Intelligible Universe in the Philosophy of Plotinus: An Analytical and Historical Study* (Hakkert: Amsterdam, 1967).

Astell, A.W., *The Song of Songs in the Middle Ages* (Ithaca, NY: Cornell University Press, 1995).

Augustine, *Confessions*, trans. Henry Chadwick (Oxford: Oxford University Press, 1991).

———, *The Confessions of St Augustine*, ed. J.J. O'Donnell, 3 vols (Oxford: Oxford University Press, 1992).

———, 'On Seeing God', trans. M.T. Clark in *Augustine of Hippo: Selected Writings* (New York: Paulist Press, 1984), pp. 365–402.

———, *The Literal Meaning of Genesis*, trans. and with intro by J.H. Taylor, 2 vols, Ancient Christian Writers 41 and 42 (New York: Newman Press, 1982).

———, *Saint Augustine: The Trinity*, trans. S. McKenna (Washington: CUPA, 1962).

Barrett, C., 'The Logic of Mysticism', in M. Warner (ed.), *Religion and Philosophy* (Cambridge: Cambridge University Press, 1992), pp. 61–71.

Beauvoir, Simone de, *Mémoires d'une jeune fille rangée (Memoirs of a dutiful daughter)* (Paris: Gallimard, 1958).

———, *The Second Sex*, trans. H.M. Prashley (Harmondsworth: Penguin, 1972).

Beckwith, S., 'A Very Material Mysticism: The Medieval Mysticism of Margery Kempe', in D. Aers (ed.), *Medieval Literature: Criticism, Ideology and History* (Brighton: Harvester Press, 1986), pp. 34–57.

Bell, D.N., *The Image and Likeness: The Augustinian Spirituality of William of Saint-Thierry*, CS 78 (Kalamazoo: Cistercian Publications, 1984).

Bell, R.M., *Holy Anorexia* (Chicago: Chicago University Press, 1985).

Bernard of Clairvaux, *On the Song of Songs I*, trans. K. Walsh, Cistercian Fathers 4 (Shannon: Cistercian Publications, 1971).

Bevans, S.B. and Shroeder, R.P., *Constants in Context: A Theology of Mission for Today* (Maryknoll, NY: Orbis Books, 2004).

Bhattacharji, S., 'Medieval Contemplation and Mystical Experience', in D. Dyas, V. Edden and R. Ellis (eds), *Approaching Medieval English Anchoritic and Mystical Texts* (Cambridge: D.S. Brewer, 2005), pp. 51– 63.

Bonaventure, *The Mind's Journey to God*, trans. P. Boehner (New York: Franciscan Institute, 1956; repr. 1990, 1998).

———, 'The Tree of Life', in *The Soul's Journey Into God; The Tree of Life; The Life of St Francis*, trans. E. Cousins (New York: Paulist Press, 1978), pp. 117–76.

Bouyer, L.E., '"Mysticism": An Essay on the History of the Word', in A. Plé et al. (eds), *Mystery and Mysticism: A Symposium* (London: Blackfriars, 1956), pp.119–37.

Bradley, A., '"Mystic Atheism": Julian Kristeva's Negative Theology', *Theology & Sexuality*, 14/3 (2008), 279–92.

Brown, D., *Tradition and Imagination: Revelation and Change* (Oxford: Oxford University Press, 1999).

Brown, P., 'The Diffusion of Manichaeism in the Roman Empire', in P. Brown, *Religion and Society in the Age of St Augustine* (London: Faber & Faber, 1972), 92–103.

Burrows, M.S., 'Raiding the Inarticulate: Mysticism, Poetics and the Unlanguageable', *Spiritus: A Journal of Christian Spirituality*, 4 (2004), 173–94.

Butler, C., *Western Mysticism*, 2nd edn (London: Constable, 1927).

Butler, J., *Bodies that Matter: On the Discursive Limits of 'Sex'* (London: Routledge, 1993)

Bynum, C.W., '"… And Woman His Humanity": Female Imagery in Religious Writing of the Later Middle Ages', in *Fragmentation and Redemption: Essays on Gender and the Human Body in Medieval Religion* (New York: Zone Books, 1991), pp. 151–79.

———, 'The Body of Christ in the Later Middle Ages: A Reply to Leo Steinberg', in *Fragmentation and Redemption: Essays on Gender and the Human Body in Medieval Religion* (New York: Zone Books, 1991), pp. 79–118.

———, 'The Female Body and Religious Practice in the Later Middle Ages', in *Fragmentation and Redemption: Essays on Gender and the Human Body in Medieval Religion* (New York: Zone Books, 1991), pp. 181–238.

———, *Fragmentation and Redemption: Essays on Gender and the Human Body in Medieval Religion* (New York: Zone Books, 1991).

———, *Holy Feast, Holy Fast: The Religious Significance of Food to Medieval Women* (Berkeley: University of California Press, 1987).

———, *Jesus as Mother: Studies in the Spirituality of the High Middle Ages* (Berkeley and Los Angeles: University of California Press, 1982).

———, *Metamorphosis and Identity* (New York: Zone Books, 2001).

———, *The Resurrection of the Body in Western Christianity, 200–1336* (New York: Columbia University Press, 1995).

————, *Wonderful Blood: Theology and Practice in the Late Medieval Northern Germany and Beyond* (Philadephia: University of Pennsylvania Press, 2007).

Caciola, N., *Discerning Spirits: Divine and Demonic Possession in the Middle Ages* (Ithaca: Cornell University Press, 2003).

————, 'Mystics, Demoniacs, and the Physiology of Spirit Possession in Medieval Europe', *Comparative Studies in Society and History*, 42/2 (2000), 268–306.

Camille, M., *The Gothic Idol: Ideology and Image-Making in Medieval Art* (Cambridge: Cambridge University Press, 1989).

Caputo, J.D., 'Apostles of the Impossible: On God and the Gift in Derrida and Marion', in J.D. Caputo and M.J. Scanlon (eds), *God, the Gift, and Postmodernism* (Bloomington, IN: Indiana University Press, 1999), pp. 185–222.

————, *The Prayers and Tears of Jacques Derrida: Religion without Religion.* Bloomington, IN: Indiana University Press, 1997.

Caputo, J.D. and Scanlon, M.J., 'Introduction: Apology for the Impossible: Religion and Postmodernism', in J.D. Caputo and M.J. Scanlon (eds), *God, the Gift, and Postmodernism* (Bloomington, IN: Indiana University Press, 1999), pp. 1–19.

————, 'Introduction: The Postmodern Augustine', in J.D. Caputo and M.J. Scanlon (eds), *Augustine and Postmodernism: Confession and Circumfession* (Bloomington, IN: Indiana University Press, 2005), pp. 1–16.

Carlson, T.A. *Indiscretion: Finitude and the Naming of God* (Chicago: University of Chicago Press, 1999).

————, 'Postmetaphysical Theology' in K.J. Vanhoozer (ed.), *The Cambridge Companion to Postmodern Theology* (Cambridge: Cambridge University Press, 2003), pp. 58–75.

Cassidy, E., 'Le Phénomène Erotique: Augustinian Resonances in Marion's Phenomenology of Love', in I. Leask and E. Cassidy (eds), *Givenness and God: Questions of Jean-Luc Marion* (New York: Fordham University Press, 2005), pp. 201–19.

Certeau, M. de, *The Mystic Fable: Volume One, The Sixteenth and Seventeenth Centuries*, trans. M.B. Smith (Chicago: University of Chicago Press, 1986).

Chadwick, H., *The Early Church* (Grand Rapids, MI: Eerdman's 1968).

Chewning, S.M. ,'"Mi bodi henge/wið þi bodi": The Paradox of Sensuality in þe Wohunge of Ure Lauerd', in S.M. Chewning (ed.), *Intersections of Sexuality and the Divine in Medieval Culture The Word Made Flesh* (Aldershot: Ashgate, 2005), pp. 183–96.

————, '"Mysticism and the Anchoritic Community: 'A Time of Veiled Infinity'"', in D. Watt (ed.), *Medieval Women in their Communities* (Cardiff: University of Wales Press, 1997), pp. 116–37.

Clark, J.P.H., *The Cloud of Unknowing: An Introduction* (Salzburg: Institut für Anglistik und Amerikanistik, Universität Salzburg, 1994).

————, *The Cloud of Unknowing*, trans. J. Walsh (New York: Paulist Press, 1981).

Coakley, S., 'Introduction: Religion and the Body', in S. Coakley (ed.), *Religion and the Body* (Cambridge: Cambridge University Press, 1997), pp. 1–12.

Cohn, N., *The Pursuit of the Millenium* (London: Secker and Warburg, 1957)

Colledge, E., 'Margery Kempe', *The Month*, 28 (1962), 16–29.

——— (ed.), *The Medieval Mystics of England* (London: John Murray, 1962).

Copeland, R., 'Richard Rolle and the Rhetorical Theory of the Levels of Style', in (ed.) M. Glasscoe, *The Medieval Mystical Tradition in England III*, Papers read at Dartington Hall, July 1984, (Cambridge: D.S. Brewer, 1984), pp. 55–80.

Courcelle, P., *La Consolation de Philosophie dans la tradition littéraire: Antécédents et postérité. de Boèce* (Paris: Études Augustiniennes, 1967).

Cousins, E., 'The Fourfold Sense of Scripture in Christian Mysticism', in S.T. Katz (ed.), *Mysticism and Sacred Scripture* (New York: Oxford University Press, 2000), pp. 118–37.

———, 'Francis of Assisi: Christian Mysticism at the Crossroads', in S.T. Katz (ed.), *Mysticism and Religious Traditions* (Oxford: Oxford University Press, 1983), pp. 163–91.

———, 'The Humanity and the Passion of Christ', in J. Raitt, (ed.), *Christian Spirituality: High Middle Ages and Reformation* (London: SCM 1996), pp. 375–91.

Cox, M., *A Handbook of Christian Mysticism* (Wellingborough: Aquarian, 1948; repr. 1986).

Crouzel, H., *Origen*, trans. A.S. Worrall (Edinburgh: T. & T. Clark, 1989).

Cutrofello, A., *Continental Philosophy: A General Introduction* (London: Routledge, 2005).

de Vries, H., 'Instances: Temporal Modes from Augustine to Derrida to Lyotard', in .J.D. Caputo and M.J. Scanlon (eds), *Augustine and Postmodernism* (Bloomington, IN: Indiana University Press, 2005), pp. 68–87.

Davies, O., *Meister Eckhart: Mystical Theologian* (London: SPCK, 1991).

Derrida, J., *Circumfession*, in J. Derrida and G. Bennington, *Derrida*, trans. G. Benington (Chicago: University of Chicago Press, 1993), pp. 3–315,

———, *Given Time: I. Counterfeit Money*, trans. P. Kamuf (Chicago: University of Chicago Press, 1994).

———, 'How to Avoid Speaking: Denials', in H. Coward and T. Foshay (eds), *Derrida and Negative Theology* (Albany, NY: State University of New York Press, 1992).

———, *Of Grammatology* (Baltimore: The Johns Hopkins University Press, 1976).

———, *Sauf Le Nom* (Paris: Galilee, 1993). In English as *On the Name*, ed. T. Dutoit, trans. D. Wood, J.P. Leavey Jr and I. McLeod (Stanford: Stanford University Press, 1995).

Derrida, J. and Marion, J.-L., 'On the Gift: A Discussion Between Jacques Derrida and Jean-Luc Marion, moderated by Richard Kearney' in J.D. Caputo and M.J. Scanlon (eds), *God, the Gift, and Postmodernism* (Bloomington, IN: Indiana University Press, 1999), pp. 54–78.

Dinzelbacher, P., 'The Beginnings of Mysticism Experienced in Twelfth-Century England', in M. Glasscoe (ed.), *The Medieval Mystical Tradition in England: The Exeter Symposium IV: Papers read at Dartington Hall, July 1987* (Cambridge: D.S. Brewer, 1987), pp. 111–31.

Dodaro, Robert. 'Loose Canons: Augustine and Derrida on Their Selves', in J.D. Caputo and M.J. Scanlon (eds), *God, the Gift, and Postmodernism* (Bloomington, IN: Indiana University Press, 1999), pp. 79–111.

Dodds, E.R., *The Ancient Concept of Progress and Other Essays on Greek Literature and Belief* (Oxford: Oxford University Press, 1985).

Dronke, P., *The Medieval Lyric* (New York: Harper Row, 1969).

Dyrness, W., *Visual Faith: Art, Theology and Worship in Dialogue* (Grand Rapids, MI: Baker Academic, 2001).

Eckhart, Meister, *Meister Eckhart: The Essential Sermons, Commentaries, Treatises, and Defense*, trans. and with intro. by E. Colledge OSA and B. McGinn, with preface by H. Smith (New York: Paulist Press, 1981).

———, *Meister Eckhart, Mystic and Philosopher: Translations with Commentary*, trans. R. Schürmann (Bloomington: Indiana University Press, 1978).

———, *Meister Eckhart: Teacher and Preacher*, trans. B. McGinn, F. Tobin and E Borgstädt (New York: Paulist Press, 1986).

Elliott, D., 'The Physiology of Rapture and Female Spirituality', in P. Biller and A. Minnis (eds), *Medieval Theology and the Natural Body* (Woodbridge: York Medieval Press, 1997), pp. 141–73.

———, 'Seeing Double: John Gerson, the Discernment of Spirits, and Joan of Arc', *The American Historical Review*, 107 (2002), 26–54.

———, *Spiritual Marriage: Sexual Abstinence in Medieval Wedlock* (Princeton, NJ: University of Princeton Press, 1993).

Epiney-Burgard, G. and Zum Brunn, E., *Women Mystics in Medieval Europe*, trans. S. Hughes (New York: Paragon, 1989).

Forman R.K.C. (ed.), *Meister Eckhart: Mystic as Theologian: an Experiment in Methodology* (Rockport, MA: Element, 1991).

———, *The Problem of Pure Consciousness: Mysticism and Philosophy* (New York: Oxford University Press, 1990).

Foucault, M., *The History of Madness* (London: Routledge, 2006).

Freeman, P.R., Bogarad, C.R. and Sholomskas, D.E., 'Margery Kempe, a New Theory: The Inadequacy of Hysteria and Postpartum Psychosis as Diagnostic Categories', *History of Psychiatry*, 1 (1990), 169–90.

Frend, W.H.C., 'The Gnostic-Manichaean Tradition in Roman North Africa', *The Journal of Ecclesiastical History*, 4/1 (1953), 13–26.

———, *The Rise of Christianity* (Philadelphia: Fortress Press, 1984).

Gertrude of Helfta, *Gertrude of Helfta: The Herald of Divine Love*, trans and ed. M. Winkworth (New York: Paulist Press, 1993).

Gillespie, V., 'Mystic's Foot: Rolle and Affectivity', in M. Glasscoe (ed.), *The Medieval Tradition In England: Papers Read at Dartington Hall, July 1982* (Exeter: Short Run Press, 1982), pp.199–230.

Gilson, É., *The Christian Philosophy of St Augustine*, trans. L.E.M. Lynch (London: Victor Gollancz, 1961).

Gimello, R.M., 'Mysticism in Its Contexts', in S.T. Katz (ed.), *Mysticism and Religious Traditions* (Oxford: Oxford University Press, 1983), pp. 61–88.

Glasscoe, M., *English Medieval Mystics: Games of Faith* (London and New York: Longman, 1993).

Gutting, G., 'French Philosophy in the Twentieth-Century', in D. Moran (ed.), *The Routledge Companion to Twentieth-Century Philosophy*. (Abingdon: Routledge, 2008), pp. 814–48.

Hadewicjh, *Hadewijch: The Complete Works*, trans. Mother Columbia Hart OSB, Classics of Western Spirituality (New York: Paulist Press, 1989).

Hamburger, J.F., *The Visual and the Visionary: Art and Female Spirituality in Late Medieval Germany* (New York: Zone Books, 1998).

Happold, F.C., *Mysticism: A Study and An Anthology* (Harmondsworth: Penguin, 1963).

Hart, K., 'The Experience of Nonexperience', in M. Kessler and C. Sheppard (eds.), *Mystics: Presence and Aporia*, Religion and Postmodernism Series (Chicago and London: University of Chicago Press, 2003), pp. 188–206.

Hendrikx, E., 'Augustins Verhältnis zur Mystik: Ein Rückblick', in C.P. Mayer and W. Eckermann (eds), *Scientia Augustiniana, Studien über Augustinus, den Augustinismus und den Augustinerorden Festschrift Adolar Zumkellar zum 60. Geburtstag*, Cassiacum 30 (Würzburg: Augustinus-Verlag, 1975), pp. 107–11.

Hilton, W., *The Scale of Perfection: Introduction*, ed. T. Bestul, online at www.lib. rochester.edu/camelot/teams/hilintro.htm.

———, *Walter Hilton: The Scale of Perfection*, ed. and trans. J.P.H. Clark and R. Dorward (New York: Paulist Press, 1991).

Hollenback, J.B., *Mysticism: Experience, Response, and Empowerment* (University Park, PA: Pennsylvania State University Press, 1996).

Hollywood, A., 'Marguerite Porete, Meister Eckhart and the Problem of Women's Spirituality' in B. McGinn (ed.), *Meister Eckhart and the Beguine Mystics: Hadewijch of Brabant, Mechthild of Magdeburg, and Marguerite Porete* (New York: Continuum, 1994), pp. 87–113.

———, *Sensible Ecstasy: Mysticism, Sexual Difference, and the Demands of History* (Chicago: University of Chicago Press, 2002).

Holsinger, B. W., *Music, Body and Desire in Medieval Culture: Hildegard of Bingen to Chaucer* (Stanford: Stanford University Press, 2001).

Horner, R., *Jean-Luc Marion: A Theo-Logical Introduction* (Aldershot: Ashgate, 2005).

Howells, E., *John of the Cross and Teresa of Avila: Mystical Knowing and Selfhood* (New York: Crossroad, 2002).

———, 'Mysticism and the Mystical: The Current Debate', in *The Way Supplement*, 102 (2001), 15–27.

———, 'Relationality and Difference in the Mysticism of Pierre de Bérulle', *Harvard Theological Review*, 102/2 (2009), 225–43.

Hudson, A., *The Premature Reformation: Wycliffite Texts and Lollard History* (New York: Oxford University Press, 2002).

Hugh of St Victor, *On the Sacraments of the Christian Faith*, trans. R. Deferrari (Cambridge, MA: Medieval Academy of America, 1951).

Inge, W.R., *Mysticism in Religion* (London: Hutchinson University Library, 1947).

Irigaray, L., 'Divine Women', in *Sexes and Genealogies*, trans. G.C. Gill (New York: Columbia University Press, 1993), pp. 55–72.

———, *Ethique de la différence sexuelle* (Paris: Gallimard, 1960).

James, W., *The Varieties of Religious Experience: A Study in Human Nature: Being the Gifford Lectures on Natural Religion Delivered at Edinburgh 1901–2* (London: Burns and Oates, 1952).

Jantzen, G.M, *Becoming Divine: Towards a Feminist Philosophy of Religion* (Manchester: Manchester University Press, 1998).

———, *Power, Gender and Christian Mysticism* (Cambridge: Cambridge University Press, 1995).

Jennings, M., 'Richard Rolle and the Three Degrees of Love', *Downside Review*, 93 (1975), 193–200.

Joby, C., 'The Extent to which the Rise in the Worship of Images in the Late Middle Ages was Influenced by Contemporary Theories of Vision', *Scottish Journal of Theology*, 60/1 (2007), 36–44.

Johnson, L.S., 'The Trope of the Scribe and the Question of Literary Authority in the Works of Julian of Norwich and Margery Kempe', *Speculum*, 66 (1991), 820–38.

Julian of Norwich, *Showings*, trans. E. Colledge OSA, and J. Walsh SJ (New York: Paulist Press, 1978).

Katz, S.T., 'The "Conservative" Character of Mystical Experience', in S. Katz (ed.), *Mysticism and Religious Tradition* (Oxford: Oxford Univesity Press, 1983), pp. 3–60.

———, 'The Diversity and Study of Mysticism', in S. Jakelic and L. Pearson (eds), *The Future of the Study of Religion: Proceedings of Congress 2000* (Boston, Brill, 2004), pp. 189–210.

———, 'Language, Epistemology, and Mysticism', in S.T. Katz (ed.), *Mysticism and Philosophical Analysis* (London: Sheldon Press, 1978), pp. 22–74.

———, 'Mystical Speech and Mystical Meaning', in S.T. Katz (ed.), *Mysticism and Language* (New York: Oxford University Press, 1992), pp. 3–41.

———, 'Mysticism and the Interpretation of Sacred Scripture', in S.T. Katz (ed.), *Mysticism and Sacred Scripture* (New York: Oxford University Press, 2000), pp. 7–67.

——— (ed.), *Mysticism and Language* (New York: Oxford University Press, 1992).

——— (ed.), *Mysticism and Philosophical Analysis* (London: Sheldon Press, 1978).

—— (ed.), *Mysticism and Religious Traditions* (Oxford: Oxford University Press, 1983).

—— (ed.), *Mysticism and Sacred Scripture* (New York: Oxford University Press, 2000).

Kay, S., 'Courts, Clerks and Courtly Love', in R.L. Krueger (ed.), *The Cambridge Companion to Medieval Romance* (Cambridge: Cambridge University Press, 2000), pp. 81–96.

Kempe, M., *The Book of Margery Kempe: A New Translation, Contexts, Criticism*, ed. and trans. L. Staley (New York: Norton, 2001).

——, *The Book of Margery Kempe: The Text From the Unique Ms. Owned by Colonel W. Butler-Bowdon Vol. 1*, ed. S.B. Meech and H.E. Allen, Early English Text Society, o.s. 212 (London: Oxford University Press, 1940).

Kenney, J.P., *The Mysticism of St Augustine: Rereading the Confessions* (Oxford: Routledge, 2005).

Kieckhefer, R., *European Witch Trials: Their Foundations in Popular and Learned Culture, 1300–1500* (London: Routledge and Kegan Paul, 1976).

King, S.B., 'Interpretation of Mysticism', *Journal of the American Academy of Religion*, 56/2 (1988), 257–79.

Kolve V.A., *Chaucer and the Imagery of Narrative: The First Five Canterbury Tales* (Stanford: Stanford University Press, 1984).

Knepper, T., 'Investigating Ineffability: What the Later Wittgenstein Has to Offer to the Study of Ineffability', *International Journal for Philosophy of Religion*, online June 2008, at www.springerlink.com/content/u1k2754gw61p11q7/fulltext.pdf.

Knowles, D., *The English Mystical Tradition* (London: Burns and Oates, 1961).

——, *The English Mystics* (London: Burns, Oates and Washbourne, 1927).

Kügler, P., 'Denys Turner's Anti-Mystical Mystical Theology', *Ars Disputandi*, 4 (2004), at www.ArsDisputandi.org.

Lambert, M.D. *Medieval Heresy: Popular Movements from the Gregorian Reform to the Reformation* (Cambridge, MA: Blackwell Publishing, 1992).

Lanzetta, B.J., *The Other Side of Nothingness: Toward A Theology of Radical Openness* (Albany: State University of New York, 2001).

——, *Radical Wisdom: A Feminist Mystical Theology* (Minneapolis: Fortress Press, 2005).

Lawes, R., 'Psychological Disorder and the Autobiographical Impulse in Julian of Norwich, Margery Kempe and Thomas Hoccleve', in D. Renevey and C.A.R. Whitehead (eds), *Writing Religious Women: Female Spiritual and Textual Practices in Late Medieval England* (Cardiff: University of Wales Press, 2000), pp. 217–43.

Lichtmann, M. 'Marguerite Porete and Meister Eckhart: *The Mirror of Simple Souls* Mirrored', in B, McGinn (ed.), *Meister Eckhart and the Beguine Mystics: Hadewijch of Brabant, Mechthild of Magdegburg and Marguerite Porete* (New York: Continuum, 1994), pp. 65–86.

Lochrie, K., *Margery Kempe and the Translations of the Flesh* (Philadelphia: University of Pennsylvania Press, 1991).

Louth, A., *Denys the Areopagite* (Wilton, CT: Morehouse-Barlow, 1989).

———, 'Dionysios the Areopagite', *The Way Supplement*, 102 (2001), 7–14.

———, *Eros and Mysticism: Early Christian Interpretations of the Song of Songs*, Lecture 241 (London: The Guild of Pastoral Psychology, 1992).

———, *The Origins of the Christian Mystical Tradition: From Plato to Denys* (Oxford: Oxford University Press, 1981).

Lyotard, J.-F., *The Confession of Augustine*, trans R. Beardsworth (Stanford: Stanford University Press, 2000).

McGinn, B., 'The English Mystics', in J. Raitt (ed.), *Christian Spirituality, Volume 2: The High Middle Ages* (London: SCM, 1996), pp. 194–207.

——— (ed. and trans.), *The Essential Writings of Christian Mysticism* (Modern Library Classics; New York: Random House, 2006).

———, *The Flowering of Mysticism: Men and Women in the New Mysticism, 1200–1350*, The Presence of God: A History of Western Christian Mysticism, vol. 3 (New York: Crossroad, 1998).

———, *The Foundations of Mysticism: Origins to the Fifth Century*, The Presence of God: A History of Western Christian Mysticism, vol. 1 (New York: Crossroad, 1991).

———, *The Growth of Mysticism: Gregory the Great through the 12th Century*, The Presence of God: A History of Western Christian Mysticism, vol. 2 (New York: Crossroad, 1992).

———, 'The Language of Inner Experience in Christian Mysticism', *Spiritus: A Journal of Christian Spirituality*, 1/2 (2001), 156–71.

———, 'The Language of Love in Christian and Jewish Mysticism', in S.T. Katz (ed.), *Mysticism and Language* (Oxford: Oxford University Press, 1992), pp. 202–35.

———, 'Love, Knowledge and Mystical Union in Western Christianity: Twelfth to Sixteenth Centuries', *Church History*, 56 (1987), 7–24.

——— (ed.), *Meister Eckhart and the Beguine Mystics: Hadewijch of Brabant, Mechthild of Magdegburg and Marguerite Porete* (New York: Continuum, 1994).

——— (ed.), *Meister Eckhart: Teacher and Preacher*, trans. B. McGinn, F. Tobin and E. Borgstädt (New York: Paulist Press, 1986).

———, *Method in Theology* (New York: Herder & Herder, 1972).

———, 'Mystical Consciousness: A Modest Proposal', *Spiritus: A Journal of Christian Spirituality*, 8/1 (2008), 44–63.

———, 'Theoretical Foundations: The Modern Study of Mysticism', in B. McGinn, *The Foundations of Mysticism: Origins to the Fifth Century*, The Presence of God: A History of Western Christian Mysticism, vol 1 (SCM Press: London, 1992), pp. 265–343.

McIntosh, M.A., *Mystical Theology: The Integrity of Spirituality and Theology* (Cambridge: Blackwell, 1998).

Macquarrie, J., *Two Worlds Are Ours*: *An Introduction to Christian Mysticism* (London: SCM, 2004).

Marebon, J., *Boethius* (Oxford: Oxford University Press, 2003).

Marion, J.-L., *Being Given: Toward a Phenomenology of Givenness*, trans. T.A. Carlson (Stanford: Stanford University Press, 2002.

———, *The Erotic Phenomenon*, trans. S.E. Lewis (Chicago: Chicago University Press, 2007).

———, *God without Being: Hors-Texte*, trans. T.A. Carlson (Chicago: University of Chicago Press, 1991).

———, 'In the Name: How to Avoid Speaking of "Negative Theology"', in J.D. Caputo and M.J. Scanlon (eds), *God, the Gift, and Postmodernism* (Bloomington, IN: Indiana University Press, 1999).

———, 'Mihi magna quaestio factus sum: The Privilege of Unknowing', *The Journal of Religion*, 85/1 (2005), 1–24.

Masters, R.E.L., and Houston, J., *The Varieties of Psychedelic Experience* (New York: Holt, Rinehart and Winston,1966).

Matter, E.A. *The Voice of My Beloved: The Song of Songs in Western Medieval Christianity* (Philadelphia: University of Pennsylvania Press, 1990).

Miles, M.R., *Image as Insight: Visual Understanding in Western Christianity and Secular Culture* (Boston: Beacon Press, 1985).

———, 'Vision: The Eyes of the Body and the Eye of the Mind in Saint Augustine's *De Trinitate* and *Confessions*', *The Journal of Religion*, 63 (1983), 125–42.

Minnis, A.J., 'Affection and Imagination in *The Cloud of Unknowing* and Walter Hilton's *Scale of Perfection*', *Traditio*, 39 (1983), 323–66.

Moran, D., *Introduction to Phenomenology* (London: Routledge, 2000).

Murphy, J.J., 'Meister Eckhart and the Via Negativa: Epistemology and Mystical Language', *New Blackfriars*, 77/908 (2007), 458–72.

Nelson, J., *Body Theology* (Louisville: Westminster/John Knox, 1992).

Nelstrop, L., 'The Merging of Eremitic and "Affectivist" Spirituality in Richard Rolle's Reshaping of Contemplation', *Viator*, 35 (2004), 387–434.

———, 'Richard Rolle and the Apophasis of Touch', unpublished paper delivered at Sources of Transformation: Revitalising Traditions of Christian Spirituality for Today Conference, St. Mary's University, Twickenham, June 2009.

Newman, B., *Sister of Wisdom: Hildegard's Theology of the Feminine* (Berkeley: University of California Press, 1987).

Nietzsche, F., *The Gay Science,* trans. J. Nauckhoff and A. Del Caro (Cambridge: Cambridge University Press, 2001).

Nygren, A., *Eros and Agape*, trans. P.S. Watson (London: Westminster Press, 1953).

Origen, 'Prologue to the Song of Songs', in *Origen: An Exhortation to Martydom, Prayer, First Principles: Book IV, Prologue to the Commentary on the Song of Songs, Homily XXVII on Numbers*, trans. R.A. Greer, Classics of Western Spirituality (New York: Paulist Press, 1979), pp. 217–44.

Otto, R., *The Idea of the Holy: An Inquiry into the Non-Rational Factor in the Idea of the Divine and Its Relation to the Rational*, trans. J.W. Harvey (Oxford University Press: London, 1931).

———, *Mysticism East and West: A Comparative Analysis of the Nature of Mysticism*, trans. B.L. Bracey and R.C. Payne (New York: The Macmillan Co., 1932).

Owen, H.P., 'Experience and the English Mystics', in S. Katz (ed.), *Mysticism and Religious Traditions* (Oxford: Oxford University Press, 1983), pp. 148–62.

Patch, H.R., *The Tradition of Boethius: A Study of His Importance in Medieval Culture* (New York: Oxford University Press, 1935).

Pattison, G., 'What to Say: Reflection on Mysticism after Modernity', in K. Vanhoozer and M. Warner (eds), *Transcending Boundaries in Philosophy and Theology: Reason, Meaning and Experience*, (Aldershot: Ashgate, 2007), pp. 191–205.

Pelikan, J., 'The Odyssey of Dionysian Spirituality', in *Pseudo-Dionysius: Complete Works*, trans C. Luibhéid and P. Rorem (New York: Paulist Press, 1987), pp. 11–24.

Pepler, C., *The English Religious Heritage* (London: Blackfriars, 1958).

Petroff, E.A., *Body and Soul: Essays on Medieval Women and Mysticism* (New York: Oxford University Press, 1994).

——— (ed.), *Medieval Women's Visionary Literature* (New York, Oxford: Oxford University Press, 1986).

Pike, N., *Mystic Union: An Essay in the Phenomenology of Mysticism* (Ithaca, New York: Cornell University Press, 1992).

Plato, *The Republic*, trans. D. Lee, 2nd rev. edn (London: Penguin Classics, 2003).

———, *Symposium and Other Dialogues*, trans. J. Warrington (New York: Dent, 1964).

Pollard, W., 'Richard Rolle and the Eye of the Heart, in W.F. Pollard and R Boenig (eds), *Mysticism and Spirituality in Medieval England* (Cambridge: Boydell and Brewer, 1997), pp. 85–106.

Porete, M., *Marguerite Porete: The Mirror of Simple Souls*, ed. and trans. E.L. Babinsky, (New York: Paulist Press, 1993).

Proclus, *The Elements of Theology: A Revised Text with Translation, Introduction and Commentary*, trans. and ed. E.R. Dodds (Clarendon Press: Oxford, 1933; rev. 2nd edn, 1969).

Pseudo-Denys, *Pseudo-Dionysius: The Complete Works* trans. C. Luibheid and P. Rorem (London: Paulist Press, 1987).

Ranft, P., *Women and Spiritual Equality in Christian Tradition* (New York: St Martin's Press, 1998).

Renevey, D., 'Margery Kempe's Performing Body: The Translation of Late Medieval Discursive Religious Practices' in D. Renevey and C. Whitehead (eds), *Writing Religious Women: Female Spirituality and Textual Practices in Late Medieval England* (Toronto: University of Toronto Press, 2000), pp. 197–216.

———, 'Richard Rolle', in D. Dyas, V. Edden and R. Ellis (eds), *Approaching Medieval English Anchoritic and Mystical Texts* (Cambridge: D.S. Brewer, 2005), pp. 63–74.

Riehle, W., *The Middle English Mystics*, trans. B. Standring (London and Boston: Routledge and Kegan Paul, 1981).

Robertson, E., *Early English Devotional Prose and the Female Audience* (Knoxville: University of Tennessee Press,1990).

Rolle, R., 'The Fire of Love', in *The Fire of Love and The Mending of Life*, trans. M.L. del Mastro (Garden City, NY: Image Books, 1981), pp. 93–264.

———, *Richard Rolle: English Writings*, trans. R.S. Allen (New York: Paulist Press, 1988).

Rollins, P., *How (Not) to Speak about God* (Brewster, MA: Paraclete Press, 2006).

Rorem, P., *Biblical and Liturgical Symbols within the Pseudo-Dionysian Synthesis* (Toronto: Pontifical Institute in Medieval Studies, 1984).

———, *Pseudo-Dionysius: A Commentary on the Texts and an Introduction to Their Influence* (New York: Oxford University Press, 1993).

Schroeder, W.R. *Continental Philosophy: A Critical Approach* (Oxford: Blackwell, 2004).

Sells, M., *Mystical Languages of Unsaying* (Chicago: Chicago University Press, 1994).

———, 'The Pseudo-Woman and the Meister: "Unsaying" and Essentialism', in B. McGinn (ed.), *Meister Eckhart and the Beguine Mystics: Hadewijch of Brabant, Mechthild of Magdegburg and Marguerite Porete* (New York, Continuum, 1994), pp. 114–46.

Shaw, G., 'Neoplatonic Theurgy and Dionysius the Areopagite', *Journal of Early Christian Studies*, 7/4 (1999), 573–99.

———, *Theurgy and the Soul: The Neoplatonism of Iamblichus* (University Park, PA: Pennsylvania State University Press, 1995).

Sheldrake, P. 'Unending Desire: De Certeau's "Mystics"', *The Way Supplement*, 102 (2001), 38-48

Smalley, B., *The Study of the Bible in the Middle Ages* (Oxford: Blackwells, 1941; 2nd edn 1952).

Smart, N., 'Interpretation and Mystical Experience', *Religious Studies*, 1 (1980), 75–87.

———, 'What Would the Buddhaghosa Have Made of *The Cloud of Unknowing*', in S.T. Katz (ed.), *Mysticism and Language* (New York: Oxford University Press, 1992), pp. 103–22.

Smith, H., 'Is there a Perennial Philosophy?', *Journal of the American Academy of Religion*, 55/3 (1987), 553–68.

Smith, J.E., 'In What Sense Can We Speak of Experiencing God?', *Journal of Religion*, 50 (1978), 229–444.

———, 'William James's Account of Mysticism; A Critical Appraisal', in S.T. Katz (ed.), *Mysticism and Religious Traditions* (Oxford: Oxford University Press, 1983), 247–79.

Sommerfeldt, J.R., *The Spiritual Teachings of Bernard of Clairvaux: An Intellectual History of the Early Cistercian Order*, Cistercian Fathers 125 (Kalamazoo: Cistercian Publications, 1991).

Spence, S., *Texts and the Self in the Twelfth Century* (Cambridge: Cambridge University Press, 2006).

Stace, W.T., *Mysticism and Philosophy* (Philadelphia: J.B. Lippincott, 1960).

———, *The Teachings of the Mystics* (New York: New American Library, 1960).

Stanford Encyclopadia of Philosophy, online at http://plato.stanford.edu.

Stephens, R.A., 'Orthodoxy and Liminality in Marguerite Porete's *Mirror of Simple Souls*' (unpublished doctoral dissertation, University of Birmingham, England, 1999).

Sullivan, L., 'Body Works: Knowledge of the Body in the Study of Religion', *History of Religions*, 30 (1990), 86–99.

Teasdale, W., *Essays in Mysticism* (Lake Worth, FL: Sunday Publications, 1985).

Teske, R., 'Augustine's Philosophy of Memory', in E. Stump and N. Kretzmann (eds), *The Cambridge Companion to Augustine* (Cambridge: Cambridge University Press, 2006), pp. 148–58.

TeSelle, E., 'Augustine', in P. Szarmach (ed.), *An Introduction to the Medieval Mystics of Europe* (New York: State University of New York Press, 1984), pp. 19–36.

Tobin, F. 'Eckhart's Mystical Use of Language: The Contexts of "eigenschaft"', *A Journal of Germanic Studies*, 8/3 (1972), 160–68.

———, *Meister Eckhart: Thought and Language* (Philadelphia: University of Pennsylvania Press, 1986).

———, 'Medieval Thought on Visions and Its Resonance in Mechthild von Magdeburg's *Flowing Light of the Godhead*, in A.C. Bartlett et al. (eds), *Vox Mystica: Essays on Medieval Mysticism in Honour of Professor Valerie M. Lagorio* (Cambridge: Brewer, 1995), pp. 41–53.

Turner, D., *The Darkness of God: Negativity in Christian Mysticism* (Cambridge: Cambridge University Press, 1995).

———, *The Dark Vision of God: Denys the Carthusian and Contemplative Wisdom* (Turnhout: Brepols, forthcoming).

———, *Eros and Allegory: Medieval Exegesis of the Song of Songs* (Kalamazoo: Cistercian Publications, 1995).

———, *Faith Reason and the Existence of God* (Cambridge: Cambridge University Press, 2004).

Underhill, E., *The Fire of Love or Melody of Love and the Mending of Life or Rule of Living*, trans. Richard Misyn, ed. F.M.M. Comper, intro. by E. Underhill. (London: Methuen, 1914; repr. 1920).

———, *Mysticism: A Study of the Nature and Development of Man's Spiritual Consciousness*, 4th edn (London: Methuen and Co., 1912).

————, *Practical Mysticism* (New York: E.P. Dutton and Company, 1915).

Vanhoozer, K.J., *Is There a Meaning in this Text?: The Bible, the Reader, and the Morality of Literary Knowledge* (Grand Rapids, MI: Zondervan, 1998).

Voaden, R., *God's Words, Women's Voices: The Discernment of Spirits in the Writing of Late-Medieval Women Visionaries* (New York: Boydell and Brewer, 1999).

von Hügel, Baron F., *The Mystical Element of Religion As Studied in Saint Catherine of Genoa and Her Friends*, 2 vols (London: J.M. Dent and Sons, 1908).

Wallace, D., 'Mystic and Followers in Siena and East Anglia: A Study of Taxonomy, Class and Cultural Mediation', in M. Glasscoe (ed.), *The Medieval Mystical Tradition in England III: Papers read at Dartington Hall, July 1984* (Cambridge: D.S. Brewer, 1984), pp. 169–91.

Ward, G., 'The *Logos*, the Body and the World: On the Phenomenological Border', in K. Vanhoozer and M. Warner (eds), *Transcending Boundaries in Philosophy and Theology: Reason, Meaning and Experience* (Aldershot: Ashgate, 2007), pp. 105–26.

Watson, N., 'The Middle English Mystics', in D. Wallace (ed.), *The Cambridge History of Medieval English Literature* (Cambridge: Cambridge University Press, 1999), pp. 539–65.

————, *Richard Rolle and the Invention of Authority* (Cambridge: Cambridge University Press, 1991).

————, 'The Trinitarian Hermeneutic in Julian of Norwich's *Revelation of Love*', in S. J. McEntire (ed.), *Julian of Norwich: A Book of Essays* (New York: Garland, 1998), pp. 61–90.

William of St Thierry, *Exposition on the Song of Songs: The Works of William of St Thierry, Volume 2*, trans Mother C. Hart OSB, with intro. by J.M. Decharet OSB, Cistercian Fathers 6 (Shannon: Cisercian Publications, 1970).

————, *The Mirror of Faith*, trans. G. Webb and A. Walker (Oxford, 1959).

Womack, S.J., 'The Jubilus Theme in the Later Writings of Richard Rolle' (unpublished PhD dissertation, Duke University, 1961).

Zaehner, R.C., *Mysticism: Sacred and Profane: An Inquiry into Some Varieties of Praeternatural Experiences* (Oxford: Oxford University Press, 1957).

Zinn, G.A., 'Book and Word: The Victorine Background of Bonaventure's use of symbols', in J.G. Bougerol (ed.), *S. Bonaventura 1274–1974*, 5 vols (Grottaferrata: Collegio S. Bonaventura, 1974), vol. 2, pp. 143–69.

Index[*]

---

[*]   This index was created with TExtract™ (www.Texyz.com).